. . . for Christ plays in ten thousand places,
Lovely in limbs, and lovely in eyes not his
To the Father through the features of men's faces.

— GERARD MANLEY HOPKINS

Christ Plays in Ten Thousand Places

A CONVERSATION IN SPIRITUAL THEOLOGY

Eugene H. Peterson

WILLIAM B. EERDMANS PUBLISHING COMPANY

GRAND RAPIDS, MICHIGAN / CAMBRIDGE, U.K.

Wm. B. Eerdmans Publishing Co.
2140 Oak Industrial Drive N.E., Grand Rapids, Michigan 49505 /
P.O. Box 163, Cambridge CB3 9PU U.K.

Published in association with the literary agency of
Alive Communications, Inc.,
7680 Goddard Street #200, Colorado Springs, CO 80920

Paperback edition 2008

Printed in the United States of America

13 12 11 10 09 08   10 9 8 7 6 5

Library of Congress Cataloging-in-Publication Data

Peterson, Eugene H., 1932-
Christ plays in ten thousand places: a conversation in
spiritual theology / Eugene H. Peterson.
p.   cm.
Includes bibliographical references and index.
ISBN 978-0-8028-6297-6 (alk. paper)
1. Spiritual life — Presbyterian Church.   I. Title.

BV4501.3.P475   2005
248 — dc22

2004056360

www.eerdmans.com

For James and Rita Houston

Contents

Acknowledgments

Three congregations gave me a long schooling in spiritual theology: Towson Presbyterian in Maryland, White Plains Presbyterian in New York, and Christ Our King Presbyterian in Maryland. These are the places and people where this conversation got its start.

Numerous schools through the years welcomed me as a visiting or adjunct professor, occasions that provided stimulus and reflection that deepened and broadened my understanding and concern for spiritual theology beyond my local circumstances. Much of what developed in this book was tested and developed while I was teaching at St. Mary's Seminary in Baltimore, Pittsburgh Theological Seminary, and Regent College in Vancouver, Canada.

Early drafts of various parts were published in *The Christian Century*, *Christianity Today*, *Crux*, *Ex Auditu*, *Journal for Preachers*, *Reformed Review*, and *The Rutherford Journal* (Scotland). The Theissen Lectures at Canadian Mennonite College, Winnipeg, and the Selwyn Lectures at Litchfield Cathedral, England, were significant in the formation of the final draft.

Pastors Michael Crowe and Steven Trotter were particularly helpful in the final stages of the writing.

To these and so many unnamed friends and colleagues, my sense of gratitude is immense for the conversations and prayers through the years that have been formational and taken form in this book. Thank you.

Preface

Two fields of work converge in these pages, the work of pastor and the work of professor. Most of my vocational life has been conducted as a pastor in a congregation. That is where most of the "field work" took place that has been written out here as an extended conversation in spiritual theology, the *lived* quality of God's revelation among and in us. Writing about the Christian life (formulated here as "spiritual theology") is like trying to paint a picture of a bird in flight. The very nature of a subject in which everything is always in motion and the context is constantly changing — rhythm of wings, sun-tinted feathers, drift of clouds (and much more) — precludes precision. Which is why definitions and explanations for the most part miss the very thing that we are interested in. Stories and metaphors, poetry and prayer, and leisurely conversation are more congenial to the subject, a conversation that necessarily also includes the Other.

But my work as a professor has also been formative. As a visiting or adjunct professor throughout the years that I was pastor, I often spent time with students and pastors to reflect on the intersection of the Scriptures, theology, history, and congregation in the work of getting the gospel lived in the actual conditions we face in North American culture. And then after thirty-three years of work as a pastor, I became a professor full-time, James M. Houston Professor of Spiritual Theology at Regent College (Canada). The overlapping fields of work, pastor and professor, cross-fertilized and provided the occasion and energy for writing this book. The wide variety of persons who have been with me for worship and learning and with whom I have been in conversation in these matters (farmers and pastors, homemakers and engineers, children and the elderly, worshipers and students, parents and scholars) accounts for the mixed style in the writing, the mixture of personal and academic. I have attempted to write spiritual theology in the same terms in which it is lived, which is to say, using language that comes at one time right out of the library and at another from a conversation over coffee in a diner, that on one page is derived from questions raised in a lecture and on another from insights accumulated while kayaking on a river. My intent is to provide the widespread but often free-floating spirituality of our time with structure and coherence by working from a scriptural foundation and with a Trinitarian imagination.

All of these conversations in congregations and schools came together in a particularly fortuitous way for me in the life and work of Dr. and Mrs. James Houston of Regent College. They embodied in their own lives the meaning and significance of spiritual theology (Jim in his teaching and mentoring and Rita in her hospitality). *Christ Plays* is dedicated to them with gratitude.

Advent 2003

Introduction

The end is where we start from. "In my end is my beginning" (T. S. Eliot).[1] Endings take precedence over beginnings. We begin a journey by first deciding on a destination. We gather information and employ our imaginations in preparing ourselves for what is to come: Life is the end of life; life, life, and more life.

The end of all Christian belief and obedience, witness and teaching, marriage and family, leisure and work life, preaching and pastoral work is the *living* of everything we know about God: life, life, and more life. If we don't know where we are going, any road will get us there. But if we have a destination — in this case a life lived to the glory of God — there is a well-marked way, the Jesus-revealed Way. Spiritual theology is the attention that we give to the details of living life on this way. It is a protest against theology depersonalized into information about God; it is a protest against theology functionalized into a program of strategic planning for God.

A sonnet by the poet and priest Gerard Manley Hopkins provides an arresting and accurate statement on the end of human life well lived:

As kingfishers catch fire, dragonflies draw flame;
    As tumbled over rim in roundy wells
    Stones ring; like each tucked string tells, each hung bell's
Bow swung finds tongue to fling out broad its name;
Each mortal thing does one thing and the same:
    Deals out that being indoors each one dwells;

Selves — goes itself; *myself* it speaks and spells,
Crying *What I do is me: for that I came.*

I say more: the just man justices;
    Keeps grace: that keeps all his goings graces;
Acts in God's eye what in God's eye he is —
    Christ. For Christ plays in ten thousand places,
Lovely in limbs, and lovely in eyes not his
    To the Father through the features of men's faces.[2]

We sense that life is more than what we are in touch with at this moment, but not different from it, not unrelated to it. We get glimpses of wholeness and vitality that exceed what we can muster out of our own resources. We get hints of congruence between who and what we are and the world around us — rocks and trees, meadows and mountains, birds and fish, dogs and cats, kingfishers and dragonflies — obscure and fleeting but convincing confirmations that we are all in this together, that we are kin to all that is and has been and will be. We have this feeling in our bones that we are involved in an enterprise that is more than the sum of the parts that we can account for by looking around us and making an inventory of the details of our bodies, our families, our thoughts and feelings, the weather and the news, our job and leisure activities; we have this feeling that we will never quite make it out, never be able to explain or diagram it, that we will always be living a mystery — but a good mystery.

Everyone alive at this moment, most emphatically including you, the person reading this page, and me, the person writing it, with no other qualification than having our eyes open and our lungs taking in air, can give personal witness to this More, this Congruence, this Kinship, this Mystery, that

Each mortal thing does one thing and the same:
    Deals out that being indoors each one dwells . . .

Our simplest word for all of this is Life.

The final lines of Hopkins's poem supply the image I have chosen for providing a metaphorical arena for working out the details of all that is involved in Christian living:

> For Christ plays in ten thousand places,
> Lovely in limbs, and lovely in eyes not his
> To the Father through the features of men's faces.

*   *   *

Hopkins's diction conveys the vigor and spark and spontaneity that is inherent in all of life. The focused conviction expressed here is that it is Christ, the God-revealing Christ, who is behind and in all of this living. The message is that all this life, this kingfisher- and dragonfly-aflame life, this tumbled stone and harp string and bell-sounding life, gets played out in us, in our limbs and eyes, in our feet and speech, in the faces of the men and women we see all day long, every day, in the mirror and on the sidewalk, in classroom and kitchen, in workplaces and on playgrounds, in sanctuaries and committees. The central verb, "play," catches the exuberance and freedom that mark life when it is lived beyond necessity, beyond mere survival. "Play" also suggests words and sounds and actions that are "played" for another, intentional and meaningful renderings of beauty or truth or goodness. Hopkins incorporates this sense of play with God as the ultimate "other" (". . . to the Father") — which is to say that all life is, or can be, worship.

Hopkins's sonnet is as good a presentation of what we are after in understanding life, the "end" of life, as we are likely to find: The vigor and spontaneity, the God-revealing Christ getting us and everything around us in on it, the playful freedom and exuberance, the total rendering of our lives as play, as worship before God. Some of us, to prevent misunderstanding or reduction, sometimes supply a defining adjective to this life and call it the *Christian* life. It is the task of the Christian community to give witness and guidance in the living of life in a culture that is relentless in reducing, constricting, and enervating this life.

And so I have chosen Hopkins's sonnet to set the tone and identify the nature of what I have set about doing in writing this book. I hope to fairly and clearly represent what the Christian church has for two thousand years now been living out in and for the world. What I am after is not unlike what Hopkins did when he made his poem. A poem is a complex matter of sounds and rhythms, meanings nuanced and plain, the ordinary and the unexpected juxtaposed, all put together in such a way as to involve us as participants in life, more life, real life. That is my intent — not primarily to explain anything or hand out information, but to enlist your play (my friends and neighbors, my family and congregation, my readers and students) in the play of Christ. I don't have anything new to say; Christians already know all the basics simply by being alive and baptized. We are already in on it, for Christ does, in fact, play "in ten thousand places." But I do hope to get you in on a little more of it, we who are the limbs and eyes and faces in and through whom Christ plays.

*   *   *

Christ Plays is a conversation in spiritual theology — "conversation" because conversation implies back-and-forthness, several voices engaged in considering, exploring, discussing, and enjoying not only the subject matter but also one another's company. Spiritual theology is a pair of words that hold together what is so often "sawn asunder." It represents the attention that the church community gives to keeping what we think about God (theology) in organic connection with the way we live with God (spirituality).

The meteoric ascendancy of interest in spirituality in recent decades is largely fueled by a profound dissatisfaction with approaches to life that are either aridly rationalistic, consisting of definitions, explanations, diagrams, and instructions (whether by psychologists, pastors, theologians, or strategic planners), or impersonally functional, consisting of slogans, goals, incentives, and programs (whether by advertisers, coaches, motivational consultants, church leaders, or evangelists). There comes a time for most of us when we discover a deep desire within us to live from the heart what we already know in our heads and do with our hands. But "to whom shall we go?" Our educational institutions have only marginal interest in dealing with our desire — they give us books to read and exams to pass but pay little attention to us otherwise. In our workplaces we quickly find that we are valued primarily, if not exclusively, in terms of our usefulness and profitability — they reward us when we do our jobs well and dismiss us when we don't. Meanwhile our religious institutions, in previous and other cultures the obvious places to go in matters of God and the soul, prove disappointing to more and more people who find themselves zealously cultivated as consumers in a God-product marketplace or treated as exasperatingly slow students preparing for final exams on the "furniture of heaven and the temperature of hell."[3]

4

Because of this spiritual poverty all around, this lack of interest in dealing with what matters most to us — a lack encountered in our schools, our jobs and vocations, and our places of worship alike — "spirituality," to use the generic term for it, has escaped institutional structures and is now more or less free-floating. Spirituality is "in the air." The good thing in all this is that the deepest and most characteristic aspects of life are now common concerns; hunger and thirst for what is lasting and eternal is widely acknowledged and openly expressed; refusal to be reduced to our job descriptions and test results is pervasive and determined. The difficulty, though, is that everyone is more or less invited to make up a spirituality that suits herself or himself. Out of the grab bag of celebrity anecdotes, media gurus, fragments of ecstasy, and personal fantasies, far too many of us, with the best intentions in the world, because we have been left to do it "on our own," assemble spiritual identities and ways of life that are conspicuously prone to addictions, broken relationships, isolation, and violence.

There is no question but that there is widespread interest in living beyond the roles and functions handed to us by the culture. But much of it ends up as a spirituality that is shaped by terms handed out by the same culture. Because of this, it seems preferable to use the term "spiritual theology" to refer to the specifically Christian attempt to address the lived experience revealed in our Holy Scriptures and the rich understandings and practices of our ancestors as we work this experience out in our contemporary world of diffused and unfocused "hunger and thirst for righteousness."

The two terms, "spiritual" and "theology," keep good company with one another. "Theology" is the attention that we give to God, the effort we give to knowing God as revealed in the Holy Scriptures and in Jesus Christ. "Spiritual" is the insistence that everything that God reveals of himself and his works is capable of being lived by ordinary men and women in their homes and workplaces. "Spiritual" keeps "theology" from degenerating into merely thinking and talking and writing about God at a distance. "Theology" keeps "spiritual" from becoming merely thinking and talking and writing about the feelings and thoughts one has about God. The two words need each other, for we know how easy it is for us to let our study of God (theology) get separated from the way we live; we also know how easy it is to let our desires to live whole and satisfying lives (spiritual lives) get disconnected from who God actually is and the ways he works among us.

Spiritual theology is the attention we give to lived theology —

prayed and lived, for if it is not prayed sooner or later it will not be lived from the inside out and in continuity with the Lord of life. Spiritual theology is the attention that we give to living what we know and believe about God. It is the thoughtful and obedient cultivation of life as worship on our knees before God the Father, of life as sacrifice on our feet following God the Son, and of life as love embracing and being embraced by the community of God the Spirit.

Spiritual theology is not one more area of theology that takes its place on the shelf alongside the academic disciplines of systematic, biblical, practical, and historical theology; rather, it represents the conviction that *all* theology, no exceptions, has to do with the living God who creates us as living creatures to live to his glory. It is the development of awareness and discernments that are as alert and responsive in the workplace as in the sanctuary, as active while changing diapers in a nursery as while meditating in a grove of aspens, as necessary when reading a newspaper editorial as when exegeting a sentence written in Hebrew.

Some may want to simplify things by keeping the spiritual and throwing out the theology. Others will be content to continue with the theology as usual and forget the spiritual. But the fact is that we live only because God lives and that we live well only in continuity with the way God makes, saves, and blesses us. Spirituality begins in theology (the revelation and understanding of God) and is guided by it. And theology is never truly itself apart from being expressed in the bodies of the men and women to whom God gives life and whom God then intends to live a full salvation life (spirituality).

*　　　*　　　*

"Trinity" is the theological formulation that most adequately provides a structure for keeping conversations on the Christian life coherent, focused, and personal. Early on the Christian community realized that everything about us — our worshiping and learning, conversing and listening, teaching and preaching, obeying and deciding, working and playing, eating and sleeping — takes place in the "country" of the Trinity, that is, in the presence and among the operations of God the Father, God the Son, and God the Holy Spirit. If God's presence and work are not understood to define who we are and what we are doing, nothing we come up with will be understood and lived properly.

"Trinity" has suffered the indignity among many of being treated as a desiccated verbal artifact poked and probed by arthritic octogenarians of the sort skewered by Robert Browning as "dead from the waist down."[4] In reality, it is our most exuberant intellectual venture in thinking about God.[5] Trinity is a conceptual attempt to provide coherence to God as God is revealed variously as Father, Son, and Holy Spirit in our Scriptures: God is emphatically *personal;* God is only and exclusively God in *relationship.* Trinity is not an attempt to explain or define God by means of abstractions (although there is some of that, too), but a witness that God reveals himself as personal and in personal relations. The down-to-earth consequence of this is that God is rescued from the speculations of the metaphysicians and brought boldly into a community of men, women, and children who are called to enter into this communal life of love, an emphatically *personal* life where they experience themselves in personal terms of love and forgiveness, of hope and desire. Under the image of the Trinity we discover that we do not know God by defining him but by being loved by him and loving in return. The consequences of this are personally revelatory: another does not know me, nor do I know another, by defining or explaining, by categorizing or by psychologizing, but only relationally, by accepting and loving, by giving and receiving. The personal and interpersonal provide the primary images (Father, Son, and Holy Spirit) for both knowing God and being known by God. This is living, not thinking about living; living with, not performing for.

And so these conversations in spiritual theology are set in this Trinity-mapped country in which we know and believe in and serve God: the Father and creation, the Son and history, and the Spirit and community.

There is far more to Trinity than getting a theological dogma straight; the country of the Trinity comprehends creation (the world in which we live), history (all that happens to and around us), and community (the ways we personally participate in daily living in the company of all the others in the neighborhood). Trinity isn't something imposed on us, it is a witness to the co-inherence of God (Father, Son, and Holy Spirit) and the co-inherence of our lives in the image of God (where we are, what is happening, and who we are as we speak and act and engage in personal relations with one another).

Trinity maps the country in which we know and receive and obey God. It is not the country itself, but a map of the country. And a most useful map it is, for God is vast and various, working visibly and invisibly. Left to ourselves we often get lost in blind alleys, get tangled up in thickets, and don't have a clue to where we are. The map locates us: it provides the vocabulary and identifies the experience by which we can explore God when there are no signs pointing to him, when there are no neatly lettered labels defining the odd shape or feeling that is in front of our eyes.

There is this also to be said about a map. Even though a map is an artifact, something made, it is not arbitrarily imposed on the land. It comes out of careful observation and accurate recording of what is actually there. It is required that maps be honest. And there is also this: maps are humble — they don't pretend to substitute for the country itself. Studying the map doesn't provide experience of the country. The purpose of the map is to show us the way into the country and prevent us from getting lost in our travels.

*   *   *

With the Holy Trinity providing structure and context, the conversations will proceed under the metaphor "Christ plays in ten thousand places" by first clearing the playing field and then exploring the three intersecting dimensions of creation, history, and community in which we live out our lives:

Clearing the Playing Field. We live in a time in which there is an enormous interest in what is popularly called "spirituality." The Christian church has no monopoly on giving out guidance on how to live life. The playing field of spirituality is fairly cluttered with debris from improvised attempts and makeshift rules in playing out this life. I will attempt to clear the playing field of this clutter and establish a common ground for conversation by getting some basic stories, metaphors, and terms in place that will prepare us to understand the Christian life in biblical and personal terms.

Christ Plays in Creation. We live in an extraordinarily complex cosmos. We live out our lives in the presence of and in relation to millions of other life-forms. There's a lot going on. We don't want to miss any of it. In an age that increasingly functionalizes everything and everyone, and in times when the sense of the sacred, the holy, whether in things or people, steadily erodes, we will explore the ways in which the Christian receives, celebrates, and honors all creation as a holy gift that has its origins and comes to its full expression in the birth of Christ.

8

Christ Plays in History. But life is not only the gift of creation. We are also plunged into history in which sin and death play a major part: suffering and pain, disappointment and loss, catastrophe and evil. In an age of burgeoning knowledge and dazzling technological proficiency it is easy to assume that a little more knowledge and technology will turn the tide and we will all soon be getting better. But we haven't. And we won't. Historians have provided thorough and irrefutable documentation that the century just lived through (the twentieth) has been the most murderous on record.[6] We need help. We will explore the ways in which Christians enter into a history that gets its definitive meaning from Christ's death and the life of salvation that derives from it.

Christ Plays in Community. The Christian life is lived with others and for others. Nothing can be done alone or solely for oneself. In an age of heightened individualism, it is easy to assume that the Christian life is primarily what I am responsible for on my own. But neither self-help nor selfishness has any standing in spiritual theology. We will explore the ways in which we are placed in the community formed by Christ's Holy Spirit and become full participants in all that the risen Christ is and does, living resurrection lives.

Clearing the Playing Field

"Come to me . . . learn from me; for I am gentle and humble in heart. . . ."

MATTHEW 11:28-29[1]

As soon as the Gospels were written, speech without experience began to dabble with the new facts proposed by the existence of the Church. . . . People tried to think the new life without being touched by it first in some form of call, listening, passion or change of heart.

EUGEN ROSENSTOCK-HUESSY[2]

There are seething energies of spirituality in evidence everywhere. To begin with this is a good thing. But spirituality is also prone to imprecisions that clutter the playing field and make it difficult to carry on a conversation. Four are common: First, spirituality easily, almost inevitably, develops elitist postures as it notices that so many of the men and women that we rub shoulders with in our work and worship are so "unspiritual." Then, in the enthusiasm of firsthand experience, spirituality imperceptibly wanders away from its basic spirituality text, the Bible, and embraces the inviting world of self-help. Now, exposed and vulnerable to a culture that is only too happy to supply the terms of discourse, spirituality is diluted or emptied of any gospel distinctiveness. Finally, in reaction to what is assumed to be "dead" theology, spirituality easily becomes theologically amnesiac and ends up isolated from any awareness of the grand and spacious God horizons, the truly vast landscapes in which we are invited to live out the Christian life.

I want to harness these contemporary but imprecise spirituality energies in biblical leather and direct them in entering the company of Jesus in preparation for joining the actual "play" of Christ in creation, history, and community. I will employ two stories, three texts, four terms, and a dance to clear the field for conversation, get rid of the clutter of misconceptions and misunderstanding in these four areas: two stories to level the playing field so that we live humbly and without pretense (countering elitism); three texts that define a scriptural foundation so that we live obediently (countering self-helpism); four terms that provide gospel foci for living accurately (countering cultural fuzziness); and a dance to bring theology prominently into the field of action so that our imagination is large enough to accommodate our life (countering the shrunken secular horizon).

Two Stories

Story is the most natural way of enlarging and deepening our sense of reality, and then enlisting us as participants in it. Stories open doors to areas or aspects of life that we didn't know were there, or had quit noticing out of over-familiarity, or supposed were out-of-bounds to us. They then welcome us in. Stories are verbal acts of hospitality.

St. John tells two stories early in his Gospel that definitively welcome all into the Christian life.

13

The first story is of Nicodemus, a Jewish rabbi (John 3). Nervous about his reputation, he came to talk with Jesus under cover of darkness. He would have lost credibility with his rabbi colleagues if it became known that he was consulting this disreputable itinerant teacher, this loose prophetic cannon out of nowhere, the no-place Nazareth in Galilee, so he came to Jesus by night. He came, it seems, without an agenda, simply to get acquainted, opening the conversation by complimenting Jesus: "Rabbi, we know that you are a teacher who has come from God; for no one can do these signs that you do apart from the presence of God" (John 3:2).

But Jesus discerned an agenda, a yet unspoken question; Nicodemus was after something. Jesus brushed aside the introductory small talk and got down to business; he read Nicodemus's heart and addressed himself to that: "Very truly I tell you, no one can see the kingdom of God without being born from above" (3:3). So *that* is what Nicodemus was there for, to inquire about getting into the kingdom of God, living under the rule of God, participating in the reality of God. That's odd.

Odd, because this is the kind of thing in which Nicodemus was supposed to be an expert. So why is he sneaking around, having a clandestine conversation with Jesus? Was it out of humility? That is plausible. Leaders who are looked up to constantly, who give out answers competently, who everyone assumes are living what they are saying, often have acute experiences of dissonance: "Who I am and what people think I am aren't anywhere close to being the same thing. The better I get as a rabbi and the more my reputation grows, the more I feel like a fraud. I *know* so much more than I live. The longer I live, the more knowledge I acquire, the wider the gap between what I know and what I live. I'm getting worse by the day. . . ."

So perhaps it was this deep sense of unease, grounded in a true humility, that brought Nicodemus that night to Jesus. He wasn't looking for theological information but for a way *in,* not for anything more *about* the kingdom of God but for a personal guide/friend to show him the door and lead him in: "How do I *enter* . . . ?"

Or was he there simply out of curiosity? Leaders, if they are to maintain their influence, have to stay ahead of the competition, have to keep up with the trends, know what sells best in the current market. Jesus was attracting an enormous amount of attention these days — so what's his angle? What's his secret? How does he do it? Nicodemus was good at his work, but he knew he couldn't simply rest on his laurels. The world was changing fast. Israel was in a vortex of cultures — Greek learning and Roman government and Jewish moral traditions mixed in with gnostic sects, mystery cults, terrorist bands, and assorted messianic adventurers and fanatics. The mix changed weekly. Nicodemus had to be alert to every shift in the wind if he was going to keep his leadership out in front and on course. Jesus was the latest attraction and so Nicodemus was there that night to dig out some useful piece of strategy or lore. This also is plausible.

But our interest in teasing out the motive that brought Nicodemus to Jesus is not shared by the storyteller, St. John. There is no authorial interest in motive here; this is a story about Jesus, not Nicodemus. Jesus does not question Nicodemus's motives, and John does not explore them. After the brief opening gambit, Jesus seizes the initiative by introducing a startling, attention-demanding metaphor, "born again" or "born from above": "I tell you, no one can see the kingdom of God without being born from above" (3:3); and then, before Nicodemus can so much as catch his breath, Jesus adds another metaphor, even odder than the first: "I tell you, no one can enter the kingdom of God without being born of water and Spirit" (3:5). Wind, Breath, and Spirit are the same word in the Aramaic that Jesus presumably spoke and also in the Greek that St. John wrote. The necessity in those languages of using the same term for the movement of air caused by a contraction of the lungs, the movement of air caused by a shift in barometric pressure, and the life-giving movement of the living God in us, required an exercise of the imagination every time the word was used: What's being talked about here, breathing or weather or God?

No sooner have we asked the question than John clarifies matters by putting the literal and the metaphorical together side by side: "The wind [*pneuma*] blows where it chooses, and you hear the sound of it, but you do not know where it comes from or where it goes. So it is with everyone who is born of the Spirit [*pneuma*]" (3:8).

Nicodemus shakes his head. He doesn't get it.

*   *   *

Another story follows, this one of the Samaritan woman (John 4). This story takes place not at night as with Nicodemus but in broad daylight by Jacob's Well in Samaria. Jesus is sitting alone when the woman comes to get water. Jesus opens the conversation by asking for a drink. The woman is surprised even to be spoken to by this man, this *Jew*, for there were centuries of religious bad blood between the two ethnic groups.

She is surprised, but is she also wary? Do we detect an edge to her voice in her reply, "How is it that you, a Jew, ask a drink of me, a woman of Samaria?" (4:9). Does she mistrust this man sitting at the well? It would seem she had good reason to. She is a woman hard-used by life. Later in the narrative we will find that she has been married five times and is now living with a sixth man without benefit of marriage. It is not difficult to conjure a scenario of serial rejections, multiple failures, year by year accumulating wounds and scars in mind and body. For her, to be a woman is to be a victim. To be near a man is to be near danger. What is this stranger going to do next, say next? Her guard is up.

Or is it just the opposite? Maybe that was not mistrust we detected in her question, but a teasing flirtatiousness. Maybe she is on the hunt. Maybe she used up those five husbands, one after another, and is now working her seductive ways on this sixth. Maybe she sees men as opportunities for gratification or access to power or advancement and when they no longer serve her pride or ambition or lust she dumps them. It is entirely possible that from the moment she saw Jesus she began calculating strategies of seduction: "Well, this is a nice surprise! Let's see what I can get out of this one."

We love playing these little games. Filling in the blanks, guessing at the reality behind the appearances, getting the inside scoop on people's lives. But again, just as in the Nicodemus story, Jesus shows no interest in playing the game and John shows no interest in exploring motives. He takes her just as he finds her, no questions asked. We realize that, as before with Nicodemus, this is a story not about the woman but about Jesus.

After the opening conversational exchange at the well, Jesus starts talking in riddles: "If you knew the gift of God, and who it is that is saying to you, 'Give me a drink,' you would have asked him, and he would have given you living water" (4:10). Soon it becomes clear to us that Jesus is using the word "water" as a metaphor with the Samaritan just as he used "wind" as a metaphor with Nicodemus. The word "water" that initially referred to well water pulled up by a bucket is now being used to refer to something quite different, something interior, "a spring of water gushing up [in them] to eternal life" (4:14). And then the earlier Nicodemus metaphor is added: "God is spirit, and those who worship him must worship in spirit and truth" (4:24).

"Spirit" again, the word that connects our sensory experience of breath and wind with the nature and activity of God. Just as the conversation is on the brink of degenerating into a squabble over where to worship, Jesus' words suddenly create a new reality in which God takes the center ground.

The woman gets it. She makes the connection between things she knows about messiah and what Jesus says to her, what he *is* to her. She is converted on the spot.

*   *   *

The striking thing about these two stories, set in parallel as they are by St. John, is that God's Spirit is at the heart of the action: the aliveness of God, the creating presence of God, the breath breathed into our lives just as it was breathed into Adam, the breath that makes us alive in ways that biology can neither command nor account for.

There is a corresponding feature: the stories taken together insist on accessibility. There is an unfortunate connotation that often accompanies the contemporary use of the word "spiritual" — a tinge of elitism, that only a select or in-the-know few can get in on it. But these two stories dismiss even a hint of that. The God-breathed life is common, it is totally accessible across the whole spectrum of the human condition. We are welcomed into life, period. There are no pre-conditions.

This realization of generous welcome is achieved first of all by the choice of vocabulary. The introductory metaphors in each story are completely accessible; everyone knows the words without using a dictionary; they come out of ordinary life. With Nicodemus it is birth; with the Samaritan it is water. We all have sufficient experience of those two words to know what is going on without further instruction. We all know what birth is: our being here is proof that we were born. We all know what water is: we drink it or wash with it several times a day. The metaphor common to both stories, wind/breath, is also plain. We all know what wind/breath is: blow on your hand, take a deep breath, look at the leaves blowing in the breeze.

And then there are these features:

The first story is about a man; the second about a woman. There is no preferred gender in the Christian life.

The first story takes place in the city, the center of sophistication and learning and fashion; the second on the outskirts of a small town in the country. Geography has no bearing on perception or aptitude.

Nicodemus is a respectable member of a strictly orthodox sect of the Pharisees; the Samaritan is a disreputable member of the despised heretical sect of the Samaritans. Racial background, religious identity, and moral track record are neither here nor there in matters of spirituality.

The man is named; the woman is unnamed. Reputation and standing in the community don't seem to count for anything.

There is also this: Nicodemus opens the conversation with Jesus with a religious statement, "Rabbi, we know that you are a teacher come from God." Jesus opens the conversation with the woman by asking for a drink of water, a sentence that doesn't sound the least bit religious. It doesn't seem to make any difference in the Christian life who gets things started, Jesus or us, or what the subject matter is, heavenly or earthly.

And in both stories a reputation is put at risk: Nicodemus risks his reputation by being seen with Jesus; Jesus risks his reputation by being seen with the Samaritan woman. There is a sense of ignoring conventions here on both sides, a crossing of the lines of caution, a willingness on both sides to risk misunderstanding. When we get close to the heart of things, we aren't dealing with assured results or conventional behavior. So —

A man and a woman.
City and country.
An insider and an outsider.
A professional and a layperson.
A respectable man and a disreputable woman.
An orthodox and a heretic.
One who takes initiative; one who lets it be taken.
One named, the other anonymous.
Human reputation at risk; divine reputation at risk.

There is also this: In both conversations "spirit" is the pivotal word. "Spirit" links the differences and contrasts in the two stories and makes them aspects of one story. In both conversations "Spirit" refers primarily to God and only derivatively to the man and the woman: In the first conversation the Spirit gives birth ("So it is with everyone who is born of the Spirit"); Spirit is an agent, a source, a cause of the birth that makes a person able to "see" and to "enter" (both verbs are used in the conversation).

In the second conversation, God is Spirit; the consequence is that we worship him in spirit and truth. It is only because God is Spirit that there is anything to say about what we do or don't do.

Finally, there is this: Jesus is the primary figure in both stories. Although Nicodemus and the Samaritan provide the occasion, it is Jesus who provides the content. In everything that has to do with living, which is the large context in which everything that we do and say takes place, Jesus is working at the center. Jesus is far more active than any one of us; it is Jesus who provides the energy.

$$* \qquad * \qquad *$$

We are not used to this. For us, "spiritual," the adjective formed off the activity of God's Holy Spirit, is commonly used to describe moods or traits or desires or accomplishments in us. The unhappy result is that the word has become hopelessly garbled. These two stories rescue us from our confusion: We will no longer consult our own experiences or feelings or performance or those of our friends as we study the ways of God among us in Jesus Christ and the ways we are welcomed into those ways. We will start with these stories and make a clearing in which to stand. We have removed some of the clutter by observing that

> spirituality is not a body of secret lore,
> spirituality has nothing to do with aptitude or temperament,
> spirituality is not primarily about you or me; it is not about personal power or enrichment. It is about God.

But because the terms "spiritual" and "spirituality" are used so widely these days quite apart from (and sometimes in defiance of) the biblical revelation, "the Christian life" will be often used in these pages (but not exclusively) as a synonym for spirituality.

$$* \qquad * \qquad *$$

The biblically instructed Christian church has always maintained an open door, a welcoming stance to "the lost," to those disenfranchised by establishment religion or deficient in education or piety or social respectability. But not infrequently, especially when the church has been adopted by the culture and is numerically successful, it has strayed in this commitment and society's outsiders have also been left out of the church. At such times marginal people have often provided voices that recovered the original welcome and re-included the left out.

Perpetual vigilance is required in all matters of spirituality. Elitism is always "couching at the door" (Gen. 4:7 RSV) — the gospel perhaps is for everyone, but in "advanced" matters in the kingdom some are more suited than others, and these "some" always seem to be socially and culturally from the middle or upper social strata. The poor and the minimally educated never seem to receive much attention in these matters. But "evangelical" brings the same energy and acceptance to the outsiders as to the insiders. The storefront mission and the prairie outpost often have deeply developed Christian spiritualities, even though their vocabularies might not fit in easily with what is heard in mountain retreat centers or large suburban churches.

Three Texts

The two stories set the word "spirit" front and center for us, inviting one and all into a life of growing intimacy with our Lord. The word "spirit," designating God's Spirit, or Holy Spirit, occupies a prominent place throughout our Scriptures and traditions, designating God's living presence at work among us. Three representative texts mark the range of the formative work of Spirit in the world we find ourselves in: Genesis 1:1-3, Mark 1:9-11, and Acts 2:1-4. Each of these texts marks a beginning and in each text it is the Spirit that initiates the beginning.

G. K. Chesterton once said that there are two kinds of people in the world: When trees are waving wildly in the wind, one group of people thinks that it is the wind that moves the trees; the other group thinks that the motion of the trees creates the wind.[3] The former view was the one held by most of humankind through most of its centuries; it was only in recent years, Chesterton said, that a new breed of people had emerged who blandly hold that it is the movement of trees that creates the wind. The consensus had always held that the invisible is behind and gives energy to the visible; Chesterton in his work as a journalist, closely observing and commenting on people and events, reported with alarm that the broad consensus had fallen apart and that the modern majority naively assumes that what they see and hear and touch is basic reality and generates whatever people come up with that cannot be verified with the senses. They think that the visible accounts for the invisible.

Having lost the metaphorical origin of "spirit" we operate, in our daily conversations (in the English language at least), with a serious vocabulary deficit. Imagine how our perceptions would change if we eliminated the word "spirit" from our language and used only "wind" and "breath." Spirit was not "spiritual" for our ancestors; it was sensual. It was the invisible that had visible effects. It was invisible but it was not immaterial. Air has as much materiality to it as a granite mountain: it can be felt, heard, and measured; it provides the molecules for the quiet breathing that is part of all life, human and animal, waking and sleeping — the puffs of air used to make words, the gentle breezes that caress the skin, the brisk winds that fill the sails of ships, the wild hurricanes that tear roofs off barns and uproot trees.

It would clarify things enormously if we could withdraw "spirit" and "spiritual" from our language stock for a while.

But these three texts can, if we attend to them, serve as signposts in the muck of imprecision in which we find ourselves. The three texts mark the three beginnings, the beginning of creation, the beginning of salvation, and the beginning of the church: holy creation, holy salvation, holy community.

Genesis 1:1-3

"In the beginning God created the heavens and the earth. The earth was without form and void, and darkness was upon the face of the deep; and the Spirit of God was moving over the face of the waters. And God said, 'Let there be light'" (RSV).

God begins. He begins by creating. This act of creation accounts for everything there is, visible and invisible, "heavens and earth." Creation takes noncreation, or anti-creation, that which is "without form and void," that which is without light ("darkness on the face of the deep"), and makes something of it, gives it form and content, and floods it with light. Noncreation or pre-creation is pictured as ocean waters deep and dark — formless, anarchic, wild, unpredictable, death-dealing.

God breathes or blows over these waters. The breath is life and life-making. We see the wind moving over these anarchic waters, these dark and lethal waters, God breathing life into this unlife, this nonlife.

And then this breath of God, no longer just an inarticulate blowing, is used to make words. The same breath/spirit that produces wind now makes language. We first *see* the effects of God's breath on the water, then we *hear* the articulation of God's breath in words: "God said. . . ." Eight times in the narrative God speaks. The eight sentences account for everything that is; the scope is comprehensive. "Create" accounts for everything that is in heaven and earth.

But there is more to this. The Spirit of God that moved over the face of the waters "in the beginning" continues to move, continues to create. The Genesis creation text is not confined to telling us how the world came into being, it is also a witness to the creation work of the Spirit of God now. The verb "create" in our Bibles is used exclusively with God as its subject. Men and women and angels don't create. Only God creates. And the most frequent use of the verb is not in the story of the beginning of heaven and earth but in a prophetic/pastoral ministry that took place among the exiled people of God in Babylon in the sixth century B.C. The Hebrew people had lost virtually everything — their political identity, their place of worship, their homes and farms. They had been force-marched across six hundred miles of desert to eke out a bare exilic existence in a strange land. They had nothing. They were stripped not only of their possessions but of their very identity as a people of God. They were uprooted and plunked down in a foreign and idolatrous society. And it was there and in those conditions that they began hearing the Genesis verb "create" in a fresh, unexpected way. The word "create" (and "Creator") occurs more times in the preaching of Isaiah of the exile than any other place in the Bible — seventeen times as compared to the six occurrences in the great creation narrative in Genesis. The Spirit of God created life out of nothing in the Babylon of the sixth century B.C. just as he had done in the formless void when the "darkness was upon the face of the deep." Through the text of Isaiah the Creator Spirit is seen as creating both a structure to live in and human lives adequate for living in it now. "Create" is not confined to what the Spirit did; it is what the Spirit *does*. Creation is not an impersonal environment, it is a personal home — *this* is where we live. The superb accomplishment of Isaiah of the exile was to bring every detail of the Genesis beginnings into this present in which we feel so uncreated, so unformed, and unfitted for the world in which we find ourselves. The work of the Spirit in creation no longer is confined to asking the questions "When did this take place? How did this happen?" We are now asking "How can I get in on this? Where is my place in this?" And praying, "Create in *me*..." (Ps. 51:10).

Mark 1:9-11

"In those days Jesus came from Nazareth of Galilee and was baptized by John in the Jordan. And when he came up out of the water, immediately he saw the heavens opened and the Spirit descending upon him like a dove; and a voice came from heaven, 'Thou art my beloved Son; with thee I am well pleased'" (RSV).

God begins again. A second beginning: Jesus is baptized and identified as God's "beloved Son."

Genesis is cosmological, presenting us with a watery chaos breathed on by God into form and fullness and light; life both inorganic and organic emerges out of no-life. The Gospel of Mark presents us with a local and named river in which Jesus is baptized, first drowned in the river and then raised from the river. Baptism is a replay of Genesis. As Jesus is lifted out of the water, God breathes life into him. The breathing is given visibility this time by means of what looks like a dove descending out of heaven.

The descending dove on Jesus provides a visual link with Genesis 1. The verb used for the "Spirit of God moving (*m⁰rachepheth*) over the face of the waters" can also be translated "hovering." It is used in Deuteronomy (32:11) of an eagle nurturingly or protectively hovering over the young in its nest.[4] The birds, hovering Genesis eagle and descending Markan dove, provide our imaginations with an image of the Spirit of God.

And as in Genesis the breathing of God that is first given visibility immediately becomes audible in speech ("Let there be . . ."), so in *Mark*: "Thou art my beloved Son; with thee I am well pleased" (Mark 1:11).

A lot has happened between the events of Genesis and the arrival of Jesus. The creation that was brought into being by the life-breath of God has been battered around a good bit. Death has become a major factor — death, anti-creation. Death, the denial of life, the elimination of life, the enemy of life. There is no energy in death, no movement in death, no words out of death. But death never prevailed. Always life — God-breathed, God-articulated life — survived, at times even flourished. As death worked its way into the creation, an extensive vocabulary of death words was developed to identify its various forms, words like "sin" and "rebellion," "iniquity" and "lawlessness." Biblically, we are given an extensively narrated story of life assaulted by death but all the time surviving death, with God constantly, in new ways and old, breathing life into this death-plagued creation, these death-battered lives. A complex plot emerges as we read this story: God creating a way of life out of this chaos and misery, God countering death, God breathing life into creation and creatures and the life-breath becoming audible in language over and over again. The vocabulary of life-words counters and surpasses the death-words: words like "love" and "hope," "obedience" and "faith" and "salvation," "grace" and "praise." Hallelujah and Amen words.

The same Spirit of God, so lavishly articulated in words that create out of formlessness, void, and darkness everything that is, "heavens and earth," fish and birds, stars and trees, plants and animals, man and woman, now descends on Jesus who will now speak salvation into reality in our death-ravished and sin-decimated world.

The God-breathed-into-life of Jesus, the God-blessed person of Jesus, at this moment begins to work out the consummation of salvation over death.

Acts 2:1-4

"When the day of Pentecost had come, they were all together in one place. And suddenly from heaven there came a sound like the rush of a violent wind, and it filled the entire house where they were sitting. Divided tongues, as of fire, appeared among them, and a tongue rested on each of them. All of them were filled with the Holy Spirit and began to speak in other languages, as the Spirit gave them ability."

And yet again, God begins. A third beginning, as God breathes on a company of 120 followers of Jesus and creates the holy community, the church.

On the day of his ascension into heaven Jesus had told his apostles that God would breathe life into them just as God had breathed heaven and earth into creation, just as God had breathed blessing into Jesus at his baptism, confirming and authorizing the completion of salvation in him. Once having been breathed into life by God — "baptized with the Holy Spirit" was the way he put it (Acts 1:5) — they would have the strength and energy to continue the God-breathed creation of heaven and earth and the God-breathed baptism of Jesus. "My witnesses" was the term he used to designate their new identity.

They believed the promise. They told other Jesus-followers. Soon there were 120 of them waiting for it to happen. They were waiting for the God-breathed creation of heaven and earth and the God-breathed baptism of Jesus to be God-breathed into them. They waited ten days.

When it happened, as it most surely did, there were surprises. The continuity with God's life-giving breath in the Genesis creation and the Jesus baptism was evident, but also augmented — the holy breathing became a holy wind, "the rush of a violent wind" (2:2), and filled the room. Soon the wind that filled the room (v. 2) filled them (v. 4). As if that were not enough, another sign was added, the sign of fire. Those gathered in the room that day were part of a tradition in which fire, commonly altar fire, was associated with the presence of God — Abraham at Moriah, Aaron in the tabernacle, Elijah on Carmel. But there was more to it here; this fire was *distributed* — each person individually was signed with a tongue of fire, each person an altar, visibly on fire with the presence of God. As the breathing of the Genesis creation and the Jesus baptism swelled into a wind, the old altar fires were multiplied into personalized fires burning above each waiting man and woman, each of them now a sign of God alive, God present.

And then, repeating the pattern of Genesis and Jesus, the breath/wind, that is, the living presence of God that filled each of them, was formed into spoken words by each of them. The tongues of fire became articulate in tongues of speech. The God-breathing that was formed into speech came out of the mouths of men and women speaking in all the languages (sixteen are named) represented in Jerusalem that day, with all the languages expressing essentially the same thing, "God's deeds of power" (v. 11).

Everyone, of course, was properly astonished. The miracle of language is what first caught their attention, the God-originated and God-witnessing speech spoken in sixteen (at least) different languages by ordinary men and women ("Galileans" — that is, provincials who presumably would know only one or two languages). The confusion of languages at Babel (Gen. 11) was reversed. The continuing miracle that continues to astonish is that the same breath (life) of God that created heavens and earth, that validated and blessed Jesus, is now being breathed into ordinary men and women and formed into words that continue to give witness to God's Genesis-creation and Jesus-salvation.

*   *   *

The three texts function like a tripod, grounding every aspect of life — creation, salvation, community — in the living (breathing) God. God alive who makes alive. God the Spirit who imparts spirit. God's Spirit is not marginal to the main action, it *is* the main action. Spirit is comprehensive. The three texts also make it clear that language is always involved in the making and saving and carrying on of life.

In the Christian tradition Spirit and Word are organically connected. They are not simply related or complementary; they are aspects of the same thing. Attempts are made from time to time to launch wordless spiritualities in which silence is set as the goal. It is no doubt true that there is too much talk in most religion or spirituality. But these three texts stand as authoritative: sooner or later something is said, reality is *spoken* into being.

Four Terms

Four terms provide a common vocabulary for exploring the nature and dynamics of the Christian life, Christian spirituality. The four terms work together as a quartet. There are no solo voices here. All are needed at once, although on occasion any one may take the lead for a brief time. Each gets its significance as much from how it sounds in relation to the others as from what it is in itself. A quartet of terms: "spirituality," "Jesus," "soul," and "fear-of-the-Lord." "Spirituality" sounds the note of comprehensiveness — anything and everything that men and women designate as they speak or think about the significance of their lives, including God and personal meaning and concern for the world. "Jesus" evokes focus and particularity. "Soul" gives voice to our unique human identity. "Fear-of-the-Lord" sets the mood and rhythm that makes it possible for the four terms to stay together, moving at the same pace.

There is nothing esoteric or obscure about any of the four terms; all are part of our common speech and may be heard if we step at random into the nearest coffee shop or hair salon or family reunion. But they are also used variously and carelessly in our culture, usually far removed from the language home in which they grew up. Since the terms provide a basic vocabulary in the pages of this book, it will be useful to reflect on how they sound and the associations they have in their more natural surroundings where they are most at home, the Christian life.

Spirituality

"Spirituality" is a net that when thrown into the sea of contemporary culture pulls in a vast quantity of spiritual fish, rivaling the resurrection catch of 153 "large fish" that St. John reports (John 21:11). In our times "spirituality" has become a major business for entrepreneurs, a recreational sport for the bored, and for others, whether many or few (it is difficult to discern), a serious and disciplined commitment to live deeply and fully in relation to God.

Once used exclusively in traditional religious contexts, the word is now used quite indiscriminately by all sorts of people in all sorts of circumstances and with all sorts of meanings. This once pristine word has been dragged into the rough-and-tumble dirt of marketplace and playground. Many lament this, but I'm not sure that lament is the appropriate response. We need a word like this.

The attempt to reclaim the word for exclusively Christian or other religious usage usually begins with a definition. But attempts to define "spirituality," and they are many, are futile. The term has escaped the disciplines of the dictionary. The current usefulness of the term is not in its precision but rather in the way it names something indefinable yet quite recognizable — transcendence vaguely intermingled with intimacy. Transcendence: a sense that there is more, a sense that life extends far beyond me, beyond what I get paid, beyond what my spouse and children think of me, beyond my cholesterol count. And intimacy: a sense that deep within me there is a core being inaccessible to the probes of psychologists or the examinations of physicians, the questions of the pollsters, the strategies of the advertisers. "Spirituality," though hardly precise, provides the catch-all term that recognizes an organic linkage to this Beyond and Within that are part of everyone's experience.

We need a term that covers the waterfront, that throws every intimation of Beyond and Within into one huge wicker basket, a term that is indiscriminately comprehensive: spirituality.

*   *   *

The word "spirituality," historically, is a relative latecomer to our dictionaries, and only very recently has it hit the streets in common, everyday speech. St. Paul used the adjective "spiritual" (*pneumatikos*) to refer to actions or attitudes derived from the work of the Holy Spirit in all Christians.[5] It was only later in the medieval church, and primarily in the context of monasticism, that the word began to be used to name a way of life restricted to an elite class of Christian, those who worked at a higher level than ordinary Christians. The lives of "spiritual" Christians, mostly monks and nuns vowed to celibacy, poverty, and obedience, were viewed in contrast to the muddled lives of men and women who married and had babies, who got their hands dirty in fields and markets in a world where "all is seared with trade; bleared, smeared with toil;/and wears man's smudge and shares man's smell...."[6] "Spirituality," then, came into use to designate the study and practice of a perfect life before God, of extraordinary holiness in the Christian life. It was a specialized word having to do with only a small number of people and so was never part of everyday speech.

The word got into our common language more or less through the backdoor. A movement developed in seventeenth-century France among Catholic laity who held the then radical notion that the monasteries had no corner on the Christian life well-lived. They insisted that the ordinary Christian was quite as capable of living the Christian life as any monk or nun — and of living it just as well. Madam Guyon and Miguel de Molinos, prominent voices in this movement, were silenced by church authorities who condemned their beliefs as "quietism." The religious establishment, with its nose in the air, used the term *la spiritualité* as a term of derogation for laypeople who practiced their devotion too intensely, a snobbish dismissal of upstart Christians who didn't know what they were doing, writing, thinking, and practicing. These were things that were best left in the hands of the experts. But the official church's attempt to silence them was too late; the cat was out of the bag.

It wasn't long, though, before the word lost its pejorative tone. Among Protestants, lay-oriented spiritual seriousness came to be expressed in Puritan "godliness," Methodist "perfection," and Lutheran "pietism." "Spirituality," this loose, vaguely comprehensive "net" word, is now used on the streets with general approval. Now anybody can be spiritual.

Interestingly, some of today's "experts" in religion are again using the term dismissively. Because there appears to be a widespread and faddish use of the term by men and women judged by credentialed insiders as misguided, ignorant, and undisciplined, some professionals are once again taking a condescending stance toward spirituality in its popular forms.

*   *   *

Living, living fully and well, is at the heart of all serious spirituality. "Spirit," in our three parent languages of Hebrew, Greek, and Latin, carries the root meaning of breath and easily offers itself up as a metaphor for life. The word figured prominently in the two stories (Nicodemus and the Samaritan) and the three texts (Genesis, Mark, Acts) that set the tone for our conversation. In each instance the spirit is God's Spirit: God alive, God creating, God saving, God blessing. God lives and gives life. God lives and brims with life. God lives and permeates everything we see and hear and taste and touch, everything we experience.

At this time in our history, "spirituality" seems to be the term of choice to refer to this vast and intricate web of "livingness." It may not be the best word, but it is what we have. Its primary weakness is that in the English language "spirituality" has been eroded to an abstraction, even though the metaphor "breath" can be detected just beneath the surface. As an abstraction "spirituality" frequently obscures the very thing it is intended to convey — God alive and active and present.

The difficulty is that the term has become widely secularized in our present culture and consequently reduced to mean simply "vitality" or "centered energy" or "hidden springs of exuberance" or "an aliveness that comes from within." For most people it conveys no sense of the life of God: *Spirit* of God, *Spirit* of Christ, Holy *Spirit*. The more the word is secularized the less useful it is. Still, it is what we have and as with many ruined or desiccated words (I think of "marriage," "love," "sin," and so on) requires constant rehabilitation. I find it best to use it as little as possible — following the precedent of our Scriptures, which have an aversion to abstractions of any kind — and prefer to use stories and metaphors that keep us involved and participating in what is right before us.

The abstracted vagueness of the word easily serves as a convenient cover for idolatry. Idolatry, reducing God to a concept or object that we

29

can use for our benefit, is endemic to the human condition. As long as the word carries connotations of sincerity and aspiration for all that is good, it is easy and common for idolatrous motives to quietly and unassumingly attach themselves to it and involve us in ways of living and thinking that are crippling.

Superficial misunderstandings can be easily disposed of: Spirituality is not immaterial as opposed to material; not interior as opposed to exterior; not invisible as opposed to visible. Quite the contrary; spirituality has much to do with the material, the external, and the visible. What it properly conveys is living as opposed to dead. When we sense that the life has gone out of things and people, of institutions and traditions, eventually (and sometimes this takes us awhile) we notice the absence. We look for a file-drawer kind of word in which we can shove insights, images, and desires that we don't have a precise name for. "Spirituality" works about as well as anything for filing purposes.

The frequent use of the word as a catch-all term is understandable in a society in which we are variously depersonalized, functionalized, and psychologized. The particularity of each life is obscured by reductionizing abstractions. Life leaks out of us as we find ourselves treated as objects, roles, images, economic potential, commodities, consumers. Even though daily life is much simplified and made easier by these various reductions, something in us rebels, at least in fits and starts. Most of us, at least at times, sense that there is something more, something vastly more. We need a word, any word, to name what we are missing.

But if we are going to use the term, and it's difficult to see how we can avoid it, our use is going to have to be marked by vigilance and attentiveness. Vigilance: discerning the de-spiritualization of spirituality by watching for and naming the many and various ways in which we fall prey to the devil's lure to "be like God" (Gen. 3:5). The primary way in which this vigilance is maintained is in a continual and careful reading of Holy Scripture.

And attentiveness: noticing the many and profligate ways in which God gives life, renews life, blesses life. Noticing and then insisting that everything in this creation is livable. The primary way in which this attentiveness is nurtured is in common worship and personal prayer.

I am quite content to work in this field of spirituality with whatever is given me, however vague and fuzzy. But I am also interested in providing as much clarity and focus as I am able by identifying life, all of life, as God-derived, God-sustained, and God-blessed: "I walk before the LORD in the land of the living" (Ps. 116:9).

Jesus

If the usefulness of the term "spirituality" is in its vague but comprehensive suggestiveness of everything Beyond and More and Deep, the term "Jesus" is useful as it gathers all the diffused vagueness into a tight, clear, light-filled focus; for in the Christian way there is nothing vague about life (although there is plenty of ambiguity involved!). Spirituality is never a subject that we can attend to as a thing-in-itself. It is always an operation of God in which our human lives are pulled into and made participants in the life of God, whether as lovers or rebels.

The Christian community is interested in spirituality because it is interested in living. We give careful attention to spirituality because we know, from long experience, how easy it is to get interested in ideas of God and projects for God and gradually lose interest in God alive, deadening our lives with the ideas and the projects. This happens a lot. Because the ideas and projects have the name of God attached to them, it is easy to assume that we are involved with God. It is the devil's work to get us worked up thinking and acting for God and then subtly detach us from a relational obedience and adoration of God, substituting our selves, our godlike egos, in the place originally occupied by God.

Jesus is the name that keeps us attentive to the God-defined, God-revealed life. The amorphous limpness so often associated with "spirituality" is given skeleton, sinews, definition, shape, and energy by the term "Jesus." Jesus is the personal name of a person who lived at a datable time in an actual land that has mountains we can still climb, wildflowers that can be photographed, cities in which we can still buy dates and pomegranates, and water which we can drink and in which we can be baptized. As such the name counters the abstraction that plagues "spirituality."

Jesus is the central and defining figure in the spiritual life. His life is, precisely, *revelation*. He brings out into the open what we could never have figured out for ourselves, never guessed in a million years. He is God among us: God speaking, acting, healing, helping. "Salvation" is the big word into which all these words fit. The name Jesus means "God saves" — God present and at work saving in our language and in our history.

The four Gospel writers, backed up by the comprehensive context provided by Israel's prophets and poets, tell us everything we need to know about Jesus. And Jesus tells us everything we need to know about God. As we read, ponder, study, believe, and pray these Gospels we find both the entire Scriptures and the entirety of the spiritual life accessible and in focus before us in the inviting presence of Jesus of Nazareth, the Word made flesh.

But while the Gospel writers present Jesus in a feet-on-the-ground setting not too different from the town and countryside in which we live, and in a vocabulary and syntax similar to the language we use when we sit down to the dinner table and go out shopping, they don't indulge our curiosity — there is much that they do *not* tell us. There is so much more that we would like to know. Our imaginations itch to fill in the details. What did Jesus look like? How did he grow up? How did his childhood friends treat him? What did he do all those years of his growing up in the carpentry shop?

It didn't take long, as it turns out, for writers to appear on the scene who were quite ready to satisfy our curiosities, to tell us what Jesus was *really* like. And they keep showing up. But "lives" of Jesus — imaginative constructs of Jesus' life with all the childhood influences, emotional tones, neighborhood gossip, and social/cultural/political dynamics worked in — are notoriously unsatisfactory. What we always seem to get is not the Jesus who reveals God to us, but a Jesus who develops some ideal or justifies some cause of the writer. When we finish the book, we realize that we have less of Jesus, not more.

This itch to know more about Jesus than the canonical Gospel writers chose to tell us started early on in the second century. The first people who filled in the blanks in the story had wonderful imaginations but were somewhat deficient in veracity; they omitted to tell us that the supplementary entertaining details were the product of their imaginations. Some wrote under apostolic pseudonyms to provide authority for their inventions. Others claimed actual Holy Spirit inspiration for their fictions. It wasn't long before the church got more or less fed up with this imaginative tinkering with and creative expansion of Jesus and said it had to stop. The church leaders rendered their decision: The Gospels of Matthew, Mark, Luke, and John are the last word on Jesus. There is nothing more to be said on the subject.

The ban on inventing new Jesus stories and sayings was not, as some have suggested, repressive. Its effect was to release the imagination for doing what is proper to it, namely, joining Mary the mother of Jesus in pondering Jesus in our hearts (Luke 2:19, 51), meditating our own selves into the presence of Jesus as presented by the Gospel writers, or meditating other settings in which Jesus is met and either crucified again or believed in again by us. And we have been doing it ever since in sermons and Bible studies, in stories and poems, in pilgrimage and silence, in hymns and prayers, in acts of obedience and service in Jesus' name.

It is essential that we honor this reticence on the part of the Gospel writers. Spirituality is not improved by fantasies. The Christian life is not a field in which to indulge pious dreams.

By accepting Jesus as the final and definitive revelation of God, the Christian church makes it impossible for us to make up our own customized variations of the spiritual life and get away with it, not that we don't try. But we can't get around him or away from him: Jesus is the incarnation of God, God among and with us. Jesus gathered up God's words spoken to and through God's people and given to us in our Holy Scriptures. He spoke them personally to us. He performed God's works of healing and compassion, forgiveness and salvation, love and sacrifice among *us*, men and women with personal names, with personal histories. Because Jesus was born in Bethlehem, grew up in Nazareth, gathered disciples in Galilee, worshiped in synagogues, ate meals in Bethany, went to a wedding in Cana, told stories in Jericho, prayed in Gethsemane, led a parade down the Mount of Olives, taught in the Jerusalem temple, was killed on the hill Golgotha, and three days later had supper with Cleopas and his friend in Emmaus, we are not free to make up our own private spiritualities; we know too much about *his* life, *his* spirituality. The story of Jesus gives us access to scores of these incidents and words, specific with places and times and names, all of them hanging together and interpenetrating, forming a coherent revelation of who God is and how he acts and what he says. Jesus prevents us from thinking that life is a matter of ideas to ponder or concepts to discuss. Jesus saves us from wasting our lives in the pursuit of cheap thrills and trivializing diversions. Jesus enables us to take seriously who we are and where we are without being seduced by the intimidating lies and illusions that fill the air, so that we needn't be someone else or somewhere else. Jesus keeps our feet on the ground, attentive to children, in conversation with ordinary people, sharing meals with friends and strangers, listening to the wind, observing the wildflowers, touching the sick and wounded, praying simply and unselfconsciously. Jesus insists that we deal with God right here and now, in the place we find ourselves and with the people we are with. Jesus *is* God here and now.

* * *

It is basic to the Christian faith that Jesus is, in actual fact, God among us. As hard as it is to believe and as impossible as it is to imagine, Christians do believe it. The entire and elaborate work of salvation from "before the foundation of the world" (Eph. 1:4) is gathered up and made complete in this birth, life, death, and resurrection — a miracle of unprecedented and staggering proportions. We acknowledge all this when we, following the example of St. Peter, add the title "Christ" to the name Jesus: Jesus Christ. Christ: God's anointed, God among us to save us from our sins, God speaking to us in the same language we learned at our mother's knee, God raising us from the dead to real, eternal life.

You would think that believing that Jesus is God among us would be the hardest thing. It is not. It turns out that the hardest thing is to believe that God's work — this dazzling creation, this astonishing salvation, this cascade of blessings — is all being worked out in and under the conditions of our humanity: at picnics and around dinner tables, in conversations and while walking along roads, in puzzled questions and homely stories, with blind beggars and suppurating lepers, at weddings and funerals. Everything that Jesus does and says takes place within the limits and conditions of our humanity. No fireworks. No special effects. Yes, there are miracles, plenty of them. But because for the most part they are so much a part of the fabric of everyday life, very few notice. The miraculousness of miracle is obscured by the familiarity of the setting, the ordinariness of the people involved.

* * *

This is still the way Jesus is God among us. And this is what is still so hard to believe. It is hard to believe that this marvelous work of salvation is presently taking place in our neighborhoods, in our families, in our governments, in our schools and businesses, in our hospitals, on the roads we drive and down the corridors we walk, among people whose names we know. The ordinariness of Jesus was a huge roadblock to belief in his identity and work in the "days of his flesh." It is still a roadblock.

In an incident reported by St. John, people who heard Jesus speak a most impressive, a truly astonishing, message in the Capernaum synagogue — offering his own body and blood as food for eternal life! — disbelieved what he said because he wasn't more impressive. "This man," they called him dismissively (John 6:52). Given their earlier attempt to discredit his extravagant claim ("I am the bread that came down from heaven," 6:41) by pointing out his unmistakable humanity ("Is not this Jesus, the son of Joseph, whose father and mother we know?" 6:42), "this man" carries the clear implication of "this nobody." Suddenly many of Jesus' followers weren't buying it any longer — they couldn't fit the miracles and the message into the unimpressive form of "this man" they were looking at. Their rhetorical question, "Who can accept it?" called for a negative answer, "Not us."

Jesus brings the undercurrent of dissension into the open: "Does this offend you? Then what if you were to see the Son of Man ascending to where he was before? It is the spirit that gives life; the flesh is useless" (John 6:61-63). Which is to say, "So, what is your problem? If you saw me levitating right here before your eyes straight up into heaven, then would you believe what I'm telling you? I guess you would, but it is the spirit, which is like the wind that you can't see, that gives life, not the flesh, not out-of-this-world wonders." Spirit again. This key word in the earlier conversations with Nicodemus and the Samaritan marks the quiet, often concealed, means by which God works his salvation among us.

They are not impressed. They walk off, followers no longer: "Because of this many of his disciples turned back and no longer went about with him" (6:66). Because of what? Because Jesus was so obviously *human* — so ordinary, so uncharismatic, so unexciting, so everyday human.

Jesus asks the Twelve if they also are going to abandon him. Here St. John supplies us with St. Peter's punch line response: "Lord, to whom can we go? You have the words of eternal life . . . you are the Holy One of God" (6:68-69). Peter has come to the place where we must all come if we are going to continue following Jesus: he does not impose on Jesus his own ideas or ambitions on how God must do his work; he is willing to let Jesus do it in his own way, *as a man.*

The perpetual threat to living a real life, an authentic and true and honest life, is to evade or dump "this man," this Jesus, this ordinary way he comes to us and this inglorious company he keeps, and pretentiously attempt to be our own god or to fashion a glamorous god or gods that appeal to our vanity.[7] When it comes to dealing with God, most of us spend considerable time trying our own hands at either being or making gods. Jesus blocks the way. Jesus is not a god of our own making and he is certainly not a god designed to win popularity contests.

Soul

When we come to understand ourselves and the men and women we work with "according to the Scriptures," our core identity comes out as persons-in-relationship. Each person is a one-of-a-kind creature made in the "image of God." Whatever else that phrase means, it conveys a sense of enormous dignity and thorough-going relationality.

"Soul" is our word for this.[8] It is the most personal term we have for who we are. The term "soul" is an assertion of wholeness, the totality of what it means to be a human being. "Soul" is a barrier against reduction, against human life reduced to biology and genitals, culture and utility, race and ethnicity. It signals an interiority that permeates all exteriority, an invisibility that everywhere inhabits visibility. "Soul" carries with it resonances of God-created, God-sustained, and God-blessed. It is our most comprehensive term for designating the core being of men and women.

"Soul" in the Hebrew language is a metaphor, *nephesh*, the word for neck. The neck is the narrow part of the anatomy that connects the head, the site of intelligence and the nervous system, with everything else; it literally keeps us "together." Physically, the head is higher than the body, at least when we are standing up, and so we sometimes speak of the higher functions of thinking, seeing, hearing, and tasting in contrast to the lower functions of digestion and excretion, of perspiring and copulating. But if there are higher and lower aspects to human life (which I very much doubt) it is not as if they can exist independently from one another. And what connects them is the neck. The neck contains the narrow passage through which air passes from mouth to lungs and back out again in speech — breath, spirit, God-breathed life. It is the conduit for the entire nervous system stemming and branching from the brain. And it is where the mighty jugular vein, an extremely vulnerable three to four inches of blood supply, comes dangerously close to the surface of the skin. Soul,

36

nephesh, keeps it all together. Without soul we would be a jumble of disconnected parts, lumps of protoplasm. Our modern passion for analysis and dissection, trying to find out what makes us tick, is not a biblical passion. Our Scriptures come at us differently; they convey a sense of wholeness, *created*. The Hebrews had a genius for metaphors and "soul" is one of their finest. Synonyms for "soul" proliferate — heart, kidneys, loins — accumulating metaphors that deepen a sense of inwardness and depth. But "soul" holds the center.

The term "soul" works like a magnet, pulling all the pieces of our lives into a unity, a totality. The human person is a vast totality; "soul" names it as such.[9]

The biblical story that gives us this metaphor in Genesis 2 makes it clear that the breath that flows through the neck/soul is God's breath. And if God's breath is gone, the human being is gone. Apart from God there is nothing to us.

Virtually every language has a word or words similar to this, words that reach for what the human being is uniquely and comprehensively. Biblically, "comprehensive" includes God and all the operations of God in men and women. Most of what makes us human is God. When we say "soul" we are calling attention to the God-origins, God-intentions, God-operations that make us what we are. It is the most personal and most comprehensive term for who we are — man, woman, and child.

But in our current culture, "soul" has given way to "self" as the term of choice to designate who and what we are. Self is the soul minus God. Self is what is left of soul with all the transcendence and intimacy squeezed out, the self with little or no reference to God (transcendence) or others (intimacy).

"Self" is a threadbare word, a scarecrow word.

"Soul" is a word reverberating with relationships: God-relationships, human-relationships, earth-relationships.

"Self" in both common speech and scientific discourse is mostly an isolating term: the individual.

"Soul" gets beneath the fragmentary surface appearances and experiences and affirms an at-homeness, an affinity with whoever and whatever is at hand.

When "soul" and "self" are turned into adjectives in colloquial speech, the contrast becomes even clearer: "soulish" gives a sense of something inherent and relational, entering the depths, plumbing the underlying sources of motive and meaning, as in soul food, soul music, the soulful eyes of a spaniel, and, negatively, "that poor lost soul"; "selfish," on the other hand, refers to the self-absorbed, uncaring, and unrelational — a life that is all surface and image.

Setting the two words side by side triggers a realization that a fundamental aspect of our identity is under assault every day. We live in a culture that has replaced soul with self. This reduction turns people into either problems or consumers. Insofar as we acquiesce in that replacement, we gradually but surely regress in our identity, for we end up thinking of ourselves and dealing with others in marketplace terms: everyone we meet is either a potential recruit to join our enterprise or a potential consumer for what we are selling; or we ourselves are the potential recruits and consumers. Neither we nor our friends have any dignity just as we are, only in terms of how we or they can be used.

Two words, widely used these days, are symptomatic of the reduction of soul to self in our society. The first of these, "resource," is commonly used of people who can help us in our work. I can still remember how jarring that word sounded to me when I first heard it used forty years ago by a man who was giving me direction in my work of developing a new congregation. He kept pushing me to identify the resource-people that I could use in my work. And then I noticed that he was using the word as a verb; he frequently offered to resource our church board, our financial committee, our planning committee.

But "resource" identifies a person as something to be used. There is nothing personal to a resource — it is a thing, stuff, a function. Use the word long enough and it begins to change the way we view a person. It started out harmlessly enough as a metaphor and as such was found useful, I guess. But when it becomes habitual, it erodes our sense of this person as soul — relational at the core and God-dimensioned.

And "dysfunctional." It is alarming how frequently people are referred to as dysfunctional: dysfunctional families, dysfunctional committees and congregations, dysfunctional leaders, dysfunctional relationships, dysfunctional politicians. But dysfunctional is not a personal word, it is mechanical. Machines are dysfunctional but not souls; bicycles are dysfunctional but not children; water pumps are dysfunctional but not spouses. The constant, unthinking use of the word erodes our sense of worth and dignity inherent in the people we meet and work with no matter how messed up they are.

We cannot be too careful about the words we use; we start out using them and then they end up using us. Our imaginations become blunted. We end up dealing only with surfaces, functions, roles.

In our present culture all of us find that we are studied, named, and treated as functions and things. "Consumer" is the catch-all term for the way we are viewed. From an early age we are looked upon as individuals who can buy or perform or use. Advertisers begin targeting us in those terms from the moment we are able to choose a breakfast cereal.

For those of us who are reared in North American culture, it is inevitable that we should unconsciously acquire this way of looking at everyone we meet. Other people are potential buyers for what I am selling, students for what I am teaching, recruits for what I am doing, voters for what I am proposing, resources for what I am building or making, clients for the services I am offering. Or, to reverse the elements, I identify myself as the potential buyer, student, recruit, resource, client, and so on. But it is consumerism either way.

I have no complaint about this at one level. I need things, other people offer what I need; I am happy to pay for and take advantage of what is offered whether it is food, clothing, information, medical and legal help, leadership in a cause that is dear to my heart, advocacy in matters of justice, or victim-rights that I care about. I'm quite happy to be a consumer in this capitalist economy where there is so much to consume.

Except. Except that I don't want to be just a consumer. I don't even want to be predominantly a consumer. To be reduced to a consumer is to leave out most of what I am, of what makes me *me*. To be treated as a consumer is to be reduced to being used by another or reduced to a product for someone else's use. It makes little difference whether the using is in a generous or selfish cause, it is reduction. Widespread consumerism results in extensive depersonalization. And every time depersonalization moves in, life leaks out.

But souls are not sieves; souls brim with life: "Bless the Lord, O my *soul!*"

Fear-of-the-Lord

Finally, we need a common and comprehensive term for referring to the way we live the spiritual life — not just what we do and say but the way we act, the way we speak. How do we go about living appropriately in this world that has been revealed to us in Jesus Christ?

This is a question that needs to be delayed for as long as possible. Most of the Christian life (and spiritual theology is responsible for maintaining vigilance in this regard) involves paying attention to who God is and what he does; but not only the who and the what but the *how*, the *means* God employs to accomplish his ends. If we get too interested too soon in what *we* do and are, we go off the rails badly. Still, we are part of it and need a term to designate the human side of spirituality, something that names the way we make our way through this complex minefield of a world in which we live out the Christian life. But it needs to be a term that does not make us the center of the subject. (The words most in use among us tend to put the emphasis on what we initiate and carry out: spiritual discipline, piety, devotional practice, quiet time, and so on.) It also needs to be a term that doesn't contribute to the dichotomizing of spirituality into God's part and the human part.

This question — "what is our part in this?" — requires considerable care in the answering. We realize how critical it is to get the right term for this when we look around and become aware of the sheer quantity of silliness, sördidness, meanness, and dullness that piles up under the roofs of enterprises given over to directing and motivating people to serve God, as our "leaders" tell us what to do and say to be distinctively God's people. Given the frequency with which men and women make hash out of the words and works of God, it might seem best to do nothing. Just get out of the way and let God do it all.

There have been teachers who have formulated just such an answer and been serious about it: the less we do for God, the better; it leaves more room for God to do something for us, which is the point of it all anyway.[10] But most of us do not find that adequate counsel. Most of us have a sense that somehow or other we need to get in on what God is doing; we *want* to be involved, we want to *do* something. But what, without getting in the way, without gumming up the works?

*   *   *

The biblical word of choice for the term we need is "fear-of-the-Lord." It is the stock biblical phrase for the way of life that is lived responsively and appropriately before who God is, who he is as Father, Son, and Holy Spirit.

None of the available synonyms in the English language — awe, reverence, worshipful respect — seems quite adequate. They miss the punch delivered by "fear-of-the-Lord." When Rudolf Otto, one of our great scholars in these matters, analyzed this core religious/spiritual attitude and response, he resorted to Latin phrases (*numen* and *mysterium tremendum*), finding that nothing in his German language worked either.[11]

The primary way in which we cultivate fear-of-the-Lord is in prayer and worship — personal prayer and corporate worship. We deliberately interrupt our preoccupation with ourselves and attend to God, place ourselves intentionally in sacred space, in sacred time, in the holy presence — and wait. We become silent and still in order to listen and respond to what is Other than us. Once we get the hang of this we find that this can occur any place and any time. But prayer and worship provide the base.

"Fear-of-the-Lord" is the best term we have to point to this way of life we cultivate as Christians. The Christian life consists mostly of what God — Father, Son, and Holy Spirit — is and does. But we also are part of it. Not the largest part, but still part. A world has been opened up to us by revelation in which we find ourselves walking on holy ground and living in sacred time. The moment we realize this, we feel shy, cautious. We slow down, we look around, ears and eyes alert. Like lost children happening on a clearing in the woods and finding elves and fairies singing and dancing in a circle around a prancing two-foot-high unicorn, we stop in awed silence to accommodate to this wonderful but unguessed-at revelation. But for us it isn't a unicorn and elves; it is Sinai and Tabor and Golgotha.

The moment we find ourselves unexpectedly in the presence of the sacred, our first response is to stop in silence. We do nothing. We say nothing. We fear to trespass inadvertently; we are afraid of saying something inappropriate. Plunged into mystery we become still, we fall silent, all our senses alert. This is the fear-of-the-Lord.

Or we don't. Uneasy with the unknown, again like children, we run around crazily, yelling and screaming, trying to put our stamp of familiarity on it. We attempt to get rid of the mystery by making our presence large and noisy. When children do this in church we call it misbehaving. But misbehavior in these matters does not consist in what we say or do as such; it is that what we say or do is incongruent with the sacred time and place. Until we know what is going on, anything we say or do is apt to be wrong, or at least inappropriate.

We all have experiences of finding ourselves in the sacred presence or on holy ground from time to time, however briefly. The most common of such experiences is being in the presence of a newborn child. Most of us are speechless and still. We don't know what to do or say. We are overtaken by the mystery of God-given life. Something deep within us responds to the sacredness of life, of sheer existence; our response becomes worship, adoration, prayer, awe — the fear-of-the-Lord.

But there is also something about the sacred that makes us uneasy. We don't like being in the dark, not knowing what to do. And so we attempt to domesticate the mystery, explain it, probe it, name and use it. "Blasphemy" is the term we use for these verbal transgressions of the sacred, these violations of the holy: taking God's name in vain, dishonoring sacred time and place, reducing God to gossip and chatter. Uncomfortable with the mystery, we try to banish it with clichés.

Every culture has stories and taboos to train and discipline its people in protecting and honoring the sacred mystery. Human beings are not gods; the moment we forget this, we violate the boundaries of our humanity and something is violated in reality itself. The universe suffers damage.

So we set out to cultivate the fear-of-the-Lord, "the quintessential rubric, which expresses in a nutshell the basic grammar that holds the covenant community together," as Bruce Waltke puts it.[12] Despite its prominence in the Bible, the term does not find wide use among North American Christians. "Fear" apparently gets us off on the wrong foot. Grammarians help us regain our biblical stride by calling our attention to the fact that fear-of-the-Lord is a "bound phrase" (syntagm). The four words in English (two in Hebrew) are bound together, making a single word. Its function as a single word cannot be understood by taking it apart and then adding up the meanings of the parts. Fear-of-the-Lord is not a combination of fear + of + the + Lord. Fear-of-the-Lord is a word all its own. So we don't look up "fear" in the dictionary, then "God," and then proceed to combine the two meanings: "fear," a feeling of apprehension, plus "God," a divine being worthy of worship, is not fear-of-the-Lord. Pursuing that analytical route gets us way off the track.

But when we let the biblical contexts provide the conditions for understanding the word we find that it means something more like a way of life in which human feelings and behavior are fused with God's being and revelation. There are upward of 138 occurrences of the term in a wide range of Old Testament books but most prominently in Proverbs, Psalms, Isaiah, Chronicles, and Deuteronomy.[13] God is active in the term; the human is active in the term. "Fear-of-the-Lord" designates a way of living that cannot be dissected into two parts, any more than a baby can be dissected into what comes from sperm and what comes from egg. "Fear-of-the-Lord" is a new word in our vocabularies; it marks the way of life appropriate to our creation and salvation and blessing by God.

A common and distressingly frequent way of answering the question, "So now, what do we do?" but one that avoids prayerful involvement with God in the presence of God, is to come up with a Code of Conduct. The Ten Commandments is the usual place to start, supplemented by Proverbs, brought to a focus by Jesus' summing up (Love God/Love your neighbor), salted by the Golden Rule, and then capped off by the Beatitudes. That might seem to be the simplest way to go about it, but religious communities that take this route have rarely, if ever, been able to let it go at that. They commonly find that the particular context in which they live requires special handling: rules are added, regulations enforced, and it isn't long before the Code of Conduct grows into a formidable jungle of talmudic regulation.

The other and opposite way of doing the Code of Conduct thing is to make it as simple as possible; get it down to the bare bones of bumper sticker spirituality: "Follow your bliss. . . . Smell the roses. . . . Do no harm. . . ." My favorite is the fragment of a poem sometimes attributed to W. H. Auden:

> I love to sin; God loves to forgive;
> The world is admirably arranged.

But the fundamental inadequacy of codes of conduct for giving direction in how to live the spiritual life is that they put us in charge (or, which is just as bad, put someone else in charge of us); God is moved off the field of action to the judge's stand where he grades our performance. The moment that we take charge, "knowing good and evil," we are in trouble and almost immediately start getting other people in trouble too.

No. However useful codes of conduct are in the overall scheme of things, they are not the place to begin answering the question, "Now, what do we do?"

*   *   *

The fact that fear-of-the-Lord cannot be precisely defined is one of its glories — we are dealing with something that we cannot pin down, we inhabit mystery, we can't be cocksure about anything, we cultivate an attentive and reverent expectation before every person, event, rock, and tree. Presumption recedes, attentiveness increases, expectancy heightens.

"Fear-of-the-Lord," as we notice the way our biblical writers use it, turns out to be a term that is plain without being reductive, clear without being over-simplified, and accurate without dissolving the mystery inherent in all dealings with God and his world. It also has the considerable advantage of evading the precise definition or "control" that we could use to locate ourselves along a spectrum of piety or goodness that would feed our instincts for coziness with God.

So what do we do, given our launch into this life of following Jesus? "Fear the LORD, you his saints" (Ps. 34:9 RSV). Fear-of-the-Lord is not studying about God but living in reverence before God. We don't so much lack knowledge, we lack reverence. Fear-of-the-Lord is not a technique for acquiring spiritual know-how but a willed not-knowing. It is not so much know-how we lack; we lack a simple being-there. Fear-of-the-Lord, nurtured in worship and prayer, silence and quiet, love and sacrifice, turns everything we do into a life of "breathing God."

And a Dance

The dance is *perichoresis,* the Greek word for dance. The term was used by our Greek theologian ancestors as a metaphor to refer to the Trinity. *Perichoresis,* wrote Karl Barth, "asserts that the divine modes of existence condition and permeate one another mutually with such perfection, that one is as invariably in the other two as the other two are in the one."[14] Imagine a folk dance, a round dance, with three partners in each set. The music starts up and the partners holding hands begin moving in a circle. On signal from the caller, they release hands, change partners, and weave in and out, swinging first one and then another. The tempo increases, the partners move more swiftly with and between and among one another, swinging and twirling, embracing and releasing, holding on and letting go. But there is no confusion, every movement is cleanly coordinated in precise rhythms (these are practiced and skillful dancers!), as each person maintains his or her own identity. To the onlooker, the movements are so swift it is impossible at times to distinguish one person from another; the steps are so intricate that it is difficult to anticipate the actual configurations as they appear: *Perichoresis* (peri = around; *choresis* = dance).[15]

The essence of Trinity, the centerpiece of Christian theology and sometimes considered the most subtle and abstruse of all doctrines, is captured here in a picture that anyone can observe in an American neighborhood barn dance or an Irish *ceilidh*.

Trinity is the most comprehensive and integrative framework that we have for understanding and participating in the Christian life. Early on in our history, our pastors and teachers formulated the Trinity to express what is distinctive in the revelation of God in Christ. This theology provides an immense horizon against which we can understand and practice the Christian life largely and comprehensively. Without an adequately imagined theology, spirituality gets reduced to the cramped world reported by journalists or the flat world studied by scientists. Trinity reveals the immense world of God creating, saving, and blessing in the name of Father, Son, and Holy Spirit with immediate and lived implications for the way we live, for our spirituality. Trinity is the church's attempt to understand God's revelation of Godself in all its parts and relationships. And a most useful work it has been. At a most practical level it provides a way of understanding and responding to the God who enters into all the day-to-day issues that we face as persons and churches and communities from the time we get out of bed in the morning until we fall asleep at night, and reaches out to bring us into participation on God's terms, that is, on Trinitarian terms. It prevents us from getting involved in highly religious but soul-destroying ways of going about living the Christian life.

*   *   *

Trinity understands God as three-personed: Father, Son, and Holy Spirit, God in community, each "person" in active communion with the others.[16] We are given an understanding of God that is most emphatically personal and interpersonal. God is nothing if not personal. If God is revealed as personal, the only way that God can be known is in personal response. We need to know this. It is the easiest thing in the world to use words as a kind of abstract truth or principle, to deal with the gospel as information. Trinity prevents us from doing this. We can never get away with de-personalizing the gospel or the truth to make it easier, simpler, more convenient. Knowing God through impersonal abstractions is ruled out, knowing God through programmatic projects is abandoned, knowing God in solitary isolation is forbidden. Trinity insists that God is not an idea or a force or a private experience but personal and known only in personal response and engagement.

Trinity also prevents us from reducing God to what we can understand or need at any one time. There is a lot going on in us and this world, far exceeding what we are capable of taking in. In dealing with God, we are dealing in mystery, in what we do not know, what we cannot control or deal with on our terms. We need to know this, for we live in a world that over-respects the practical. We want God to be "relevant" to our lifestyle. We want what we can, as we say, "get a handle on." There is immense peer pressure to reduce God to fit immediate needs and expectations. But God is never a commodity to use. In a functionalized world in which we are all trained to understand ourselves in terms of what we can do, we are faced with a reality that we cannot control. And so we cultivate reverence. We are in the presence of One who is both before and beyond us. We listen and wait. Presumption — God-on-demand on our terms — is exposed as simply silly. Defining God down to the level of our emotions, and thinking and then demanding that God work by the terms of our agenda, is set aside in favor of a life of worship and prayer, obedience and love — a way of life open and responsive to what *God* is doing rather than one in which we plot strategies to get God involved in what *we* are doing. Trinity keeps pulling us into a far larger world than we can imagine on our own.

And Trinity is a steady call and invitation to participate in the energetically active life of God — the image of the dance again. It is the participation in the Trinity (God as he has revealed himself to us) that makes things and people particularly and distinctively who they are. We are not spectators to God; there is always a hand reaching out to pull us into the Trinitarian actions of holy creation, holy salvation, and holy community. God is never a nonparticipant in what he does, nor are any of us. There are no nonparticipants in a Trinity-revealed life. We need to know this. It is a lot easier to guide, motivate, plan, and direct from a distance, whether in our homes or in our work. So we keep a little distance, find ways to delegate so we don't have to get too involved. But the reality of the Trinity does not permit it. If we are going to know God we have to participate in the relationship that is God. We discover ourselves as unique participants — each of us one-of-a-kind — in the life of God. The Christian life is not preprogrammed; it is a release into freedom. Trinity keeps us alert and responsive to the freedom that derives from participation in the life of God. And every act of participation is unique.

Every expression of spirituality, left to itself, tends toward being more about me and less about God. Spiritual theology counters by giving witness to the living God, using the largest and most comprehensive and involving terms possible. Trinity provides these terms, a theological language that enables us to maintain our Christian identity in God's image rather than in what we see in our mirrors each morning.

I

Christ Plays in Creation

[Christ is] the firstborn of all creation; for in him all things in heaven and on earth were created. . . .

COLOSSIANS 1:15-16

It is not allowable to love the Creation according to the purposes one has for it, any more than it is allowable to love one's neighbor in order to borrow his tools.

WENDELL BERRY[1]

Exploring the Neighborhood of Creation

We wake up each morning to a world we did not make. How did it get here? How did *we* get here? We open our eyes and see that "old bowling ball the sun" career over the horizon. We wiggle our toes. A mocking bird takes off and improvises on themes set down by robins, vireos, and wrens, and we marvel at the intricacies. The smell of frying bacon works its way into our nostrils and we begin anticipating buttered toast, scrambled eggs, and coffee freshly brewed from our favorite Javanese beans.

There is so much *here* — around, above, below, inside, outside. Even with the help of poets and scientists we can account for very little of it. We notice this, then that. We start exploring the neighborhood. We try this street, and then that one. We venture across the tracks. Before long we are looking out through telescopes and down into microscopes, curious, fascinated by this endless proliferation of sheer Is-ness — color and shape and texture and sound.

After awhile we get used to it and quit noticing. We get narrowed down into something small and constricting. Somewhere along the way this exponential expansion of awareness, this wide-eyed looking around, this sheer untaught delight in what is here, reverses itself: the world contracts; we are reduced to a life of routine through which we sleepwalk.

But not for long. Something always shows up to jar us awake: a child's question, a fox's sleek beauty, a sharp pain, a pastor's sermon, a fresh metaphor, an artist's vision, a slap in the face, scent from a crushed violet. We are again awake, alert, in wonder: how did this happen? And why this? Why anything at all? Why not nothing at all?

Gratitude is our spontaneous response to all this: to *life*. Something wells up within us: Thank you! More often than not, the thank you is directed to God, even by those who don't believe in him. Johnny Bergman was a young man in my congregation. He and his wife were enthusiastic participants, but then the weeds of a distracting world choked their young faith. They acquired children. They became suddenly wealthy and their lives filled up with boats and cars, house-building and social engagements. They were less and less frequently in worship. After a two-year absence, on a bright sunshiny Sunday, Johnny was there again. Surprised to see him I said, "Johnny! What brought you to worship today?" He said, "I woke this morning feeling so good, so blessed — so *created* — I just had to say thank you, and this is the only place I could think to say it rightly, adequately — I wanted to say it to Jesus." The next Sunday his string of absences resumed, but, all the same, the moment struck me as epiphanic, and so very accurate.[2] The sheer wonder of life, of creation, of this place where we find ourselves alive at this moment, requires response, a thank you. There is something so deeply congruent with the world we live in and who we are that when we become aware of it we exclaim at the miracle and wonder of it. In the ancient world, Plato observed that all philosophy begins in wonder. In the modern world Heidegger used the phrase "radical astonishment" to underline Plato. Leibniz asked the question that continues to provoke our endless ruminations on finding ourselves plunked down in this place, in this time: "Why is there not nothing?"[3]

Wonder. Astonishment. Adoration. There can't be very many of us for whom the sheer fact of existence hasn't rocked us back on our heels. We take off our sandals before the burning bush. We catch our breath at the sight of a plummeting hawk. "Thank you, God." We find ourselves in a lavish existence in which we feel a deep sense of kinship — we *belong* here; we say thanks with our lives to life. And not just "Thanks" or "Thank it," but "Thank *you*." Most of the people who have lived on this planet earth have identified this *you* with God or gods. This is not just a matter of learning our manners, the way children are taught to say thank you as a social grace. It is the cultivation of adequateness within ourselves to the nature of reality, developing the capacity to sustain an adequate response to the overwhelming giftedness and goodness of life.

Wonder is the only adequate launching pad for exploring a spirituality of creation, keeping us open-eyed, expectant, alive to life that is always more than we can account for, that always exceeds our calculations, that is always beyond anything we can make.

Kerygma: Jesus' Birth

Naturally, we are interested in what is behind all this: the meaning, the purpose, the implications. We begin by believing in God. Creation is not something we figure out, or deduce, or argue, or simply appreciate as is — it is what we believe: *credo*. "By faith we understand that the world was created by the word of God, so that what is seen was made out of things which do not appear" (Heb. 11:3 RSV).

But creation in itself does not compel belief in God. There are plenty of people who take creation on its own terms, often designated simply as "nature," and approach it as if its meaning, its "spirituality," were inherent in it. There is something very attractive about this; it is so clean and uncomplicated and noncontroversial. And obvious. We get a satisfying sense of the inherently divine in life itself without all the complications of theology, the mess of church history, the hypocrisies of men and women who insist on taking up space in church pews, the incompetence of pastors, and appeals for money. Creation on its own seems perfectly capable of furnishing us with a spirituality that exults in beautiful beaches and fine sunsets, surfing and skiing and body massage, emotional states and aesthetic titillation. But for all its considerable attractions, it is considerably deficient in person.

Our Christian Scriptures take quite a different tack: God reveals himself most completely in a named person: Jesus.

The Genesis stories of creation begin with "heaven and earth," but that turns out to be merely a warm-up exercise for the main event, the creation of human life, man and woman, designated "image of God." Man and woman are alive with the very breath ("spirit") of God. If you want to look at creation full, creation at its highest, you look at a person — a man, a woman, a child. The faddish preference for appreciating creation in a bouquet of flowers over a squalling baby, for a day on the beach rather than rubbing shoulders with uncongenial neighbors in a cold church — creation with the inconvenience of persons excised — is understandable, but it is also decidedly not creation in the terms it has been revealed to us.

All this comes together as good news, creation as God's gift of life and the conditions necessary for life, *our* lives, in the birth of Jesus. This is truly good news, what the Greeks named *kerygma,* a public proclamation that brings what it proclaims into historical reality. The birth of Jesus provides the kerygmatic focus for receiving, entering into, and participating in creation, for *living* the creation and not just using it or taking it for granted. This birth is also, our Gospel writers Matthew and Luke give us to understand, a "virgin birth."

In St. John's Gospel rewriting of Genesis we read, "the Word became flesh and lived among us" (John 1:14). St. Matthew and St. Luke begin their Gospels with detailed accounts of Jesus' birth. St. Paul in the first written reference to Jesus' birth calls Jesus the "firstborn of creation" (Col. 1:15).[4]

In the act of believing in creation, we accept and enter into and sub-

mit to what God does — what God made and makes. We are not spectators of creation but participants in it. We are participants first of all by
simply being born, but then we realize that our births all take place in the
defining context of Jesus' birth. The Christian life is the practice of living
in what God has done and is doing. We want to know the origins of things
not to satisfy our curiosity about fossils and dinosaurs and the "big bang"
but so that we can live out of our origins. We don't want our lives to be
tacked on to something peripheral. We want to live *origin*-ally, not derivatively.

So we begin with Jesus. Jesus is the revelation of the God who created heaven and earth; he is also the revelation of the God who is with us,
Immanuel. Karl Barth goes into immense detail (he wrote four fat volumes
on it) to make this single point: "We have established that from every angle Jesus Christ is the key to the secret of creation."[5]

*   *   *

The birth story of Jesus as told by St. Luke is the most extensive that we
have. Gabriel, God's messenger, opens with the kerygmatic Annunciation
to Mary: "Greetings, favored one! The Lord is with you" (Luke 1:28), at
which she is properly astonished (*diatarachthē*). Gabriel reassures her that
everything is going to be all right and then delivers his gospel message:
"you will conceive in your womb and bear a son" (v. 31). Only then does
Mary learn that the conception of her son will be the work of God's Holy
Spirit: "The Holy Spirit will come upon you, and the power of the Most
High will overshadow you; therefore the child to be born will be called
holy, he will be called Son of God" (v. 35). Mary welcomes and receives this
impregnating, life-generating gospel word, and becomes pregnant with
Jesus: "Here I am, the servant of the Lord; let it be with me according to
your word" (v. 38).

The story of Mary's pregnancy continues in the context of another
pregnancy, that of Mary's elderly cousin Elizabeth. Mary goes to Elizabeth
for a "pregnancy test." The two pregnancies are parallel but contrasting
wonders: the old barren woman and the young virgin girl, both impossi-
bly pregnant. Elizabeth, already six months pregnant, confirms Mary's
new pregnancy: "Blessed are you among women, and blessed is the fruit of
your womb" (v. 42). And Mary makes joyful response with her magnificent Magnificat.

"My soul magnifies the Lord,
and my spirit rejoices in God my Savior. . . ."

(vv. 46-55)

When Mary gives birth to her Holy Spirit–conceived child, Luke uses the same word that Paul had earlier used to describe Jesus Christ to the Colossian Christians as "the firstborn *(prototokos)* of all creation" (Col. 1:15), identifying Mary's baby, Jesus, as "her firstborn son" *(prototokon)* (Luke 2:7). The birth is then greeted across the entire range of creation, heaven and earth, angels' song and shepherds' welcome. The highest (angels) and the lowliest (shepherds) join in wonder and welcome of Jesus, born "to you" (2:11), or, perhaps, "for you" *(etechthe humin)*. This birth most emphatically has to do with us.

The Spirit that comes upon Mary and conceives the Savior echoes the Spirit that hovered over the waters in the account of creation (Gen. 1:2). As Raymond Brown writes, "The earth was void and without form when that Spirit appeared; just so Mary's womb was a void until the Spirit God filled it with a child who was His Son."[6]

This basic, defining creation story begins with God's word preached (by messenger Gabriel) — a word that conceives life (by the Holy Spirit) and results in a pregnancy that attracts wonder and blessing (Elizabeth's greeting and Mary's Magnificat) — and concludes in a birth that brings heaven's angels and earth's shepherds together in joyful, validating witness and worship.

*   *   *

Five earlier stories of conception and birth in our Scriptures also reveal God as critically and intimately involved in the creation of human life.

Abraham and Sarah and the birth of Isaac: "the LORD did for Sarah as he had promised. Sarah conceived and bore Abraham a son in his old age" (Gen. 21:1).

Manoah and his unnamed wife and the birth of Samson: "And the angel of the LORD appeared to the woman and said to her, 'Although you are barren, having borne no children, you shall conceive and bear a son'" (Judg. 13:3).

Boaz and Ruth and the birth of Obed: "The LORD made her conceive, and she bore a son" (Ruth 4:13).

Elkanah and Hannah and the birth of Samuel: "Elkanah knew his wife Hannah, and the LORD remembered her. In due time Hannah conceived and bore a son. She named him Samuel" (1 Sam. 1:19-20).

Zechariah and Elizabeth and the birth of John: "they had no children, because Elizabeth was barren. . . . Elizabeth will bear you a son. . . . Elizabeth conceived" (Luke 1:7, 13, 24).

And now this final conception and birth story in which God is explicitly revealed as the Creator: Joseph and Mary and the birth of Jesus.

The work of God in the conception and birth of Jesus through Mary is continuous with these five previous "impossible" births, but it is also different. In the mothers ranging from Sarah to Elizabeth, a barren womb was the impossible condition to be overcome; these women very much wanted a child. But in Mary the "impossible" condition is virginity; here there is no yearning for or expectation of a child. Conception and birth for Mary is the surprise of creation. "This is God's initiative going beyond anything man or woman has dreamed of," writes Brown.[7] This is the birth that will now set all births under the conditions of God's creative initiative.

These six "insider" birth stories take the so-called natural processes of reproduction, conception, pregnancy, and birth, and reveal God working in impossible conditions, barrenness and virginity, to bring forth life.

*   *   *

That Jesus, in St. Paul's phrase, is "born of woman" (Gal. 4:4) quietly insists that Jesus is most emphatically human, the "firstborn of *creation*." That Mary is at the same time a virgin insists that the birth of Jesus cannot be reduced or accounted for by what we know or can reproduce from our own experience. Life that is unmistakably *human* life is before us here, a real baby from an actual mother's womb; there is also miracle here, and mystery which cannot be brushed aside in our attempts to bring the operations of God, let alone our own lives, under our control. The miracle of the virgin birth, maintained from the earliest times in the church and confessed in its creeds, is, in Karl Barth's straightforward phrase, a "summons to *reverence and worship*." Barth maintained that the one-sided views of those who questioned or denied "born of the virgin Mary" are "in the last resort to be understood only as coming from dread of reverence and only as invitation to comfortable encounter with an all too near or all too far-off God."[8]

Artists, poets, musicians, and architects are our primary witnesses to the significance of the meaning of "virgin" in the virgin birth as "a summons to reverence and worship." Over and over again they rescue us from a life in which the wonder has leaked out. While theologians and biblical scholars have argued, sometimes most contentiously, over texts and sexual facts and mythological parallels, our artists have painted Madonnas, our poets have provided our imaginations with rhythms and metaphors, our musicians have filled the air with carols and anthems that bring us to our knees in adoration, and our architects have designed and built chapels and cathedrals in which we can worship God.

Madeleine L'Engle's poem "After Annunciation" tells us why:

This is the irrational season
When love blooms bright and wild.
Had Mary been filled with reason
There'd have been no room for the child.[9]

Conception, pregnancy, and birth language that feature God as the Creator occupy a prominent place in our Scriptures as they give witness to the Christian life. Jesus' words to Nicodemus, "You must be born anew" (John 3:7 RSV), are certainly the most well known. Jesus and Nicodemus between them use the word "born" seven times in the course of their conversation. Paul's language is also significant. Writing to the Christian community in Rome, he views the entire creation as a birth process — "We know that the whole creation (*pasa hē ktisis*) has been groaning in labor pains until now" (Rom. 8:22) — and then immediately parallels it with what goes on in us: "we ourselves, who have the first fruits of the Spirit, groan inwardly while we wait for adoption, the redemption of our bodies" (8:23). Another time, writing to the Christians in Galatia, he goes so far as to identify himself to them as a mother in the pains of childbirth, "again in travail until Christ be formed in you!" (Gal. 4:19).

*   *   *

The story of Jesus' birth is our entry into understanding and participating in the play of creation. But every birth can, if we let it, return us to the wonder of Jesus' birth, the revelation of sheer life as gift, God's life with us and for us.

God is the Creator and his most encompassing creation is human life, a baby. We, as participants in creation, do it too. When we beget and conceive, give birth to and raise babies, we are in on the heart of creation. Every birth is kerygmatic. There is more gospel in all those "begats" in the genealogical lists of our Scriptures ("And Ezekias begat Manasses; and Manasses begat Amon; and Amon begat Josias . . .") than we ever dreamed.

*   *   *

A few years ago I was invited by my daughter-in-law to be present at the birth of her third child. She knew how disappointed I was in never being permitted to be in on the births of my own three children. In the days Jan and I were having children, fathers were banished to outer darkness ("where there is weeping and gnashing of teeth") at the time and place of birth. So, what I had missed with my own children, by her generosity I experienced with this grandchild. The birthing took place a few days after Christmas, so my mind and heart were well saturated with the songs and stories of Jesus' birth as my wife and I drove at 2 A.M. to the hospital in Tacoma in anticipation of experiencing this birth.

Nowhere I have ever been and nothing I have ever done in God's creation rivals what I experienced in that birthing room. The setting was austere — antiseptic and functional — but the life, the sheer life, exploding out of the womb that night, transformed it into a place of revelation. My son received the baby into his hands as she came into the world: "Welcome, Sadie Lynn!"

I have climbed mountain peaks that gave me views of glaciated mountains in wave after wave of ranges, but none of those breathtaking vistas was comparable to seeing that baby enter the world; I have heard the most delicate and exquisite birdsong and some of the best musicians in the world, but no sounds rivaled the cries of that baby.

I was a latecomer to this firsthand experience common to most fathers today and common to the human race as a whole. Does anyone ever get used to this? I was captured by the wonder of life, the miracle of life, the mystery of life, the glory of life.

The day after the birth I was in the grocery store getting some vegetables and grains for the family. There were several mothers shopping up and down the aisles with young children in tow — many of them snarling and snapping at the over-lively, curiosity-filled, wildly energetic kids. I wanted to grab the mothers, embrace them, tell them, "Do you realize what you have done? You have given birth to a child, a *child* — this miracle, this wonder, this glory. You're a Madonna! Why aren't you in awe and on your knees with the magi, with the shepherds?" Luckily, I restrained myself. "Madonna" probably would not have had the same meaning for them as it had for me.

Birth, any birth, is our primary access to the creation work of God. Jesus' virgin birth provides and maintains the focus that God himself is personally present and totally participant in creation, which is good news indeed. Creation itself is kerygmatic. The birth of Jesus, kept fresh in our imaginations and prayers in song and story, keeps our feet on solid creation ground and responsive to every nuance of obedience and praise evoked by the life all around us.

Threat: Gnosticism

But this has never been an easy truth for people to swallow. There are always plenty of people around who will have none of this particularity: human ordinariness, bodily fluids, raw emotions of anger and disgust, fatigue and loneliness. Birth is painful. Babies are inconvenient and messy. There is immense trouble involved in having children. God having a baby? It's far easier to accept God as the Creator of the majestic mountains, the rolling sea, the delicate wildflowers, fanciful unicorns, and "tygers, tygers burning bright" (to quote William Blake).

When it comes to the sordid squalor of the raw material involved in being human, God is surely going to keep his distance from that. We have deep aspirations native to our souls that abhor this business of diapers and debts, government taxes and domestic trivia. We imagine that we were created for higher things, that there is a world of subtle ideas and fine feelings and exquisite ecstasies for us to cultivate.

Somewhere along the way some of us become convinced that *our* souls are *different* — a cut above the masses, the common herd of philistines that trample the courts of the Lord. We become connoisseurs of the sublime.

As it turned out, the ink was barely dry in the stories telling of the birth of Jesus when a small industry was already up and running, putting out alternate stories that were more "spiritual" than those provided in our

Gospels. A rash of apocryphal stories, with Jesus smoothed out and universalized, flooded the early church. They were immensely popular. They still are. And people are still writing them. These alternate stories prove very attractive to a lot of people.

In these accounts of the Christian life, the hard-edged particularities of Jesus' life are blurred into the sublime divine. The hard, historical factuality of the incarnation, the word made flesh as God's full and complete revelation of himself, is dismissed as crude. Something finer and more palatable to sensitive souls is put in its place. Jesus was not truly flesh and blood, but entered a human body temporarily in order to give us the inside story on God and initiate us into the secrets of the spiritual life. And of course he didn't die on the cross, but made his exit at the last minute. The body that was taken from the cross for burial was not Jesus at all, but a kind of costume he used for a few years and then discarded.

It turned out in these versions that Jesus merely role-played a historical flesh-and-blood Christ for a brief time and then returned to a purely spiritual realm. Anyone who accepts that version of Jesus is then free to live the version: we put up with materiality and locale and family for as much and as long as necessary, but only for as much and as long as necessary. The material, the physical, the body — history and geography and weather — is temporary scaffolding; the sooner we realize that none of it has anything to do with God and Jesus, the better.

The attractions of this kind of thing are considerable. The feature attraction is that we no longer have to take seriously — that is, with eternal seriousness, *God* seriousness — either things or people. Anything you can touch, smell, or see is not of God in any direct or immediate way. We save ourselves an enormous amount of inconvenience and aggravation by putting materiality and everydayness of every kind at the edge of our lives, at least our spiritual lives. Mountains are nice as long as they inspire lofty thoughts, but if one stands in the way of my convenience, a bulldozer can be called in to get rid of it. (And didn't Jesus say something like this, that faith was useful for getting rid of mountains? If a bulldozer can do the same thing, isn't it already pre-sanctioned by Jesus?) People are glorious as long as they are good-looking, well-mannered, bolster my self-esteem, and help me fulfill my human potential, but if they smell badly or function poorly they certainly deserve to be dismissed. (It's what Jesus did, isn't it? When Peter proved incompetent spiritually, Jesus curtly dismissed him with the rebuke, "Get behind me, Satan!") If we are going to be truly spiritual beings, we need to free ourselves of all that is unspiritual.

The accompanying attraction to this refined life is that when we engage in it we find ourselves members of an elite spiritual aristocracy. We are insiders to God, privileged members of the ultimate "club" — the Inner Ring of Enlightened Souls.

This all sounds and feels so good that there are very few among those of us who have been involved in the Christian faith who haven't given it a try. No church is safe from its influence. No one who desires to live a godly life is impervious to its attraction.

*   *   *

"Gnostic" is the term we often use to designate this most attractive but soul-destroying spirituality. Philip Lee has given careful study to the various and subtle ways in which gnosticism has infected the post-Reformation churches of North America across the board, evangelical and liberal alike. In his analysis, Protestant churches are more liable to the infection than Roman Catholic and Orthodox, but no one is unaffected. He identifies five elements, some or all of which carry the virus of gnosticism and threaten the health of the Christian gospel.[10]

First, gnosticism works out of a deep metaphysical alienation. The cosmos is a colossal error. Creation is alien to our deepest and truest soul. God, the true God, had and has nothing to do with it, and so the less we have to do with it the better.

Second, there is a secret lore, a knowledge (gnosis) that can save us from this hopeless condition. But it isn't open knowledge; it has to be acquired by initiation and intuition. A certain spiritual aptitude has to be developed and nurtured.

Third, escapism is the strategy for survival, beginning with an escape from the God of creation. The escapism is nearly total: we escape from everything except the self, we escape from the world into the self.

Fourth, the few souls who learn this secret lore and embark on this escapist life constitute an elite, each a divinity in herself or himself.

And fifth, each person is free to assemble any ideas or stories or techniques at hand to accomplish this way of life; no institution or authority is permitted to interfere or tell the "gnostic" (the one "in the know") what to believe or do.

Against the good creation of the Christian, the gnostic posits a bad creation.

Against knowing the God who saves, the gnostic sets a secret knowledge, a mystic lore that can be used to free the self from human ordinariness and defilement. It is, in effect, a formula for self-salvation.

Against living life as a pilgrimage in the company of Abraham, Isaac, Jacob, Moses, David, and Isaiah, and following Jesus, the gnostic plans an escape.

Against the life of the community of children of God, commanded to love one another, the gnostic is absorbed in the self.

Against the life of the ordinary, an embrace of family and work, cooking and sewing, helping the poor and healing the sick — all the foolish, weak, low, and despised "in the world" honored by St. Paul (1 Cor. 1:27-28) — the gnostic claims a special status among the elite that exempts him or her from the sacred ordinary.

Against the particular revelation of God in Jesus, "the Word made flesh," the gnostic refuses to be bound to anything particular, least of all the particularity of Jesus — "Christ crucified, a stumbling block to Jews and foolishness to Gentiles" (1 Cor. 1:23).

Gnosticism is a virus in the bloodstream of religion and keeps resurfacing every generation or so advertised as brand new, replete with a new brand name. On examination, though, it turns out to be the same old thing but with a new public relations agency. "Gnosticism is all over the world today," Eugen Rosenstock-Huessy writes. "The Churches themselves are filled with it."[11] Gnosticism offers us spirituality without the inconvenience of creation. Gnosticism offers us spirituality without the inconvenience of sin or morality. Gnosticism offers us spirituality without the inconvenience of people we don't like or who aren't "our kind." And, maybe most attractive of all, gnosticism offers us a spirituality without God, at least any god other than the spark of divinity I sense within me.

Grounding Text (1): Genesis 1–2

Our entire Scriptures are vigorously arrayed against this dematerialized, elitist self-spirituality, but Genesis in the Old Testament and John in the New are basic.

The Bible opens with two creation stories, set side by side: Genesis 1 and 2. Genesis 1 and 2 have been studied meticulously for two thousand years by some of our very best scholars, Jewish and Christian. The accumulated insights and truths stagger our imaginations. There is so much here to consider and ponder, to appreciate and respond to. It is not possible to over-appreciate these scholars, whether living or dead.

But what is sometimes missed in this cascade of exegetical brilliance is how skillfully and well these texts prepare and lead each of us as ordinary working Christians in "the land of the living" (Ps. 116:9) right now. These two creation stories, set at the entrance to our Bibles, are primarily texts for living in the time and place that we wake up into each morning.

Creation Now

I missed the personal immediacy of Genesis 1–2 for a long time. Early on I was distracted by the arguers and polemicists who were primarily interested in how things got started. As an adolescent I got mixed up with friends who loved using these texts to pick fights with evolutionists and atheists. Still later I became intoxicated with the words and images and syntax, comparing and evaluating them in the study of the contrasting but still fascinating worlds represented in the ancient Sumerian and Assyrian, Babylonian and Egyptian civilizations.

Then I became a pastor and gradually realized what powerful texts Genesis 1 and 2 are for dealing with life just as it comes to us each day. As pastor my work was to pray and teach and preach these Holy Scriptures into the lives of mothers and fathers raising their children, farmers in their wheat fields, teachers in their classrooms, engineers building bridges, sergeants and captains and colonels keeping watch over our national security, and not a few arthritic octogenarians in nursing homes.

In the course of this work, I've come to think that Genesis 1 and 2, prominent as they are in launching us into the grand narrative of the Bible, are among the most under-interpreted and under-used texts for shaping an obedient and reverent life of following Jesus in our daily, ordinary, working and worshiping lives.

My shift from reading Genesis 1–2 primarily as an account of the beginning of all things to reading it as a text for beginning to live right now took place early in my pastoral work. As I was learning how to lead my congregation into an obedient life of worshiping and following Jesus, I was struck by how extensively the cultural and spiritual conditions in which I was working matched the exile conditions of the Hebrews in the sixth century before Christ: the pervasive uprootedness and loss of place, the loss of connection with a tradition of worship, the sense of being immersed in a foreign and idolatrous society. I felt that I and my congregation were starting over every week; there was no moral consensus, no common memory, all of us far removed from where we had grown up. The lives of my parishioners seemed jerky and spasmodic, anxious and hurried, with little sense of place or grounding. When I realized that these were the same exile conditions lived through by the people of God in the sixth century B.C., I started preaching and teaching the exile texts of Isaiah, those great pastoral messages to people who had lost touch with their time and place in the world. In doing that I discovered that one of the most important Isaianic words used with these exiled people was "create." "Create" is a word that is used in the Bible exclusively with God as the subject. Men and women don't, *can't*, create. But God does. When nothing we can do makes any difference and we are left standing around empty-handed and clueless, we are ready for God to create. When the conditions in which we live seem totally alien to life and salvation, we are reduced to waiting for God to do what only God can do, create. The words "create" and "Creator" occur more times in the exilic preaching of Isaiah than in any other place in the Bible — sixteen times as compared to the six occurrences in the great creation narratives of Genesis 1–2.[12] As I pursued this pastoral task, I realized how immediate and powerful, how convincing and life-changing, the creation work of God is among a people who feel so uncreated, so unformed and unfitted for the world in which they find themselves. While under Isaiah's influence I was moving from my pulpit to hospital rooms and family rooms, coffee shops and community gatherings, praying with and listening to bored or devastated men and women, "create" emerged out of the background of what happened long ago in Canaan and Egypt and Babylon into prominence in my community as an actively gospel word of what God is doing today among the exile people with whom I was living.

After several years of this, I came back to Genesis 1–2 in a fresh way and found in these texts an urgency and freshness and immediacy that surprised me. No longer was I reading Genesis and asking, "What does this mean? How can I use this?" I was asking, "How can I obey this? How can I get in on this?"

These are grounding texts for forming us and leading us into living well, *playing* well, to the glory of God in the great gift of creation. Genesis 1 is formational for receiving and living into the creation gift of time; Genesis 2 for the creation gift of place.

The Creation Gift of Time

The understanding and honoring of time is fundamental to the realization of who we are and how we live. Violations of sacred time become desecrations of our most intimate relations with God and one another. Hours and days, weeks and months and years, are the very stuff of holiness.

Among the many desecrations visited upon the creation, the profanation of time ranks near the top, at least among North Americans. Time is the medium in which we do all our living. When time is desecrated, life is desecrated. The most conspicuous evidences of this desecration are hurry and procrastination: Hurry turns away from the gift of time in a compulsive grasping for abstractions that it can possess and control. Procrastination is distracted from the gift of time in a lazy inattentiveness to the life of obedience and adoration by which we enter the "fullness of time." Whether by a hurried grasping or by a procrastinating inattention, time is violated.

Genesis 1 is not in a hurry. And Genesis 1 does not procrastinate.

*   *   *

Sister Lychen prepared me for the lived quality of Genesis 1. I grew up in a spiritual culture that was dismissive, if not outright contemptuous, of time. Time, ordinary time, was just "putting in time" until the final intervention of God would put an end to time and usher in eternity. Meanwhile, there was a lot to do: witness to our friends, send out missionaries, hold street meetings, go to the jail every Sunday afternoon and sing and preach to the prisoners. But nothing held our attention for very long. We had to make sure we were ready and then hurry and get everybody we knew ready for the end, the rapture, the second coming of Jesus. We had no time for anything but the briefest of vacations, no time to go to college, no time for games. Time was just about up. Time was not honored for its own sake; its only value was to get ready for the end time. End time was the only sacred time. Everything else, days and weeks, minutes and hours, was to be used in service of the end time. If you were not using it for some sanctified project or some Spirit-anointed goal, you were wasting time.

Sister Lychen (every adult in our small congregation was either a "sister" or a "brother") was a significant figure in this world. She was an ancient, small wisp of a woman, five feet tall and shrinking. She lived in a small house in our neighborhood. The shades were always drawn. I walked or rode my bike past her house often. I never saw her step out of her always darkened house except on Sunday each week when we picked her up and drove her to church. During the testimony and prayer time, with liturgical regularity in our defiantly anti-liturgical pentecostal worship, she stood to her feet and said that our Lord had revealed to her that she would not die before his second coming in glory. He told her that she would be caught up with all the saints in the clouds and meet him in the air (1 Thess. 4:17). Every Sunday. Word perfect. I was very impressed. When I was about eight years old, I started calculating how much time I had on earth, for I took it for granted that I also would be "caught up." She was at least ninety years old. Given her increasing feebleness and loss of stature — she was shrinking at the rate of about an inch a year — I figured she might live and therefore the rapture be held off for another five or six years. I would be fourteen when the rapture occurred. That meant that I'd never get to drive a car. A big disappointment.

When I was ten years old, Sister Lychen died.

I can still remember my confusion during the funeral service. I kept waiting for Pastor Jones to say something about the Second Coming but he didn't. Silence. The next Sunday one of the pillars of my childhood experience of worship was gone. The building was still standing. The accustomed congregation was still there. Intact. No rapture. And nobody even seemed to notice. Ten years is not a propitious age to figure out matters eschatological and so I eventually dropped it. Two or three years later I was plunged into adolescence, the age in which biology virtually obliterates eschatology — everything was present, now, immediate, firsthand, with no connections between past and future. Past and future alike took on a shadowy existence.

But eventually I found myself dealing with it again. As I worked my way into adulthood, I was reading my Bible with more diligence, paying attention to how this gospel of Jesus got lived, not just talked about, not just given witness to, not just studied and memorized. I gradually realized that ordinary time is not what biblical people endure or put up with or hurry through as we wait around for the end time and its rocket launch into eternity. It is a gift through which we participate in the present and daily work of God. I finally got it: end time influences present, ordinary time, not by diminishing or denigrating it but by charging it, filling it with purpose and significance. The end time is not a future we wait for but the gift of the fullness of time that we receive in adoration and obedience as it flows into the present.

Rhythm

Back to Genesis 1. The most prominent feature of Genesis 1 is its rhythmic structure. The creation account is arranged in a sequence of seven days. Six times a segment of creation work is introduced with the phrase, "And God said . . ." and six times a segment is concluded with the phrase, "And there was evening and there was morning . . ." followed by the number of the day, one through six.

But the seventh day is treated very differently and that difference sets it off for special emphasis and attention. Instead of the number being in the concluding phrase, it is in the introductory: "And on the seventh day. . . ." This number seven is then repeated twice more in successive sentences. So "seventh" is repeated three times, giving this seventh day an emphasis far beyond that of the first six.

So here is what we notice: God's work of creation is conveyed to us rhythmically: 1 2 3 4 5 6 7 7 7. There are two sets of three days each of creation activity. The first set of three gives form to the pre-creation chaos of verse 2 (the *tohu*); the second set of three fills the pre-creation emptiness (the *bohu*). These two sets of creation days, days 1-3 forming the "without form" and days 4-6 filling the "void," are then followed by the seventh day of creation rest in triple emphasis.

There is another interesting rhythmic variation. The third day of each three-day set comprises a double creation. So the cadence becomes: 1 2 3/3, 4 5 6/6, followed by the triple 7 7 7.

When we speak this text aloud, or listen to it being spoken (which is how most people would have done it in biblical times), the text gets inside us. We enter the rhythms of creation time and find that we are internalizing a creation sense of orderliness and connectedness and resonance that is very much like what we get from music. As we assimilate Genesis 1, we find ourselves "keeping time": one two three-three, four five six-six, seven seven seven.

Bruce Waltke conveys the musical and rhythmic character of Genesis 1 by naming this text the "libretto for all of Israel's life."[13] Think of Genesis 1 as an opera or oratorio of creation life; as we get this text, this libretto, into our way of living, these rhythms get into us and are expressed in our language and work.

It is the very nature of time to be rhythmic; it is the rhythm that keeps us participant and present, inhabiting time, tapping our foot, instead of being a mere onlooker to it, measuring it with a clock. This rhythmic core is reinforced in Genesis 1 with many repeated phrases. We have already noted the framing repetitions that initiate ("And God said 'Let there be . . .'") and conclude ("And there was evening and there was morning") the six days of creation work. In addition to the eight major creation acts, verbs are used in a grammatical form that we translate "let it be" four more times, giving us twelve named acts of bringing into being. And there are many, many other repetitions that deepen the regularity of the pulse and the variations of the rhythms of creation time and keep us both participant (the pulse) and alert (the variations).[14]

We are created to live rhythmically in the rhythms of creation. Seven days repeated in a sequence of four weeks place us in the rhythm of the twenty-eight-day phases of the moon circling the earth. This lunar rhythm gets repeated twelve times in the annual sweep of earth and moon around the sun. These large encompassing rhythms call forth regularities of spring births, summer growth, autumn harvest, and winter sleep. Creation time is rhythmic. We are immersed in rhythms.

But we are also composed of rhythms. Physiologically we live out rhythms of pulse and breath. Our hearts beat steadily, circulating our blood through our bodies in impulses of sixty or eighty or a hundred times a minute. Our lungs expand and contract, pushing oxygen through our bodies fifteen or twenty or thirty times a minute.

The interesting thing about rhythm is that we can slow down or quicken the tempo, but we cannot eliminate the beat, the cadence. This can be realized most readily in music and dance, but the very creation itself is this way. This is the nature of the creation of which we are part. We are embedded in time, but time is also embedded in us. Creation is called into being, not haphazardly and not in a cacophony of noise but rhythmically; as we listen and observe we find ourselves integrated into the rhythms. The great creative cadences keep sounding and resounding around and within us: And God said . . . and God created . . . and God blessed . . . and God made . . . and God gave . . . and God called. . . .

Genesis "has a certain liturgical flavor . . . a highly regular and repetitive description of the *process* of creation, step by step, day by day," writes Jon Levenson.[15] We continue to be part of this process as the Genesis text gets us in tune with, puts us in step with, keeps us present to creation time: light and darkness . . . sky and sea . . . earth and vegetation . . . sun, moon, and stars . . . fish and birds . . . animals and humans. As we enter each night's rest and each day's work, the great formative rhythms keep us aware of and participant with God's formational words: "and God said . . . be fruitful and multiply and fill . . . according to its kind . . . and it was good . . . and it was so . . and there was evening and there was morning. . . ."

There is much more in Genesis 1, of course. There is the work of each of the six days by which we are guided to attend to everything that is going on around us. But the gift of time is, first, that by which we become present and participant in the work. Nothing in this creation is here merely to be studied, analyzed, figured out; each element, each day's "work," is here first of all to be received as an integrated and coherent "note" in the all-encompassing rhythms of the creation oratorio, in which we breath the same air that God breathed over the deep, and from deep in our lungs — our lives! — we sing and play to the glory of God.

Recovering the Rhythm

But I'm not done with Sister Lychen. I imagine a scenario in which I am again ten years old; it is a month or so before Sister Lychen dies. I go to her house and knock on her door. She opens it and invites me in. I am no stranger there, for my mother occasionally sent me over with a plate of cookies. The usual routine was that after she let me in she would go to the kitchen and bring me a glass of milk. We would sit there in her knick-knack–crowded living room with the shades pulled. I would eat my cookie and drink my milk in the darkened, sunless room. But this day, in my fantasized scenario, while she is in the kitchen getting the milk, I let up the blinds from all the windows. As she returns with the milk, I exclaim, "Sister Lychen, look! The world!" Startled, she drops the milk and shatters the glass. In her confusion I take her hand and lead her across the street and down a trail to a swampy place, Lawrence Slough, where I and my friends loved to go. I show her the turtles and the frogs — she had never seen either. I show her a nesting osprey waiting for the next fish, the downy heads of its chicks just visible on the nest. She is amazed. Just then a white-tailed deer leaps from a tangle of cattails. She asks what it is and I tell her it is one of Solomon's gazelles. She is astonished. I am afraid that she is getting too excited and so lead her back home and help her clean up the spilled milk and broken glass.

The next Sunday in worship, she stands to her feet at the usual time but she doesn't say the usual words. This time she says, "An angel visited me this week and showed me wonders I'd never seen. He said he'd come back on Thursday and show me more. I'm not sure I want to leave and 'be with the Lord' yet."

Each succeeding Thursday I go to her house, take her by the hand, lead her down the path into Lawrence Slough, and show her more wonders. One day we stay late in the evening and watch the setting sun throw a kaleidoscope of color over the surface of the water. She is in awe. One afternoon we watch the kingfisher catch minnows and fly off singing his triumphant scratchy imitation of a rusty gate. She is enthralled. Another day I bring sandwiches and half a loaf of stale Wonder Bread; we sit on a log at the edge of the water, eat our lunch, and feed two swans and seven or eight mergansers who are showing off their dashing swept-back hairdos. She loves it. As we walk home, holding hands, she says, "And to think all this has been going on practically in my backyard!" Each Thursday she notices and comments on connections or echoes between the Sunday hymns, psalms, and Scriptures and what she is feeling, seeing, and remembering from her childhood as we meander in Lawrence Slough. Sunday is no longer a rehearsal of escape, an anticipation of the final escape; it is an exposition of the week, or at least the Thursday segment of it. She never gives me credit as the angel, but each Sunday she does give an accounting of that week's Thursday angel revelation. And each week the congregation remarks on the lessening enthusiasm in Sister Lychen for being raptured from behind her drawn shades. The concluding sentence of her weekly report in the testimony time takes on a Genesis rhythm: "I'm not sure I want to leave quite yet."

And then, after four weeks of this, Sister Lychen dies.

*　　　*　　　*

This is all fantasy, of course, casting my ten-year-old self in the role of ministering angel. But my fantasy has a factual base in those childhood years of listening to Sister Lychen's rhythm-obliterating end time liturgy each Sunday. And for me now, the fantasy has turned into a way of life: the lived quality of Genesis 1 fuels my efforts in trying to raise the blinds in the living quarters of so many people I know and have known; to raise the blinds and get them out of the house between Sundays to enter into this vast, rhythmic extravaganza, seeing and hearing, tasting and touching and smelling what God has created and is creating by his word: sky and earth, plants and trees, stars and planets, fish and birds, Jersey cows and basset hounds, and the crowning touch, man and woman — look at them! — wonder of wonders, male and female!

So here is what I want to say: the *way* in which this Genesis 1 text on the creation gift of time gets inside us is through the act of worship, believingly listening, obediently receiving the Word of God, but if the blinds are down all week, we cut ourselves off from the textures and rhythms of ordinary time that is the context of that worship. Worship is the primary means for forming us as participants in God's work, but if the blinds are drawn while we wait for Sunday, we aren't in touch with the work that God is actually doing. These Genesis work-rhythms are reproduced in our lives and brought to focus in the Sabbath-rest command that enables our participation. When we walk out of the place of worship, we walk with fresh, recognizing eyes and a re-created obedient heart into the world in which we are God's image participating in God's creation work. Everything we see, touch, feel, and taste carries within it the rhythms of "And God said . . . and it was so . . . and it was good. . . ." We are more deeply in and at home in the creation than ever.

The Creation Gift of Place

Genesis 1 is structured in time, a seven-day sequence of God's speaking creation into being. The formative effect is rhythmic, using metrical and repeated melodic phrases to pull our distracted, anxious, and sometimes lethargic lives into the steady, sure, unhurried pace of God as he speaks his reliable and effective word across a sequence of six days. These rhythms are then resolved in an all-embracing seventh-day Sabbath, in which we become present to all of creation time, assimilated and realized. It is by means of this contemplative seventh day that we become participants in creation.

Genesis 2 is structured by place. Time provides the medium by which we become present to the moment and the rhythmic relation of this moment to all other moments, moments past and moments future, giving us a history by securing us in a living way to our past; at the same time it provides us with seeds of hope that grow into anticipation and purpose and fulfillment, tying us into a future. Place is a companion gift to go with time; it locates us on the earth where we become oriented, find work, experience freedom in obedience, and find companionship in a community of others.

If the first creation account has its closest analogy in music with its sequence of rhythms and repeated melodic-like themes, the second creation account is more like a story with a setting in place where a plot begins to form and characters are introduced. We see the human being taking his or her place in the context of country and work and community.

The Place

This second account of creation is set in geography. The first creation account opens with "In the beginning . . . God created the heavens and the earth" and is structured across a sequence of seven days. This second account reverses the pairing of nouns, putting earth in first place, followed by heaven; all the action takes place in a single location on earth, a garden. The first account is comprehensive, the entire cosmos and everything in it. The second account zooms in on earth and then on one place on earth.

The place is defined as a garden as opposed to a wilderness. A garden implies boundaries and intention. It is not a limitless "everywhere" or "anywhere"; it is local: "The LORD God planted a garden in Eden, in the east" (Gen. 2:8).

Everything that the Creator God does in forming us humans is done in place. It follows from this that since we are his creatures and can hardly escape the conditions of our making, for us everything that has to do with God is also in place. All living is local: this land, this neighborhood, these trees and streets and houses, this work, these people.

This may seem so obvious that it doesn't need saying. But I have spent an adult lifetime with the assigned task of guiding men and women in living out the Christian faith in the place where they raise their children and work for a living, go fishing and play golf, go to bed and eat their meals, and I know that cultivating a sense of place as the exclusive and irreplaceable setting for following Jesus is mighty difficult.

For twenty-five years of Sundays a nuclear scientist sat in my congregation and listened as I preached a thirty-minute sermon. I preached texts of Jesus' message of forgiveness and salvation, mercy and love, grace and justice. As he left the sanctuary after the benediction, he was always warm in his appreciation: "Thank you pastor — powerful words, great message." There was hardly a Sunday in which he did not respond positively to the text and its exposition. I never had reason to suppose that he was anything but sincere. But when he returned home — the primary place for him where forgiveness and love and justice could be enacted — he treated his mother-in-law who lived with him with sneers and disdain, acting out years of accumulated grudges. The word of God for this man never got located in his garden, never got *placed*.

Variations on that story are endless.

I have always loved teaching Bible studies, especially in homes or retreat settings with a dozen or so women and men. There is a kind of low-voltage thrill that comes as diverse personalities and temperaments discuss and comment and exclaim over the revealed text of God's word, and their words get woven by the Spirit into something coherent and beautiful, the picked-up themes improvised and elaborated into something almost musical. But then later as I would meet these same friends in their workplaces or homes, I observed little, often no, continuity between the electrifying insights of the Bible study and the conditions of work or home. It is so easy to get excited and enthusiastic about the gospel outside our gardens. But it is in our gardens that we have been placed.

One of the seductions that bedevils Christian formation is the construction of utopias, ideal places where we can live totally and without inhibition or interference the good and blessed and righteous life. The imagining and then attempted construction of such utopias is an old habit of our kind. Sometimes we attempt it politically in communities, sometimes socially in communes, sometimes religiously in churches. It never comes to anything but grief. Utopia is, literally, "no-place." But we can live our lives only in actual place, not in an imagined or fantasized or artificially fashioned place.

Several times when my place seemed inadequate for my vision of what I wanted to do for God, a story held me fast to my place, the story of

Gregory of Nyssa, who lived in Cappadocia in the fourth century. His older brother Basil, a bishop, arranged for his brother to be appointed bishop of the small, obscure, and decidedly unimportant town of Nyssa. Gregory objected; he didn't want to be stuck in such an out-of-the-way place. His brother told him that he didn't want Gregory to obtain distinction from his church but rather to confer distinction upon it.[16] Gregory went where he was placed. And he stayed there. The preaching and writing that he did in that backwater community continues its invigorating influence to this day. One of the features of his biblical expositions was the thoroughness and intensity with which he read Scripture as a text for living, not just for truth or ideas, but as a formative text for Christian faithfulness and obedience. In obscure Nyssa, apart from the high-adrenalin stimulus of the city, Gregory looked around and recognized his *place* in creation, noticed the script of God's revelation in the created world around him, noticed the intricate relationships and resonances between his place and the Christ of creation.

This garden, this place, in which the human is placed, has a name: Eden. The word has a good sound to it, "bliss." A good place to live. But as we know from the story as it develops, Eden is not an ideal place, not a perfect place. It is possible that bad things can happen here; in fact, a bad thing does happen here — a catastrophe, no less. An inconspicuous and seemingly innocent sin sets off an avalanche of sin that continues to pick up momentum right into our own time, dumping debris and chaos into every community on this planet earth.

This place, this garden, is not utopia, is not an ideal no-place. It is simply place, locale, geography, geology. But it is also a good place, Eden, because it provides the form by which we can live to the glory of God.

*   *   *

Our Scriptures that bring us the story of salvation ground us unrelentingly in place. Everywhere and always they insist on this grounding. Everything that is critically important to us takes place on the ground. Mountains and valleys, towns and cities, regions and countries: Haran, Ur, Canaan, Hebron, Sodom, Machpelah, Bethel, Bethlehem, Jerusalem, Samaria, Tekoa, Nazareth, Capernaum, Mt. Sinai, Mt. of Olives, Mt. Gilboa, Mt. Hermon, Caesarea, Gath, Ashkelon, Michmash, Gibeon, Azekah, Jericho, Chorazin, Bethsaida, Emmaus, the Valley of Jezreel, the Kidron Valley, the Brook Besor, Anathoth. And heading the list, Eden.

What we often consider to be the concerns of the spiritual life — ideas, truths, prayers, promises, beliefs — are never in the Christian gospel permitted to have a life of their own apart from particular persons and actual places. Biblical spirituality/religion has a low tolerance for "great ideas" or "sublime truths" or "inspirational thoughts" apart from the people and places in which they occur. God's great love and purposes for us are all worked out in messes in our kitchens and backyards, in storms and sins, blue skies, the daily work and dreams of our common lives. God works with us as we are and not as we should be or think we should be. God deals with us where we are and not where we would like to be.

People who want God as an escape from reality and the often hard conditions of this life don't find much to their liking in this aspect of our Scriptures, our text for living. But there it is. There is no getting around it.

But to the man and woman wanting *more* reality, not less, this insistence that all genuine life, life that is embraced in God's work of salvation, is *grounded, placed,* is good news indeed.

"Eden, in the east" is the first place name in the Bible. It comes with the unqualified affirmation that place is good, essential, and foundational for providing the only possible creation conditions for living out our human existence truly.

The Human

Twice in the text we are told that the human was placed in the garden: "there he put the man whom he had formed" (v. 8) and "the LORD God took the man and put him in the garden" (v. 15). The place that forms the setting for human life is where man is placed, *put.*

The human is the most conspicuous resident in this place, this garden planted by God and watered by a great river that divides and flows around the four quadrants of the earth.

The terminology is significant: the term for the human is *adam,* which later in the narrative will assume the dignity of a proper name, Adam. The term for ground is *adamah.* The human, *adam,* is derivative of *adamah,* the ground. It is unfortunate that we have no satisfactory way in our language to represent this. We could attempt "earth" and "earthling" but that sounds a little like science fiction fantasy. Or we could try "dust" and "dusty," but that sounds like slang out of a Western movie.

Still, we need to pay attention to the relentless verbal repetitions in this narrative that accumulate resonances between the human and the ground from which the human is formed. Eighteen times we have *adam,* the human; five times *adamah,* the ground, supplemented by earth (three times), field (three times), land (twice), garden (five times), and dust (once). Adding up all the earth terms, the terms that designate what the human is formed from and the terms that designate where the human is placed, we get nineteen, nearly symmetrical with the eighteen uses of *adam,* that term that associates the human with that out of which he is formed and where he is placed.

In the next chapter *adam* will become a proper name but here it seems clear that *adam* is generic, as it is in Genesis 1:27 where *adam* is inclusive of both male and female. So, *adam,* usually translated "the man," is simply the human being as such; this is us: you, me, her, him.

Since this Genesis text is not just about how things got started but how things are going right now, it might be more accurate to replace the "in general" translation of *adam* as "the human" or "the human being" with personal pronouns: we, you, us.

We are the identical stuff with the place in which we have been put. God formed us from dust, from dirt — the same stuff that we walk on every day, the same stuff on which we build our houses, the same stuff in which we plant our gardens, the same stuff over we which construct our roads and on which we drive our cars.

Wendell Berry dislikes the term "environment" as a synonym for creation because it puts too much distance between us and where we live. He thinks it sounds as though we think of earth as simply a place where we happen to be camping. But creation, he insists, is not something apart from us; it is part of us and we are part of it. When the land is violated, when animals are exploited and abused, when the streams are polluted, that is the stuff of our personal creation that is desecrated.[17]

We don't own this place and so we can't do with it whatever we wish. We *are* this place, an identity that we have in common with all our earth-neighbors.

The Latin words *humus,* soil/earth, and *homo,* human being, have a common derivation, from which we also get our word "humble." This is the Genesis origin of who we are: dust — dust that the Lord God used to make us a human being. If we cultivate a lively sense of our origin and nurture a sense of continuity with it, who knows, we may also acquire humility.

The gospel of Jesus Christ has no patience with a spirituality that is general or abstract, that is all ideas and feelings, and that takes as its theme song, "This world is not my home, I'm just a passing through." Theology divorced from geography gets us into nothing but trouble.

Why is it so difficult to *stay put*, to cultivate the garden in which we have been placed? Ideas and causes and projects are important, but if they are not worked out in the garden where we have been put they distract us from present work and company, and hamstring the fine and delicate co-ordination between freedom and necessity that is at the heart of a life of free obedience.

Annie Dillard in her brilliant tour de force, "Expedition to the Pole," sets stories of polar expeditions alongside stories of people like you and me who enter churches to worship God. She exposes the disaster that overtakes people, whether on a polar expedition or sitting in a church pew, who on a search for the Absolute, the Sublime, ignore or are indifferent to what she calls "conditions" and what I am about to name "necessity." "On the whole," she writes, "I do not find Christians, outside of the catacombs, sufficiently sensible of conditions."[18]

The fact is that we can do God's work only in God's place: "The LORD God planted a garden in Eden . . . and there he put the man whom he had formed" (Gen. 2:8).

Freedom and Necessity

We are not, of course, merely dust. The Lord God breathed into the nostrils of this dust-man who then became "a living being." As the breath of God infuses this form that we humans are, an enormous dignity accumulates around and within us.

The dignity takes particular shape as a shift occurs in the narrative plot: in the first half of the chapter (vv. 4-14) the Lord God forms and places us; he deals with us in a more personal, relational way in the last half (vv. 15-25).

First, God involves us in a continuation of his creation work: "The LORD God took the man and put him in the garden of Eden to till it and keep it" (v. 15). We are put to work, which is to say, we have something useful to do, participating in God's creation under God's direction. We are not outsiders to this place, this earth, this stuff of which we are made. The work we are given to do, working the soil and tending it, is congruent with

77

what we are made of and where we are placed. The verb "keep" *(shamar)* has the sense of "taking good care of it." "Conserve" is an appropriate translation in the context: we keep watch with an eye to maintaining and preserving. Conservation of the place in which we live is the first work assignment that occurs in our Scriptures.

We live in a good place, planted with trees "that are pleasant to the sight and good for food" (v. 9), good for the eyes and good for the stomach. Lewis Mumford, in his study of the kind of thing that Genesis 2 is concerned with, made the astute comment that "The workings of the natural environment and human history provide even the poorest community with a rich compost, far more favorable to life than the most rational ideal schemes would be if they lacked such a soil to grow in."[19]

Then following the assignment to work in the soil of our creation, God issues a command: "You may freely eat of every tree of the garden; but of the tree of the knowledge of good and evil you shall not eat, for in the day that you eat of it you shall die" (vv. 16-17). The command announces our capacity for freedom. If place marks the necessary conditions in which live, the command marks the freedom to say yes or no, choose this or that, go here or there, think our own thoughts and sing our own songs. It is a freedom absolutely unique in the total scheme of creation.

I am not right now interested so much in the intriguing significance of the "tree of the knowledge of good and evil" as in the significance of the command simply as command. The command assumes a capacity for freedom. We are not slaves to necessity; we are in a fundamental sense free. Our place, this creation, is given to us as is. It comprises the necessary conditions in which we live: gravity and the second law of thermodynamics, procreation and our genes, weather and the seasons, for a start. But within this world of necessity we are able to live in freedom. Necessity, this place we have been given to live in, is not as such limitation but the field in which we can practice and exercise freedom. The permission, "You may freely eat of every tree of the garden" (v. 16), and the prohibition, "of the tree of the knowledge of good and evil you shall not eat" (v. 17), in combination plunge us into a world of freedom and necessity. This garden in which we have been placed (and there is no other!) is where we learn to live in the land of the free.

Getting to know the neighborhood, the nature and conditions of the neighborhood, is fundamental to living to the glory of God. It is slow and complex work. It involves learning to live in the interlocking, shifting combinations, the endless variations in this country mapped between the uninhabitable poles of necessity and freedom.

This command, which presumes the freedom to obey or disobey, is the first command given in our Scriptures. It defines us as creatures of freedom: We can decide which road to travel; we are not pre-determined. We have the capacity to say, "Yes, I'll do that," or "No, I don't think I'll do that." We are not doomed to living out, as some of our friends say, our karma. We are the only part of the creation that has this ability, the only creature that can say no — or yes. The swallows that we envy, sweeping so effortlessly through the air, appearing so invitingly free, are not free at all; virtually everything they do is instinctive. And the warblers whom we admire catching insects and building nests and then, at just the right time in the autumn, migrating to Nicaragua without a map — incredibly intricate procedures all — accomplish faultlessly each of these marvelously skilled and timed and executed tasks, without deciding a single detail of one of them. They are incapable of either assent or protest. "Free as a bird" is not free. If we live in Minnesota, we can leave in October for Hawaii for a winter of sunshine, or stay at home and shovel snow. It's up to us. We are free. The birds are not.

Freedom does not mean doing whatever pops into our heads, like flapping our arms and jumping off a bridge, expecting to soar lazily across the river. Freedom is, in fact, incomprehensible without necessity. Freedom and necessity are twinned realities. Much of the art of living consists in acquiring skill in negotiating with them. But here's the thing: It is in the arena of place, the gift of place, that freedom and necessity engage us in constant dialectic. Living out this dialectic is at the heart of the human condition, at the heart of what we do as we join Christ in his play in the creation.

If we slight necessity, our so-called freedom is nothing but blundering and flailing about, maiming ourselves and others, whether morally or physically — usually both. If we slight freedom, submitting passively to necessity, we become sluggish, forfeit the unique particularity of our humanness, and sink into the parasitic state of the consumer and spectator.

It is only by taking our *place* seriously, studying its nature, familiarizing ourselves with its conditions, learning the texture and feel of this place where we work and play, eat and sleep, that we begin to acquire firsthand experience in the realities of freedom and necessity and learn that they are both gifts of God, that each is equally good, and that there can be no shirking of either.

Intimacy

After forming and placing us (the necessary conditions for living), assigning us work and commanding us (plunging us into a life of freedom), God introduces us to human relationship, brings us into intimacy with the other. God announces that "It is not good that the man should be alone; I will make him a helper as his partner" (Gen. 2:18).

Just as our launch into a life of freedom was prefaced by an assignment of responsibility, working and caring for the garden, so our launch into a life of intimacy is also prefaced by an assignment, this time using language: God formed animals and birds and "brought them to the man to see what he would call them" (v. 19). The first use of language in the Garden is naming animals and birds. It has been suggested that Adam, by naming the animals, was the first poet, but I think that comes later. Given the present context, it is more likely that he was the first naturalist. Naming identifies. Naming, when done well, captures something of the essence of the life so named.

A name is particular and calls attention to the particular, the "nature," the specific. Two friends enter a forest. One sees a mass of trees, the other sees spruce and oak and pine and elm. One looks at the ground and sees tangles of needles and brush, the other looks down and sees bloodroot and hepatica and arnica. One looks up and sees a blur of motion through the leaves, the other looks up and sees a Red-Eyed Vireo and a McGillivray Warbler and the Least Flycatcher. Which of the two is more alive to the garden and more in relation to the life spilling out and reverberating all through it in colors and songs, forms and movements — and to God who planted the garden and put us in it? And which of the two is better trained to exercise the glorious freedom of obedience in the context of the intricate necessities of the place?[20]

The men and women who train me in naming what is in the garden, seeing and hearing the proliferation of life around me, are as important as those who teach me to know and understand the Father, Son, and Holy Spirit. John Muir in his journals, Annie Dillard exploring Tinker Creek, and Wendell Berry working his Kentucky farm take their places alongside Moses in Genesis as companions in acquiring fluency of language in the creation garden. Loren Wilkinson and Luci Shaw are as important as Karl Barth, P. T. Forsyth, and John Calvin in helping me feel at home in this world that is spoken into being and formed into the purposes of salvation by the Lord God.

But naming the living creatures is only the first step on the way to relational intimacy. The naming, wonderful and useful and important as it is, is not enough. God's language assignment also exposes incompleteness. The naming, a precondition for intimacy, does not in itself produce intimacy. The creatures named don't know their names. They themselves don't speak. They don't answer and their not answering exposes a need that mere naming cannot fulfill, a need for relational answering, for intimacy. The unfulfilled need is expressed succinctly in the Genesis sentence, "but for the man there was not found a helper fit for him" (v. 20 RSV). A "helper fit for him" in the context suggests a person who can also use language, who can answer back, who can converse. In short, an equal. However glorious the animals and birds, they cannot engage us in conversation. We need another whom we can be over against and in relationship with. "A helper fit for him" suggests a "fit," *kᵉnegdo*, a creature other than me but enough like me to be in intimate relationship, marked from the beginning, unlike the animals and birds, by the use of language.

And so the Lord God made another human, a companion, to fill the need for intimacy, "a helper fit," in this garden of necessity and freedom that is our home. This is not simply another creature to name and identify and care for, but a person with whom we can be intimate. In contrast to the dust used to form man, a rib, a bone taken out of the critical center of the body, is used to form the other, the "fit": the woman. The man's immediate response to this other is by means of language:

> "This, at last, is bone of my bones
>   and flesh of my flesh;
> she shall be called woman,
>   because she was taken out of man."
>
> (v. 23)

Earlier the man used language in naming the animals and birds, but we were not given the words. These are the first words of human speech reported to us. In these initial Genesis chapters we have been hearing God's word in profusion: God creating, God making, God resting, God blessing, God commanding. Now we hear the first human words to be reported. They turn out to be words of intimate recognition ("bone of my bones, and flesh of my flesh") and words of intimate relationship ("she shall be called woman, because she was taken out of man").

Significantly, these intimacy-expressing phrases come to us in the form of poetry, our basic intimacy language — the language used by gurgling and cooing infants, by lovers, by pray-ers. This is not the distancing, objective language of prose but the involving, participating diction of poetry, revealing who I am and drawing the other into the personal revelation.

Thus the creation gift of place: man and woman, placed in the necessary garden for work and freedom and language, and now crowned with the dignity of intimacy.

*   *   *

There is a great deal of so-called creation appreciation, or "love of nature," that prefers to look the other way when men and women appear on the scene. Genesis 2 will not permit it. Men and women are as integral to creation as the garden with its trees and rivers, its animals and birds.

Several years ago one of my students who lived a distance away and rode a crowded bus to the college each day said to his wife as he went out the door one morning, "I'm just going to go out and immerse myself in God's creation today." The next day his parting words were the same. On the third day, she called him back, "Don't you think you ought to go to class today? A couple of days of walking in the woods or on the beach is okay, but don't you think enough is enough?"

He said, "Oh, I've been going to class every day."

"Then what," she said, "is all this business about immersing yourself in creation?"

"Well, I spend forty minutes on the bus each morning and afternoon. Can you think of a setting more thick with creation than that — all these people *created*, created in the image of God, created male and female?"

"I never thought of that," she said.

"You mean you've never read Genesis?"

*   *   *

I'm not suggesting it is easy, this maintaining of an observant Genesis connection between the animals and trees in the garden and the people in the garden, honoring the continuities in the God-formed man or woman right before us with the God-formed trees and birds around us. I'm only insisting that it is necessary.

Years ago when my children were young, our family was driving through Yellowstone National Park on holiday. Our national parks are among the great accomplishments that our not-always-accomplished governments have provided for us. Just as our churches and places of worship serve to sanctify time,[21] so these parks have always seemed to me to mark sacred space. As they accompanied their mother and me into these beautiful and glorious stretches of protected beauty and wildness, our children were subjected to as much biblical talk as when in church. One phrase that they heard a great deal was "leave nothing but footprints, take nothing but pictures." It is a motto used by the Sierra Club, but it was years before our children knew that. They assumed it was a Bible verse.

On this particular Yellowstone Park holiday, relishing the blessing of the sacred place, we had pulled to the side of the road to view a meadow of wildflowers. About twenty yards away a five- or six-year-old girl was picking a bouquet of fringed gentians. The gentian is a stunning blue alpine flower and one of my favorites. The little girl had an innocent fistful of these beauties, probably picked for her mother. When I noticed her, I was suddenly indignant at this violation of the sacred ground; I yelled at her, "Don't pick the flowers!" The poor little girl, terrorized by my bark, dropped the flowers and looked at me with total bewilderment and dismay, her face clouding over and then spilling out tears.

Immediately my children were all over me: "Dad, what you did is a lot worse than what she did. How could you do that to her? The God who made the flowers also made her! You ruined her day! You've probably scarred her for life!" And on and on and on for the rest of the day, ruining *my* day.

And of course they were right. How could I be so selective in my sense of kinship with creation? How did it happen that I felt so sensitive to the fringed gentian that had been formed out of the same dust as me, and so insensitive to the little girl also formed out of that same dust, or even something more like my own rib?

The same dust: the fringed gentian, the little girl, me. Desecration of the one is of a kind with desecration of the others. If we are going to enjoy and celebrate and live this gift of place in which the Lord God has placed us, we are going to have to embrace the people around us with the same delight as we do the hawks soaring above us and the violets blooming at our feet. Men and women, children and the elderly, the beautiful and the plain, the blind and the deaf, amputees and paralytics, the mentally impaired and the emotionally distraught — each a significant and sacred detail of nature, of God's creation.

*   *   *

The two creation stories are the same in that the subject in each is God at work in creation. Genesis 1: God (*Elohim*, the sum of all creative powers) is the exclusive subject of all the verbs (thirty-five of them) used in the seven days of creation. Creation in time. Genesis 2: The LORD God (*Elohim* compounded this time with *Yahweh*, the unique and personal name revealed to Moses) is the exclusive subject of the verbs that form man, plant a garden, assign work, give commands, form animals and birds, release the gift of language, and shape a relationship of communion and intimacy. Creation in place.

Genesis 1 and Genesis 2 work from the same base: when we wake up in the morning and look around us, wondering who we are, where we are, how we got here, where we came from, how we fit into what's going on, the answer is the same: "In the beginning . . . God created the heavens and the earth" (1:1); and, "In the day that the LORD God made the earth and the heavens" (2:4).

If we are going to live as intended, which is, to the glory of God, we cannot do it abstractly or in general. We have to do it under the particularizing conditions in which God works, namely, time and place, here and now. Genesis 1 and 2 reveal the forms that are formative for our living. Genesis 1 locates us formatively in time; Genesis 2 locates us formatively in place.

Hans Urs von Balthasar has written passionately and at length on the necessity for understanding and appreciating form as fundamental to life with its focus in the Christian life: "What is a person without a life-form, that is to say, without a form which he has chosen for his life, so that his life becomes the soul of the form and the form becomes the expression of his soul."[22]

We are not disembodied angels. We have a street address where God can find us. And we have ten fingers and ten toes, two eyes and two ears and a nose, along with assorted other items that form a body that is emphatically *us*. That's enough for a start.

*   *   *

A primary but often shirked task of the Christian in our society and culture is to notice, to see in detail, the sacredness of creation. The marks of God's creative work are all around and in us. We live surrounded by cherubim singing Holy, Holy, Holy.

It is easy to miss it. Sin-graffiti disfigure both land and people. Death is a frequent visitor. Blasphemies assault our ears. And our sin-blurred eyes and sin-dulled ears miss the glory that is right before us. But no excuses. We have a huge responsibility and an enormous privilege to live daily in such a way that we give witness to the immense and sacred gifts of time and place. The good news of Jesus Christ, "the firstborn of *creation*," has its context in these Genesis-revealed gifts of time and place. It is far too common in our fast-paced and technologically depersonalized society, impatient and zealous to get out the gospel message, to skip the Genesis context and slap together something improvisatory so that we can quickly get on with our urgent mission. More often than not these improvisations are dismissive of the intricacies and beauties of God's gifts of time and place. But the good news entrusted to God's people is the good news of Jesus Christ, the firstborn of, yes, *creation*. Jesus' life and work, crucifixion and resurrection, are thoroughly established and worked out in the creation gifts of time and place. We dare not put asunder what he joined together.

Grounding Text (2): St. John

St. John's Gospel is a rewriting of Genesis 1–2. The Gospel of John is the creation story with Jesus Christ presented as simultaneously the revelation of Creator and creation. Creator, God's Word that spoke creation into being (Gen. 1), comes into view in John's Gospel as Jesus, as the Word who spoke but also continues to speak creation into being. Creation, that which is summed up and completed in man and woman (Gen. 2), is now presented by St. John to our understanding as this same Jesus, the "Word

[that] became flesh," who entered our history and "dwelt among us" (John 1:14 RSV).

Our ancestors kept the "both/and" identity of Jesus in attentive focus with the phrase "very God and very man." By "very" they meant totally and completely: undiluted divinity, unadulterated humanity. In Jesus Christ we see the Creator at work among us (very God); in him we also see the creation of which we are a part (very Man).[23]

*   *   *

St. John's Gospel is an extensive presentation of Jesus Christ, Creator and creation, "at play" in the Genesis creation. This is Genesis elaborated, personalized, and grounded in a recognizable geography and history. The Christian life is in perpetual danger of dissolving into wonderful ideas or sublime feelings or ambitious projects; John's Gospel, undergirded by Genesis 1–2, prevents dilutions and dissolutions that are so fatal to living robustly to the glory of God. This Gospel continues, century after century, generation after generation, as one of our very best defenses against a spirituality that is abstracted from the actual lives in which we follow Jesus, one step at a time, walking from kitchen to bedroom, from parking lot to workplace, from sanctuary to cemetery, from classroom to playing field, slugging it out with "the things in the world . . . the lust of the flesh and the lust of the eyes and the pride of life . . ." (1 John 2:15-16 RSV).

Everything that comes into view in Genesis 1–2 is lived out in the person of Jesus among men and women like us and under the conditions (sunshine and rain, buying and selling, birth and death, sickness and oppression, sex and religion — whatever) in which we live. The word that gives precision to this comprehensive revelation of God in human form, living (not merely admiring or discussing) the creation, is *incarnation:* "the Word became flesh and dwelt among us" (John 1:14 RSV). Incarnation, *in-flesh-ment*, embodiment.

It is not uncommon among people like us to suppose that if we lived in another place or a better neighborhood with more congenial living conditions, voted in a better government, built finer schools, then we would most certainly live a more spiritual life. St. John's Gospel says, Forget it.

It is also common among people like us to look for ways to free ourselves from the humdrum, escape as often as possible into ecstasy, devise ways to live separated from the clamor of traffic and family, associate so far as possible only with people of like mind, and engage in disciplines and ways of dress and speech that set us apart from "the others." John's Gospel says, Forget it.

*   *   *

Here is how St. John does it. He writes a story that picks up features of the Genesis 1–2 accounts of creation and presents Jesus as God's Genesis Word continuing to speak creation into existence. Somewhere along the line, things went wrong (Genesis tells that story too), and they are in desperate need of fixing. The fixing (like the making in the first place) is all accomplished by speaking — God speaking the new creation into being in the person of Jesus. But Jesus in this story not only speaks the word of God; he *is* the Word of God.

Keeping company with these words, we begin to realize that our words are more important than we ever supposed. Saying "I believe," for instance, marks the difference between life and death. Our words accrue dignity and gravity in conversations with Jesus, for Jesus doesn't impose this new creation as a solution; he *narrates* us into this creation through leisurely conversation, intimate personal relationships, compassionate responses, passionate prayer, and — putting it all together — a sacrificial death. Keeping company with Jesus we become insiders to the creation. It is not something "out there" that we can adopt or ignore as we will. We can't walk away from creation in order to attend to the spiritual life. We are embedded in the creation, we are integral to the creation.

St. John signals the Genesis connection by starting his Gospel with the opening Genesis words "In the beginning . . ." (but in Greek: *en archē*). In a dazzling passage of theological poetry, John then identifies Jesus with that Genesis Word. The same Word that brought all creation into being is Jesus, who now brings a new creation into being. John expresses this both succinctly and comprehensively in his incomparable sentence: "And the Word became flesh and dwelt among us, full of grace and truth; we have beheld his glory, glory as of the only Son from the Father" (1:14 RSV).

John's task is to show Jesus completely and utterly at home in the Genesis creation with the intent of making us completely and utterly at home in this same holy creation. There is far more to life, of course, than creation. There is holy history and holy community (parts two and three in this volume), in the living of which Jesus is also definitive. But creation is where we begin. We cannot skip the beginning and enter at a higher grade: we live one day after the other, not in timeless reveries; we live in dirt and with animals and birds, not in cloud castles; we live male and female, not in undisturbed solitariness; we are flesh that requires feeding and cleaning and clothing. We cannot live God's gifts of salvation history and holy community apart from God's creation conditions. Jesus didn't and we can't.

Was St. John dealing with people who were trying to shortcut creation in order to get to the "real heart of things," to plunge into the "deeper life," to live on a "higher spiritual plane" than the others around them — what we have identified earlier as the "gnostic" virus? It would be a surprise if he were not, for wherever concerns for God and a godly life surface, these kinds of creation detours also show up.

*　　*　　*

St. John is a consummate writer, skilled in nuance and allusion. There is an inviting simplicity in John's writing, but it is a simplicity that conceals depths of insight. It would be both irreverent and a violation to reduce or summarize his Gospel to a few "truths" or "principles" (the gnostic way of doing things). We must let him do his work in his own way. Our task is to submit ourselves to John's narrative art and let him ground us with Jesus in the creation, this creation in which Jesus is revealing the fullness of God to us; and then to follow John in embracing a Jesus-believing life in which the fullness of a creation-grounded life takes shape in us.

John writes the Jesus story in quite a different way from his canonical companions, Matthew, Mark, and Luke, who all follow a different outline. John's approach gives us the same story, but the shift in perspective and tone engages us differently. Novelist John Updike observes that if we view Matthew, Mark, and Luke as progressively sedimentary, John is metamorphic — all the strata violently annealed into something quite different.[24]

John's storytelling consists primarily of Jesus' conversations. In John's rewriting of the Genesis creation the most conspicuous feature is that Jesus *speaks*. He is, after all, the Word. But unlike the terse Genesis sentences, Jesus' words flourish into conversations and discourses. John's opening sentence, "In the beginning was the Word . . . ," is elaborated in conversations that Jesus has with all sorts and conditions of people, conversations brief and lengthy, conversations pithy and elaborate, but *conversations*. The conversations develop and accumulate: conversations between Jesus and his mother, Jesus and his disciples, Jesus and Nicodemus, Jesus and the Samaritan, Jesus and the paralytic, Jesus and the blind man, Jesus and the Jews, Jesus and Martha, Jesus and Mary, Jesus and Caiaphas, Jesus and Pilate, and, without any change of tone or diction, Jesus and God, the Son and the Father. Several times the conversations develop into discourses but the conversational tone is always maintained. These are not declamations to a generalized "world" but person-to-person conversations. The Lord of language uses language not to "lord it over" anyone but to engender relationships of grace and love, creating community and bringing it to maturity in prayer.

In this richly conversational Gospel world, three elements give a distinctively "creation" cast to the story: the *egō eimi* formula, the use of the term "sign," and the frequent mention of glory.

Egō Eimi

When God appeared to Moses at the burning bush and told him that he was to lead his people out of Egyptian slavery, Moses was understandably cautious. He asked God to identify himself by name; the answer was, "I AM WHO I AM. . . . [S]ay this to the people of Israel, 'I AM has sent me to you'" (Exod. 3:14). The phrase became the unique personal name for God in Israel, in its original Hebrew form "Yahweh" but in Greek translation *egō eimi*. *Egō eimi*, "I am," is the most personal name for God in the Scriptures.

The phrase is often on Jesus' lips. Every time he says *egō* or *egō eimi* we hear an echo of the divine name "Yahweh," Jesus taking the Name as his own. All the Gospel writers have Jesus employing this God-identifying formula, but John far more than the other three combined. Virtually everyone who has reflected on this feature realizes, as G. M. Burge puts it, that "Jesus is publicly applying the divine name of God — God's authoritative presence — to himself."[25]

The frequency of Jesus' justly famous assertion, "I am . . . " throughout these conversations makes the story work at two levels (or in two dimensions) simultaneously: We hear Jesus using God's new name, "I am," as his own name and we hear it in the simplest and most accessible diction and grammar, the personal use of the verb "to be." Through these accumulating conversations we realize that God is speaking in this Jesus voice, the God who called all creation into being, the God who identified himself to Moses as the savior of Israel; *this* God, speaking in these Jesus conversations and discourses — God's Word and words.

Jesus' boldest use of the Name came during the Feast of Tabernacles in the Jerusalem temple: the Feast, associated with messianic expectation; the temple, God's honored place. At precisely that time and place Jesus said, "Very truly, I tell you, before Abraham was, I am" (John 8:58). Reynolds Price, one of our finest novelists, who has many pungent observations on the various ways and circumstances in which Jesus employs the "I am," calls this "the towering crest of Jesus' claim for himself."[26] The immediate response of his listeners shows that they understood immediately that he was saying, "I am God himself, here and now; I have always been, will always be."

But Jesus' hearers knew their Bibles: "One who blasphemes the name of the LORD shall be put to death; the whole congregation shall stone the blasphemer" (Lev. 24:16). Jesus' words immediately transformed the congregation into a lynch mob; there were plenty of stones from the temple construction scattered around, "so they picked up stones to throw at him" (John 8:59). But Jesus escaped.

Seven times Jesus uses the "I am/*egō eimi*" formula with a predicate, a metaphor that serves as a parable that fills in details of who he is and what he is up to: the bread of life (John 6:35), the light of the world (8:12), the gate for the sheep (10:7), the good shepherd (10:14), the resurrection and the life (11:25), the way and the truth and the life (14:6), the true vine (15:1).

All these metaphors are simple, ordinary words, words that we commonly use on the street and in the kitchen as we go about our work, walking and seeing, believing and loving. In fact, there is hardly a word anyplace in St. John's storytelling that we have not used with comprehension since we were five years old. We are included in these conversations marked by intimacy and leisure; we are welcomed as participants.

Intimacy. Jesus, by means of John's story, invites us into his life, God's life, in terms and in circumstances that are immediately accessible. The simplest grammar is employed to invite us in as participants in the story. Jesus doesn't try to impress us with big words or highfalutin concepts; he doesn't flaunt his credentials; he doesn't bully or intimidate with a show of authority. Jesus is in conversation with the same kinds of people we talk to most days, and many of them we recognize in ourselves.

And leisure. John is a most leisurely storyteller. He takes his time, he repeats, he circles back upon himself. He uses words lovingly, savoring them. Or he holds a sentence up to the light and then rearranges the words, sometimes only slightly, to shift the angle of refraction and bring out another color. Austin Farrer characterized John's style in this regard as "divinatory brooding."[27] The brisk narrative pace so pronounced in his three Gospel-writing predecessors slows to a meditative Sunday stroll in John.

Edward Dahlberg, in trying to recover Thoreau's prophetic bite for us, insisted that "*Walden* cannot be rushed into men's hearts. . . . Persuade and hint."[28] And if Thoreau's *Walden* cannot be rushed, much less can John's Gospel. To read this story, to *heart-listen* to his story, John's millions of appreciative readers have slowed themselves to John's pace, submitting themselves to the tidal rhythms of the conversations, rejecting time-saving doctrinal summaries that tell us what John *means* theologically without going to all the trouble of listening to him say it. We are not in John's storytelling company long before we realize that he is not nearly as interested in telling us anything new *about* Jesus (although he also does plenty of that along the way) as he is in drawing us into an increasingly intimate relationship *with* Jesus. "Believe" and "love" are the characteristic verbs; neither can be accomplished in a hurry.

And so in the quartet of Gospel writers, John gets the final storytelling word. As generation follows generation there is danger that the creation will be reduced to mere nature study on the one hand or mere doctrine on the other. John renews the original personal quality of God's creation, exquisitely designed for believing and loving. Robert Browning's poem "A Death in the Desert," named by William Temple "the most penetrating interpretation of St. John in the English language,"[29] has John, accounting for why he wrote his Jesus story the way he did, say,

> . . . truth, deadened of its absolute blaze,
> Might need love's eye to pierce the o'erstretched doubt.[30]

John supplies "love's eye." To this day, whenever the brightness of the creation story is dulled by depersonalized study or fogged by clichés, John's story is the Gospel of choice to penetrate to the original Genesis blaze.

The Signs

Most of us have a hankering for "signs" — supernatural phenomena and marvels of various sorts. The vast field of religion is commonly assumed to provide ground for the miraculous, and the more fertile the soil the more miracles per acre. So it often comes as a surprise to learn that Jesus was distinctly cool to the subject as a whole. Without debunking miracles as such, Jesus flatly denied that they were evidence of authenticity and gave a stern warning against being duped by them: "false messiahs and false prophets will appear and produce great signs and omens, to lead astray, if possible, even the elect" (Matt. 24:24; see also 2 Thess. 2:9 and Rev. 19:20). Jesus also, though he performed a number of miracles in the course of his life, bluntly refused to use a miraculous sign as validation or proof of his divine authority and had harsh words for those who asked for one: "An evil and adulterous generation asks for a sign" (Matt. 12:39; see also Luke 23:8 and 1 Cor. 1:22).

That seems to be clear enough and, with Jesus as the speaker, sufficiently authoritative: Don't be impressed by signs; don't go out looking for signs. The miraculous is no proof of truth or reality. Supernatural marvels have wonderful entertainment value, but not much else. There is a basic sense in which we cannot avoid the miraculous. We live in a world, after all, in which God is supernaturally active, visibly and invisibly, both around and within us, far beyond our capacity to notice or explain, control or manage. It would be odd if we did not at least occasionally catch a glimpse of this "beyond" in our backyards and remark on it — a sign, a sign of God's presence or work where we had not expected to see or hear it and in circumstances in which we cannot account for it. But such signs are not for advertising or entertainment.

John uses the term "sign" in this chastened way.[31] It is one of his signature words. He presents Jesus' signs not to prove or parade Jesus as superior to or exempt from the creation, but to give us a look *into* the creation instead of just *at* it, to show us how Jesus who created all these things and holds them all together still (Col. 1:15-20) continues to work in this same stuff of creation. Everything Jesus does, he does with his hands deep in the soil and flesh of creation.

Jesus is openly impatient and even dismissive of those who ask for miraculous proof that will validate his authority. The episode in John's Gospel immediately following the "first of his signs," the changing of water into wine at the wedding at Cana (John 2:11), tells the story of Jesus routing those who had set up shop in the temple courts during Passover to sell sacrificial animals and to engage in money-changing for worshipers who had arrived with foreign currencies — both highly profitable businesses. Jesus denounced their profiteering with his stinging "you shall not make my Father's house a house of trade" (2:16 RSV). The religious professionals ("the Jews," in this case) challenged his right to interfere with the accepted routines and disrupt their temple way of life, throwing everything into confusion: "What sign can you show us for doing this?" (2:18). Which is to say, "Show us your papers. Who authorized you to barge in here and act like you owned the place? And what's this 'Father' talk? These are sacred precincts and this is the holiest festival of the year. *We* are in charge here. Present us with a sign that authorizes this outrage."[32] Jesus refuses. His response ("Destroy this temple . . .") is an enigmatic non-answer that they could not possibly understand and only serves to provoke them further. It seems that Jesus has no time for people who demand the sensational to validate truth or confirm God's presence among them.

Signs and wonders, miracles and mighty works are certainly part of the story, yes, an essential part of the biblical story and its continuation and outworking in the Christian life; but out of context, apart from God's revelation of himself in Jesus, severed and then removed from their organic positionings in the intricate and detailed formation of God's people, they are simply things, miracle-commodities that are bought and sold on the religious stock exchange.

It has long been customary by readers of this Gospel to count seven signs, acts of Jesus described in some detail by which we may come to recognize and believe the revelation of God in Jesus. "Believe" is the critical verb here. It is to evoke belief, which is to say trust and obedient participation, that John writes his Gospel.

The seven signs show Jesus continuing the work laid out in Genesis in the seven days of creation. It would be difficult to tell these Jesus stories without conveying some sense of wonder, awe that we are being let in on something extraordinary, a realization that these signs are evidence that God is still at work in this creation and not just its maintenance engineer. All the same, John downplays the element of wonder and makes certain we understand that none of the signs were compelling, forcing a unanimous verdict from the jury, "God did this!"

The too often disregarded scriptural rule is that we cannot be *made* to believe. Belief by its very nature requires assent and participation, trust and commitment. When we believe we are at our most personal and intimate with another, with the Other. Belief cannot be forced. If we are bullied or seduced or manipulated to believe, we do not end up believing, we end up intimidated or raped or used. And we are less, not more.

John maintains this sense of participation and freedom by embedding each sign in a story; a sign is not a detached item to be studied as a thing in itself, but a moment or event of realization: Jesus is God at work right here, now. John also maintains this sense of uncoerced participation by making it clear that the sign as such was not compelling: the sign is a signpost, it points beyond itself, it may or may not be followed.

At the first sign, the changing of water to wine at the wedding at Cana (John 2:1-11), most of the guests don't appear to have even known that the miracle occurred. The servants, Jesus' mother, and his disciples knew, but the text mentions only the disciples as those in whom the sign accomplished its purpose: they "believed in him." The "chief steward," who was in charge of the whole affair, strikes me as a snooty fellow, self-important in his role and aloof from his servants. He seems to have been completely in the dark, oblivious to the miracle, calling the bridegroom over and, I would think with some disapproval, expert as he was in the fine etiquette of wines, remarking how extraordinary it was to save such good wine for the end when most of the guests wouldn't be in a position even to notice.

The second sign has its beginning in this same village of Cana but is completed in Capernaum (4:46-54). It contains within it both a criticism and an affirmation of signs. The sign gets its start in Cana when an official, probably an appointee of Herod Antipas, comes from Capernaum to ask Jesus to accompany him to Capernaum and heal his son. Jesus' response is negative, "Unless you see signs and wonders you will not believe" (v. 48), not unlike the unfavorable assessment of signs that Matthew reports (Matt. 12:39).[33] But the father, undeterred, persists, as if to say, "I don't care about signs, I want you to heal my son!" And then comes the interesting part: Jesus tells him, "Go; your son will live"; and "the man believed" and left, *without any evidence of the healing,* which is to say, quite apart from sign or wonder. The father responded believingly to Jesus without benefit of a sign, we might almost say without the distraction of a sign. Jesus' word, not the sign, formed the man's belief. It was not until the next day as he neared home — it was a twenty-mile hike between Capernaum and Cana

— that he learned that his son got well at the very time on the day before that Jesus, in Cana, had said that he would.

The third sign, the healing of the paraplegic, is set in Jerusalem at the pool of Bethzatha (John 5:1-18). This sign was spectacular: the man had been paralyzed for thirty-eight years. And the setting was dramatic: a large pool not far from the busy temple court on the holy Sabbath, and bordering the pool five porches crowded with invalids hoping for healing in the supposedly therapeutic waters. Jesus healed the man with a question ("Do you want to be made well?") and a command ("Take up your mat and walk"). When the people realized what Jesus had done, restored this precious but damaged "God's image" in creation, we would expect a response of grateful and awed belief in Jesus. After all, the wretch had been hanging around the pool for as many years as their ancestors had trekked through the wilderness! But the self-appointed religious police attacked Jesus on the grounds of Sabbath-breaking, an attack that escalated into an assassination plot when they heard Jesus call God his Father ("making himself equal with God"). The sign, a window that showed God at work in Jesus, in this case provoked murderous hostility, the polar opposite of belief.

The fourth sign, the feeding of the five thousand, takes place back in Galilee on a hill on the north shore of the Sea of Tiberius around the season of Passover (John 6:1-15). Associations with the exodus from Egypt, the salvation Passover meal, and the years of miraculous provision of manna in the wilderness must have quickly sprung to mind among those being fed. Prompted by Deuteronomy 18:15 they concluded with enthusiasm that the new Moses was there with them: "When the people saw the sign which he had done, they began to say, 'This is indeed the prophet who is to come into the world'" (v. 14). But they got the sign only half right. In the sign they saw rightly that Jesus was from God and was leading them to salvation and providing a miraculous meal. But they misunderstood the sign when they "took it over" as a mandate to force Jesus into becoming a political king who would free them from Roman rule. Jesus escaped into the hills. We cannot make Jesus do what we think he ought to do. A sign is not a blank ticket that we can use to write our agenda for Jesus. The next day, back in Capernaum (6:25-30), Jesus tried to correct their misinterpretation of the sign as an invitation to just get what they wanted for themselves ("your fill of the loaves") instead of a revelation of God at work in Jesus, a sign of God's giving of himself to them ("the food that endures for eternal life, which the Son of Man will give you"). But they still didn't get it, asking for another sign, "that we may see it and believe you."

The misunderstanding provoked the magnificent "I am the bread of life" discourse (6:35-59) but also much murmuring and disputation. It eventually led to a major defection from the ranks of followers (6:66). Signs reveal Jesus as God at work among us, but they also reveal how unready so many of us are to accept and embrace what is revealed and how contentious we can become when the God in heaven that we worship turns out to be involved in the details of our daily lives on this earth in ways that don't fit our preconceptions.

The fifth sign, tucked into the context of the fourth, is the quieting of the sea storm as the disciples rowed back to Capernaum on the night following the feeding of the five thousand (6:16-21). This sign is unique among the seven, the only sign, as it turns out, to be free of ambiguity. The sign reveals Jesus as sovereign in creation, gladly received and welcomed as such by the disciples. And, most significantly, there is this: the narration of the sign is centered in the *egō eimi* expression in verse 20: "It is I; do not be afraid." As we have observed, this is the form of the divine name with which Jesus identifies himself and that John skillfully and continuously weaves in and out of the fabric of his Gospel storying. This sign, set in the context of the sign that was so beset by inadequate responses, counters the wrongheaded "make him a king (of Galilee)!" with the assertion of uncluttered sovereignty over all creation, doing for his disciples what they, for all their strenuous rowing, could not do for themselves, and taking them where they were unable to get by themselves.

The sixth sign, the healing of the man born blind, takes place back in Jerusalem (John 9:1-41). The sign reveals Jesus as the incarnation of the Genesis Word, "Let there be light." It was the first day of light for the man born blind, but there was no Genesis consensus in the Jerusalem community that it "was good." Like the third sign at the pool of Bethzatha, this one took place on the Sabbath. The city's religion experts didn't see the healing as a sign of anything other than one more case of Sabbath-breaking that had to be dealt with. They did this by kicking the so-recently-blind man out of the synagogue. The sign, as sign, was also lost on the man's parents, whose concern with their standing with the religious establishment blinded them to God at work right before them. Jerusalem was full of blind men and women that day who "loved darkness rather than light" (3:19). But the man blind from birth saw. He not only saw the city around him for the first time but saw the sign to which everyone else was blind — he saw God present and at work in his life and he believed. "Believe" occurs three times in as many sentences and finds its terminus in worship: "he worshiped him" (9:35-38).

The seventh sign is the raising of Lazarus from his tomb in the small town of Bethany (John 11:1-54). This is the most elaborately narrated of the signs, gathering into the story a large cast, including family members, grieving friends from nearby Jerusalem, Jesus' disciples, and the hostile chief priests and Pharisees meeting in council. Five of the cast are named: Lazarus and his sisters Mary and Martha, the disciple Thomas, and the high priest Caiaphas. This is unusual. The other sign stories, except for the name Jesus, are sparing of names. The first sign (water into wine) names Mary, and the fourth (feeding the five thousand) Philip and Andrew, but that's it. The signs are not human interest stories; they are God-revealing stories. But eventually, of course, they have an impact on every human concern. So in this final named sign, John, having held our human curiosity in check long enough as he kept our attention focused on what was being revealed in Jesus, steps back and lets us see a spectrum of human emotions and responses in the raising of Lazarus, the "resurrection and life" sign.

Thomas, learning that Jesus intended to return to the neighborhood where they had so recently escaped arrest and stoning (10:31-39; 11:7-8), assumed they would all be killed and rallied his fellow disciples to stick with Jesus and die with him. Jesus himself weeps in sympathy with the mourners and for love of his dead friend. He is visibly and deeply moved. The sisters Mary and Martha each in turn express their disappointment that Jesus did not come when they had sent word of their brother's illness — do we catch a tone of rebuke in their voices? And Caiaphas? For him this was the last straw. He promptly set the machinery in motion to kill Jesus.

*   *   *

Signs and sayings are woven throughout this Gospel to provide us with a comprehensive basis for belief that "Jesus is the Messiah, the Son of God, and that through believing you may have life in his name" (John 20:31). All the same, signs are not easy to read and they are certainly not compelling — opposition was aroused more often than belief. God reveals himself in Jesus, but the revelation rarely conforms to our expectations. We have such stereotyped ideas of what God does and how he does it that we frequently misread the signposts. As John makes us insiders to these seven named signs, we realize how often in our preoccupation with our self-importance we miss seeing what is going on right under our eyes (the steward at the wedding); how, with our fixed idea of how God works, we dismiss what is overwhelmingly obvious (the Sabbath healings); how, in a flush of blessings, we try to grab Jesus and enlist him for our personal agendas (the feeding of the five thousand); how easily and quickly devastation or death or its emotional and circumstantial equivalent (the circumstances around the death and raising of Lazarus) pushes Jesus out of the center to the margins while we get on the best we can with what we have: courage and resignation (like Thomas), accusation and weeping (like Mary), or retaliation even to the extent of murder (like Caiaphas). Martha, like the Capernaum official earlier in the Gospel, was the only one in the Lazarus cast who believed in Jesus previous to the completion of the sign (11:27).

But not always. One sign, the stilling of the storm, was read by the disciples without confusion or ambiguity. They all saw Jesus in majestic sovereignty, heard him speak his God-identifying name, and received him gladly.

*   *   *

"Although he had performed so many signs in their presence, they did not believe in him" (John 12:37). John quotes Isaiah to confirm that this is nothing new. This is the way it is with us. We don't find it easy either to recognize the signs of God's glory or to receive him on the terms that he comes to us. The good news, though, is that the signs are everywhere. God is not stingy in revelation. But neither does he shortcut our participation. God will not interfere with our freedom or our dignity by using signs that overpower or intimidate. We are not used to this. When someone wants us to do or buy something, we are used to being argued with, shown irrefutable evidence, promised side benefits, flattered, and sometimes even threatened. When a gift or blessing is offered to us apart from such demeaning means and meddling methods, we hardly know what to do. Keeping company with John and his canonical brothers and sisters brings us into a way of life in which God's life is given to us in God's way, in Jesus, and can be received only under the modes of believing and loving. It's going to take us a while, but given the conditions of creation in which we inescapably find ourselves, the signs point the way clearly enough: submit to and receive Jesus as revealed whenever and wherever, follow and worship him. And look for the glory.

The Glory

"Glory" is a light-filled word spilling out the extravagant brightness that marks God's presence among us. It is also used to ascribe honor and dignity and "weightiness" to mountains and weather and men and women, but the most prominent use in our Scriptures is in relation to God. "No one has ever seen God" (John 1:18) but we do see his glory, the bright splendor that marks God's presence, present among us here and now: at Sinai, in the tabernacle, in the temple, and, most of all and most personally, in Jesus: "we have beheld his glory, glory as of the only Son from the Father" (1:14 RSV).

John's fondness for the term "glory," in his retelling of the meaning of our participation in the creation, is noteworthy. "Glory," a prominent word throughout our Scriptures, is nowhere more prominent than in John's Gospel.

"Dwelt among us" on the first page of the Gospel (RSV) is an arresting image and paints a picture that pulls the entire Gospel within its frame. To say that Jesus, the Word that has become flesh, "dwelt among us" sends tentacles of association far back into the Hebrew Bible to Exodus, when the recently saved people of God were instructed to pitch an elaborate tent, the tabernacle, that became the place on earth where God revealed himself and was worshiped (Exod. 25:8-9).

Centuries later, Joel prophesied of a coming time when "you shall know that I, the LORD your God, *dwell* in Zion" (Joel 3:17; italics added here and in following passages).

When Israel returned from Babylonian exile, they heard a sermon in which Zechariah preached, "Sing and rejoice, O daughter of Zion! For lo, I will come and *dwell* in your midst" (Zech. 2:10).

God, showing Ezekiel a vision of the perfected temple, told him, "this is the place of my throne . . . where I *will dwell* in the midst of the people of Israel forever" (Ezek. 43:7 RSV).

So when John tells us that Jesus, the flesh and blood Jesus that everyone can see, *dwelt among us,* he clearly means us to understand that Jesus is the new tabernacle and temple of the Hebrew people. Do you want to see God present among you, do you want to come into the presence of God and worship him? Here he is making himself at home among you: Jesus — pitching his tent, building a house, setting up shop.

There is another possible word-triggered association here. In rabbinic times, many years after the Hebrew Bible was completed, the Hebrew verb "dwell" was given a noun form, *shekinah,* which was widely used in the Hebrew religious community to mark God's presence, God dwelling among his people accompanied by a visible display of bright glory. There are frequent connections made in our Scriptures between the presence of God and the glory of God (Exod. 24:15-16 at Sinai; Exod. 40:34 with the tabernacle; 1 Kings 8:10-11 at Solomon's temple; Ezek. 44:4 in the vision of the restored temple). *Shekinah* became the word that marked this visible, light-spilling presence of God among us. *Shekinah* became a virtual synonym for God. When John immediately follows "And the word became flesh and dwelt among us" with "and we beheld his glory . . . ," many readers of his Gospel, noticing the frequent references to glory (thirty-four times) in relation to Jesus, may well have heard echoes of *Shekinah,* the God-revealing glory evident in Jesus (but especially in his prayers: 12:27-28; 17:1, 4, 5, 10, 22, 24).

By a sheer but happy accident of language the consonants in the Greek term "dwell" — S, K, and N *(skēnei)* — are similar to the consonants in Hebrew "dwell" — SH, K, and N *(shakan* and *shekinah).* The respective words in Greek and Hebrew not only meant the same thing but *sounded* the same, reinforcing the associations between the place where the people met and worshiped God and the person of Jesus in whom the people met and worshiped God.

Jesus is the person in whom we see God present among us, God dwelling among us, God here and now. Jesus calls us out of our libraries and classrooms and lecture halls where we are studying the rich and storied past of God's revelation; Jesus challenges our obsessive preoccupations with scenarios of how and when God will finally accomplish his purposes with us and all humankind. "Look at what is right before you: *I am.*" The signs are all over the place, the sayings are echoing in our minds and hearts. The glory.

But once we take a careful John-guided look at Jesus, we have to revise our understanding of glory considerably. The thunder and lightning of Sinai, the elaborate rituals and fabrics and designs for worship in the wilderness tent, the architectural splendors of the Solomonic temple, the spinning, gyroscopic cherubim dazzle of Ezekiel's throne, the thunderous Psalm 29 poem/prayer that conducts the entire creation into symphonic harmonies — all this is now background to the glory that we see in Jesus. Nothing of the splendor that is conveyed in these earlier expressions of the glory is to be dismissed or minimized in any way. But this glory must now be reimagined and received and entered into as Jesus reveals it: Jesus ignorable, Jesus unimpressive, Jesus dismissed, Jesus marginal, Jesus suffering, Jesus rejected, Jesus derided, Jesus hung on a cross, and — the final and irrefutable indignity — Jesus dead and buried. All this is included in the content of "we beheld his glory."

At the pivotal centerpoint of his Gospel, John gives us Jesus' most significant and critical, but also most disconcerting, statement on the glory. Jesus is anticipating his imminent death. He says, "The hour has come for the Son of man to be glorified. Very truly, I tell you, unless a grain of wheat falls into the earth and dies, it remains just a single grain; but if it dies, it bears much fruit. . . . Now is my soul troubled. And what should I say — 'Father, save me from this hour'? No, it is for this reason that I have come to this hour. Father, glorify your name" (12:23-28).

Jesus, it seems, has an option. He can ask the Father to save him from the hour of death. He can ask the Father to deliver him from the fiery furnace and the lions' den. He can ask the Father to glorify the Son in triumph, in a Moses Red Sea Crossing, a Joshua Jericho March, in Elijah's Fiery Chariot. He can ask for another way than a sacrificial death. He considers it, or at least he knows it is a possibility. But he doesn't do it.

These words are precipitated by Philip and Andrew coming to Jesus and telling him that some Greeks want to see him. Jesus has a great evangelistic opportunity to build on their "seeker" curiosity to recruit the Greeks as followers. But Jesus ignores the request, what we would be apt to call the "opportunity." Maybe Jesus sensed that the Greeks were tourists and were only in Jerusalem that Passover week to see the sights, one of the sights being Jesus.

Jesus begins and ends this passage with the term "glory." Glory, the brightness of God's presence right here on our home ground, clearly has something, maybe everything, to do with his approaching death and burial. This is going to take some relearning. The dictionaries and word studies in Hebrew and Greek, the etymologies and definitions that we are so fond of, at this moment are radically relativized. Jesus takes the brightest word in our vocabularies and plunges it into the darkest pit of experience, violent and excruciating death. Everything we ever associated with glory has to be recast: We have entered a mystery.

But it is not a total mystery. Every gardener knows something of this: each spring we bury seeds in our gardens and in a few weeks enjoy the bloom of flowers and the nourishment of vegetables. The metaphor enables our participation. Jesus, as he so often did, uses a familiar experience that we all have, in this case planting a seed in the soil, to lead us into the unfamiliar, the mystery that he wills us to enter: glory.

Glory is what we are after. Whatever else glory is, it is not just more of what we already have or the perfection of what we already have. Do we suppose that the Christian life is simply our human, biological, intellectual, moral life developed and raised a few degrees above the common stock? Do we think that faith in Jesus is a kind of mechanism, like a car jack, that we use to lever ourselves up to a higher plane where we have access to God?

Jesus' imagery, to be followed soon by his sacrifice, is totally counter to our culture of more, more. Could Jesus have made it any clearer? We don't become more, we become less. Instead of grasping more tightly to whatever we value, we let it all go: "He who loses his life will save it." "Blessed are the poor in spirit" is another way that Jesus said it.

Here's the thing: we must let Jesus define the glory for us or we will miss it entirely. The astonishing thing from our perspective is that so few people who were around Jesus "saw his glory." They were looking right at the glory and didn't see it. They variously perceived in Jesus ignorance, lack of sophistication, blasphemy, lawlessness, an excellent not-to-be-missed opportunity to exploit, a threat that would destroy a privileged way of life, and finally, at the crucifixion, abject failure.

One of the extraordinary things about John's Gospel is that even though it explicitly states that it is written so that we might believe in Jesus as the Son of God, few people did in fact believe in him. In the presence of all those signs, despite all those conversations and prayers and discourses in which Jesus over and over again identified himself as God's Word, *egō eimi*, speaking creation and salvation and wholeness of life into being, not many saw the glory.

*   *   *

One of the severe handicaps under which the church operates is the cover-up of the glory with respectable substitutes such as acceptance and honor, success and "relevance." Over and over again, we miss it. The Greeks missed it. Tourists at the holy sights, cameras at the ready, guidebooks in hand, tried to hire Philip as a tour guide to Jesus. But Jesus wouldn't pose for their photographs. Jesus was already praying his way to the cross. Jesus had been giving hints of the glory that was about to be displayed fully ("The hour has come for the Son of man to be glorified") but in a way that no one anticipated, death — a most horrible but freely chosen death.

Tell the Greeks to go back home and take pictures of the Parthenon.

Not many hours after this stunning, baffling juxtaposition of glory and death, Jesus prays for his disciples that they (we are included) will be glorified with the same glory: "The glory that you have given me I have given them, so that they may be one, as we are one" (John 17:23).

The glory with which Jesus was glorified and the glory for which Jesus prayed for us is quite different from the kinds of glory that we are conditioned to want and admire. This glory is not conspicuous. It is not glamorous. It is not the glory that gets featured in glossy magazines or travel posters. It is not a glory noticed by fashion editors. It is not a glory that flatters our lusts and egos.

But it is no less glory for all that. This glory, once we perceive it, is the brightness radiating from God as he moves into our neighborhood. Followers of Jesus regularly have to relearn the meaning of words corrupted by our culture and debased by our sin. Jesus is the dictionary in which we look up the meaning of words. When we look up the glory in Jesus we find — are we ever ready for this? — obscurity, rejection and humiliation, incomprehension and misapprehension, a sacrificial life and an obedient death: the bright presence of God backlighting what the world despises or ignores.

Just as the glory was evident in Jesus throughout his life for those who were watching the signs and discerning clues from his words, so also among contemporary followers of Jesus. Christians don't have to wait until we die to die. We don't have to wait until after our funerals to get in on the glory. As St. Teresa, one of our most irreverent and audacious saints, used to say, "The pay starts in this life."[34]

*   *   *

I have translated verse 14 of John's first chapter:

> The Word became flesh and blood
>> And moved into the neighborhood.
> We saw the glory with our own eyes,
>> The one-of-a-kind glory,
>> Like Father, like Son,
> Generous inside and out,
>> True from start to finish.

"Moved into the neighborhood" triggers another childhood memory from that year when I was ten years old. It was late August in the small Montana town in which I grew up. A moving truck rolled up our street and stopped at the house next door, a house that had been empty for several months. My friends and I were thoroughly bored, having exhausted the resources for play and entertainment through the vacation months. We had been waiting all summer for someone to move in, wondering who our new neighbors might be. And then everything changed with the arrival of the moving van at the unoccupied house next door. It was a North American Van Line vehicle, majestic in its red, white, and blue logo, a huge truck half a block long. It was the first time I had ever seen a moving van. It dominated the street, bringing with it an aura of expectancy, the promise of new life in the neighborhood.

In our town, if you moved from one house to another, you called up everyone you knew who had a pickup truck and asked them for help. On moving day there would be five or six pickups there to move you. I got in on most movings because my father's red, half-ton GMC truck was in much demand. Carrying out things from houses I had only seen from the outside, discovering the secrets of attics and basements, getting a look at the behind-the-scenes lives of people — all this was high adventure for me, and I relished every bit of it. I evaluated each family's life by its furniture and pictures, formed opinions based on the cleanliness or messiness of the closets, sifted through discarded junk for clues that revealed the way they lived. The pickups were always loaded high. In my memory now it seems that there was always a mattress on top with kitchen chairs roped to the sides, the load balanced precariously as we drove off in a caravan across town to the new house.

But this was a new experience: a moving van, holding more than eight or ten pickups could carry. Moving in our town was mostly a matter of rearrangement of residences of people we already knew or the arrival of relatives who for the most part were a variation on the same old thing. But this was promising. I and my two friends Freddy and Bob were there watching with anticipation to see how our lives were about to be changed. We were ready for change. With the late summer boredom of schoolchildren, we were ripe for excitement.

The new owners of the house didn't arrive for another two days so the only evidence we had for assessing these people was what we observed as the van was unloaded. Who were these people? What would they be like? We watched the movers unload the van, alert for evidence of how our lives would be changed. We were there all day, watching everything that came off that truck, making deductions and guesses about these people moving into our neighborhood.

Two bicycles came off early — that meant there were children in the family and we would have playmates. Then skis came off. We lived in ski country but none of us had ever skied; only rich kids did that — it was obvious that the neighborhood was being upgraded. Then a motorcycle. I had never been close to a motorcycle before — maybe we'd be taken for a ride. Every item that came off the van was a clue to what we might expect from our new neighbors. When an immense plate glass mirror appeared we knew these people were wealthy. All the furniture looked expensive. We had hit the jackpot. These people whom we didn't know, simply by moving into the neighborhood, were already transforming our lives. We would never be bored again. We would never be ordinary again.

Two days later our new neighbors arrived: Mr. and Mrs. Tipton with their teenage children Billy and Cynthia. Their expensive Chrysler sported New York license plates. That was the icing on the cake: we could feel the culture and celebrity of the fabled East rubbing off on us. Our neighborhood was suddenly better and more interesting and important. We couldn't wait for what was coming next.

St. John sets us up to engage in a similar process of observation — looking for signs, listening to what is said, and interpreting the signs and sayings — when he tells us that Jesus "dwelt among us," moved into the neighborhood. John enlists our curiosity and anticipation. We want to know what God is up to in his creation — we're all eyes, all ears.

But in that Montana summer, from the moment the Tiptons actually showed up things more or less fell apart. Billy and Cynthia hated being in our little town. They called it a bush town and called us hicks or little Montana hayseeds. We never got near the chrome-trimmed Harley Davidson, got nothing but sneers from the new kids on the block. To hear it from them, all they had done in their previous life was lie in the sun on Jones beach, go to Yankee baseball games, ride the carriages in Central Park, and stroll down Broadway spotting celebrities. Mr. Tipton never spoke to us. Self-important, he came and went with an immense black cigar in his mouth that you could smell from across the street. After a few days our mothers made plates of cookies and my two friends and I brought them to the door and knocked. Mrs. Tipton opened the door, took the cookies, thanked us unsmiling, and closed the door. We had hoped that we might get a look inside, might see how rich and important easterners lived. Among ourselves my friends and I took our revenge by speculating on which dog in the neighborhood Mr. Tipton had followed to pick up that thing he was so fond of chewing on. The event that had promised so much delivered nothing. Nothing but disappointment. We were shut out. As it turned out, we had misinterpreted every sign.

But in John's Gospel the people looking for clues, the signs and sayings that John brings to our attention as Jesus "moved into the neighborhood," found themselves in a new creation. At the end of the day, some at least of those who had watched and listened knew that not only the neighborhood but they themselves had changed forever: they had seen ("beheld") the glory.

*　　*　　*

We have observed the Genesis word, "in the beginning," that John used to open his Gospel-rewriting of the creation story. Another word near the end of the Gospel triggers a similar realization of correspondence between Genesis and John, inviting a continuing reflection on how personal and present the creation becomes to us as we follow Jesus. On the evening of his resurrection, Jesus appears to his disciples — his fearful disciples, huddled and cowering with all the life knocked out of them — and breathes on them, saying, "Receive the Holy Spirit" (John 20:22). The phrase "breathed on them" is the identical phrase (in Greek, *enephusēsen*) used in Genesis 2 when the Lord God breathed life into Adam, who at once became a "living soul." The Genesis "in the beginning" that opens John's Gospel is now complemented by the Genesis "breathed into his nostrils the breath of life" (Gen. 2:7) as Jesus breathes his life-creating Spirit into his disciples. The same Spirit that moved over the chaos and became articulate in the eight "God said . . ." commands that created the heavens and the earth, now moves in the disciples so that they can continue the creation work of the "firstborn of creation."

Is it not clear by now that John's Jesus story is a rewrite of the Genesis creation story with Jesus making himself personally at home in the same conditions of creation that we now inhabit? At home in time: unhurried and leisurely in the Genesis week, its seasons and days and years (Gen. 1:14) as these find focus in "that day" (John 14:20; 16:23), "my time" (John 7:6), "my hour" (John 2:4), "the hour" (John 4:21; 5:25, 28; 16:2 RSV; 16:25, 32; 17:1), "this hour" (John 12:27). And at home in place: the Genesis Garden of Eden with its trees and four rivers now extending to Cana and Bethany, Galilee and Jerusalem, Samaria and Bethzatha, Siloam and Golgotha, Capernaum and Kidron — places where Jesus walked, his feet on the ground, spoke names, touched men and women, ate and drank, went to trial, was killed and buried. Never, impatient with the limitations of time, did Jesus slip through some time-warp and bypass the waiting. Never, chafing under the limitations of place, did Jesus replace the local with some generalized and ethereal spiritual "presence." Anything and everything in creation was an occasion for the glory, the entire creation manifesting the bright presence of God, even in, *especially* in, the most unlikely times and places; the line between supernatural and natural constantly was blurred. Very God in the utterly ordinary — waterpots, mud, fragments of bread, basin and towel, the 153 fish — that we continue to handle and deal with wherever we live. And Very Man speaking simple words that give content to salvation — vine, door, shepherd, water, light — words that we continue to speak as we go about our daily work.

The two primary verbs that John uses to bring us into a willing and obedient participation in the creation, so that we are not mere spectators to it whether appreciative or disgruntled, are "believe" and "love." Both verbs involve us in a reality that is more and other than ourselves. No Gospel writer has used the two verbs to greater effect in getting us in on the work of Creator and creation.[35]

When we believe, we respond embracingly to what we cannot see, the things of heaven. Belief is worked out in a life of worship and prayer to God, Father, Son, and Holy Spirit.

When we love, we respond embracingly to what we can see and

touch and hear, the things of earth. Love is worked out in lives of intimacy and care among the people in our families and neighborhoods and workplaces.

John skillfully uses both verbs to cultivate responsiveness in us, via Jesus, to the entire range of creation work in which we are immersed simply by being born, but even more intensely by being born again.

Jesus is our access to creation as the time and place to believe. Jesus immerses us in everything material, from the water pots at the Cana wedding to Lazarus's stinking corpse at Bethany. Things, stuff, bodies are holy. As we think and act sacramentally we learn to believe. Jesus draws us into a pervasive awareness of Spirit, training us as "detectives of divinity"[36] to interpret the signs and understand the sayings as evidence of the unseen yet unmistakable presence of God. We learn to recognize the glory.

Jesus is our access to creation as the time and place to love: "For God so loved the world that he gave his only Son, that whoever believes in him should not perish but have eternal life" (John 3:16 RSV). Jesus is our access to creation as time and place to believe: "these are written that you may believe that Jesus is the Christ, the Son of God, and that believing you may have life in his name" (John 20:31 RSV). Believe and love — our ways into creation as participants.

Cultivating Fear-of-the-Lord in Creation: Sabbath and Wonder

The Christian community has never supposed that its work was done simply by attending to Genesis and John and affirming creation as it is revealed in these texts. The community *has* done this. We need to know the creation-reality in which we are placed. But we also have to cultivate a fear-of-the-Lord appropriate and adequate to this reality. We need to live in a way that is congruent with where we are.

Quoting Kierkegaard, Karl Barth warns against the blasphemy of glibly using what we know of God to support a life of so-called righteousness and piety tailored to our personal specifications, "without the trembling which is the first requirement of adoration."[37]

So, what do we do to cultivate this "trembling," this fear-of-the-Lord, this life of reverent responsiveness before a holy God, under the conditions of creation? How do we live so that the wonder and astonishment that so often comes to us unbidden and spontaneously isn't dissipated in trivial pursuits?

Albert Borgmann has given us the phrase "focal practice"[38] to guide us into an engagement with life — the way we "take up with the world" is his phrase — that doesn't reduce the complexities into something meager, that doesn't abstract them into something lifeless, that doesn't manipulate them into something self-serving. A focal practice enables us to stay personally engaged and socially responsible in a culture that is increasingly depersonalized and alarmingly fragmented. The focal practice that enables us to take up with creation is Sabbath-keeping. The early church put its stamp on the Mosaic commandment with "Keep the Lord's Day." The practice, as focal practices need to be, is clear, succinct, and unequivocal.

Sabbath

The mind that comes to rest is tended
In ways that it cannot intend:
Is borne, preserved, and comprehended
By what it cannot comprehend.

Your Sabbath, Lord, thus keeps us by
Your will, not ours. And it is fit
Our only choice should be to die
Into that rest, or out of it.

Wendell Berry[39]

The most striking thing about keeping the Sabbath is that it begins by not doing anything. The Hebrew word *shabbat,* which we take over into our language untranslated, simply means, "Quit . . . Stop . . . Take a break."

As such, it has no religious or spiritual content: Whatever you are doing, stop it. . . . Whatever you are saying, shut up. . . . Sit down and take a look around you. . . . Don't do anything. . . . Don't say anything. . . . Fold your hands. . . . Take a deep breath. Creation is so endlessly complex and so intricately interconnected that if we are not very careful and deeply reverent before what is clearly way beyond us, no matter how well-intentioned we are, we will probably interfere, usually in a damaging way, with what God has done and is doing. So begin by not doing anything: attend, adore.

But it soon appears that there is more to this than simply not-doing, not-talking. The word arrives on the page of Genesis in the context of creation, God making heaven and earth. When the work was complete God rested — stopped speaking, stopped making (Gen. 2:1-4). The seventh-day[40] not-doing, in other words, took place in the context of much-doing.

As it turned out in Israel's practice, Sabbath was never a day of mere not-doing — the context wouldn't permit it. Human not-doing became a day of God-honoring. God worked in creation, which means that all our work is done in the context of God-work. Sabbath is a deliberate act of interference, an interruption of our work each week, a decree of no-work so that we are able to notice, to attend, to listen, to assimilate this comprehensive and majestic work of God, to orient our work in the work of God.

In reading Genesis, many have noted how differently the seventh day is described in contrast to the first six days. In the narration of each of the first six days the first and last lines are identical and there are frequent repetitions of familiar words and phrases. Both of these features are abandoned in describing the seventh day. Here the day's number is repeated three times — seventh . . . seventh . . . seventh. This hasn't happened before.

It looks very much as if Genesis "points to the seventh day as the clue to the meaning of creation."[41] The evidence accumulates that if we are to live out the reality and meaning of creation we are going to be inextricably involved with Sabbath-keeping.

"Time," insisted Peter Forsyth, "is a sacrament of eternity."[42] Sabbath is a workshop for the practice of eternity. "The other life then is the other life now" is the way Forsyth put it.

The Commands

Our involvement in the creation is made explicit in the Sinai command to keep the Sabbath holy. The seventh day is the only Genesis day, that is, the only element of creation, to be picked up and used as material for a commandment in the Sinai revelation given to Moses (Exod. 20:8). The immediate and obvious meaning of this is that God's sabbatical rest is something in which humans may participate. If Genesis is a text for getting us in on and participating in God's creation work, Sabbath is our point of entry. The Jewish scholar Jon Levenson stresses this: "Genesis accentuates the possibility of human access [through Sabbath-keeping] to the inner rhythm of creation itself."[43]

The Sinai command to keep the Sabbath holy is the fourth in the listing of the ten°revealed to Moses. It is given in two forms, one in Exodus and the other in Deuteronomy. The commands are nearly identical in the two listings but the reasons supporting the commands differ. The reason given in Exodus is that this is what God did; God worked six days and quit working on the seventh (Exod. 20:8-11). The reason given in Deuteronomy is that when God's people were slaves in Egypt it was work, work, work — incessant, unrelieved work; they must never themselves perpetuate such oppression; they must quit work each seventh day so that their slaves and livestock and children will get a day off (Deut. 5:12-15). The Exodus reason supports a life of believing in God — Sabbath-keeping is a way to get in on what God does; the Deuteronomy reason supports a life of love — Sabbath-keeping is a way to love your neighbor, a simple act of justice.

The Exodus command to remember the Sabbath is backed up by the precedent of God, who rested on the seventh day. When we remember the Sabbath and rest on it we enter into and maintain the rhythm of creation. We keep time with God. Sabbath-keeping preserves and honors time as God's gift of holy rest: it erects a weekly bastion against the commodification of time, against reducing time to money, reducing time to what we can get out of it, against leaving no time for God or beauty or anything that cannot be used or purchased. It is a defense against the hurry that desecrates time.

The Deuteronomy command to observe the Sabbath is backed by a sense of social justice in the neighborhood. We remember the Sabbath and rest on it in order to enter into and maintain the freedom of creation, to experience and share God's deliverance and love for others. Sabbath-keeping preserves and honors time as God's gift of holy freedom: it erects a weekly bastion against the lethargic procrastination that breeds oppression, that lets injustice flourish because we are not attending in holy obedience and adoring love to the people and animals and things God has placed around us.

*   *   *

The prominence of the Sabbath command is conspicuously reaffirmed by Jesus. In the Judaism of Jesus' time, the Sabbath was being meticulously observed but it had been ripped out of its creation/salvation context and turned into a cruel instrument of oppression. There are five recorded occasions (four of them miraculous healings) when Jesus exposed Sabbath distortions and restored Sabbath as a gift for living in free obedience before and with God (Mark 2:23-28; 3:1-6; Luke 14:1-6; John 5:1-18; 9:1-41).

Worship

So how do we get these creation and Sabbath-keeping rhythms into our lives so that we can work congruently with God at work, live more or less in step with God and his creation? The obvious answer (at least judging by its popularity) might be to get a pair of binoculars and take up bird-watching, becoming familiar with the amazing and colorful ways of hawks and warblers; or to get a fly rod and learn to read the rivers, studying which insects are fancied by the fish and how to cast a line lightly and unobtrusively over waters that are home to rainbow trout; or to get a camera with a bag full of lenses and photograph wild flowers and humming-birds.

But the obvious answer in this case is not the right answer. We could do worse than watch curlews and angle for salmon and photograph wild orchids. But the way of Israel and Church is to embed Sabbath-keeping in weekly acts of worship in the company of the people of God. We keep Sabbath best when we enter a place of worship, gather with a congregation, and sing and pray and listen to God.

This is ancient wisdom and we disregard it at our peril. There is widespread evidence accumulated from many civilizations and through many millennia that connects world-making, that is, creation, with temple-building, which serves worship. Creation and the ordering of the world is over and over and over again associated with the building of a place of worship and the ordering of worship in it. The point of building a place of worship is to "realize and extend creation through human reenactment."[44] This is done not only by prayer and praise but by rehearsing and embracing the commandments and promises and blessings in order to put them into action in the creation that we live in. I like Garrison Keillor's comment: "Sunday feels odd without church in the morning. It's the time in the week when we take our bearings, and if we miss it, we're just following our noses."[45]

Creation rhythms get inside us through the act of worship in place and time. Worship is the primary means by which we immerse ourselves in the rhythms and stories of God's work, get a feel for proper work, creation work. When we go to work it must not be helter-skelter improvisation; it must be congruent with the *way* God works. And that begins with Sabbath-keeping: the resting, blessing, and hallowing without which the creation week is not complete. God's creation rhythms, brought to completion in the Sabbath rest commands, are reproduced in our lives through acts of worship in a structure and place and time that enable our participation. When we walk out of the place of worship we walk with fresh, recognizing eyes and a re-created, obedient heart into the world in which we are God's image participating in God's creation work. Everything we see, touch, feel, and taste carries within it the rhythms of "And God said . . . and it was so . . . and it was good. . . ." We become adept at discerning the Jesus-signs and picking up on the Jesus-words that reveal the presence and the glory. We are more deeply at home in the creation than ever.

*   *   *

The story that lays this out for us and makes the connection between creation and worship is in the book of Exodus. Here's the story:

Moses came down from Mount Sinai something over three thousand years ago with the stone tablets of God's commands in his arms and the word of God on his lips. He had just been instructed by God in how to train and lead the Hebrews into a life of mature, obedient, and holy freedom. But these people who had just been delivered from a world of oppressive slavery and were now free — saved and free — had generations of slave-identity bred into them. This was not going to be easy, and certainly not quick — no easier and certainly not any faster for them than it is for us.

After Moses at Mount Sinai delivered an overview of God's revealed commandments and instructions to the people (Exod. 20:1-24:11), he returned to the mountain for further briefing, which turned out to involve an elaborate set of instructions for worship (Exod. 24:12-31:18). Everything was laid out in detail: the structure for worship, the materials for worship, the sacrifices for worship, the leadership for worship. These instructions were presented in a Genesis-structured seven: seven addresses by God to Moses (25:1; 30:11; 30:17; 30:22; 30:34; 31:1; 31:12). The seventh and final address deals with the Sabbath.

But Moses was gone a long time, forty days and nights. Meanwhile, the people, impatient to get on with their new life of freedom, decided that they wanted to develop their own worship, worship that, in the phrase of our times, "we can get something out of." So they talked their associate pastor Aaron into providing them with worship that satisfied their desire for novelty and excitement, something that turned out to be pretty much a reflection of the gaudy Egyptian world in which they had so recently been oppressed but which they also, as oppressed people often do as excluded outsiders, had lusted after and envied.

And we know what happened (Exod. 32–33). Their golden calf worship, self-defined and self-serving — refusing to wait, contemptuous of rest, defiant of contemplation — nearly destroyed them. But Moses graciously interceded and started over. He again went up and then came down the mountain (Exod. 34). On his return this time, he put the people to work, preparing them for what was to become the central action of their lives, namely, worship (Exod. 35–40).

Moses makes it clear that the construction of this building is for worship, first and last. The first set of Sinai commands concluded with instructions on keeping Sabbath; this second set begins with the Sabbath instructions. Worship is the primary way in which the people of God stay in rhythm with their creation, find their place in creation, who they are and where they come from, internalizing the creation cadences of God who made heaven and earth, who said "Let there be light," who created male and female, who said "Be fruitful and multiply, and fill the earth and subdue it," who "saw everything that he had made, and behold, it was very good," who rested and sanctified the seventh day. Our text is unequivocal: Remember and observe this Sabbath day; take the Genesis week into your lives in this grand practice of contemplation; get creation into your nervous system; receive the great creation verbs into your souls; make friends with this world of sky and sea, fish and bird, cattle and plants, male and female.

Two verbal echoes of Genesis in the Exodus worship instructions tie creation and worship together even more tightly. The first regards Bezalel, the master builder in charge of preparing the place and materials for worship. Twice we are told that Bezalel is filled with the "Spirit of God," first as the plans for worship are proposed (Exod. 31:3 NKJV) and later after the golden calf disaster as the plans are executed (Exod. 35:31 NKJV). This is the identical phrase *(ruach elohim)* used when the creation of heavens and earth began: "the Spirit of God was moving over the face of the waters" (Gen.

114

1:2). Bezalel building the place of worship is in continuity with God creating heaven and earth.[46]

The other phrase from the Genesis creation story now echoed in the Exodus work of worship is "finished his work." The Genesis "God finished his work" (Gen. 2:2) is picked up at the end of Exodus, "So Moses finished the work" (Exod. 40:33). Again, creation and worship set in parallel.

There has been no end of imaginative proposals connecting the Genesis creation and the act of common worship, reaffirming and deepening the creation/worship continuities. Many of them are more fanciful than exegetical but at least they convey the sound intuition that our common citizenship on earth (the world of creation) and in heaven (the world of worship) requires thoughtful attention.[47]

Work

We cannot understand either the character or the significance of Sabbath apart from work and workplace. Work doesn't take us away from God; it continues the work of God through us. Sabbath and work are not in opposition; Sabbath and work are integrated parts of an organic whole. Either apart from the other is crippled.

The obvious way to comprehend this is to observe that God comes into view on the first page of our Scriptures as a worker. We see God in his workplace (and yes, our workplace) working. And throughout his so leisurely Gospel, John tells us over and over again, insistently (twenty-seven times!), that Jesus is working: "My Father is still working, and I also am working" (John 5:17). This is so important. Jesus embraces the creation as his workplace; he anticipates his crucifixion as the finishing touch to his work week — "[I have] accomplished the work which thou gavest me to do. . . . Father, glorify thou me in thy own presence" (John 17:4-5 RSV) — in parallel with the seventh Genesis day's "God finished the work which he had done . . ." (Gen. 2:2). God in Genesis and Jesus in John are not abstractions — "higher power" or "eternal love" or "pure being" — but named workers working in a workplace that all of us continue to work in. Creation is our workplace, providing the light we work by, the ground under our feet and the sky above us, the plants and trees that we grow, the rhythms of the year, fish and birds and animals in the food chain. As God works through the days of the week and detail after detail comes into being, a refrain develops: "God saw that it was good." Good . . . good . . . good.

Seven times across six days we hear it, "And God saw that it was good." The final statement, the seventh, is a superlative, "and indeed, it was very good" (Gen. 1:31). Good work. Good workplace.

And then Sabbath. But only then. We cannot rightly understand Sabbath apart from work nor rightly understand work apart from Sabbath. Wendell Berry makes workday and Sabbath rhythmic with one another in another of his Sabbath poems:

> ... workday
> And Sabbath live together in one place.
> Though mortal, incomplete, that harmony
> Is our one possibility of peace.[48]

Sabbath is the final day in a series of workdays, each of which are declared good by God. The work context in which Sabbath is set is emphasized by the three-time repetition of the phrase, "the work that he had done ... all the work that he had done ... all the work that he had done in creation." But the distinctive Sabbath character is conveyed by four verbs: God *finished* his work ... he *rested.* ... God *blessed* the seventh day ... and *hallowed* it (Gen. 2:2-3).

The four verbs take us beyond the workplace itself. There is more to work than work — there is God: God in completion, God in repose, God blessing, God making holy. Most of us spend most of our time in the workplace. But without Sabbath, in which God goes beyond the workplace (but not away from it), the workplace is soon emptied of any sense of the presence of God and the work becomes an end in itself. It is this "end in itself" that makes an un-sabbathed workplace a breeding ground for idols. We make idols in our workplaces when we reduce all relationships to functions that we can manage. We make idols in our workplaces when we reduce work to the dimensions of our egos and control.

There is considerable attention given in the business world these days to Sabbath-keeping. Sabbath-keeping has been discovered to yield benefits to the workplace in matters of health and relationships and productivity. This all may be true, but that is not why we keep Sabbath. We are not primarily interested in a longer life, or emotional maturity, or a better golf game, or higher productivity. We are interested in God and Christ being formed in us. We are interested in creation completed in resurrection.

Sabbath is not primarily about us or how it benefits us; it is about

God and how God forms us. It is not, in the first place, about what we do or don't do; it is about God completing and resting and blessing and sanctifying. These are all things that we don't know much about; they are beyond us but not beyond our recognition and participation. But it does mean stopping and being quiet long enough to see, open-eyed with wonder — resurrection wonder. As we stand or sit in surprised and open receptivity to what is beyond us, what we cannot control, we cultivate the fear-of-the-Lord. Our souls are formed by what we cannot work up or take charge of: We respond and enter into what the resurrection of Jesus continues to do on the foundations of creation, our work and workplace.

*　　*　　*

If there is no Sabbath — no regular and commanded not-working, not-talking — we soon become totally absorbed in what we are doing and saying, and God's work is either forgotten or marginalized. When we work we are most god-like, which means that it is in our work that it is easiest to develop god-pretensions. Un-sabbathed, our work becomes the entire context in which we define our lives. We lose God-consciousness, God-awareness, sightings of resurrection. We lose the capacity to sing "This is my Father's world" and end up chirping little self-centered ditties about what *we* are doing and feeling.

This is a most difficult command to keep, a most difficult practice to cultivate. It is one of the most abused and distorted practices of the Christian life. Many through the centuries have suffered much under oppressive Sabbath regimens. And more than a few of us have been among the oppressors. It is difficult to assemble a congregation of Christians today that does not number in its company both oppressed and oppressors. John gives us accounts of two of Jesus' Sabbath healings (chapters 5 and 9) that serve as serious warnings against glib or legalistic or oppressive Sabbath practices. Jesus spent a good deal of his time at odds with people who had wrong ideas about keeping Sabbath. (See also Mark 3:1-6; 3:23-30; Luke 14:1-6.) And one contributing cause of their wrong ideas was that they had severed the connection between Sabbath and work.

But I don't see any way out of it: if we are going to live appropriately in the creation we must keep the Sabbath. We must stop running around long enough to see what he has done and is doing. We must shut up long enough to hear what he has said and is saying. All our ancestors agree that without silence and stillness there is no spirituality, no God-attentive, God-responsive life.

*   *   *

Sabbath-instructed Christians can begin by reimagining, restructuring, and restoring the Lord's Day as a day that cultivates not-doing, not-saying — freeing the people around us to do nothing on the Lord's Day. Gathering for Sunday worship has a long and honorable tradition among us and provides the best way for most of us to listen to and adore the resurrection Jesus. But we need to keep it simple.

Pastors and congregational leaders commonly cram the Lord's Day with work: committees, meetings, projects, mission and social activities. Much doing and much talking displace Sabbath quietness and stillness. Typically, congregational leaders, knowing that they have these people all to themselves for a few hours on just one day a week, conspire to get them involved in anything and everything they think will be good for their souls and good for the church. Well-intentioned but dead wrong. All the leaders do is get them so busy for the Lord that they have no time for the Lord, pour in so much information about God that they never have a chance to listen to God.

If we are serious about living well in God's creation, we can start by clearing out the clutter of Sundays, and then engage in corporate ways to do nothing, to say nothing: "In returning and rest you shall be saved; in quietness and in trust shall be your strength" (Isa. 30:15). Cultivate solitude. Cultivate silence. There is nothing novel here; this counsel is at the center of the counsel of those who have led us into an obedient and faithful life of mission and prayer for twenty centuries now. I have nothing new to say on the subject; but I am convinced that it is critical to say it again, to say it urgently, to say it in Jesus' name backed by Moses' authority: keep Sabbath — attend to creation . . . adore the Creator.

If we are not to simply contribute a religious dimension to the disintegration of our world, join company with the mobs who are desecrating the creation with their hurry and hype in frenzy and noise, we must attend to what we have been given and the One who gives it to us. One large step in the renewal of the creation today, this field upon which the resurrection Christ plays with such exuberance, is to not take the next step: stand where we are, listen to our Lord: attend . . . adore.

Wonder

What has really happened during the last seven days and nights? Seven times we have been dissolved into darkness as we shall be dissolved into dust; our very selves, so far as we know, have been wiped out of the world of living things; and seven times we have been raised alive like Lazarus, and found all our limbs and senses unaltered, with the coming of the day.

G. K. Chesterton[49]

The attentiveness and adoration that Sabbath-keeping cultivates develops into a capacity for wonder under the conditions of creation that permeate the days of the week. The resurrection of Jesus is our showpiece narrative for seeing that process at work and getting in on the practice.

In John's rewriting of Genesis, the resurrection of Jesus completes the creation story. The week of the Genesis creation was complete as Jesus rested ("was buried") on the seventh day, the Sabbath. Then Jesus presented himself alive to his friends and followers early in the morning following the Sabbath. Over time they realized that they were now involved in a new creation week marked by this "eighth day" resurrection. Gradually, the traditions and commands associated with Sabbath were transferred to Sunday, referred to as "the first day" (Mark 16:2 and John 20:19) and "the Lord's Day" (Rev. 1:10).

Resurrection Wonder

Our four Gospel writers all complete their narrations of the Gospel of Jesus with a story or stories of Jesus' resurrection. They come at it from different directions and provide different details, but one element is common to them all: they all convey a sense of wonder, astonishment, surprise. Despite the several hints scattered through the Hebrew Scriptures, and Jesus' three explicit statements forecasting his resurrection, when it happened it turned out that no one expected resurrection — no one had any idea that there was to be a *new* creation. The first people involved in Jesus' resurrection were totally involved in dealing with death; now they had to do a complete about-face and deal with life. As they did it they were suffused with wonder.

*   *   *

As we meditate the four resurrection accounts, our sense of creation-wonder, now recast as resurrection-wonder, accumulates. The four stories are spare, compact, economically narrated. From this bedrock narrative austerity a few things emerge with clarity, things that are significant for us as we ponder our cultivation of the wonder that is inherent in living well in creation.

First, however many resurrection "hints followed by guesses"[50] there may have been in the centuries preceding this, when it happened it took those who were closest to the event and best prepared for it totally unawares. We are never in a position to know very much about the ways in which God's Spirit forms our lives under the conditions given in creation. Nothing here is quite analogous to the usual categories by which we understand ourselves — psychological development, for instance, or moral metaphysics. We inhabit a mystery. We must not pretend to know too much.

Second, it is obvious that no one involved in the resurrection appearances did anything to prepare for what actually happened. There was no "working up" a readiness for wonder. The two Jewish religious groups who at the time were working most diligently to prepare the messianic ground for something like this "new heavens and earth" inaugurated by Jesus, namely, the Pharisees and the Essenes, were looking the other way and missed it. Everyone is a beginner in this business. There are no experts. Given the care that we, in our way of going about things, take to prepare and plan and train for something that is big and important, that's more than a little disconcerting. Sabbath-wonder, creation-wonder, resurrection-wonder, is not something that we master. It is not something over which we have much, if any, control. Buddhists talk of cultivating the "beginner mind." Jesus said we can only enter the kingdom "as a little child" (Mark 10:15).

Third, in the resurrection stories, marginal people (in this case, women) play a prominent role in perception and response, although recognized leaders (Peter and John) aren't excluded. Mary Magdalene, perhaps the most marginal of any of the early followers of Jesus, is the chief resurrection witness and the only person to appear in all four accounts. The only fact we know about Mary Magdalene before she joined Jesus was that she had been possessed by and delivered from "seven devils." The "seven devils" could refer to an utterly dissolute moral life or to an extreme form of mental illness. Either or both of these pre-Jesus conditions coupled with being a woman in a patriarchal society puts her at the far edge of marginality.

Given the importance that we, in our society, give to celebrity endorsements, this means that we need to pay serious attention to other voices. The men and women who are going to be most valuable to us in cultivating fear-of-the-Lord wonder are most likely going to be people on the edge of respectability: the poor, minorities, the suffering and rejected, poets and children.

Fourth, the resurrection was a quiet business that took place in a quiet place without publicity or spectators. There was, of course, much energy and emotion (tears and running, astonishment and bewilderment and joy), but nothing to catch the attention of outsiders. (Matthew's earthquake is a partial exception to this, but the only people we're told were affected were the Roman guards who were knocked insensible by it.)

Given our accustomed ways of surrounding important events with attention-getting publicity and given the importance of this event to the gospel and everything connected with it, that's a big surprise. Bright lights and amplification are not accessories to the cultivation of wonder.

And fifth, and most important, is the fact that *fear* is the most frequently mentioned response to Jesus' resurrection. We're afraid when we're suddenly taken off guard and don't know what to do. We're afraid when our presuppositions and assumptions no longer account for what we are up against and we don't know what will happen to us. We're afraid when reality without warning is shown to be either more or other than we thought it was. Fear-of-the-Lord is fear with the scary element deleted. And so it is often accompanied by the reassuring "fear not." The "fear not" doesn't result in the absence of fear, but rather its transformation into "fear-of-the-Lord." But we still don't know what is going on. We still are not in control. We still are deep in mystery.

In the four resurrection stories there are six occurrences of various forms of the root word "fear" (*phobos*): twice as a word to express terror — the Roman guards before the dazzling angel at the empty tomb (Matt. 28:4) and the confounded disciples later running away from that same tomb (Mark 16:8); Luke tells of the women being frightened but immediately reassured in the presence of the angel at the tomb (Luke 24:5); in Matthew, the first angel and then Jesus say "Do not be afraid" in reassurance (28:5, 10); sandwiched between these reassurances the word conveys a sense of reverent joy (28:8). They are accompanied by several other wonder-evoking words: amazed (*exethambēthēsan, ekthambeisthe*; Mark 16:5, 6 RSV); trembling and astonishment (*tromos* and *ekstasis*; Mark 16:8 RSV); perplexed (*aporeisthai*; Luke 24:4); frightened (*emphobōn*; Luke 24:5 RSV); wondering (*thaumazōn*; Luke 24:12 RSV).

The ease with which the same root word (first as noun then as verb) can be used so differently but without confusion in the context is evident in the Matthew reference: "And *for fear of him* the guards trembled and became like dead men. But the angel said to the women, '*Do not be afraid* . . .'" (Matt. 28:4-5 RSV, italics added).

These six references to fear take place in a tradition of story-telling (the Hebrew culture and Scriptures) in which the word "fear" is frequently used in a way that means far more and other than simply being scared. But, and here's the thing, it *includes* all the emotions that accompany being scared — the disorientation, the not-knowing what is going to happen to me, the realization that there is far more here than I had any idea of. And that "more and other" is God. When that happens, we begin to get in on the fear-of-the-Lord.

Fear-of-the-Lord is the cultivated awareness of the "more and other" that the presence or revelation of God introduces into our lives: I am not the center of my existence; I am not the sum-total of what matters; I don't know what will happen next.

Fear-of-the-Lord keeps us on our toes in the play of creation, keeps our eyes open — something's going on here and I don't want to miss it. Fear-of-the-Lord prevents us from thinking we know it all and therefore from closing our minds or perceptions off from what is new. Fear-of-the-Lord prevents us from acting presumptuously and therefore destroying or violating some aspect of beauty or truth or goodness that we didn't recognize or didn't understand.

No matter how much we travel throughout the creation, no matter how many pictures we take of its flowers and mountains, no matter how much knowledge we acquire, if we fail to cultivate wonder we risk missing the very heart of what is going on.

*   *   *

Wonder cultivated in Sabbath-keeping permeates these resurrection stories. The five elements of surprise here — the unpreparedness, the uselessness of experts, the prominence of marginal companions, the quiet out-of-the-wayness, and the fear — give a rich texture to the wonder. Wonder doesn't travel along the lines of our expectations, especially expectations that we bring to something we consider important and life-changing. And if Jesus' resurrection is at the center of the Spirit's work of forming our lives, which I am convinced it is, then a sense of wonder is a big part of what goes on: surprise, puzzlement, astonishment — *God* at work. And right here — in Jesus, in you, in me!

Without wonder we approach life as a self-help project. We employ techniques; we analyze gifts and potentialities; we set goals and assess progress. Spiritual formation is reduced to cosmetics.

Without wonder the motivational energies for living well get dominated by anxiety and guilt. Anxiety and guilt restrict; they close us in on ourselves; they isolate us in feelings of inadequacy or unworthiness; they reduce us to ourselves at our worst. Instead of being formed by the Spirit that hovered over the waters and raised Jesus from the dead, we are malformed into lives of moral workaholism or pious athleticism.

The Deconstruction of Wonder

Unfortunately, we do not live in a world that promotes or encourages wonder.

Wonder is natural and spontaneous to us all. When we were children we were in a constant state of wonder — the world was new, tumbling in on us in profusion. We staggered through each day fondling, looking, tasting. Words were wondrous. Running was wondrous. Touch, taste, sound. We lived in a world of wonders. We became Christians and found to our delight that all this is confirmed in Genesis and John (and so many other places), and we realized that the wonder is deep and eternal, that we are part of a creation that is "very good."

But gradually a sense of wonder gets squeezed out of us. There are many reasons, but mostly the lessening of wonder takes place as we develop in competence and gain in mastery over ourselves and our environment.

The workplace is where this diminishing of wonder goes on most consistently and thoroughly. It's difficult to cultivate a sense of wonder in the workplace. Information and competence are key values here. We don't want any surprises. We don't want to waste time just staring at something, wondering what to make of it. We are trained and then paid to know what we are doing.

Some of us go to work that excites us; it demands our best and rewards us with recognition and satisfaction — we are doing something significant that makes a difference, makes the world better, makes people's lives better, makes us useful, makes money to take care of ourselves and our dependents. Work is a wonderful thing. We are involved, firsthand, in God's creation and among God's creatures. But after a few weeks or months, sometimes years, doing this work, the feelings and convictions and ideas that clustered around our becoming Christians become background to the center-stage drama of our work with its strenuous demands, energizing stimuli, and rich satisfactions.

Along the way the primacy of God and his work in our lives gives way ever so slightly to the primacy of *our* work in God's kingdom, and we begin thinking of ways that we can use God in what we are doing. The shift is barely perceptible, for we continue to use the vocabulary of our new identity; we continue to believe the identical truths; we continue to pursue good goals. It usually takes a long time for the significance of the shift to show up. But when it does it turns out that we have not so much been worshiping God as enlisting him as a trusted and valuable assistant.

On the job, we are dealing with what *we* know, and what we are good at, and what we know is our work. Why not ask God to help us in our work? He invited us to, didn't he, when he said, "Ask and you shall receive..."? Well, yes, he did. The problem is that, taken out of the context of creation/resurrection wonder, any prayer soon becomes an act of idolatry, reducing God to what I can use for my purposes, however noble and useful.

It rarely occurs to us to name such seemingly innocent and natural behavior as idolatry. We wouldn't think of placing a plastic St. Christopher on our Pontiac dashboard to prevent accidents, or installing a big-bellied Buddha in a shrine in our family room to put a brake on our helter-skelter running around pursuing illusions, or planting a Canaanite fertility Asherah grove in our backyards to promote bigger tomatoes in our gardens and more babies in our nurseries. But it is idolatry all the same — using God instead of worshiping God. Not full-grown idolatry at first, to be sure, but the germs of the kind of idolatry that thrives in the workplace.

For others of us, the work we go to every day is sheer drudgery, a boring, lackluster job through which we drag ourselves day after day, week after week. If and when we acquire a Christian identity, the new creation that we now have displaces the boredom of the workplace. Prayers murmur quietly like a mountain stream under the surface of our speech; songs of praise reverberate in our imaginations; we see everything and everyone with fresh eyes — we are new creatures set down in a world of wonders.

And then one day we realize that the "all things new" into which we have been introduced by Christ doesn't include our workplace. We're still in the same old dead-end job in which we've been stagnating for ten, twenty, thirty years. With our new energy and the sense of unique identity and purpose sparked by our conversion, we look around for a way out; we fantasize about jobs in which we can wholeheartedly work, in the wonderful phrase, "to the glory of God." A few people risk everything and break out. But most of us do not: We have a mortgage to pay, children to put through college; we don't have the training or schooling necessary; our spouse is content just as things are and doesn't want to jeopardize the security of familiarity. And so we accept the fact that we're stuck and return to slogging through the daily mud and boredom of our routines.

But what we also do is look around for ways to affirm and cultivate our new life in Christ outside our workplace. And we soon find, quite to our delight, that there is a lot to choose from. A huge religious marketplace has been set up in North America to meet the needs and fantasies of people just like us. There are conferences and gatherings custom-designed to give us the lift we need. Books and videos and seminars promise to let us in on the Christian "secret" of whatever we feel is lacking in our life: financial security, well-behaved children, weight-loss, exotic sex, travel to holy sites, exciting worship, celebrity teachers. The people who promote these goods and services all smile a lot and are good-looking. *They* are obviously not bored.

It isn't long before we are standing in line to buy whatever is being offered. And because none of the purchases does what we had hoped for, or at least not for long, we are soon back to buy another, and then another. The process is addictive. We have become consumers of packaged spiritualities.

This also is idolatry. We never think of using this term for it since everything we are buying or paying for is defined by the adjective "Christian." But idolatry it is nevertheless: God packaged as a product; God depersonalized and made available as a technique or program. The Christian market in idols has never been more brisk or lucrative.

*   *   *

Every Christian man or woman who gets out of bed and goes to work walks into a world in which idolatry is the major temptation for seducing him or her away from the new life of being formed by resurrection into the likeness of Christ.

There are endless variations and combinations of the "good" and "bad" workplaces I have sketched, but possibilities — in fact, probabilities — of idolatry are ever present. If we work, and most of us do (the obvious exceptions are children, the elderly, the disabled, and the unemployed), we live most days and most of the hours of those days in a world permeated with the making and purchasing of idols.

Most of us spend a lot of time at work. This means that our Christian identity is being formed much of the time under uncongenial if not downright hostile conditions — that is, conditions marked by the intolerance of mystery (information and know-how are required in the workplace), conditions in which a premium is put on our competence and being in control (incompetence and out-of-control behavior will get us dismissed in short order), and conditions in which personal relationships are subordinated and conformed to the nature of the work to be done.

Technology is one of the primary promoters of idolatry today. Ironic, isn't it? Idolatry, which is associated, at least in the popular imagination, with superstition — the unenlightened, uneducated, primitive child-mind with its myths and mumbo-jumbo — now finds itself with a new lease on life with the help of technology, which is associated with no-nonsense scientific research, with using the pure language of mathematics to create a world of computers that dominate the workplace. Before technology, before computers, virtually everybody is bowing down in respectful reverence — to impersonal *things* that dominate our time and imagination, offer extravagant promises of control and knowledge, and squeeze all sense of mystery and wonder and reverence out of our lives.

The workplace has always been a threat to the Sabbath-mind because it is the place where we don't wonder very much; wonder is pretty much banished on principle. In the workplace we know, we are competent; or we are bored and inattentive. But in today's culture, the threat posed by life diminished in wonder has accelerated many times over.

That is why Christian formation demands endless vigilance. The workplace is the arena in which idolatry is constantly being reconfigured by putting us in the position of control and giving us things and systems that enable us to exercise our skills and carry out our strategies in the world.

Wonder, that astonished willingness to stop what we are doing, to stand still, open-eyed and open-handed, ready to take in what is "more and other," is not encouraged in the workplace.

Wonder in the Workplace

Does that mean that we put spiritual formation "on hold" during working hours and pick it up again after hours and on weekends?

I don't think so.

For here is the striking thing: The opening scene in the resurrection of Jesus occurs in the workplace. Mary Magdalene and the other women were on their way to work when they encountered and embraced the resurrection of Jesus. I'm prepared to contend that the primary location for spiritual formation is the workplace.

So how do we who work for a living and so spend a huge hunk of our time each week in a workplace that is unfriendly to wonder, cultivate wonder, the resurrection-wonder in which spiritual formation thrives?

*　　*　　*

The first participants on the day of resurrection — Mary Magdalene and the other Mary, Joanna, Peter, John, and Cleopas along with the other unnamed followers of Jesus (Luke 24:10, 18; John 20:1-10) — had presumably spent the previous day keeping the Sabbath. They were devout Jews, after all, and it is unlikely that the habits of a lifetime would be discarded. On the previous Friday evening, shortly after Jesus had been taken from the cross and placed in Joseph's tomb, devout Jews in Jerusalem and Nazareth, Bethlehem and Capernaum, Alexandria and Babylon, Athens and Rome lit two candles and welcomed the Sabbath: "Blessed art Thou, O God, King of the Universe, who hast sanctified us by Thy commandments and commanded us to kindle the Sabbath lights."

One candle was lit for the Exodus command: "Remember the Sabbath day, and keep it holy . . . you shall not do any work. . . . For in six days the LORD made heaven and earth, the sea and all that is in them, but rested the seventh day . . ." (Exod. 20:8-11).

The second candle was lit for the Deuteronomy command: "Observe the Sabbath day, to keep it holy . . . you shall not do any work . . remember that you were slaves in Egypt . . ." (Deut. 5:12, 14-15).

On Saturday at sundown the prayer was repeated, the candles again lit, and the final prayer, the Havdilah, was said, closing the holy day of rest.

It is not far-fetched to imagine Jesus' friends and followers spending the twenty-four hours of Jesus' Sabbath rest in the tomb, also resting — remembering and observing. The entire city was keeping Sabbath; they would also be keeping it. It is unlikely, I think, that they would have gone to synagogue or temple; worshiping with the leaders who had conspired in the crucifixion of Jesus would have put their own lives at risk. The one thing we know that they did not do on that Sabbath day was embalm Jesus' body, which was what they, at least the women among them, most wanted to do, what they were most motivated to do. They didn't do it because they were keeping Sabbath, remembering and observing God's work of creation and their deliverance from slavery. I'm not supposing that they talked or prayed about these things formally by having a Bible study, say, but I am imagining that a lifelong habit of Sabbath-keeping was working subconsciously in them, providing an underlying awareness of the immensity of God at work in the world and the personal immediacy of God at work for and in them. I am thinking that their Sabbath observance set them in a far larger context than was reported to them by the crucifixion events of Friday or their own feelings of devastation. The huge catastrophe and horror and disappointment of crucifixion was settling into a larger context of God's world-making work and soul-making salvation. Nothing that they could do or wanted to do was important enough to take precedence over what God had done and was doing in creation as it came into focus in the Exodus and Deuteronomy commands and was internalized in a lifetime of Sabbath-keeping.

I'm imagining what effect a lifetime of keeping Sabbath had on those women as they returned to their homes at the close of Sabbath, and rose the next morning, the first day of the week, and set out for work to embalm Jesus' body. Is it beyond belief that in the throes of their devastation, there would also be a deeply developed instinct for God in them, a capacity to respond in wonder to mysteries that were beyond them, a readiness to be surprised by what they did not understand and could not anticipate? Their Sabbath-keeping was weekly housecleaning. The day after keeping Sabbath they entered the work week uncluttered with idols — all those subtle but obsessive attempts that daily get tracked into kitchens from off the street to serve as a god or a routine or a program that can be handled and used. Sabbath-keeping provided a detachment from the world's way of doing things and from their own compulsions to take things into their own hands. Keeping Sabbath, a day of studied and vowed resistance to doing any work so they could be free to see and respond to who God is and what he is doing, was basic in the lives of the women and men who found Jesus alive on the first day of the new creation week.

The capacity to see God working in our place in creation (our workplace) and to respond in resurrection wonder requires detachment from the workplace. How do we cultivate such detachment? Here it is again: Keep Sabbath.

William Willimon puts it well: "Sabbath keeping is a publicly enacted sign of our trust that God keeps the world, therefore we do not have to. God welcomes our labors, but our contributions to the world have their limits. If even God trusted creation enough to be confident that the world would continue while God rested, so should we."[51]

II

Christ Plays in History

"This child is destined for the falling and the rising of many in Israel, and to be a sign that will be opposed . . . and a sword will pierce your own soul. . . ."

LUKE 2:34-35

[T]he world which surrounds us is temporary and its laws were negated by the Son of God's act of submission to them. The Prince of this World triumphed, and as a result he lost.

CZESLAW MILOSZ[1]

Exploring the Neighborhood of History

When we first look around the neighborhood we are struck by the sheer profusion of life — a rose in blossom, a red-tailed hawk in flight, a cat on the prowl. White oak and blue whale, amoeba and giraffe give fresh and eloquent witness to a mystery that ever eludes us but never, if we take the time for it, fails to put us on our knees in adoration. This is especially the case with human life. Every time a baby is born the gospel is preached. The virgin birth of Jesus provides the kerygmatic center to all this world of experience in which we receive the revelation of God as Christ plays in creation.

But we are not on our knees in adoration for very long, taking in the wonder of creation, before we find that everything is not so wonderful. Mosquitoes invade our picnic, a patch of black ice sends our car careening off a winter wonderland road into a ditch, our carefully tended garden is trashed by the neighbor's playful Dalmatian. And we are not up on our feet very long, alive with an awareness of our participation in the creation, resurrection-eager and ready to love, before we find that not everybody thinks that human life is so wonderful. The lovely baby cries, gets sick, interrupts our sleep, invades our comfortable routines — and then begins to grow and turns into a disobedient, defiant brat: he refuses to eat what we prepared for supper; she leaves her room a mess. It's not long before we are having headaches and sleepless nights over this child that not long ago we were cuddling in our arms.

If the world is so wonderful, if life is so amazing, why all this trouble, this mess? We pick up this lovely apple and bite into it, and find that there is a worm in the apple. This is the world of experience in which we receive the revelation of God as Christ plays in history. We have a glorious beginning. But things took a bad turn long before we entered the scene, and it isn't long before we find that we are living with the consequences of catastrophe. Much of life, much of *our* lives, consists in picking up the pieces of history, cleaning up the mess.

Popular forms of spirituality tend to avoid history, at least in its messier aspects, as subject matter and context for nurturing the soul. The sensory-rich outside world of mountains and seashores and the inner world of thoughts and emotions enhanced by poetry, song, and meditation are more congenial.

History is bounded by birth and new birth, by the virgin birth of Jesus and the resurrection of Jesus — life, life, and more life. But between those two life-giving moments there is also death, death, and more death. When we are born we find ourselves in a world in which death and dying are major preoccupations; when we are born again it is still the same world. History consists of what happens in this world. History is the accounting we make of the human endeavor. More often than not it is an accounting of the mess we make of things: brutality, war, famine, hate, quarrelling, exploitation. History deals with what happens, what has happened, what is happening and what will happen. It means dealing with a world where things rarely turn out the way we think they should. It means dealing with corrupt politicians, birth defects, floods and volcanoes, divorce and death, starvation and famine, the arrogance of the rich and the destitution of the poor. Something is wrong here, dreadfully wrong. We feel it in our bones. The most conspicuous event in history that arouses within us this spontaneous sense of violation, of outrageous sacrilege, is the suffering and death of Jesus, a suffering and death in which eventually we will all find ourselves involved whether we like it or not. History.

*   *   *

I had a delayed but abrupt introduction into the mess of history. I grew up in a Christian home with good parents. I was told the story of Jesus and instructed in the right way to live. I was loved and treated well. In my memory it was a fair approximation of the Garden of Eden — a good and wonderful creation. Life. Our modest house was on a gravel road on the edge of a small Montana town, three or four blocks beyond where the sidewalks ended. It was a neighborhood with plenty of playmates, none of whom went to church, but their unbaptized state never seemed to make any difference in that pre-school life of games (kick-the-can, hide-and-seek, softball) and imagination (pretending to be explorers like Lewis and Clark and Indians like Chief Joseph and Sacajawea). There were trees to climb and a creek to swim in. There was a meadow bordering our backyard in which cows grazed. We used the dried cowflop for bases in our ball games.

And then I went off to school and discovered what St. John named "the world" — the society that does not regard God with either reverence or obedience. This knowledge came into my life in the person of Garrison Johns. Garrison was a year older than me and the school bully. He lived in a log house a couple of hundred yards beyond where I lived, the yard littered with rusted-out trucks and cars. I had been in that house only once; it was a cold winter day and his mother, a beautiful willowy woman as I remember her, invited me and the Mitchell twins in to warm us up with a bowl of moose meat chili that was simmering on the back of the wood stove. Struggling through deep snow, we were taking a shortcut home through her backyard; we must have looked half frozen — we *were* half frozen — and she had compassion on us. But Garrison wasn't there. I had never seen him close up, only at a distance — he wore a red flannel shirt, summer and winter, and walked with something of a swagger that I admired and tried to imitate. Being a year older than me and living just far enough away, he was beyond the orbit of my neighborhood games and friendships. I knew of his reputation for meanness, but the memory of his mother's kindness tempered my apprehension. I wasn't prepared for what was to come.

About the third day in school, Garrison discovered me, took me on as his project for the year, and gave me a working knowledge of what twenty-five-years later Richard Niebuhr would give me a more sophisticated understanding of in *Christ and Culture*. I had been taught in Sunday School not to fight and so had never learned to use my fists. I had been prepared for the wider world of neighborhood and school by memorizing "Bless those who persecute you" and "Turn the other cheek." I don't know how Garrison Johns knew that about me — some sixth sense that bullies have, I suppose — but he picked me for his sport. Most afternoons after school he would catch me and beat me up. He also found out that I was a Christian and taunted me with "Jesus-sissy." I tried finding alternate ways home by making detours through alleys, but he stalked me and always found me out. I arrived home every afternoon, bruised and humiliated. My mother told me that this had always been the way of Christians in the world and that I had better get used to it. I was also supposed to pray for him. The Bible verses that I had memorized ("Bless ..." and "Turn ...") began to get tiresome.

I loved going to school, learning so much, finding new friends, adoring my teacher. The classroom was a wonderful place. But soon after the dismissal bell each day I had to face Garrison Johns and get the daily beating that I was trying my best to assimilate as my "blessing."

March came. I remember that it was March by the weather. The winter snow was melting but there were still patches of it here and there. The days were getting longer — I was no longer walking home in the late afternoon dark. And then one day something unexpected happened. I was with my neighborhood friends on this day, seven or eight of them, when Garrison caught up with us and started in on me, jabbing and taunting, working himself up to the main event. He had an audience and that provided extra incentive; he always did better with an audience.

That's when it happened. Something snapped within me. Totally uncalculated. Totally out of character. For just a moment the Bible verses disappeared from my consciousness and I grabbed Garrison. To my surprise, and his, I realized that I was stronger than he. I wrestled him to the ground, sat on his chest and pinned his arms to the ground with my knees. I couldn't believe it — he was helpless under me. At my mercy. It was too good to be true. I hit him in the face with my fists. It felt good and I hit him again — blood spurted from his nose, a lovely crimson on the snow. By this time all the other children were cheering, egging me on. "Black his eyes! Bust his teeth!" A torrent of vengeful invective poured from them, although nothing compared with what I would, later in my life, read in the Psalms. I said to Garrison, "Say 'Uncle.'" He wouldn't say it. I hit him again. More blood. More cheering. Now the audience was bringing the best out of *me*. And then my Christian training reasserted itself. I said, "Say, 'I believe in Jesus Christ as my Lord and Savior.'"

And he said it. Garrison Johns was my first Christian convert.

Garrison Johns was my introduction into the world, the "world" that "is not my home." Creation is wonderful, but history is a mess. He was also my introduction to how effortlessly that same "world" could get into me, making itself at home under cover of my Christian language and "righteous" emotions.

That happened sixty-five years ago. I have recently moved back and taken up residence once more in this Montana valley in which I grew up, was beaten up by Garrison Johns almost daily for seven months, and on that March afternoon in 1938 bloodied his nose and obtained his Christian confession. The other day I drove down the street where the evangelistic event took place and pointed out the spot to my wife. When I got home, I thought, "I wonder what has become of Garrison Johns?" I opened the telephone book and sure enough his name is listed with an address that locates him about ten miles from my present home. Should I call him up? Would he remember? Is he still a bully? Did the ill-gotten Christian confession "take"? Would a meeting result in a personal preview of Armageddon in which I would end up on the losing side? I haven't called him yet. I am putting off the judgment.

Meanwhile I continue to reflect on what it means to be plunged into history. God made everything good. But in that good creation, soon or late each of us, one after another, gets discovered by Garrison Johns and finds that not everyone thinks that our place in this creation life is so wonderful. We are plunged into pain and disappointment and suffering. Sometimes it recedes for a while; other times it threatens to overwhelm us.

The final verdict on all of this is death. We die. Strangely, virtually every death, even of the very old, feels like an intrusion and more or less surprises us. Tears and lament give witness to our basic sense that this is *wrong* and that we don't like it one bit. Death provides the fundamental datum that something isn't working the way it was intended, accompanied by the feeling that we have every right to expect something other and better.

Kerygma: Jesus' Death

The birth of Jesus provides our entrance into the reality and meaning of creation: this is the world of the Father revealed by Jesus. Jesus shows us that the creation is something to be lived, not just looked at, and the way he did it becomes the way we do it.

In a parallel way, the death of Jesus provides our entrance into the reality and responsibilities of history: mostly, but not always, it is a mess: the daily round of failed plans, disappointed relations, political despair, accidents and sickness and neighborhood bullies. In this same mess of history in which we find ourselves, Jesus found himself. The remarkable thing is that he embraced it. This embrace involved him in enormous suffering and an excruciating death. The life of Jesus is not a happy story, not a success story. What it is (and we are coming to this) is a salvation story. His birth precipitated a bloody massacre of babies (Matt. 1–2); his entrance into public ministry plunged him into a forty-day wilderness ordeal in which he went to the mat with evil, tested to the limit of body and soul (Matt. 3–4). At the moment of what seemed to be a breakthrough understanding of his messianic identity among the disciples at Caesarea Philippi, Jesus' lead disciple, Peter, turned out to have more affinity for Satan than for his Master (Matt. 16:15-23). And when Jesus was surrounded with the acclaim of Hosannas in that great Passover parade into Jerusalem, certainly a moment of festive celebration if there ever was one, Jesus wept (Luke 19:28-44; Matt. 23:37-39), wept for the suffering of body and the pain of soul in store for these men and women and children who were having such an innocently good time.

History is lubricated by tears. Prayer, maybe most prayer (two thirds of the psalms are laments), is accompanied by tears. All these tears are gathered up and absorbed in the tears of Jesus.

*   *   *

The death of Jesus outside Jerusalem "under Pontius Pilate" — the date according to our calendars is AD 30 — placed in the larger context of his birth, resurrection, and ascension is essential to the gospel kerygma. Jesus' death becomes the proclamation that our salvation is accomplished. This death is not out of the blue; it is the final entry in a long history of suffering and death embraced and prayed in our Scriptures.

Jesus was born into a people of God that had a long and still-living tradition of taking history seriously as the arena in which God carries out his work of salvation. A deeply pervasive sense of history — the dignity of their place in history, the presence of God in history — accounts in large part for the way in which the Hebrew people talked and wrote. They did not, as was the fashion in the ancient world, make up and embellish fanciful stories. Their writings did not entertain or explain; they revealed the ways of God with men and women and the world. They gave narrative shape to actual people and circumstances in their dealings with God, and in God's dealings with them.

For the prophets and priests and writers who preceded Jesus and in whose footsteps Jesus continued, there was no secular history. None. Everything that happened, happened in a world penetrated by God. The Hebrew people were intent on observing and participating in what happened in and around them because they believed that God was personally alive and active in the world, in their community, and in them. Life could not be accounted for by something less than the life of God, no matter how impressive and mysterious their experience was, whether an eclipse of the sun, spots on the liver of a goat, or the hiss of steam from a fissure in the earth. God could not be reduced to astronomical, physiological, geological, or psychological phenomena. God was alive, always and everywhere working his will, challenging people with his call, evoking faith and obedience, calling them into a worshiping community, showing his love and compassion, and working out judgments on sin. And none of this "in general" or "at large," but at particular times, in specific places, with named persons: history.

For biblical people, God is not an idea for philosophers to discuss or a force for priests to manipulate. God is not a part of creation that can be studied and observed and managed. God is person — a person to be worshiped or defied, believed or rejected, loved or hated, in time and place. That is why the biblical revelation is so profuse with names and dates, places and events. God meets us in the ordinary and extraordinary occurrences that make up the stuff of our daily lives. It never seemed to have occurred to our biblical ancestors that they could deal better with God by escaping from history, "getting away from it all" as we say. History is the medium in which God works salvation, just as paint and canvas is the medium in which Rembrandt made works of art. We cannot get closer to God by distancing ourselves from the mess of history.

But most of us have a difficult time understanding history with God as the major and definitive presence. We have grown up getting our sense of history from so-called historians, scholars, and journalists for whom God is not germane or present in what they study and write. We are thoroughly trained by our schools, daily newspapers, and telecasts to read history solely in terms of politics and economics, human interest and environmental conditions, military operations and diplomatic intrigue. If we have a mind for it, we can go ahead and fit God in somewhere or other. But the biblical writers do it the other way around; they fit us into the history in which God is the primary reality.

This is a difficult mindset for us to acquire, but if we are to understand ourselves truly and live appropriately in the history in which we find ourselves, we must acquire it. Otherwise we will fall prey to dodges and denials that incapacitate us for actively participating in the actual world in which God is present and at work.

Reading and praying our way through these history-saturated pages of Scripture, we gradually get it: This is what it means to be a woman, a man — mostly it means dealing with God, God using the authenticating reality of our daily experience as the stuff for working out his purposes of salvation in us and in the world. We immerse ourselves in the Scripture narratives and realize that God is the commanding and accompanying presence that provides both plot and texture to every sentence. The interlocking stories and prayers, reflections and guidance, sermons and decrees, train us in perceptions of ourselves, our sheer and irreducible humanity, that cannot be reduced to personal feelings or ideas or circumstances. If we want a life other than mere biology, we must deal with God, and God on his own historical turf. If we want anything to do with God as biblically revealed there is no escaping history.

The biblical way is not to present us with a moral code and tell us "Live up to this," nor is it to set out a system of doctrine and say, "Think like this and you will live well." The biblical way is to tell a story that takes place on solid ground, is peopled with men and women that we recognize as being much like us, and then to invite us, "Live into this. This is what it looks like to be human. This is what is involved in entering and maturing as human beings." We do violence to the biblical revelation when we "use" it for what we can get out of it or what we think will provide color and spice to our otherwise bland lives. That results in a kind of "boutique spirituality" — God as decoration, God as enhancement.

One of the remarkable characteristics of the biblical way of training us to understand history and our place in it is the absolute refusal to whitewash a single detail. God is equally present and active in the history recorded in the Scriptures and the history recorded in our contemporary textbooks. Biblical history deals with the same historical materials as European, African, Asian, and American history. When the name of God is left out of the history of, say, the Exploration of the Amazon, God is not left out; he is still as present and involved as in the history of the Crossing of the Jordan. History is history, biblical history and modern history alike. The history in which our Scriptures show that God is involved is every bit as messy as the history reported by our mass media in which God is rarely mentioned apart from blasphemies. Sex and violence, rape and massacre, brutality and deceit do not seem to be congenial materials for use in developing a story of salvation, but there they are, spread out on the pages of our Scriptures. It might not offend some of us so much if these flawed and reprobate people were held up as negative examples with lurid, hellfire descriptions of the punishing consequences of living such bad lives. But the story is not told quite that way. There are punishing consequences, of course, but the fact is that all these people, good and bad, faithful and flawed, are worked into the plot of salvation. God, it turns out, does not require good people in order to do good work. As one medieval saying has it, "God draws straight lines with a crooked stick." He can and does work with us, whatever the moral and spiritual condition in which he finds us. God, we realize, does some of his best work using the most unlikely people.

*   *   *

This is the history that we learn to enter and embrace as God works his salvation on earth. Once we realize this — and it is unavoidable if we let these Scriptures shape our imaginations — we will not be seduced into the usual detours that evade the biblical way: intimidation by history and exploitation of history.

Intimidation. It always appears that history is dominated by powerful forces that totally overshadow people of faith in God: powerful politicians, powerful armies, powerful financiers, powerful institutions. What good are prayer and worship compared to these "principalities and powers"? The temptation, then, is to live small, settle for domestic coziness, retreat to the sidelines, create a ghetto in which we can carry out our life of faith in God with as little interference as possible from "the world."

Timid people (intimidated people) often secretly admire those whom they fear. They constantly compare themselves unfavorably with them, but would very much like to be one of them. As a consequence their imaginations are shaped by a history that exhibits the power of the human and has no sense of God's presence and action in it. They are left with a feeling that God is involved only in the privacies and domesticities of their inner lives — what they think of as their souls.

Exploitation. Others observe that the movers and shakers of history get their way by using power and violence, position and status, money and influence and conclude that the only way to be relevant to the reality of history is to join history on its own terms. "On its own terms," of course, means without God, without prayer and worship, without forgiveness and love, without justice and grace. Christians have a long and sorry record of employing this strategy. The Holy Roman Empire, the Crusades, and Cromwell are textbook citations, but there is hardly a congregation or mission movement or school that has not been touched by it — doing God's work in the world's way.

There is another option: we can enter and embrace history on Je-

sus' terms, on gospel terms, on the terms that we are prepared to understand and accept by our centuries-long Scripture training in reading history as the arena in which God works out our salvation on his terms. We
are now freed from retreating from history, intimidated by its bluster
and swagger. We are now protected from exploiting history, supposing
that we can compete with it on its terms and using God as our trump
card.

*   *   *

The death of Jesus is the centerpiece for learning how to deal with the fundamental violation of life, this sacrilege visited on creation that makes up
so much of what happens in and around us — history. We begin to deal
with the "what's wrong with the world" at the place where the gospel deals
with it: Jesus dead and buried.

The death of Jesus confirms and validates our experience that there
is, in fact, something terribly wrong and that this wrong is not simply a
logical working out of cause-effect, of the way things are. Jesus, born of a
virgin, dies on a cross — there is no logic, physical or spiritual, between
those two clauses.

Jesus' suffering, recorded in his laments, tears, and death, provides
the authoritative Gospel text for finding our place in history — this history that seems to be so much at variance with what is given and promised
in the creation itself, in the life abundant all around us.

Jesus suffered and died. This is the plot that provides the structure of
the gospel story. Our four Gospel writers, each in his own way, tell the
story of Jesus' passion — his suffering and death — and then write out an
extended introduction. The passion story takes place in one week, but it is
given space far out of proportion to its chronology. Matthew gives a quarter of his pages to the passion; Mark a third; Luke a fifth; and John almost
one half. It was to tell this story, Jesus' suffering and death, that each evangelist wrote his Gospel. Each Gospel writer does the extended introduction in his own way, but when it comes to this core material, they all write
it pretty much the same way. This, this suffering and death, is important,
repeated four times. We need to know that this happened and how and
why it happened. The Gospel writers are determined to get us in on this,
and not just in general; we need to know exactly, detail by detail, what it is
we are getting in on.

142

*　　*　　*

If "life" is the thematic word woven into creation, "death" is the equivalent theme word for history. Suffering and death are huge megaphonic voices, human voices backed up by the whole creation groaning in travail (Rom. 8:22), throughout history calling attention to the *need* for salvation; Jesus' suffering and death is the definitive historical proclamation of the *means* for this salvation.

Our Scriptures are full of this suffering and death language: the Gospel passion stories spill over into the Epistles and the apocalypse — our sufferings continuously set in the context of Christ's sufferings; Christ's sufferings placed insistently alongside ours.

"Christ also suffered for you, leaving you an example, so that you should follow in his steps" (1 Pet. 2:21).

"I want to know Christ and . . . [share] his sufferings by becoming like him in his death" (Phil. 3:10).

"I saw under the altar the souls of those who had been slaughtered for the word of God" (Rev. 6:9).

Jesus died. There is no avoiding this. This is fundamental. And I am somehow or other going to die. There is no avoiding this: this also is fundamental. This conjunction of deaths, Jesus' and mine, is where I begin to understand and receive salvation.

Paul distills the entire scheme of God's working in our lives to this and only this: "Jesus Christ, and him crucified" (1 Cor. 2:2), a crucifixion death in which he finds himself a willing participant (Gal. 2:20).

Nothing in the story of Jesus could be clearer or more plainly presented than this: that Jesus chose the way of suffering and death, that he did this in continuity with the entire history of the people of God before him, and that this suffering and death was kerygmatic. Suffering and death, the worst that life can hand us, is the very stuff out of which salvation is fashioned.

And that means that if we want to live as followers of Jesus, live the way Jesus wants us to live, receive Jesus' life as our life, our restored identity in the image of God, then we also follow him into this so-called mess of history. History is not what we keep at arm's length in impersonal study and analysis. It must not be avoided or denied by withdrawal. It has to be embraced. The way Jesus did it becomes the way we do it.

The intricate and elegantly written early church sermon named the

Letter to the Hebrews is our most detailed and vivid working out of the kerygmatic impact of Jesus' suffering and death. In the letter, all Christ's suffering and death is distilled into salvation prayer for all who suffer and die, which is to say, for all of us: "In the days of his flesh, Jesus offered up prayers and supplications, with loud cries and tears, to the one who was able to save him from death, and he was heard because of his reverent submission. Although he was a Son, he learned obedience through what he suffered; and having been made perfect, he became the source of eternal salvation for all who obey him, having been designated by God a high priest according to the order of Melchizedek" (Heb. 5:7-10).

"Prayers and supplications, with loud cries and tears": Jesus descended into the depths of history, took it into his very heart, and in that action "became the source of eternal salvation. . . ." Jesus' suffering and death, his passion, is the fuel for salvation.

Jesus' death is our way into salvation. There is no other way.

Threat: Moralism

But however much we admire Jesus, and however many hymns we write and sing about the death of Jesus, however many years we repeat the cycle of Lent and Holy Week in our churches, this death talk doesn't go down well with us. We can't avoid it in our preaching and hymnody and calendars, but we do manage to find ways to dodge it in the way we live.

The most common way that we in the Christian community have of avoiding or marginalizing Jesus' death is by constructing a way of life that is safe and secure and guilt-free. We have a lot of information on how to live rightly before God. The Ten Commandments provide the classic structure for living the way we are supposed to live. And we have considerable stores of wisdom accumulated through the Hebrew and Christian centuries on how to conduct our lives decently and pray effectively. We take on heavy commitments to teach our children and others, "line upon line, line upon line, here a little, there a little" (Isa. 28:10).

When things go wrong, whether at home or in society, in church or in government, it is easy to find a moral reason: disobedience or ignorance of the biblical commandments is obviously at the root of a lot of what is wrong with the world. We conclude that if only we can educate our children and our parents, our politicians and our professors, our business leaders and our celebrities in right thinking and right behavior, things will improve dramatically.

All this is true enough.

But the moment this becomes our basic orientation for dealing with what is wrong with the world, we have turned our backs on the cross of Christ, on Jesus as our Savior. The moment the moral life defines our way of life we turn our backs on most of what is revealed in our Scriptures, refuse to admit the presence of God in what is happening around us (history), but worst of all, refuse to deal with the most significant thing we know about Jesus, having replaced the real Jesus with a crude, one dimensional cardboard cutout. It amounts to a defiant denial of Jesus. We place ourselves in a position to receive Jesus' most serious rebuke: "Get behind me, Satan. You are a stumbling block to me; for you are setting your mind not on divine things but on human things" (Matt. 16:24). When we rip the moral life from the living context of the Christ life, pull it up by the roots from the nourishing, loamy soil of Scripture, we end up holding a withered, drooping, and finally dead flower, a cut flower.

I am going to use the term "moralism" to designate this common, seemingly inoffensive, but in fact disastrous betrayal of Jesus. But note the word carefully. The root of the word is "moral," a glorious and necessary word. Morality is built into reality as deeply and inescapably as atoms and protons and neutrons. We are moral beings to the core — the very universe is moral. Right and wrong are embedded in the creation. It matters what is done, said, believed, even thought. Morality is fundamental and non-negotiable.

But moral*ism* is something quite different. Moralism means constructing a way of life in which I have no need of a saving God. Moralism is dead; morality is alive. Moralism works off of a base of human ability and arranges life in such a way that my good behavior will guarantee protection from punishment or disaster. Moralism works from strength, not weakness. Moralism uses God (or the revelation of God) in order not to need God any longer. Moral codes are used as stepping stones to independence from God.

Moralism works from the outside: it imposes right behavior on oneself or others. There is no freedom in it, and no joy. Moralism is a moral grid that is set on life. Up against this grid, I can see exactly where I fit or don't fit, where you fit or don't fit, what actions are right and which are wrong. And once I know that, what else is there? I either do it or don't. And you either do it or don't. Simple.[2]

There is a wonderful Greek myth that tells this story. Procrustes had a house alongside a well-traveled road in Greece, a strategically placed bed-and-breakfast. Somewhat stout, he seemed an affable man with a gracious manner. He liked things clean and tidy. And he wanted his guests to leave his hospitable place better than when they arrived, looking like a perfectly proportioned Greek statue. Most days he could be seen sitting comfortably in his rocking chair on the porch of his house, smoking his pipe, welcoming travelers and offering them hospitality. Smoke from his pipe conveyed a homey fragrance and his beard was a reassuring grandfatherly white. The house was neat and well-kept. It looked like a safe haven to tired travelers. Most evenings there was a guest or two. After welcoming them and providing them dinner, Procrustes showed his guests their rooms. Procrustes had a bed in his house that he described as having the unique property that it would exactly fit the frame of whoever slept in it. What Procrustes didn't say was how this was the case: After his guests were fast asleep, Procrustes would enter their rooms and complete his hospitality. A short person would be stretched on a rack until he or she filled the bed; for a tall person whatever hung over of arms and legs would be cut off to fit the bed. Everyone was made over to fit the dimensions of the bed, either by stretching or by amputation. When his guests left the next morning, whether aching or hobbling, they measured to the dimensions of a perfect Greek.

Procrustes and his bed are the stuff of moralism: a strategy carried out by people who are contemptuous of our particularities and force us to fit a preconceived pattern.

The great attraction to all this is that in a stroke we eliminate the mess of history. Also, once we go out and buy Procrustean beds and install them in our churches and homes there is no longer any need for Jesus and his cross except in a decorative way. If what fixes the world is simply getting everyone forced or conditioned into good behavior, we don't need salvation anymore; we need education and training, political reforms and a cultural renaissance, a stronger police presence and a superior military, more information and more power.

The word "sacrifice" is used over and over in our Scriptures and theology to define what took place on the cross of Jesus. The word gets its content from centuries of Hebrew practice, much of it deriving from the

Passover meal, developed in the Levitical sacrifices and worked out in the tabernacle and temple rituals of worship. This is all a far cry from the bed-and-breakfast hospitality of Procrustes.

*   *   *

We have considered how easy and common it is to avoid or sidestep Christ as he plays in creation. It is certainly plain enough that God reveals himself in the birth of Jesus to affirm life and all that is involved in life and then to involve us in it. But there are people who only want to pick out the convenient parts and discard the rest, which usually includes discarding Jesus as he is revealed to us. "Gnostic" is our shorthand term for them.

It is also common and easy to shut our eyes and take a nap as Christ appears on the field and plays in history. There is no question but that God reveals himself in the death of Jesus as he embraces all that has gone wrong in life and by means of that sacrificial death saves the world, getting us involved in the salvation. Why are there so many people who want to stand aloof from the mess and Christ in the mess and clean it up at arm's length by hiring some teachers and posting some regulations? They are determined to substitute a Procrustean bed for a Christian altar. "Moralist" is our shorthand term for them.

Grounding Text (1): Exodus

If creation provides the setting for the play of Christ, history supplies the people and circumstances among whom and in whom, "lovely in limbs, lovely in eyes not his," Christ plays. "Salvation" is the single word that most succinctly characterizes this play of Jesus in history. If the phrase had not long ago been reduced to a cliché, "Jesus saves" would serve admirably as an adequate summary for what our Scriptures have to say on the subject. But bumper stickers and graffiti have isolated the phrase so completely from the story to which it is the punch line that all the meaning has been drained out of the words. We need to recover the salvation *story* if the salvation *words* are to mean anything. Salvation is not a one-night stand. It cannot be isolated from the thick texture of history; it is all-encompassing, pulling everything that has happened and happens, and every person named and unnamed, into relationship with the work of God in history.

My choice of texts for grounding Christian identity in the historical reality in which salvation is revealed and received is Exodus and St. Mark's Gospel. These two texts in combination are paradigmatic for revealing the presence and work of God in history, the play of Christ in all the circumstances and events that occur in time and place. Game, used as a metaphor, is useful for gathering up all that goes on in history into a coherent image. Salvation is the name of this game that is history. But it must be understood that this game is no diversion from the main business of history. This *is* the main business. Salvation is the game that brings everything that happens, including everything that happens to each one of us, onto the playing field of history and into the play of Christ. This is a game in which there are no spectators — we are all in it; the meaning and outcome of our lives is at stake. The results are eternal.

*   *   *

In reading Exodus our assignment is to get a feel for the way salvation actually works in history. Exodus is "the basic revelation of the pattern of divine salvific activity in all ages."[3] It is essential that we rid our imaginations of understandings inappropriate to the reality of the salvation story as it is revealed in our biblical witness. It is far too common among us to turn "save" and "salvation" into abstractions or principles that we then fill out with our fantasies or ideas. What salvation definitely is not is a last ditch effort to salvage a few planks and timbers from a wrecked ship. "Save" and "salvation" come to us not as isolated words or phrase fragments but embedded in a large story that has plot and characters centuries in the development and telling. The energies of salvation send out tentacles into every nook and cranny of history. Salvation is an immense ecological system, surpassing creation in complexity, in which everything affects and is affected by everything else: the book of Exodus becomes "the basic revelation of the pattern of divine salvific activity in all ages."

*   *   *

Exodus opens by establishing continuity with Genesis, particularly with the family of Jacob ("seventy souls") that had emigrated from Canaan to Egypt to escape a Canaanite famine. They escaped the famine but eventually ended up as cruelly used slaves.

Exodus then picks up the salvation story with the people of God deeply mired in history at its worst: they have been slaves in Egypt for 430 years, "their lives bitter with hard service in mortar and brick . . ." (Exod. 12:40 and 1:14). Professor Don Gowan in his penetrating study of Exodus writes that "if we read the story as it is told and compare it with other low points in Israel's history as the Old Testament tells it, we may conclude that this has been depicted as the darkest moment of all."[4] This is a significant discernment. It means that our classic story of salvation does not build on anything that we have done or can do either as individuals or societies. It is initiated in conditions of human impossibility, all odds stacked against it. We are blocked from going into a huddle and calculating our chances. At that historical dead end our imaginations, unencumbered with social, political, and therapeutic strategies, are free to pay attention to God.

It is conventional for historians to assemble the achievements of nations and civilizations in order to establish the nature and meaning of their influence in the course of human affairs. Kings and generals are prominent. Buildings and monuments are given respectful attention. Language is studied and literary remains carefully assessed. Trade routes with their economic implications are traced. Battles and treaties, floods and famines all leave their mark.

Egypt is a showcase for such attention by historians. For over two hundred years now, ancient Egypt has come under the delighted and avid scrutiny of archaeologists and philologists. Napoleon Bonaparte kicked off the rediscovery of ancient Egypt in 1798 by sailing from France and challenging the power of England in Egypt. His military campaign soon failed but there was an unexpected benefit: he had brought scholars and artists with him and they gathered a rich harvest of ancient documents. One particularly dramatic prize was the Rosetta Stone, a slab of black basalt with an inscription in three languages, one of which was Egyptian written in impenetrable hieroglyphs. A young French scholar, Jean François Champollion, after many years of hard labor, succeeded in deciphering the hieroglyphics. The year was 1822. Men and women have been searching ever since through the gigantic tombs and temples of Egypt, reading the texts and reconstructing the history of this magnificently impressive world-dominating civilization. We know so much! The Giza pyramids and sphinx, the Karnak Temple, the military triumphs and defeats, the storied and carved gods and goddesses. The American scholar James Henry

Breasted (1865-1935) set himself to translating and putting all the evidence together. He has been followed by a succession of great scholars and by an unending gaggle of tourists traipsing along behind with cameras and camels, oohing and aahing in the presence of such magnificence. The evidence of power and beauty imposed on that desert landscape three and four and five thousand years ago never fails to stagger our imaginations.

But the biblical writers ignore all that. They have little interest in the spectacular achievements of men and women. They are not interested in arrogant displays of ego. They are interested in God and know better than to look for signs of his presence and activity in the big, the multitudinous, the in-your-face assertive. They come at history more in the spirit and manner of poet William Meredith:

> I speak of the unremarked
> Forces that split the heart
> And make the pavement toss —
> Forces concealed in quiet
> People and plants. . . .[5]

So it is significant that the first names that appear in this grounding account of God at work in history are Shiphrah and Puah, two midwives from the lowest social and economic strata of that society. The two women defy the order of the Egyptian king and by that act of defiance set in motion the chain of historical events that eventually, set alongside the story of Jesus, will become the paradigmatic account of salvation for all of history. The king of Egypt, also referred to as Pharaoh, perhaps the most powerful world ruler at the time, is not even dignified with a personal name.[6]

But these two obscure Hebrew women are named and by virtue of being named are not obscure: Shiphrah and Puah. They are midwives. Their job is to bring babies into the world. When the world-powerful king orders them to kill these same babies, they simply and without fanfare defy him. We won't forget this. Salvation is not imposed from above or from without; it emerges out of the conditions in which we find ourselves as life is confronted with death. Shiphrah and Puah, working daily at the times and places in which human life breaks out of the womb into history, are defiant of the command to kill babies. The will to life crosses with the command to kill. The command to kill comes from the impersonal anonymity of privilege and power; the will to life comes from the marginal but very personal Shiphrah and Puah, representatives of the oppressed and powerless. History as told from the place of invincibility is mostly about death; history as told from the place of vulnerability is mostly about life. World leaders are minor players in the biblical way of writing and participating in history. People like Shiphrah and Puah play decisive roles. Until we understand this and embrace it, this *placing* of the action, this primacy of grounding in the personal and the ordinary, we will never be in a position to participate wholeheartedly in the main action of salvation.

*   *   *

Moses and Aaron, who led the people of God through the historical circumstances in which salvation was revealed and experienced, came from the same neighborhood as Shiphrah and Puah, the neighborhood in which babies were under threat of death by the "powers that be." If Shiphrah and Puah had done their Pharaoh-commanded work, Moses and Aaron would have been dead on arrival.

We know little about Moses and even less about his brother Aaron. What is clear is that, like their angel midwives, they come from the margins of society: Moses' rescue from the bulrushes and adoption by the Egyptian princess, his murder of the Egyptian bully and escape to Midian, his samaritan intervention on behalf of Reuel's seven shepherd daughters and later marriage to one of them, Zipporah. Each of these incidents reinforces his outsider position.

As to leadership, he is presented as singularly ill-equipped. He has no confidence, no, as we like to say, "self-esteem." When God gets his attention with the burning bush, Moses is curious but diffident. The conversation that develops between God and Moses turns out to be one long wrangle, God calling Moses to confront Pharaoh and lead God's people out of Egypt and Moses raising objection after objection:

> God says: I will send you to Pharaoh to deliver my people (Exod. 3:10).
> Moses says: Who am I to do this? (3:11).
> God says: But I am with you (3:11-12).
> Moses says: What's your name? (3:13).
> God says: I AM. Tell them my name; they'll listen to you (3:14-22).
> Moses says: They won't believe me (4:1).

God says: Take this rod; perform these signs; they'll listen (4:2-9).

Moses says: But I don't talk well; I stutter (4:10).

God says: I'll teach you (4:11-12).

Moses says: Send someone else (4:13).

God, losing patience, says: I'll send your brother Aaron to help you (4:14-17).

At that, Moses, finally compliant (but, as we can well suppose, reluctant), prepares to leave for Egypt.

It's difficult to imagine a more unlikely candidate for taking on leadership in these particular historical circumstances. The work of salvation led by this dilatory, indecisive, foot-dragging loser? The work of salvation entrusted to this argumentative, excuse-making man who shows no sign of reverence before God, no readiness to obey God's clear command?

But maybe that is the point. Salvation is God's work: *Jesus* saves. Incompetence may be the essential qualification, lest we impatiently and presumptuously take over the business and start managing a vast and intricate economy that we have no way of comprehending. To be sure, we get intimations; we are in touch with stories that reveal God's salvation work at certain moments in history to which we have access. We know enough to get in on the life of salvation personally by repenting and believing and following Jesus, the architect and pioneer of salvation. But when all is said and done, we don't know very much. Most of what goes on in salvation is beyond us; we live a mystery. We make our way through life in a "cloud of unknowing."

In the light of this, Moses is not a model placed above us to strive toward but a companion who shows us what it means to keep our feet on this ground where God works savingly in the people and circumstances that make up the piece of history that we find ourselves in.

Later, when we read the opening pages of Luke's Gospel, we will catch an interesting echo of this Exodus set of "leaders" in the work of salvation. Luke also starts out with two marginal women who, like Shiphrah and Puah, give life in the powerful and death-dominated empire of Rome, but with the difference that Elizabeth and Mary do it as mothers, not as midwives. And Luke begins with two marginal men, Zechariah and John, father and son, Levites like the brothers Moses and Aaron, one of whom at least (John) also comes out of the desert to assume a place of leadership in the salvation plot.

God

But all this is preliminary, getting a feel for the circumstances in which salvation is worked out. The essential and primary focus of the story is God. The salvation story is a God story. It is God doing for us what we cannot do for ourselves. It is also God doing this in his own way and not to our dictates or preferences. He does not consult us regarding matters of timing.

This requires constant iteration. We humans, with our deep-seated pretensions to being gods, are endlessly preoccupied with worrying and tinkering with matters of salvation as if we were in charge of it. But we are not. God carries out the work of salvation; not, to be sure, without our participation, but it is God's work done in God's way.

The Absence of God

The story in which God does his saving work arises among a people whose primary experience of God is his absence. We are made to face this at the very outset of Exodus when we realize that these people have been in Egyptian slavery for over 430 years. Where was God all this time? Did not those covenantal words God made with Abraham, Isaac, and Jacob have any continuing validity? Didn't the providential Joseph years in Egypt leave a lasting mark?

The experienced absence or silence of God for the over four hundred years preceding the Exodus is a frequently overlooked but important element in the salvation story. This vast story of salvation is not a whitewash. There are stretches of time (400-plus years is a long time!) when nothing remotely like salvation seems to be happening. Donald Gowan observes, "Many commentators have noted that God is rather conspicuously absent from the first two chapters of Exodus, but no one has seen fit to make much of that."[7] That they haven't made much of it is unfortunate, for this seemingly unending stretch of the experience of the absence of God is reproduced in most of our lives, and most of us don't know what to make of it. We need this Exodus validation that a sense of the absence of God is part of the story, and that it is neither exceptional nor preventable nor a judgment on the way we are living our lives.

Whether the experience of absence is measured in weeks, months, or years, for most of us it doesn't fit into what is "normal" in our understanding of salvation.

But it is normal.

From our basic prayerbook, the Psalms, the prayers of our ancestors that the Holy Spirit continues to use to teach us to trust and follow and praise God, we also learn how common it is to experience the absence of God. Belief in God does not exempt us from feelings of abandonment by God. Praising God does not inoculate us from doubts about God. Meditating devoutly on God's word does not establish us securely in "the arms of Jesus," does not insulate us from all feelings of abandonment, darkness, and aridity. Psalm 22 is bruisingly stark but not at all atypical:

> My God, my God, why have you forsaken me?
> Why are you so far from helping me, from the words
>   of my groaning?
> O my God, I cry by day, but you do not answer;
> and by night, but find no rest.

(vv. 1-2)

Jesus hanging on the cross used this same prayer at the very moment that he was completing the work of salvation. On Jesus' lips this prayer validates the experience of the absence of God as integral to our participation in salvation.

Questions and protests regarding God's absence are not marginal to salvation. The psalmists are neither shy nor apologetic in giving us license to pray our complaints about the way this whole salvation business is being conducted:

> Why dost thou stand afar off, O LORD?
> Why dost thou hide thyself in times of trouble?

(Ps. 10:1 RSV)

> How long, O LORD? Wilt thou forget me forever?
> How long wilt thou hide thy face from me?

(13:1 RSV)

> Why hast thou forgotten me?

(42:9 RSV)

Rouse thyself! Why sleepest thou, O Lord?
  Awake! Do not cast us off forever!
Why dost thou hide thy face?
  Why dost thou forget our affliction and oppression?

(44:23-24 RSV)

My eyes grow dim
  with waiting for my God.

(69:3 RSV)

O God, why dost thou cast us off forever?

(74:1 RSV)

How long, O LORD? Wilt thou be angry forever?

(79:5 RSV)

O LORD, why dost thou cast me off?
  Why dost thou hide thy face from me?

(88:14 RSV)

How long, O LORD? Wilt thou hide thyself forever?

(89:46 RSV)

Return, O LORD! How long?

(90:13 RSV)

My eyes fail with watching for thy salvation. . . .

(119:123 RSV)

This random and cursory selection of phrases from our Psalms prayerbook is ample evidence that in the centuries following the Exodus salvation, just as in the centuries preceding it, the absence of God was a common experience in the company of the saved.

These psalmists along with Job, Jeremiah, and, never forget it, Jesus, develop and enrich our vocabularies of God's absence, enabling us to honestly face and courageously live through all that we don't like and don't understand. We pray in rhythm with our biblical companions who neither liked nor understood all that is involved in salvation any more than we do.

R. S. Thomas is another useful companion in times of God's felt absence. Thomas was an Anglican pastor all his working life in a grim rural culture set in a brutal Welsh countryside. He was also acclaimed by many as "the finest Christian poet" of the twentieth century (he died in September of 2000).[8] No poet since St. John of the Cross has explored the lived dimensions of the feeling of God's absence as thoroughly. His poem "Via Negativa" is representative:

> Why no! I never thought other than
> That God is that great absence
> In our lives, the empty silence
> Within, the place where we go
> Seeking, not in hope to
> Arrive or find. He keeps the interstices
> In our knowledge, the darkness
> Between stars. His are the echoes
> We follow, the footprints he has just
> Left. We put our hands in
> His side hoping to find
> It warm. We look at people
> And places as though he had looked
> At them, too; but miss the reflection.[9]

These witnesses to the experience of God's absence in the country of salvation are enormously important. They are rarely celebrated, whether in or out of church — this is not an area of life that most of us take kindly to — and not infrequently suppressed. But given our consumerist tendencies to shop for a god or goddess who will cater to our appetites for coziness and good feelings, they are necessary. Necessary to keep us alert and attentive to the mystery of God whose "ways are past finding out." Necessary to prevent us from reducing God Almighty to god-at-my-beck-and-call. Necessary to place disciplined constraints on our collective (especially North American) "spiritual sweet tooth."[10] Necessary to enlarge our readiness for salvation beyond our carefully fenced in and devoutly tended backyard spirituality gardens.

Any understanding of God that doesn't take into account God's silence is a half truth — in effect, a cruel distortion — and leaves us vulnerable to manipulation and exploitation by leaders who are quite willing to fill in the biblical blanks with what the Holy Spirit never tells us.

The Presence of God

I AM THAT I AM is the clearest and most convincing revelation of the presence of God that we have (always, of course, excepting Jesus, the Word-made-flesh). The sentence is seismic.

God became present to Moses as he was tending a flock in the Midian wilderness. A burning bush that didn't burn up caught Moses' attention; he approached it to see what was going on. God spoke Moses' name from the flames of the bush and Moses answered. Conversation between God and Moses developed. God announced his intention to deliver his people from Egyptian slavery and told Moses that he wanted him to lead them out to "a good and broad land." Moses was reluctant but after a lengthy back-and-forth exchange agreed, received his instructions, and the action was launched (Exod. 3–4).

I AM THAT I AM is God's answer to Moses' request for an identifying name. I AM THAT I AM — God's name for himself — tells Moses that God is alive, present to him, and ready to enact salvation. This God-revealing name, and the understandings that developed as it was used in prayer and obedience by the Hebrew people, marks the deconstruction of every kind and sort of impersonal, magical, manipulative, abstract, coercive way of understanding God. Listening to and answering I AM THAT I AM placed the Hebrew people as participating witnesses in the grand historical drama of salvation that challenges and brings about the eventual dissolution of every counter way of life, the world principalities and powers against which Paul would later issue a call to arms (Eph. 6:10-20); "all the kingdoms of the world and their splendor" that Jesus refused to bargain for with the devil (Matt. 4:8-10). Worshiping I AM THAT I AM developed into a way life in Israel in which love defined relationships — all of them, no exceptions: God, neighbor, stranger, enemy, family. Serving and obeying I AM THAT I AM became an exploration in all the dimensions of freedom, freedom from sin and oppression and damnation.

I AM THAT I AM, this verb-dominated, life-emphatic sentence by which God willed to be understood, was shortened to a verbal noun of four letters, *YHWH*, probably pronounced Yahweh (and usually translated as LORD in English). It became the primary term among the Hebrews for address and reference to the self-revealing God of Israel, used 6,700 times in the Old Testament as compared to the 2,500 occurrences of the generic Semitic term for divinity, *Elohim* (translated into English simply as "God").

The name spoken from the burning bush marked the definitive revelation of God as present to us and personal with us — God here among us, a living God in relation with us. No more gods of sticks and stones. No more gods to be appeased or bribed or courted. No more gods decked out in abstractions for philosophical speculation. No more gods cast as major players in cosmic war and sex myth dramas.

*   *   *

On the day that Moses stood before the bush in Midian, three or so hundred miles to the west the Egyptian civilization, already well over a thousand years old, flourished. It was a civilization impressive in its engineering and architecture (those incredible pyramids and temples!), its elaborate religion and accompanying priesthood that sought to control every detail of daily life, its aggressive armies intent on subduing everyone within reach to subservience. Egypt dominated the Middle Eastern world.

But it was a dominion of death. The pyramids, the most conspicuous monuments on their landscape, were tombs. They were very elaborate tombs, tombs that by their incredibly intricate art and design, and the engineering ingenuity required for their construction, evoked wonder. By their sheer size they would seem, under the guise of immortality, to defy anything, even death, especially death, and get the last word. All the same, they were tombs, hosts to a mummy, houses for the dead. As we ponder those pyramids, symbolic of so much that went on in Egyptian civilization, emotions of awe and derision compete in us. But not for long — awe can't compete with derision here. The awe that springs spontaneous in us as we stand before such engineering and art is soon overcome by derision at the absurdity of supposing that inanimate stone could provide a passage to immortal life. Egyptian civilization was obsessed with immortality achieved by the stonemason's mallet and chisel and the embalmer's art.

In the biblical story, Egypt is synonymous with death. All Egyptian magnificence and arrogance was reduced at that burning bush to its essence, a small heap of ash. The antonym of death-dealing Egypt is life-giving Yahweh, God here and present, alive and saving.

The name from the bush is not invoked or conjured. Moses is minding his own business, remote from the so-called action, miles and years away from Egyptian wealth and power and religion. The name, the verb in the first person, I AM, takes the initiative. That marked the historical turning point in what has become the long, continuing collapse of using death and the fear of death in the lucrative and complex business of selling religious insurance, playing on people's fear and superstitions.

A millennium plus a couple of centuries later, Jesus will continue and then complete the event at the bush; he will take these very words, these I AM words, on his lips and flesh them out in salvation meetings and salvation conversations with lost and dying, confused and bedeviled, sick and guilty slaves of sin and lead them into a new life. St. John's Gospel will provide a Jesus conclusion to the revelation at the bush.

*   *   *

The name, I AM THAT I AM, has been studied, examined, probed, and meditated by an endless succession of scholars and saints in many languages in attempts to pin it down, define it, say what it means. The most conspicuous result of this mountainous effort stretching now for well over two thousand years is how inconclusive it is. There is no "result."

God cannot be defined. "Yahweh" is not a definition.[11] God cannot be reduced to an "object" of our inquiry or search. The earlier God names among the people of God are all nouns: the generic God *(Elohim)*, God of the Fathers *(Elohey Avoth)*, God Almighty *(El Shaddai)*, God the Most High *(El Elyon)*, and God of Hosts *(Elohey Tsvaoth)* continue to be useful but they all now must be understood under the primacy of the verb that cannot be pinned down, cannot be put under the scrutiny of an examination but can only be received or responded to. God is actively present to us and our only option is to be actively present in our turn, or not. In this regard Th. C. Vriezen emphasizes the actuality of God: "'I am who I am' means, 'I am there, wherever it may be.... I am really there!'"[12] The parallel in Exodus 33:19 confirms this.

Is the name purposely enigmatic? Revelational but not telling everything? Disclosing intimacy, personal presence, but preserving mystery, forbidding possession and control? A verbal icon for all God-initiated relationships in faith and friendship and marriage?

I think so.

The bush and the name are in contrast to everything that was going on in Egypt at the time. Egypt represented the ultimate in control, controlling a large slave population, controlling the afterlife, controlling a world empire, controlling a huge stable of gods and goddesses, as if by reducing them to stone, gigantic and magnificent as the stones were, they could through their elaborate priestly machinations control history. But that is anti-history. History is a field for salvation. Dealing with people as objects is a violation of the primary work of history, which is salvation. And reducing God to an object (or idea or definition) so that we can control God is an outrageous absurdity no matter how solemnly carried out (and the Egyptians were nothing if not solemn). In the revelation of the name at the bush, God, by withholding a definition, preserves his freedom so that we can have our freedom. Gerhard von Rad puts it this way: "what is of greatest importance is that this name could not properly be objectified and disposed of — its secret could not in any way be reduced to a theological interpretation of its meaning, not even the one in Ex. 3:14. Yahweh had bound it up with the free manifestation in history of his self-revelation in history."[13]

Exorcism

A major difficulty in embracing history as the field for salvation (some find it insurmountable) is the sheer mass of relentless and assertive counter-evidence. The loudest and most conspicuous players on the field of history are playing quite a different game than Christ is. Most people — and certainly those who get the most attention and their names in the history books — are playing other games by different rules: war games, self games, money games, board games, baseball games, hunting and fishing games, card and roulette games, church games, sex games, games ranging from lethal to trivial. Sin and death games.

Many if not all of these games are associated with outright claims or implicit assumptions that the games will lift the lives of those who play them out of the ordinary to something more interesting, more exciting, more meaningful: banish boredom; invite excellence; offer company with the elite; establish power. It is not difficult to detect at least a hint of transcendence in all this, to pick up muted god-voices and god-claims advertising their wares, pretending to help, save, entertain, improve, empower. Even if the word is not used, and it seldom is, some variation or other on salvation is suggested — we will be rescued from a condition in which we feel stuck, anything ranging from boredom to misery, and have a better life. But in the long run, the offers don't amount to much, and certainly not to anything that would qualify as salvation.

Christian spirituality makes bold to claim that there is only one game on the field of history and that is salvation. Everything that happens, everything that men and women do, happens on this playing field on and over which God is sovereign, the field in which Christ "plays in ten thousand places."

But it takes some doing for us to see that. It took some doing for Israel to see that, but see it they did, and here is how it came about.

*   *   *

In approximately 1250 B.C., the people of Israel were living in Egypt as slaves and had been for over four centuries. Egypt at this time was a world power and had been for a long time. Egypt had developed and perfected one of the most impressive god-games of all, dominating the landscape, dominating the imaginations of people far and near, a totalitarian society ruled by a dictator whom everyone believed was also a god. The splendor surrounding the dictator-god made it believable: breathtaking architecture, dazzling art, everything magnificent in gold. But the splendor was all external; inside the place was crawling with maggots — abuse, cruelty, superstition, degradation. The Hebrews were right there in the middle of it but obviously and hopelessly on the losing side. Were there pockets of people who kept the old stories of "the fathers" in clandestine circulation? Probably, but for most it would seem Egypt was the only game in town. After 430 years in Egypt the memory of Abraham, Isaac, Jacob, and Joseph would have been well-nigh obliterated.

Under these conditions, it is difficult to apprehend what God is doing in history, or even if he is doing anything at all. In order for the people of God to be able to recognize and respond to God's revelation and work as I AM THAT I AM, they are going to have to see this Pharaonic morass of lies and oppression, this pervasive and outrageous violation of human life, for what it is — evil; but an evil which is *not* ultimate, *not* the last word. They require a massive renovation in their understanding of Egyptian reality. Typically, people who suffer long and much come to see their oppressors as powerful, *world*-powerful, and therefore at the top of the hierarchy of human achievement. The Hebrews had suffered long and much, an oppression underwritten by a most impressive religion — all those temples and statues and priests! Everywhere they looked they could see that not only were the Egyptians against them, the *gods* were against them.

However much they protested their place as oppressed slaves in the system, the system was the only reality they knew. It was impossible to imagine anything else. If by some miracle they became free of their slave condition, they would almost certainly take their place higher up in the chain of oppression and function as oppressors themselves. This kind of thing happens all the time — in families, businesses, revolutionary governments, bureaucracies, and churches.

So how was Moses to rip off the veneer of all this power and majesty and beauty and success and expose it as evil so that when he led his people out of Egypt they would not carry their Egyptian experience with them for the rest of their lives as the approved reality, the only reality, and then simply reproduce it when they arrived in the country of their salvation? If Moses led them out of Egypt with their imaginations still controlled by Egypt, it wouldn't be long before they would be repeating the "way of Egyptian success" themselves. As far as they knew, this is what worked, and had worked for at least a thousand years. If their imaginations were not thoroughly cleansed from the evil they were immersed in, they would end up doing the same thing as soon as they were in power themselves, oppressing the weak and trampling on the helpless, bullying those under them with might and size in the name of whatever gods there were.

$$*\qquad*\qquad*$$

This is where the ten plagues come in. The ten plagues were employed to expose the emptiness of evil, to purge the Hebrew minds of all envious admiration of evil, to systematically demolish every god-illusion or god-pretension that evil uses to exercise power over men and women. William Blake wrote of the necessity of cleansing the "doors of perception"[14] if we want to see what is really going on in life — salvation, in this case — not just what is reported in the newspapers. Each of the ten plagues was an ammonia-laced scrub-bucket of suds for just such a cleansing.

When our minds and spirits succumb to the *rule* of evil, not just its physical effects, we come under the sway of the demonic. Pharaoh was the embodiment of such rule in Egypt. The ten plagues were an elaborate exorcism, a casting out of the demons, that freed the imaginations of the Hebrews from domination by evil so that they were free to hear and follow their Savior and worship God "in spirit and truth" (John 4:24). When Moses began his work with his Hebrew brothers and sisters, their spirits were "broken" (Exod. 6:9) and the only "truth" they had access to was this huge Egyptian lie. But Egypt and Pharaoh were not the "real world." They were the real world defaced, desecrated, demonized. The ten plagues deconstructed this magnificent fraud item by item and piece by piece until there was nothing left of it to hold the imagination of the people of God. The exorcising drama of the ten plagues freed the Hebrews from this Egyptian way of understanding reality, clearing the mind to accept God's revelation reality, energizing their spirits to live in the world of salvation. The intent was that by the time they left Egypt, they would not only be physically free of the evil oppression but mentally free of the evil imagination that had crushed the life out of them for so long. The ten plagues would cleanse the "doors of perception" so that Israel could see life in a totally different way — the unreality of Egypt exposed; the untruth of Egypt laid bare — and would set them free to live a different life when they get out of Egypt, free to live the freedom of salvation. For over four hundred years they had lived in a world that fused political power and religious myth to form a demonic culture of arrogance and privilege for a few and slavery and degradation for many. This way of experiencing the world had penetrated deep into their genes by this time. Radical surgery was required to get it out. The ten plagues were that surgery.

*   *   *

Scholars have not made much progress in establishing the "meaning" of each of the plagues by identifying its significance in terms of the culture, although it has not been for lack of trying. But we don't need the help of scholars to see that what is primarily at issue in the ten plagues is sovereignty. Each of the ten plagues was a staging ground for a test of sovereignty. Who is in charge here? Who is running this show? The god Ra represented by the Pharaoh? Or Yahweh represented by Moses? Each plague in turn deals with that question, another round in the World Cup Sovereignty Match. Pharaoh embodies the person and presence of the great Egyptian god Ra; Moses is the prophet of God who revealed himself to Israel as I AM THAT I AM.

Pharaoh and Moses confront one another, round after round, the whole country an arena packed with spectators. Egyptians and Hebrews alike watch every move. The stakes are high. Interest is intense. Two ways of life are at stake. Ten times they go at each other. The first two rounds end in a draw; each time after that, Moses wins.

The overall significance of the plagues is that each plague has to do with some aspect or another of creation or the workings of creation, a part of the way things worked in the natural, ordinary course of everyday life, with which everyone was familiar. None of the plagues is supernatural as such; each is part of the natural order. And everyone, of course, knew that Pharaoh was in charge of them all, in charge of keeping the cosmic order — that's what a Pharaoh did, that was his job description.

But as Pharaoh and Moses repeatedly go head to head, one after another of the life-forms and forces over which everyone had always assumed that Pharaoh was sovereign turn out to be at Moses' beck and call, not Pharaoh's. Everyone in the arena — it's a full house, the entire population packed in — sees that Pharaoh is completely out of control. Each successive plague displays his humiliating impotence on a large screen. Moses, prophet of Yahweh, launches and then banishes each plague. Pharaoh's vaunted sovereignty is systematically dismantled. The grandiose, elaborately maintained fraud, that Pharaoh controls the behind-the-scenes workings of the world, is exposed as a lie. Moses makes a monkey of Pharaoh (Exod. 10:2).

Or, to change the image, the plagues are like a dramatic production in ten scenes, with the nation assembled in a playhouse. In each scene a huge steel wrecking ball is swung from a great height and smashes another piece of the Egyptian way of life, each strike a demolition, reducing item by item the intricately fashioned myth of Egyptian invulnerability, of Pharaonic sovereignty. The massive Egyptian world, sanctioned by thousands of years of precedence, staggered the imagination, especially the slave imagination, with its gigantic statues of gods, its elaborate temples, and then, the biggest lie of all, those immense pyramid tombs rising out of the desert with their bold claim to be preserving the corpse of a mummified king for transport into everlasting life. If you live in a country like that, there is not much room to imagine anything other than that. There is a bullying quality to might and size.

Each plague, relentless, inexorable, crashed into the pretensions of Egyptian sovereignty, blow by blow by blow. The ten plagues drama gets off to a somewhat slow start. The first two plagues that Moses brings on stage, blood and frogs, were matched by Pharaoh's magicians — a standoff. By the third, the mosquito plague, the magicians were clearly out of their depth, no longer able to match Moses blow for blow. After the sixth, the boils plague, the magicians were not only bested, they were incapacitated, put out of action by the boils. We hear no more of them. The four final plagues, anchored by the death plague, settle the sovereignty issue decisively. Pharaoh is skunked.

For the people in the theater, there may even have been a slapstick, cartoon-like quality to the succession of plagues as the steel wrecking ball did its work:

Blood (Pow!)
Frogs (Pow!)
Mosquitos (Pow!)
Flies (Pow!)
Pestilence (Pow!)
Boils (Pow!)
Hail (Pow!)
Locusts (Pow!)
Darkness (Pow!)
Death (Pow!)

Each blow further loosened the hold of that immense, world-dominating Egyptian/Pharaonic lie on the people, until there was nothing left but a pile of rubble, garbage, and corpses. The demolition drama, in ten scenes, played to a packed house for a little over eight months.

It has long been conventional to interpret the ten plagues as acts of judgment on Egypt. But that is not the way the story is told. For one thing, the word "judgment" is used only three times (Exod. 6:6; 7:4; 12:12), and even these uses have more to do with God's power and righteousness than with Egyptian sin. And the word "sin" is used only once, and that comes from Pharaoh's lips about himself (9:27).

No. The ten plagues are used to discredit the Pharaoh's claim to sovereignty and to establish the sovereignty of Yahweh in its place. Just that.

*   *   *

But they also serve an important function in calling attention to a major concern in spiritual theology, namely, the critical passage involved in the transition from one sovereignty to another. In the Exodus narrative the ten plagues (chs. 7–11) function as a transition from the preparation for salvation (chs. 1–6) to the accomplishment of salvation (chs. 12–15). I want to consider the effect the ten plagues had on the people who observed and then embraced this change of sovereignties. I have used several images to convey the effect of the ten plagues on those who experienced them: exorcism, surgery, an athletic contest, a demolition drama. Of these, exorcism is most useful in capturing the heart of the matter, for exorcism conveys the radical inwardness of what has to be done, freeing us from the grip of the demonic that is defiant of God's rule and oppresses our imagination, the "spirit of slavery" cited by Paul (Rom. 8:15).

The ten plagues exorcise the demonic assumptions and understandings that prevent a full embrace, body and soul, of God's salvation. In the Exodus story the Israelites are being prepared for salvation; in order to continue in the salvation life they require a disciplined and chastened imagination, free of the dirt and stink and abuse in which they had lived for so long, free to hear the word of grace and forgiveness, to recognize the world of providence and blessing, to live a life of free obedience and joyful worship.

This assessment of the spiritual effect of the ten plagues is supported by the careful exegesis of Donald Gowan. Gowan points out that "know" runs through the entire plague section (chs. 6–14) "like a thread that holds it all together" (6:7; 7:5, 17; 8:10, 22; 9:14, 29; 10:2; 11:7; 14:4, 18).[15] That observation sends us back to the first meeting of Moses and Aaron as they ask Pharaoh for permission to take the Hebrews into the wilderness to sacrifice. Pharaoh is sarcastic: "Who is the LORD, that I should heed him and let Israel go? *I do not know the LORD,* and I will not let Israel go" (5:2, emphasis added). We, who know what is coming, think, "Well, he certainly will get to know — and very soon!" He is about to be sent to school to repair his ignorance. The ten plagues will be the curriculum. But it is not just the Pharaoh who will be in that classroom — the whole country will be there, with the Israelites in the front rows. Gowan again: "Knowledge is the expressed aim of the plagues."

They (and we!) have so much to learn. The ten plagues, by exorcising the evil sovereignty from their imaginations, go a long way toward ridding the Israelites of their ingrained Egyptian view of history so that they are free to conceive the immense country of salvation under the sovereignty of I AM THAT I AM, knowledge that provides a solid structure for their unfolding life.

*   *   *

Salvation is a far larger country than creation. Creation is immense, a vast and intricate web of elements ranging from the ordinary to the wondrous. Everything is laid out for us to take in: from the light-year stretches of the cosmos beyond us to the proliferation of life-forms all around us and down, down, down to the many-layered paleolithic strata of rock beneath us. But salvation is even more extensive; it takes in all of history where things *happen* — everything that happens to men and women up and down the corridors of history. In creation we can put our subject under a microscope or bring it into focus in a telescope or observe it in a laboratory. It more or less stays put while we study it. And it doesn't lie — an amoeba is what you see; no more, no less. But human beings lie and dissemble — a lot. A Canadian politician may or may not be what he says. An American advertiser may or may not be telling us the truth. It is difficult to discover what is going on in creation, immensely difficult, requiring rigorously disciplined and trained observers. But the difficulties increase exponentially in history, this field in which salvation takes place, where lies are constantly being told; so training is necessary lest we misunderstand, prematurely read our own presuppositions into what is going on and remain ignorant of the ways in which God works, confuse our Egyptian experience of reality with salvation, the new reality into which we are being led.

The knowledge that we acquire by being in the ten plagues school is primarily the knowledge of God and how he works in contrast to Pharaoh and how he works. Pharaoh employs size and force and prestige to control and oppress. God employs an eighty-year-old desert shepherd and his brother, their only weapon a stick, and a ragtag company of despised slaves to bring about freedom and salvation for the whole world.

The knowledge that comes in the ten plagues school may better be termed "discernment," for it is not knowing bare facts that is essential here (although they also will have their place) but having a clear mind and spirit that can discern between good and evil, having the ability to penetrate the sweet and easy illusions of the devil and embrace hard-edged and demanding truth.

*   *   *

Jesus in his temple cleansing compressed the eight-month drama of the ten plagues exorcism into the work of a single day. Each of the Gospel writers, aware of the Exodus background, gives the cleansing a prominent place in their narration — John early in the ministry as a whole (John 2:13-16), the others early in Holy Week (Matt. 21:12-13; Mark 11:15-19; Luke 19:45-46). Jesus, the prophet like Moses (Deut. 18:15), was about to complete the work of salvation, bring it out into the open where everyone could see it take place. Like Moses, Jesus also worked in an Egyptian-like setting, the Jerusalem temple — a godless place, extravagantly conceived and ingeniously constructed by the godless King Herod and presided over by the equally godless Caiaphas, a place where the sovereignty of God was obscured beyond recognition. It was the site of enormous corruption and oppression, religion there being used to oppress the weak and the poor. The oppression was especially evident at Passover, the great feast initiated under Moses in Exodus. During the week of the feast, the elite priestly class, the Sadducees, led by their high priest Caiaphas, gouged immense amounts of money from pilgrims arriving at the feast from all over the world. Just as back in Egypt twelve hundred years earlier, gold and power and magnificence again dominated people's imagination at the precise time and place in which salvation was up for grabs. Jesus challenged the Caiaphas/Sadducee sovereignty by confronting, humiliating, and banishing the "den of robbers" (Mark 11:17) who had taken over the place of worship. The leaders rightly interpreted Jesus' action as a sovereignty issue: "By what authority are you doing these things?" (Mark 11:28). Who here would prove to be sovereign? Rich Caiaphas or poor Jesus? Jesus stood in that temple court, a lone figure, a Moses-like figure, dwarfed by wealth and power. How was Jesus, poor himself, without priestly and temple sanctions, to be seen for what he was, the architect of salvation? He needed to clear the deck so that he could be seen as himself, in contrast to the showy Egyptian fraudulence. And so he cleansed the temple: drove out the oppressors and imposters, upset the routines and accepted practices of a successful, godless religion, spoke the words that established the sovereignty of God in that place in his own person. In the act of cleansing the temple, he cleansed the people's understanding, purged their imagination — an exorcism so that the people, clear-eyed on the matter of God's sovereign authority, would be able to perceive and embrace salvation without distraction, without clutter. We catch a clear echo of the ten plagues in the temple cleansing.

Following the biblical precedents of exorcism in the ten plagues and the cleansing, the pre-Constantinian church developed practices that continue to be modified and adapted, as Christians prepared to embrace the radical new submission to God's sovereignty that takes place in the country of salvation.

The Epistle of Hippolytus gives us our first look at the post-biblical development. Converts to the faith were required to enter a probationary period (in some parts of the church it lasted for two years) in which candidates for baptism were taught the meaning of following Jesus. They were called "catechumens" and were not permitted to receive the Eucharist until they had completed their training. The church didn't want to risk them mucking up salvation with words and ideas that they had picked up in the gutters and streets, bazaars and brothels, schools and workplaces of their pre-conversion Egyptian lives. Salvation is a radical new way of participating in history. Their imaginations were, in effect, retrained so that they could understand their lives and the history in which they lived in the vocabulary and images that God used to reveal himself and his ways to us; their imaginations were cleansed from Egyptian assumptions and thinking.[16] During Lent, in the last five or six weeks of this probationary period, preparation intensified into a time of fasting and prayer and exorcism, with baptism at Easter.

The work continues, the work of the ten plagues in Egyptian times, of the cleansing in the Herodian temple, of the catechumenate in the culture of Roman/Greek paganism. This is a major and never-ending task, this exorcism of the culture's lies and pretensions from the Christian imagination so that God's sovereignty in history can be received in a life large with salvation.

Salvation

It is impossible to exaggerate the historical significance and the endless personal ramifications of salvation. It always exceeds our powers of understanding and imagining. We will never get our minds around it. We see well enough what is going on: God is at work in history; he heals and helps; he forgives and blesses; he takes a creation in ruins because of human willfulness and patiently begins to make a new creation of it; he takes a world corrupted by evil and begins the long, slow work of transforming it into a holy place. But we see all this in bits and pieces, moments and fragments. It is understandable that we often reduce salvation to a handful of these moments or fragments. But we must not. We are dealing with

God's work in history on a scale of comprehensiveness that ever eludes us. St. Paul, wrapping up his excursus on God's salvation work in history in his Letter to the Romans, is appropriately in awe of what we will never grasp: "O the depth of the riches and wisdom and knowledge of God! How unsearchable are his judgments and how inscrutable his ways!" (Rom. 11:33).

But if we can't overstate the significance of salvation we can certainly misconstrue it. We can read our own ideas into what we think salvation ought to be. We can spin escapist fantasies of salvation that project either our ignorance or our sin (usually both) onto a large screen of desire. When we do that we incapacitate ourselves from entering into the actual salvation that God is working right now all around us. We also commonly end up with a lot of anger or frustration or bitterness when we find that God doesn't do all the things that we imagined he must do if he is any kind of God at all.

Exodus goes a long way to prevent such misunderstandings of salvation by embedding it in a story, remembering it in a meal, and singing it in a song. The story, the meal, and the song turn like gears in a transmission, one off the other, to keep our understanding of and participation in salvation entire and healthy. Each part is essential to the others. Otherwise salvation becomes our "thing," a strategy or program for doing something that will make us and the world around us fit for heaven pretty much on our own terms. But salvation is never our thing. It is God's work in history in "ways past finding out." The story, the meal, and the song keep us in living touch with what God is doing in history.

The Story

That very day the LORD brought the Israelites out of the land of Egypt, company by company.

Exod. 12:51

Our salvation text doesn't provide us with a dictionary definition of salvation; what we get is a salvation story, frequently remembered and often told. The Hebrew way to understand salvation was not to read a theological treatise but to sit around a campfire with family and friends and listen to a story. It is the very nature of storytelling to include us, the hearers, in the story. It is important to recognize this at the outset, for salvation is not the spiritual diagnosis of souls, one here, one there; it is the story of a people, a community with a past, with ancestors, with common experience.

The central episode in the thousand-year-long salvation story laid out in the Old Testament has Israel leaving Egypt and marching east to freedom. The death plague in which Pharaoh lost his firstborn son was the precipitating cause after eight months of maddeningly indecisive negotiation. Pharaoh and all of Egypt had finally had enough — "Be gone!" (*leki*; Exod. 12:32) — and felt glad to be rid of them. But instead of taking a direct route to their new land, Israel was led south toward the wilderness and camped at the shore of the Red Sea, a dead end as it turned out. Pharaoh, meanwhile, with time to think things over, realized that he had made a terrible mistake in letting all that slave labor get away, changed his mind and set off with horses and chariots in full pursuit. He caught up with them camped there at the Red Sea. Israel's few days of euphoric freedom ended abruptly. They were doomed, trapped with no conceivable way of escape. They braced for a massacre. And then Moses spoke: "Fear not, stand firm, and see the salvation of the LORD, which he will work for you today; for the Egyptians whom you see today, you shall never see again" (14:13 RSV). At that the pillar of cloud came between the two armies, an insulating barrier that kept them apart for the night. In the morning Moses stretched his shepherd's staff over the Sea. The Sea divided and Israel walked through on dry land. The Egyptians saw what had happened and gave chase but their chariot wheels clogged in the mud and there they were, stuck in the middle of the path through the sea. That finished the Egyptians. A rout. The Hebrew expression is colorful: God "flicked off" the Egyptians (14:27), like fleas from bedclothes.[17] With Israel now safe on the other side, Moses again stretched his arm and the waters closed in on the Egyptians. "Thus the LORD saved Israel that day . . ." (14:30).

It is a memorable story and memorably told. The ten plagues provide a long introduction, that relentless, deliberate deconstruction of Egyptian sovereignty, item by item, ending in a sudden rush to freedom on the night of the tenth plague, the death plague. Israel free! Then the delicious exuberance of freedom, denied them for so long, was cruelly snatched away — they were caught between the jaws of Egyptian chariots and the Red Sea. A brief freedom about to be wiped out in a massacre. And then, without them doing one thing — Moses had told them, "You have only to keep still" (Exod. 14:14), and they were — the waters parted and they were saved. Israel never forgot it. Through frequent storytelling it became woven into the fabric of their imaginations.

All the critical verbs in the core story (Exod. 13:17 to 14:31) are powered by God. The people cry out and complain. Moses obeys a few orders. But God, and God only, does the salvation work; twelve God-activated verbs carry the action of the story, with "saved" as the summarizing final verb.

The Hebrew language has a rich vocabulary to tell what God does to help his people, but "save" is by far the richest in connotations and the most common (as a noun, 146 times; as a verb 354 times in the Old Testament). In the reading of our Scriptures, we come on the word for the first time in this Exodus salvation story, first as a noun ("stand firm, and see the salvation of the LORD," 14:13 RSV) and then as a verb ("thus the LORD saved Israel that day," 14:30). "Salvation" and "save" frame the story.

The word, whether as noun or verb, is reserved almost exclusively for what God does: God is the subject, people are the object. God does it, we get in on it. Apparently, the Hebrews were the only people among their neighbors who had this exclusive sense that salvation was God's work, and only God's work. There is only one occurrence of the word (except in proper names) outside the Hebrew language and that is in the ninth-century B.C. Mesha inscription from Moab.

The Wonder at the Sea[18] is meant to be understood as miracle without qualification. It was not even qualified by Israel's faith. Brevard Childs makes the trenchant observation that "Israel failed to believe right up to the moment of her deliverance."[19] At the very outset we are meant to understand that salvation is not limited by conditions, by impossibilities, by conventions. The Wonder at the Sea establishes it as fundamental that salvation consists in what God does; it is not a human project. We see and fear and believe (14:31) and that's it. This is difficult to digest, for we grow up with and are surrounded with "salvation projects" on all fronts (many of them in churches) that insist that what we do, how we get involved, is critical to their success. When was the last time that we heard one of our pastors or evangelists or politicians tell us, "You have only to keep still"? But that is what we are told here. This is as indisputable and as clear as our storyteller can make it: Our showcase salvation story anchors "save" in the sheer, unqualified miracle of the Wonder at the Sea. Only God did this and only God could do it.

But there is more to it. It is essential now to observe that subsequent to this salvation story, as "save"/"salvation" continues to be used in our Scriptures, the word nearly always (but not quite exclusively) tells us that God, rather than removing us from the trouble we are in, brings something into the human situation that is not already there.[20] I AM THAT I AM enters and is present with us in the conditions; he doesn't abolish the conditions. The conditions stay the same. From Exodus on, save/salvation is the distinctive and miraculous work of God among us that he works seriously and savingly with us in our troubles and difficulties, our sicknesses and addictions, our devastations and disappointments, through assault and opposition. This does not in any way diminish the miraculous element in salvation; it does, though, convey to us that the salvation that is God's work in history is not a repudiation of history, not typically a *deus ex machina*[21] that the Greeks were so fond of using in their cheaper theater productions.

Anyone who promises or demands something of salvation other than this is giving us a half truth that ends up being a lie.

The Meal

"This day shall be for you a memorial day, and you shall keep it as a feast to the LORD; throughout your generations you shall observe it as an ordinance for ever."

Exod. 12:14 RSV

The people of Israel prepared and ate a meal together on the night that they left Egypt. Along with the story, the preparation and eating of this meal is also essential for understanding salvation. The essential place the meal has in understanding and embracing salvation is underlined by God's command that they eat this meal together "for ever" — year after year after year on the fourteenth day of the spring month Nisan.

Salvation is the biggest thing. Genesis 1–2 told the story of creation, an immense subject in its own right, but then our attention was turned to the work of salvation being worked out in history. Sin and death entered the picture, then judgment and promise, then covenant and blessing. The story gathered momentum as Abraham and Sarah, Isaac and Rebekah, Jacob with Rachel and Leah, Joseph and his brothers, and now Moses, each in his or her turn entered the story. We are getting a feel for the ways of God among us. We are now at the place in the revelation where all the ele-

173

ments of salvation that we know of are, so to speak, in embryo. All these details brought to our awareness in the Genesis-Exodus exposition issue in an event that will pull them into a single event: the Wonder at the Sea. Salvation.

And here's the thing: The triggering move that sets off this final and definitive burst of wonder, God's salvation act, unprecedented and unsurpassable, is a meal, an ordinary meal, a meat and potatoes meal, prepared and eaten by a family in their own kitchen. The emphasis is on ordinariness, the ordinariness of the place (home), the ordinariness of the food (meat and bread), the ordinariness of those who eat (family members). It is definitely not a gourmet meal, certainly not an elaborate banquet with wine and servants and seven courses. Not a meal accompanied by flowers and candles on the tables, music and dancing, and everyone dressed to the nines.

This is so characteristic of biblical spirituality: the ordinary and the miraculous are on a single continuum. Anything and everything that we believe about God finds grounding in what we do in the course of any and every ordinary day. We are not permitted to segregate our salvation away from the details of getting around and making a living. "Pass the broccoli" and "Hear the Word of God" carry equal weight in conversations among the saved. The sacraments are served in kitchen and chancel alike.

But this ordinary meal does have a special name, Passover. The day before Israel left Egypt, every family slaughtered a year-old lamb for the evening meal. Blood from the lamb was gathered in a basin and splashed on the lintel and entrance posts of their homes with a whisk of hyssop sprigs. They roasted the lamb and served it with vegetables (bitter herbs) and bread (unleavened). They ate the meal dressed for travel, walking stick in hand. They were instructed to eat the meal within their house behind closed doors and stay there until morning.

As the people of Israel were preparing and eating this meal, shut up in their homes behind closed doors, in every Egyptian home from palace to hovel the firstborn boy died. In every Egyptian barn or barnyard the firstborn animals died. It was the night of the tenth plague. Meanwhile, every Hebrew firstborn, protected by the sign of blood from the sacrificed lamb and nourished by the meal of lamb, herbs, and bread, lived. The firstborn is the sign and carrier of life in each family — inherent in the firstborn is evidence of new life and the promise that life continues. The people of God remembered the eating of that meal as the night that God went through Egypt and killed every firstborn boy and beast but *passed over* the Hebrew homes marked with the lamb's blood. It has been the Passover meal ever since. The verb "passed over" *(pesach)* is livelier in Hebrew, something more like "skipped over" the Hebrew homes. For all the solemnity of that night, do we also detect a light, celebratory note in that skipping?

When morning came, they left Egypt a free people.

That night of the tenth plague and the Passover meal marked the final and conclusive, life and death test of sovereignty: Pharaoh sovereign over a nation filled with death, every home mourning the death of its firstborn; Moses leading a congregation of an estimated million men, women, and children to a life of freedom, alive and on their way to worship the living God, I AM THAT I AM.

*   *   *

Moses commanded the people of Israel to repeat this Passover meal every year in the spring, "throughout your generations" (12:14, 17, 42). In his instructions for future observance, the Passover meal expands from a day into a week of remembrance, a week of eating only flatbread (unleavened), anchored to the night of the Passover meal. The festival lasts seven days, the time God took to create heaven and earth. The week begins on the fourteenth of the month and concludes on the twenty-first, a week bracketed by Sabbaths. The week of salvation mirrors the week of creation. The people of God learn that the God who creates is the God who saves. Creation and salvation are of one piece.

Isaiah of the exile saw creation and salvation in parallel. Immediately after referring to the act of driving back the waters of chaos in creation, he picks up the story of the Red Sea when God again drove back the waters for "the redeemed to cross over" (Isa. 51:10). Creation and salvation are juxtaposed.[22]

It is significant that this salvation meal was not an exclusively Israelite meal. Hospitality was inherent in it. A "mixed crowd" left Egypt with the Hebrews that morning (Exod. 12:38). Slaves, whatever their race or origin, as well as the natives and strangers among the several ethnic groupings in the area, could become Israelites through circumcision and be spiritually adopted into the family and welcomed to eat the Passover meal. Only "foreigners" were excluded, but "foreigner" *(ben nekhar)* here means "son of a strange god" — not an alien as such but a pagan polytheist

175

(12:43-49). Any person could become an Israelite by choice (cf. Rom. 9:7). Thus Passover (salvation) is God's gift, through Israel, to all people, male and female, Jew and Gentile, bond and free alike.

The Song

Then Moses and the people of Israel sang this song to the LORD:

> "I will sing to the LORD, for he has triumphed gloriously;
>   horse and rider he has thrown into the sea."

Exod. 15:1

Salvation is God's act. The only appropriate response, therefore, is to attend to this God who saves. But the *way* in which this attention is given is critical. So far in Exodus, response has taken the form of telling the story and remembering the event in a ritual meal. What comes next? For many the next step in understanding salvation follows along the lines of study and analysis; we get out our concordances and lexicons and sharpen our pencils. But not here: here the God of salvation is *worshiped*. Story and ritual are now taken up into an act of worship that makes every Israelite a participant in salvation. Not a single Israelite, not even Moses, did one, solitary thing to bring about salvation.[23] There is nothing to sing about on that front. So if neither Moses nor the Israelites are the subject and if human experience is not the subject, that leaves God as the subject: "I will sing to the LORD. . . ."

Song is heightened speech. The heightening does not come through the addition of more words or turning up the volume of the words but by singing the words. So what does the singing do? It obviously does not add to the meaning, at least the objective, dictionary meaning. Something else is going on and that something eludes precise accounting. Song does not explain, it expresses; it gives witness to the trans-literal. Song is more than words and there are no words to convey what that "more" is precisely. Song is one of the two ways (silence is the other) of giving witness to the transcendent.

And so biblically formed people do a lot of singing as they worship. "Psalms, hymns, and spiritual songs" (Col. 3:16), not theological or Hebrew and Greek word studies, provide the primary language for embracing and savoring what God does and who God is in all matters of salvation. "Music," writes George Steiner, "makes utterly substantive . . . the real presence in meaning where that presence cannot be analytically shown or paraphrased. Music brings to our daily lives an immediate encounter with a logic or sense other than that of reason. It is, precisely, the truest name we have for the logic at work in the springs of being that generate vital forms."[24]

Because God, and therefore the worship of God, cannot be reduced to the rational, song has always been basic to the act of worship. Music is not added to the words to make them more pleasing; it is integral to the way the words are being used as openings to the transcendent, as windows to the mystery, as joining in the dance of the Trinity.

Any approach to salvation that does not eventually become worship, and the sooner the better, distorts and reduces salvation to a concept or a program or a technique that we can master and therefore control. But, of course, if we can do it or at least manage it, it is no longer salvation. We walk out on God and set up our own private enterprise salvation shops. We attempt to cover up the banality of the salvation projects we are promoting by slick advertising or by vigorously competing with rival shopkeepers. For the most part, all that these projects do is distract the customers from noticing that the salvation products for which we are making such grand claims are, on sober examination, shams. It is not easy to deal with God in his comprehensive work of salvation and so we go for something lesser. Anne Edwards, a fictional woman in an important American novel that fearlessly plots a quest for God's presence, notices how few ever notice the actual ways of God:

> God was at Sinai and within weeks, people were dancing in front of a golden calf. God walked in Jerusalem and days later, folks nailed Him up and then went back to work. Faced with the Divine, people took refuge in the banal, as though answering a cosmic multiple-choice question: If you saw a burning bush, would you (a) call 911, (b) get the hot dogs, or (c) recognize God? A vanishingly small number of people would recognize God, Anne had decided years before. . . .[25]

Salvation is God doing for us what we cannot do for ourselves. Salvation is a work of God that we cannot approximate or rival or reproduce. Salvation is of God and so the experience and response to salvation also has to do with God. We are certainly involved — the song begins with a grammatical flurry of first-person verbs and first-person pronouns: three first-person verbs, five first-person pronouns. This is no cool, objective laboratory dissection of a theological proposition. We are head-over-heels in on this. But we don't manage it. We don't direct it. What we do is worship. We "sing to the Lord" the Song of Salvation. The song doesn't explain, the song witnesses. As Moses and the Israelites sing the song they witness. In that worshiping witness they participate in the mystery. And so do we.

*   *   *

But however mysterious, that is, irreducible to reason or pragmatic reckoning, it is impossible not to notice the impact of the act of salvation on the way we live our lives: the salvation song redefines history. Apart from what is expressed and sung in the Song of Moses, history is sin-defined. But the Wonder at the Sea draws us into an understanding and participation in history that is salvation-defined. The Wonder at the Sea and the worshiping response in the Song of Moses proclaims and celebrates a salvation-defined history by those who participate in the history.

History considered extra-biblically deals with sin and the ramifications of sin. History as revelation deals with salvation and the ramifications of salvation. The Wonder at the Sea turns our sin-defined understanding of history on its head. Something happened under the leadership of Moses that day at the Red Sea that forever marked Israel's understanding of the way the world worked. The Wonder at the Sea is taken up into an act of worship: in the remembering that is worship the act of salvation is established in Israel's life as the fulcrum of history. This fulcrum provides the place of leverage by which everything that happens, in their lives and the lives of the nations, is understood and dealt with as an aspect of salvation.

In a salvation-defined history, sin is not diminished — if anything we are even more aware of it — but it is no longer definitive; salvation is definitive. Salvation provides the terms that set the limits, establish the boundaries, inform the conditions in which wars are fought, gardens planted, marriages arranged, goods and services bought and sold, elections conducted, funerals held, football games played, and meals cooked. These limits are grand, exceeding by far what we are used to. Only worship can approximate such conditions.

Given the onslaught of sin-evidence that hits us in the face every day, salvation-defined history is hard to believe. With centuries of Egyptian oppression behind them and still more centuries of Canaanite enmity ahead of them, it was hard for Israel to believe. But it is also quite clear that Israel, against all the evidence that history threw at them, did believe. They didn't always live what they believed, but they certainly believed it: they told the story, ate the supper, and sang the song that continuously set forth history as salvation-defined and not sin-defined. They also, although admittedly in a jerky stop-and-go fashion, expressed their belief in salvation in lives of prayer and obedience, social structures of justice and compassion, and a moral life that honored their core identity, male and female, as the image of God.

A sin-defined history understands history as primarily the experience of what men and women, some better and some worse than us, do. Both the statistics and stories are appalling: cruelty, hurt, injuries, betrayal, unfaithfulness, torture, killing, rape, abuse, injustice. There are bright spots, to be sure, but even the bright spots are hopelessly compromised by bad faith, corrupt motives, conscienceless exploitation, ignorant good intentions. It is impossible to find a single passage in history that displays humankind as sheer goodness, pure beauty, or flawless truth. Some historians take particular delight in picking up much admired and celebrated "great" men and women and making a public exhibit of their dark sides, the sins and crimes that they managed to conceal while preening on fame's pedestal. But it doesn't take a historian of genius to do it. The evidence, though sometimes suppressed, is abundant — any of us can play that game.

By contrast, a salvation-defined history accepts all the sin-evidence but penetratingly discerns the sovereignty of God and the work of salvation "in, through, and under" all of it. St. John put Israel's salvation perspective in an epigram: "he who is in you is greater than he who is in the world" (1 John 4:4). The "he who is in the world" is thoughtlessly and ignorantly presumed to be definitive for history. John, compressing the biblical salvation work into a phrase, says "not so — he who is in you is greater." We say, "Greater? Are you sure? Can this be true? Is this evangelical bluff? Pious bombast? Maybe this is 'spiritually' true but certainly not historically true."

But Israel never spiritualized salvation. The Song of Moses is emphatically historical, something *happened*. And what happened continues to happen.

The song is bracketed (by vv. 1-3 and 18) and then centered (vv. 11-12) in affirmations regarding this God who saves. Between the brackets and around the center it is all history: what happened at the Sea (vv. 4-10) and what will happen after the Sea as they are led into their new land (vv. 13-17). Given our habit of using the word "salvation" almost exclusively in terms of the individualized soul, a spiritual condition that deals with our interiority, our "relationship with God," this is significant.

Salvation does, of course, deal with the condition of the soul, but "soul," remember, is a totalizing term; there is no soul apart from history, with all of its economics and politics, science and geography, literature and arts, no soul apart from work and family, body and the neighborhood. The song expands the jurisdiction of salvation to cover everything that has happened and is happening and will happen. It is hardly a private affair between men and women and their God. Pharaoh's "picked officers" and the "chiefs of Edom" are also in the cast, the Sea behind them and the Land ahead of them.

The "he who is in the world" appears in history under many aliases: the Antichrist, the Serpent, the Devil, the Satan, the Tempter, Beelzebub, Rahab and Behemoth and Leviathan, the Great Dragon, the Roaring Lion, the Enemy, the Liar. These days "he who is in the world" for the most part works anonymously but can be discerned in the much reported "works of darkness."

It is easy, and common, for this perception of evil's omnipresence and omnipotence to bully many into a kind of moral/spiritual apathy, the "nothing-can-be-done" disease, and some into outright unbelief. And far too many Christians, uninstructed in the biblical story, adapt to the mood of the age. Failing a convinced knowledge that "greater is he that is in you than he that is in the world," that is, without a firmly *historical* grasp of salvation, many end up living timidly, scurrying like scared rabbits into religious holes where they maintain their faith in reduced dimensions; others over-compensate by living obnoxiously, like barking dogs voicing spiritual contempt for and superiority over history.

If we are to live fully and to the glory of God in history — which is to say, in the circumstances of our homes and workplaces, in the happenings of our nation and world — we simply must have an adequate, which is to say, a *biblical*, grasp of the pivotal, ongoing salvation action of God in history: God incessantly, relentlessly, effectively *saving* — "unresting, unhasting, and silent as light."[26] Salvation is comprehensive. Never mind that the saving is for the most part hidden and unreported. The huge, definitive historical fact for Israel is that "the horse and rider he has thrown into the sea."

*   *   *

What happened at the Sea became Israel's earliest confession and a stock element in their worship;[27] and the Song of Moses became their national anthem. It places their entire life as a people of God firmly in history. It does not offer an alternate "spiritual" world. It does not reduce their life to "mere" history by glorifying Israel or Israel's leaders. This is a God-sovereign world and the primary work of this God is salvation. This is who they are and where they live. This is how they came to be and what they are here for.

What is true for Israel is true for us: a saved people immersed in salvation-determined history in which we maintain a believing, participating involvement by worshiping the God of history.

Grounding Text (2): St. Mark

My choice for a grounding text for salvation from the New Testament is the Gospel of St. Mark. It makes a fine companion piece to Exodus. No one had ever written a Christian Gospel before Mark took up his pen. He created a new genre. It turned out to be a form of writing that quickly became both foundational and formative for living the Christian life. We are accustomed to believing that the Holy Spirit inspired the content of the Scriptures (2 Tim. 3:16), but it is just as true that the form is inspired, this new literary form that we call Gospel. There was nothing quite like it in existence, although Mark had good teachers in the Hebrew storytellers who gave us the books of Moses and Samuel.

The Bible as a whole comes to us in the form of narrative, and it is within this large, somewhat sprawling biblical narrative that St. Mark writes his Gospel. "We live mainly by forms and patterns," Wallace Stegner, one of our great contemporary storytellers, tells us; "if the forms are bad, we live badly."[28] Gospel is a true and good form, by which we live well. Storytelling creates a world of presuppositions, assumptions, and relations into which we enter. Stories invite us into a world other than our-

181

selves, and, if they are good and true stories, a world larger than ourselves. Bible stories are good and true stories, and the world that they invite us into is the world of God's creation and salvation and blessing.

Within this large, capacious context of the biblical story we learn to think accurately, behave morally, preach passionately, sing joyfully, pray honestly, obey faithfully. But we dare not abandon the story as we go off and do any or all of these things, for the minute we abandon the story, we reduce reality to the dimensions of our minds and feelings and experience. The moment we formulate our doctrines, draw up our moral codes, and throw ourselves into a life of discipleship and ministry apart from a continuous re-immersion in the story itself, we walk right out of the concrete and local presence and activity of God and set up our own shop.

The distinctiveness of the form "Gospel" is that it brings the centuries of Hebrew storytelling, God telling his story of creation and salvation through his people, to the story of Jesus, the mature completion of all the stories, in a way that is clearly revelation — that is, divine self-disclosure — and in a way that invites, more, *insists* on, our participation.

All this is in contrast to the ancient preference for myth-making, which more or less turns us into spectators of the supernatural. It is also in contrast to the modern preference for moral philosophy and "cracker barrel" wisdom that puts us in charge of our own salvation. "Gospel story" is a verbal way of accounting for reality that, like the incarnation that is its subject, is simultaneously divine and human. It *reveals,* that is, it shows us something we could never come up with on our own by observation or experiment or guess; and at the same time it *engages,* brings us into the action as recipients and participants, but without dumping the responsibility on us for making it turn out right.

This has enormous implications for the way we live, for the form itself protects us against two of the major ways in which we go off the rails: becoming frivolous spectators who clamor for new and more exotic entertainment out of heaven; or becoming anxious moralists who put our shoulders to the wheel and take on the burdens of the world. The very form of the text shapes responses in us that make it hard to become a mere spectator or a mere moralist. This is not a text that we master, it is one that we are mastered by.

It is significant, I think, that in the presence of a story, whether we are telling it or listening to it, we never have the feeling of being experts — there is too much we don't yet know, too many possibilities available, too much mystery and glory. Even the most sophisticated of stories tends to bring out the childlike in us — expectant, wondering, responsive, delighted — which, of course, is why the story is the child's favorite form of speech; why it is the Holy Spirit's dominant form of revelation; and why we adults, who like to pose as experts and managers of life, so often prefer explanation and information.

*   *   *

We don't read very long in this text by St. Mark before we realize that it is about some things that happened in and around Jesus in a thin slice of ancient history in Palestine under Roman rule; before we have finished we realize that it is about God working out our salvation in Jesus Christ. Jesus himself put it succinctly: The Son of man came "to give his life as a ransom for many" (Mark 10:45).

In some respects this is an odd kind of story, this Jesus salvation story. It tells us very little of what interests us in a story. We learn virtually nothing about Jesus that we really want to know. There is no description of his appearance. Nothing about his origin, friends, education, family. How are we to evaluate or understand this person? And there is very little reference to what he thought, to how he felt, his emotions, his interior struggles. There is a surprising, and disconcerting, reticence in regard to Jesus. We don't figure Jesus out, we don't search Jesus out, we don't get Jesus on our terms. Jesus and the salvation that he embodied are not consumer items.

There are others in the story, of course, many others — the sick and hungry, victims and outsiders, friends and enemies. And, by implication, all of us. But Jesus is always the subject. No event and no person appear in this story apart from Jesus. Jesus provides both context and content for salvation. Salvation turns out in practice (when we let St. Mark shape our practice) to be the attention and response we give the God-revealing Jesus. The text trains us in this attention and response. Line after line, page after page — Jesus, Jesus, Jesus. None of us provides the content for our own salvation; it is given to us. Jesus gives it to us. The text allows for no exceptions.

Colobodactylus

Our earliest traditions tell us that Mark wrote his Gospel in Rome in the company and presumably under the direction of St. Peter. Peter, leader of the original twelve apostles, placed first in every listing of the apostles, was in Rome being readied for martyrdom. In his presence and under his influence Mark wrote his story of Jesus. That, at least, is the tradition.

Somewhere along the way, St. Mark acquired a nickname: Colobodactylus, "stumpfinger." One suggestion accounting for the name is that Mark was a large man whose fingers were disproportionately small — stubby fingers. It sounds like an affectionate nickname, the kind we give to friends that we kid around with: Shorty, Slim, Blue-Eyes, Kitten, Colobodactylus, "Stumpfinger." It is easy to imagine that it originated in the circle of friends in Rome who saw him working away day by day writing his Gospel, who watched those short, thick fingers push that pen (stylus) back and forth across the parchment and jokingly noted the incongruity between the clumsy-looking fingers holding the pen and the swift-paced drama of the sentences laid down. There may have been at the same time a joking hint of congruity between Mark's conspicuously inelegant hands and what Reynolds Price calls his "pawky roughness of language."[29]

The apostle whom he served also had a nickname: *Peter*, Greek for "rock." But unlike his master's, Mark's nickname did not stick — only in Rome was Mark known as Colobodactylus. Tradition has it that after Peter's martyrdom, Mark went to Alexandria where he became the bishop. "Stumpfinger" probably did not seem appropriate for a bishop, and so he recovered his proper name.

*   *   *

St. Mark's story-telling is fast-paced, austere, and compellingly dramatic. Mark does not linger, does not elaborate, does not explain, does not digress. Event follows event, narrative details piling up pell-mell, seemingly without design. Careful observation discovers a design, a stunning and intricate design, but unobtrusive and concealed.[30] Mark as storyteller is entirely unpretentious. He hides his art, stripping the story of all finery or sophistication in either diction or syntax. This is drama without melodrama. Every detail is chosen with meticulous care and put in its place with great skill. The carefully rationed accumulation of narrative lines moves Jesus from the obscurity of itinerant teaching and healing in out-of-the-way Galilee into a suddenly floodlighted public notice in Jerusalem. There Roman and Jewish leaders together, fearing that he will prove fatal to their respective political and religious regimes, kill him. And here is the marvel: without the narrator's intruding into the story with comment or announcement, we end up convinced that Jesus is the anointed of God, here to save us from our sins and show us the way to live rightly: Follow this person!

This most unpretentious of storytellers (Stumpfinger!) wrote this most demanding and revealing story.

In the writing, a feature emerges that requires notice. Though St. Mark writes his story under the influence of the greatest of the apostles, Peter, he practically writes Peter out of the story by making clear that Peter is, in actual fact, the lead sinner. The true relation between Jesus and his followers is at stake here. Peter as the lead apostle has the potential for moving into a place of prominence alongside Jesus. By portraying Peter as the lead sinner, Mark makes sure that will not happen. If Peter as leader can be prevented from moving into the limelight with Jesus, it is accomplished for all Christians forever. And that is what Mark does. It may be his finest accomplishment as storywriter — in Peter's presence and under Peter's authority and influence, he keeps Peter from taking over the story. The glorification of Peter is blocked at the source. Whatever stellar qualities Peter acquired through his leadership and preaching in the early church, they are excised from the story; only his weaknesses and failures are kept. The Jesus story includes a colorful company of others, but none of them is presented in such a way as to obscure or compromise the unique and unprecedented centrality of Jesus. Peter is portrayed as a bungler, as a blasphemer, and as a faithless human being. But not *merely* Peter, Peter as *leader*. Nor do the other chosen disciples become examples for us to look up to or follow. Thick-skulled and dull-witted, they turn out to be a pack of cowards. Sir Edwin Hoskyns and Noel Davey remark on the "staggering brutality" with which Mark writes the disciples out of any part of Jesus' work.[31]

St. Mark, in other words, tells this foundational salvation story in such a way as to prevent us from setting apart any of our leaders as spiritually upper-class, to prevent us from putting them on pedestals. This is a salvation story and the Savior is Jesus. Nothing in the storytelling is permitted to divert our attention from Jesus. There is nothing here that will play into our preference for dealing with famous celebrities instead of the despised Jesus. There is nothing glamorous or inspiring about even the best of the leaders: every one, down to the last man and woman, is saved by grace.

Maintaining that simplicity and focus — that salvation is by God's initiative and grace in Jesus — has proved to be one of the most difficult things to maintain in the Christian community. In the course of the generations, Mark's storytelling has not prevented us from developing celebrity cults, elevating Peter and others to prominence, and thereby providing seemingly easier ways of dealing with our souls than dealing with God in Jesus. And it has not prevented us from being diverted by spiritual and religious novelties that promise shortcuts to soul entertainment. But Mark's story continues to provide the honest ground to which we all return from our God-detours and soul-diversions.

The Death of Jesus

In reading St. Mark's salvation text, it doesn't take us long to see that the entire story funnels into the narration of a single week of Jesus' life, the week of his passion, death, and resurrection. Of these three items, death gets the most extensive and detailed treatment. If we are asked to say as briefly as possible what Mark's Gospel consists of, we must say "the death of Jesus."

This doesn't sound very promising, especially for those of us who are looking for a text by which to live, a text by which to nurture our souls. But there it is. There are sixteen chapters in the story. For the first eight chapters Jesus is alive, strolling unhurriedly through the villages and backroads of Galilee, bringing men, women, and children to life — delivering them from evil, healing their maimed and sick bodies, feeding them, demonstrating his sovereignty over storm and sea, telling marvelous stories, gathering and training disciples, announcing that they are poised on the brink of a new era, God's kingdom, which at that very moment is breaking in upon them.

And then, just as he has everyone's attention, just as the momentum of life, life, and more life is at its crest, he starts talking about death. The last eight chapters of the Gospel are dominated by death talk.

The abrupt shift in Jesus' language from life to death (the shift occurs at 8:31-34) also signals a change of pace. As the story is told through the first eight chapters, there is a leisurely and meandering quality to the narration. Jesus doesn't seem to be going anywhere in particular — he more or less drifts from village to village, goes off by himself into the hills to pray, worships in the synagogues, gives the impression that he has time to take meals with anyone who invites him over, to go boating with his friends on the lake. We do not construe this relaxed pace as aimlessness or indolence, for energy and intensity are always evident. But through these Galilean years, Jesus appears to have all the time in the world, which, of course, he does have.

But with the death announcement that changes. Now he heads straight for Jerusalem. Urgency, gravity, and a goal now characterize the narration. The direction changes, the pace changes, the mood changes. Three times in three successive chapters Jesus is explicit: he is going to suffer and be killed and rise again (8:31; 9:31; 10:33).

And then it happens: death. Jesus' death is narrated carefully and precisely (Mark 14–15). No part of his life is told with the detail given to his death. There can hardly be any question about Mark's intent: the plot and emphasis and meaning of Jesus is his death.

This death emphasis is not an idiosyncrasy of Mark, a morbid obsession of his that distorted the basic story, for this same sequence and proportion is preserved by Mark's successors in Gospel narration, Matthew and Luke. They elaborate Mark's basic text in various ways, but preserve his proportions. John, who comes at the story from quite a different angle, dazzling us with images of light and life, actually increases the emphasis on death, giving half of his allotted space to the passion week. All four Gospel writers do essentially the same thing; they tell us the story of Jesus' death and write their respective introductions to it. And Paul — exuberant, passionate, hyperbolic Paul — skips the narration completely and simply punches out the conclusion, "Christ died for us" (Rom. 5:8-9); "I decided to know nothing among you except Jesus Christ, and him crucified" (1 Cor. 2:2).

But there is far more here than the simple fact of death, although there is that most emphatically. This is a carefully *defined* death. It is defined as voluntary. Jesus did not have to go to Jerusalem; he went on his own volition. He gave his assent to death. This was not accidental death; this was not unavoidable death.

His death is further defined as sacrificial. Jesus accepted death that others might receive life, "his life a ransom for many" (10:45). He explicitly defined his death as sacrificial, that is, as a means to life for others, when he instituted the Eucharist: "he took a loaf of bread. . . . Take; this is my body. . . . Then he took a cup. . . . This is my blood of the covenant, which is poured out for many" (14:22-24).

And this death is finally defined in the company of resurrection. Each of the three explicit death announcements concludes with a statement of resurrection. This death is a means to life, a means to salvation. This doesn't make it any less a death, but it is a quite differently defined death than we are accustomed to dealing with.

In contrast to this portrayal of death in Mark's Gospel — Jesus' intentionality regarding it, its sacrificial nature, and its resurrection context — our culture (whether secular or ecclesial) typically either characterizes death as tragic or deals with it by procrastination.

The view of death as tragic is a legacy of the Greeks. The Greeks wrote with elegance of tragic deaths — lives pursued with the best of intentions but then enmeshed in circumstances that brought a fatal flaw into play and, indifferent to heroism or hope, cancelled the intentions.

The death of Jesus is not tragic.

Procrastinated death is a legacy of modern medicine. In a culture where life is reduced to heartbeat and brainwave, death can never be accepted as having meaning beyond itself. Since there is no more to life than can be accounted for by biology — no meaning, no spirituality, no salvation — increasingly desperate attempts are made to put it off, to delay it, to deny it.

The death of Jesus is not procrastinated.

We counter our culture's attitudes to death by letting Mark's salvation story shape our understanding of Jesus' death as precisely a death that is, as our Nicene Creed has it, "for us and for our salvation."

*   *   *

The story of Jesus' death as told by St. Mark is a sharply etched dramatic sequence of twelve scenes. Two sentences (14:1-2) introduce the death-of-Jesus drama. The time is precise, two days before Passover, as thousands of lambs are being killed for the annual ritual celebration of the Exodus salvation, the defining event of Jewish history. At the same time religious leaders are on the hunt to catch and kill Jesus. Death is in the air.

1. The Anointing (14:3-11). The passion story begins in the domestic setting of Simon the Leper's home in Bethany where Jesus and some friends have been invited for a meal. During the meal a woman comes and anoints Jesus by breaking a jar of very expensive perfume and pouring it over his head. Some of the guests are irate and openly criticize the woman for her wasteful extravagance. They think the perfume should have been sold and the money given to the poor. Jesus intervenes and defends the woman's action as "a beautiful thing" and interprets it as anointing "my body beforehand for burying." Jesus' murder, which at the moment is being plotted, is accepted as a fait accompli. The woman preempts the murder with her anointing. By her lavish act this body that will soon be a corpse is pre-anointed for its burial.

Judas immediately counters the woman's extravagance by making a shrewd business deal with those plotting the murder. If the woman insists on wasting money on the death-marked Jesus, Judas will make money on it.

2. The Supper (14:12-25). The next day is Passover. The disciples, instructed by Jesus, prepare the meal. All over Jerusalem lambs are being slaughtered and this Passover meal is being prepared following the Exodus instructions. This is the annual ritual with its story and supper and song that keeps salvation at the center of their identity. The Twelve are well aware that their people have been preparing and eating this supper for over a thousand years. On this night, Jesus presides over the supper. While they eat, Jesus tells his disciples that he is about to be betrayed to those who will kill him and then proceeds to identify the bread they are eating and the wine they are drinking with himself, his body and blood: "this unleavened bread that you are eating — this is me, my flesh; this wine you are drinking, this is me, the blood from the sacrificial killing of the Passover lamb in this chalice here on the table before you. My death is going to become your life."

3. The Prayer (14:26-42). They leave the supper table and walk a mile or so east toward the Mount of Olives. As they walk, Jesus speaks darkly to them about their imminent faithlessness, but speaks in the very next sentence of his sure faithfulness to them (v. 28). They come to Gethsemane, a garden at the base of the Mount of Olives. Jesus tells the disciples to wait there for him, while he prays. He takes Peter, James, and John with him to his place of prayer. He goes on a little further, off by himself, and prays. It is an agonizing prayer: he prays to his Father, asking that he not be killed

("this cup"); he also prays his willingness to be killed. He comes back to his three closest disciples and finds them sleeping. He reprimands them — he was expecting them to be praying with and for him. The sequence — Jesus' praying, the disciples' sleeping, Jesus' reprimand — is repeated three times. Then Jesus tells them that it is time to go, time to keep his appointment with death.

4. The Arrest (14:43-52). Judas shows up right on time, leading a mob prepared for violence. Judas identifies Jesus with his famous betrayal kiss and Jesus is taken into custody. A sword is swung, the high priest's slave loses his ear, but that's as far as resistance goes. The disciples hightail it from Gethsemane, the place of their prayer meeting, leaving Jesus to his fate.

5. The Trial before the Jewish Council (14:53-65). The Jewish leaders assemble in the courtyard of the high priest. They recruit witnesses who will bring accusations that will justify a death sentence against Jesus. They have no trouble getting the witnesses (doesn't it surprise us that it was so easy to find people eager to assist in killing Jesus?), but since the witnesses weren't properly coached their stories end up contradicting one another. The high priest, impatient with the dithering of the kangaroo court, interrupts and confronts Jesus directly: "Are you the Messiah, the Son of the Blessed One?" "I am," Jesus replied. The high priest judged the "I am" as blasphemy. That settled it. The verdict: Guilty. The sentence: Death.

6. The Denial by Peter (14:66-72). At the same time that Jesus is being tried before the Jewish council by the high priest, Peter is on trial (informally) in the courtyard below with the high priest's maid in the dual role of prosecutor and judge. We are well aware that Peter was the first to confess Jesus as the Christ, the identity on which the high priest has just based his death sentence on Jesus. At the very moment that the high priest questions Jesus on his Christ identity, the high priest's serving maid questions Peter on his association with this Christ. While Jesus is admitting, simply and without qualification, that, yes, he is the Christ, Peter, with curse-punctuated vehemence, is denying that he has ever laid eyes on Jesus. And not only once; three times. Peter, the "first" apostle: first to confess Jesus, first to deny Jesus.

7. The Trial before the Roman Court (15:1-15). It is now morning. The Jewish council marches Jesus, their death-sentenced criminal, in handcuffs to the Roman court. Jerusalem is an occupied city under Roman rule and the Jews have no authority to kill Jesus. So they deliver Jesus to the Ro-

man governor, Pilate. He examines Jesus on political grounds, "Are you the King of the Jews?" Jesus replies, "You say so." Neither a denial nor an admission; in effect, "Those are your words, not mine." The Jewish leaders jump in with a flurry of scattershot accusations. Jesus is silent.

Pilate, well-trained in judicial procedures and matters of justice (Rome was famous for its justice system), senses that this is a put-up job and so attempts to release Jesus. It was customary during Passover for the Romans to release one prisoner. It would be a convenient way to set Jesus free from the hysterical, mob-like conditions that Pilate found himself dealing with. But when he tries to do it, the crowd, prompted and incited by the Jewish leaders, asks instead for Barabbas, an imprisoned political murderer. "But what about Jesus?" asks Pilate. The crowd, now in a frenzy, shouts "Crucify him." Pilate asks, "On what grounds?" But there was no answer to that, only the hysterical, "Crucify him."

Pilate caved in to the pressure of the Passover crowd. He released Barabbas, whipped Jesus, and turned him over to be killed by crucifixion. So much for Roman justice.

8. The Mock Worship (15:16-20). Jesus is now in the hands of the Roman soldiers who will crucify him. The soldiers, probably bored through inactivity, now have some fun with Jesus. They had heard Pilate's question, "Are you the King of the Jews?" They pick up on it and put on a skit — throw a royal purple robe across Jesus' shoulders, place a thorn-plaited crown on his head, proclaim his kingship, bang on his head with sticks, spit on him, and kneel before him in mock homage. Great fun. Then they take him out to kill him on a throne cross.

9. The Crucifixion (15:21-32). Simon of Cyrene carries the cross that Jesus had earlier assigned to all who would follow him (8:34). The soldiers use that cross to kill Jesus on the gruesomely named Skull Hill (Golgotha) at nine o'clock in the morning on the political charge of sedition ("King of the Jews"). Two robbers are also crucified with him, one on either side. The atmosphere is anything but solemn: soldiers are throwing dice for his clothes, passersby taunt him, the Jewish leaders mock him, even his two criminal companions in crucifixion join in the black gallows humor. Crucifixion is a merciless fusion of shame and pain drawn out to the extremity.

10. The Death (15:33-39). Three hours later, it is high noon, the sky grows dark, a darkness that continues for the next three hours while Jesus dies a slow death. At three o'clock in the afternoon, Jesus cries out loudly,

"My God, my God, why hast thou forsaken me?" People who are standing around the cross scurry around wondering if something supernatural is about to take place — one man puts a vinegar-soaked sponge on a pole and sticks it in Jesus' face (to revive him, keep the action going?). But there is no miracle — at least, not the kind they were looking for. Jesus cries out again, loudly. He gives his last breath. Across town in the temple the curtain that encloses the Holy of Holies is ripped from top to bottom. Jesus has been on the cross for six hours. The centurion assigned to the crucifixion has seen the whole thing; he delivers his witness, "Truly this man was God's Son!" Jesus is dead.

11. The Women (15:40-41). Women, "many" women, are there at the cross, looking on, a merciful presence throughout those six hours of humiliation and pain, abandonment and derision. They stay, a loyal, prayerful presence through the hard hours. The women are friends from Galilee who accompanied and served Jesus. They stick with him to the end. Three of them are named.

12. The Burial (15:42-47). Evening approaches, Friday evening. Sabbath begins at sundown. One of the Jewish leaders, Joseph of Arimathea (not all of the Jewish leaders were in on the plot to kill Jesus), asks Pilate for the body of Jesus so that he can bury him. After Pilate makes sure that Jesus is really dead (the centurion provides that assurance), he gives him the body. Joseph reverently wraps Jesus' body in a linen shroud, with dignity places him in a nearby rock tomb, and rolls a stone wheel across the entrance for protection. Two of the women who had kept vigil at the cross (the two Marys) see him do it.

*   *   *

The dramatic narrative can be visualized as a pyramid (see p. 193). Scenes 1 and 12 form the base; the two opposing sides then ascend in pairs: 2-11, 3-10, 4-9; but instead of an apex, the final pairs, 5-8 and 6-7, form a square capstone.

The *first and last* segments are burial scenes: The anointing for burial ("she has anointed my body beforehand for its burial"), and the actual burial ("laid it in a tomb") by Joseph of Arimathea.

The *second and eleventh* scenes are eucharistic gatherings of Jesus' friends in the setting of his death: The disciples with Jesus as he enacts his death in the bread/flesh and wine/blood of the Passover meal; the women

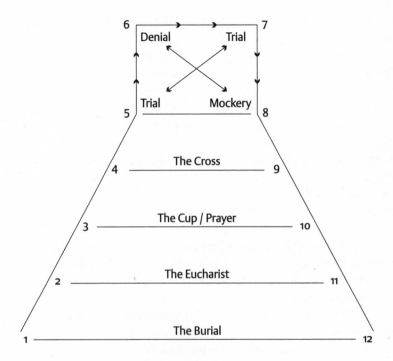

followers of Jesus present with Jesus at the cross throughout the six-hour breaking of his flesh and pouring out of his blood.

The *third and tenth* scenes are prayers of Jesus: Jesus' prayer in Gethsemane that the death cup might pass from him and the prayer of dereliction on the cross as he drinks that very cup.

The *fourth and ninth* scenes contrast the man who betrays Jesus with the man who helps Jesus: Judas betrays Jesus to his death by crucifixion and Simon of Cyrene carries his cross for him to Golgotha, the place of crucifixion.

Scenes *five, six, seven, and eight* together form the capstone. Here the pattern is more complex. *Five and six* are sequential, scene *five* set in the high priest's court as the high priest condemns Jesus on the religious charge of blasphemy ("the Messiah, the Son of the Blessed One") in the trial before the Jewish council, and scene *six* set in the high priest's courtyard as the high priest's maid evokes Peter's denial of Jesus in the courtyard trial. Scenes *six and seven* place Peter in parallel with Pilate, the leader of the apostles denying Jesus and the leader of the Romans condemning Jesus — a double rejection: the person closest to Jesus and the person most remote from Jesus rejecting him; the foreign outsider who hasn't the slightest idea of who Jesus is or might be now paired with the apostolic insider who was the first to recognize and confess Jesus' messianic identity, both teaming up to say "no" to Jesus. Scenes *seven and eight* follow the sequential pattern of the high priest's court/courtyard (as in five and six) but this time in the Roman governor's court where Jesus is tried on political charges ("Are you the King of the Jews?"), the Roman governor presiding over the parody of justice that delivered Jesus to crucifixion as "King of the Jews" (scene seven) followed by the Roman soldiers staging a cruel mockery of Jesus as that King (scene 8).

A chiastic pattern can also be discerned in these four "capstone" scenes: Peter's denial of Jesus as the Christ in scene *six* connects diagonally to the soldiers' mockery of Jesus as King in scene *eight*; and the Jewish religious trial of Jesus in scene *five* connects diagonally to the Roman political trial of Jesus in scene *seven*.

St. Mark's death narrative is an intricately interwoven web of echoes, parallels, contrasts, allusions, and repetitions. The death of Jesus gathers everything into it and fashions the finished work of salvation. Everything that goes into the work of salvation is found in this death. And everything that goes into our involvement in salvation is found in this death.

This death, in all its details, has penetrated the Christian imagination as nothing else has. Music, art, literature, drama, architecture. But most of all its effects continue to be on display in the unnumbered men and women who daily give up their own attempts to save themselves, trying to make something out of their lives on their own terms, and take up Jesus' cross and follow him. St. Mark has given us the story of Jesus' death in such a way that it continues to resonate and reverberate in our lives as nothing more nor less than salvation.

Our Salvation

It was clear in Exodus and it is clear in Mark's Gospel that we contribute nothing to our salvation. But we are invited to participate. In the first half of the Gospel all sorts of people are drawn into the life of Jesus, experience his compassion, his healings, his deliverance, his call, his peace. We find ourselves implicitly included. In the second half of the Gospel, this experience of personal participation becomes explicit.

At the center of the Gospel there is a bridge between the Galilean years narrating the life of Jesus and the final Jerusalem weeks closing in on the death of Jesus. This bridge turns out to be strategic for guiding us into a participation in salvation in a way that is congruent with Jesus' life and death as Mark so carefully narrates it. It goes without saying, I think, that Mark was not a journalist, writing daily bulletins on the first-century activities of Jesus. Nor was he a propagandist, attempting to enlist us in a cause that had designs on history. His Gospel is spiritual theology in action, a form of writing that draws us into a living participation with the text.

Mark 8:27–9:9 is the bridge passage, set at the center of the story so that one half of the Gospel, the multiple Galilean evocations of life, falls symmetrically on one side, and, on the other side, the single-minded travel to Jerusalem and death.

The transitional passage consists of two stories. The first story, Jesus' call for renunciation as he and his disciples start out on the road to Jerusalem, provides the ascetic dimension in salvation (8:27–9:1). The second story, Jesus' transfiguration on Mount Tabor, provides the aesthetic dimension in salvation (9:2-9).

The stories are bracketed by affirmations of Jesus' identity as God among us: first, Peter saying, "You are the Messiah" (8:29); second, the voice out of heaven saying, "This is my beloved Son" (9:7 RSV). Human testimony at one end, divine attestation at the other.

Before considering the two stories, I want to insist that we keep them in context and that we maintain their connection, one with the other. The context is the life and death of the God-revealing Jesus. Mark's Gospel has Jesus as its subject. Out of context, these stories can only be misunderstood. They do not stand on their own. They do not give us a spiritual theology that we can walk off with and exploit on our own terms.

And these stories are organically connected. They must not be torn apart. They are the two-beat rhythm in a single life of salvation, not two alternate ways of being in history, of participating in God's salvation work in history. The stories bring together the ascetic and aesthetic movements, the no and the yes that work together at the heart of the life of salvation. Participation in salvation, as revealed in Jesus, requires appropriate and discerning employment of both words, the yes and the no.

The Ascetic

First, let us consider the ascetic movement, God's "no" in Jesus. Jesus' words are brief and stark: If any want to become my followers, let them deny themselves and take up their cross and follow me (8:34). The ascetic life deals with life on the road with Jesus to his death.

Two verbs leap from the sentence and pounce on us: deny yourself and take up your cross. Renunciation and death. It feels like an assault, an attack. We recoil.

But then we notice that these two negatives are bracketed by the positive verb, "follow," first as an infinitive, then as an imperative. "If anyone wants to follow *(akolouthein)*" opens the sentence; "you follow me *(akoloutheitō)*" concludes it. Jesus is going someplace; he invites us to come along. There is no hostility in that. It sounds, in fact, quite glorious. So glorious, in fact, that the great verb "follow" sheds glory on the negative verbs that call for renunciation and death.

There is always a strong ascetic element in salvation. Following Jesus means *not* following the death-procrastinating, death-denying practices of a culture that by obsessively pursuing life under the aegis of idols and ideologies ends up with a life that is so constricted and diminished that it is hardly worthy of the name.

Grammatically, the negative, our capacity to say "no," is one of the most impressive features of our language. The negative is our access to freedom. Only humans can say "no." Animals can't say "no." Animals do what instinct dictates or what training embeds in them. "No" is a freedom word. I don't have to do what either my glands or my culture tells me to do. The judicious, well-placed "no" frees us from careening down many a blind alley, from bushwacking through many a rough detour, frees us from debilitating distractions and seductive sacrilege. The art of saying "no" sets us free to follow Jesus.

If we adhere carefully to St. Mark's text, we will never associate the ascetic with the life-denying. Ascetic practice sweeps out the clutter of the god-pretentious self, making ample space for access to Father, Son, and Holy Spirit; it embraces and prepares for a kind of death that the culture knows nothing about, making room for the dance of resurrection. Whenever we are around someone who is doing this well, we notice the lightness of step, the nimbleness of spirit, the quickness to laughter. H. C. G. Moule wrote that these dominical negatives "may have to carve deep lines in heart and life; but the chisel need never deface the brightness of the material."[32]

The Aesthetic

Alongside St. Mark's ascetic is his aesthetic. This is God's yes in Jesus. Peter and James and John see Jesus transfigured before them on the mountain into cloud-brightness in the company of Moses and Elijah, and hear God's blessing, "This is my beloved Son; listen to him" (9:7 RSV). The aesthetic deals with life on the mountain with Jesus.

The word "beauty" does not show up in the story, but beauty is what the disciples experienced, and what we find ourselves experiencing — the beauty of Jesus transfigured, Law and prophets, Moses and Elijah absorbed into the beauty of Jesus, the beautiful blessing "My beloved . . .": everything fitting together, the luminous interior of Jesus spilling out onto the mountain; history and religion beautifully personalized and brought into deep, resonating harmony, the declaration of love.

There is always a strong aesthetical element in salvation. Climbing the mountain with Jesus means coming upon beauty that takes our breath away. Keeping company with Jesus involves contemplating his glory, listening in on this vast, intergenerational conversation consisting of Law and Prophet and Gospel that takes place in Jesus, hearing the divine confirmation of revelation in Jesus. When God's Spirit makes its appearance, we recognize the appearance as beautiful.

Jesus transfigured: Jesus is the form of revelation, "and the light does not fall on this form from above and from outside, rather it breaks forth from the form's interior."[33] The only adequate response that can be made to light is to keep our eyes open, to attend to what is illumined — adoration.

The aesthetic impulse in salvation has to do with training in perception, acquiring a taste for what is being revealed in Jesus. We are not good at this. Our senses have been dulled by sin. The world, for all its vaunted celebration of sensuality, is relentlessly anaesthetic, obliterating feeling by ugliness and noise, draining the beauty out of people and things so that they are functionally efficient, scornful of the aesthetic except as it can be contained in a museum or a flower garden. Our senses require healing and rehabilitation so that they are adequate for receiving and responding to visitations and appearances of Spirit, God's Holy Spirit, for, as Jean

Sulivan says, "The fundamental insight of the Bible . . . is that the invisible can speak only by the perceptible."[34]

These bodies of ours with their five senses are not impediments to a life of faith; our sensuality is not a barrier to spirituality; it is our only access to it. Thomas Aquinas was convinced that *asensuality* was a vice, the rejection of one's senses too often leading to sacrilege.[35] When St. John wanted to assure some early Christians of the authenticity of his spiritual experience, he did it by calling on the witness of his senses of sight, hearing, and touch — "what we have heard . . . seen with our eyes . . . touched with our hands, concerning the word of life" (1 John 1:1). In the opening sentences of 1 John he calls on the witness of his senses seven times.

St. Mark's strategically placed stories are essential guidance as we participate in the salvation worked out in the person of Jesus, this glorious affirmation juxtaposed to the stern negation. In company with Jesus, these bodies of ours so magnificently equipped for seeing, hearing, touching, smelling, and tasting, climb the mountain (itself a strenuous physical act) where, in astonished adoration, we are trained to see the light and hear the words that reveal God to us.

*   *   *

This seems simple enough. And it is. St. Mark does not go in for subtleties — he sets it before us plainly. But he also knows that, simple and obvious as it is, it is easy to get it wrong. Peter's initial response in both the ascetic road story and the aesthetic mountain story was wrong.

On the road, Peter tried to avoid the cross; on the mountain he tried to grab the glory. Peter rejected the ascetic way by offering Jesus a better plan, a way of salvation in which no one has to be inconvenienced. Jesus, in the sternest rebuke recorded in the Gospels, called him Satan and sent him to his room. Peter rejected the aesthetic way by offering to build memorial chapels on the mountain, a way of worship in which he could take over from Jesus and set up a salvation franchise, provide something hands-on and practical. This time Jesus just ignored him.

Peter's propensity to get it wrong keeps us on our toes. Century after century we Christians keep getting it wrong — and in numerous ways. We get the ascetic of salvation wrong; we get the aesthetic of salvation wrong. Our history books are full of ascetic aberrations, full of aesthetic aberrations. Every time we get sloppy in reading St. Mark's salvation text and leave the company of Jesus, we get it wrong.

*   *   *

One more thing. These two stories, strategically placed at the center of the Gospel, are not the center of the story. St. Mark's story, we keep reminding ourselves, is a story about Jesus, not us. In fact, if we deleted this section (8:27–9:9) from the text it would still be the same story. Nothing in this road and mountain narrative is essential to understanding the story of Jesus as he lived, was crucified, and rose from the dead. If we deleted his account of the road and the mountain, we would still know everything Mark chose to tell us about Jesus as the revelation of God, a full accounting of Jesus' work of salvation.

But what we would not know, at least not nearly as well, is our place in the salvation story. Here in this bridge passage, Mark takes us aside and invites us to become full participants in salvation and shows us how to do it. We are not simply *told* that Jesus is the Son of God; we not only *become* beneficiaries of his atonement; we are invited to die his death and live his life with the freedom and dignity of participants.

And here is the marvelous thing: we enter the center of the story without becoming the center of the story.

Salvation is always in danger of self-absorption. When I become intrigued with matters of my soul there is the ever-present danger that I begin to treat God as a mere accessory to my experience. And so salvation requires much vigilance. Spiritual theology is, among other things, the exercise of this vigilance. Spiritual theology is the discipline and art of training us into a full and mature participation in Jesus' story while at the same time preventing us from taking over the story.

For this, Mark's Gospel, with Exodus as precedent, is our grounding text. The stories at the center, the road and mountain stories, are clearly proleptic — they anticipate Jesus' crucifixion and resurrection. They immerse us and train us in the ascetic negations and aesthetic affirmations, but they don't leave us there; they cast us forward in faith and obedience into the salvation life that is finally and only complete in the definitive no and glorious yes of Jesus crucified and risen.

Cultivating Fear-of-the-Lord in History:
Eucharist and Hospitality

Given all of this, the mess of history in which we find ourselves, the kerygmatic death of Jesus announcing the good news of salvation, the ever-present dangers of a moralism that offers to put us in charge of our lives, the great grounding texts of Exodus and Mark's Gospel, what do we do? What is there left for us to do?

Continuing to use Albert Borgmann's phrase, "focal practice," we come upon the dominical command, "Do this . . .": Eat the bread and drink the cup, Jesus' body and blood. Receive the Eucharist.[36] This is what Jesus told us to do. And this is what Christians have done ever since (1 Cor. 11:23-26; Luke 22:19). We receive Jesus crucified. We remember Jesus' death and receive his broken body and poured-out blood for the remission of our sins. We hold out our open hands and receive what God does for us in Jesus. We don't take what we are given and then go off and do whatever we will with it; we sit at the Table and eat and drink. We become what we receive. Christ is, we are. In receiving the Eucharist we re-affirm our identity, "Christ in you [me!], the hope of glory" (Col. 1:27). In receiving the Eucharist we relive, remember, the Exodus Passover and the Last Supper.[37] Each time we receive the Eucharist we again let Jesus take us with him into the comprehensive drama of his death that pulls us as praying participants into the life of salvation. Before *we do* anything for God, we receive what God in *Christ does* for us.

It is nothing less than astonishing, considering the conflicts and variations in practice that mark the Christian church across the continents and centuries, that this Supper has been eaten so consistently and similarly under Jesus' command "do this. . . ." We have come up with different reasons, developed different theologies for understanding what Jesus is doing as he feeds us in this Meal and what we are doing as we receive it, but as we sit at Table (or kneel or stand) with Jesus as host we do and continue to do exactly as he commanded us: we eat the bread and drink the cup in "remembrance of me" and "proclaim the Lord's death until he comes." Spread across a spectrum of highly liturgical Greek Orthodox, Roman Catholic, and Anglican congregations clustered at one end, and storefront missions, independent Bible-believing gatherings, and charismatic congregations at the other, with a middle made up of establishment Baptists, Methodists, Presbyterians, and Congregationalists, we have done this. (Quakers, as I will note again later, are the one exception.)

The Eucharist

> Bread of the world in mercy broken,
> Wine of the soul in mercy shed,
> By whom the words of life were spoken,
> And in whose death our sins are dead;
>
> Look on the heart by sorrow broken,
> Look on the tears by sinners shed;
> And be Thy feast to us the token
> That by Thy grace our souls are fed.
>
> Reginald Heber[38]

We receive the Eucharist. Receiving the Holy Eucharist is our focal fear-of-the-Lord practice as we participate in the play of Christ in salvation.[39] St. Paul's instructions tell us that two things take place in the Eucharist, remembrance of Jesus and proclamation of Jesus.

"Remembrance of me." The Greek term, *anamnēsis*, translated "remembrance," is more than a mental activity; it is a reenacting in the Supper itself what Jesus did. It involves more than just refreshing the memory of what Jesus did; it involves us in participating right now, around this Table, in what he did and now continues to do.[40] The remembrance combines words and actions: the whole Christ is re-presented, speaking to us in words, offering himself in actions. Luther and Calvin, preeminent among Reformation theologians, were bold to assert the real presence of Christ in the Eucharist — this ritual *anamnēsis* of God's physical-spiritual way of saving, from the Exodus through Jesus to now.

"Proclaim the Lord's death." This is the second thing that takes place as the Eucharist is received. Jesus died on the cross to save us (the world! — John 3:16) from our sins. The Supper is a preached parable, a proclamation in word and action of Jesus' sacrificial death as the "[Passover] Lamb of God who takes away the sin of the world" (John 1:29). The primary thing that we do in the world of salvation, the foundational act of obedience for the Christian who wants to continue and deepen participation in salvation, is to receive the body and blood of Christ in the Supper. Salvation is accomplished in this death, and only in this death.

Remember and proclaim are the magnetic poles of the Eucharist: they operate simultaneously but in polarity, the "remember" a continuous reorientation to the North Pole in the action of Christ on the cross that accomplishes salvation, and the "proclaim" a continuous reorientation to the South Pole, the articulation of that crucified Christ in kerygmatic words and acts, for "how are they to hear without someone to proclaim him?" (Rom. 10:14). If the "remember" and the "proclaim" get isolated from one another, the eucharistic compass that keeps our salvation-participating lives headed the same direction and in step with the salvation-accomplishing life of Christ malfunctions.

The Eucharist stands as a bulwark against reducing our participation in salvation to the exercise of devotional practices before God or being recruited to run errands for God. It is hard to get through our heads, but the fact is that we are not in charge of salvation and we can add nothing to it. Left to ourselves to decide what is appropriate, we will only distract or dilute. Salvation is a way of life in which what we cannot do for ourselves is done for us by Jesus on the cross. At the Supper we renew our understanding and obedience in this salvation reality and receive over and over again what we cannot take or perform for ourselves but only receive. "Do this." This Supper, received in the fear-of-the-Lord, is the remembrance and the proclamation that keep salvation rooted and grounded in Christ, and only in Christ.

Just as Sabbath-keeping protects creation from the sacrilege of being taken over by us, so Eucharist protects salvation from being dominated by our feelings and projects. Whatever we do in this world of salvation has to be rooted and grounded in the death of Christ on the cross. Receiving the Eucharist is the definitive practice, the focal practice that keeps us attentive and responsive to Jesus as present and saving. The cultivation of this awareness and responsiveness is fundamental to anything that we do.

Receiving the Eucharist, like other aspects of the fear-of-the-Lord, is rooted deep in the soil of not-doing. In this intentional, disciplined passivity we become aware that the work of salvation is far wider and deeper than just us. It *is* a work in us — most emphatically in us — but it is also far more and other than us. All of history is subject to God's salvation. A deep understanding of this prevents our salvation lives from becoming ghettoized. We cultivate fear-of-the-Lord so that salvation, God's way of dealing with what is wrong with the world and with us, will develop and mature in us on God's terms, not ours.

By grounding ourselves in not-doing we gain time and space to realize that there is far more being done to us than we will ever comprehend.

In God's saving work, God does for us what we cannot do for ourselves —
and so we simply let God do it. Much of what other people tell us about
ourselves (not all of it) is wrong. And much of what we understand ourselves to be (not all of it) is wrong. Which means that much of what we do
and think we need and ask for is also wrong — not sinful necessarily, but
inappropriate in a life of salvation.

The Eucharist is the definitive action practiced in the Christian community that keeps Jesus Christ before us as the Savior of the world and our
Savior, and ourselves as sinners in need of being saved. The Eucharist is
the sacramental act that pulls us into actual material participation with
Christ (eating and drinking bread and wine) as he gives his very life "for us
and for our salvation" (Nicene Creed). Without the Eucharist as focal practice, it is very easy to drift off into imagining Jesus as our Great Example
whom we will imitate, or our Great Teacher from whom we will learn, or
our Great Hero by whom we will be inspired. And without the Eucharist it
is very easy to drift into a spirituality that is dominated by ideas about Jesus instead of receiving life from Jesus. The Eucharist says a plain "no" to
all that. The Eucharist puts Jesus in his place: dying on the cross and giving
us that sacrificed life. And it puts us in our place: opening our hands and
receiving the remission of our sins, which is our salvation.

The Christian community is never going to give up teaching moral
behavior, giving instruction in the commandments of Moses and the imperatives of Jesus and the exhortations of Paul, dealing with the ideas and
truths given in the Scriptures, and training Christians to follow and obey
Jesus in the many and varied conditions of history in which we find ourselves. But however important all of these things are, they cannot serve as
the center. We cultivate our participation in the play of Christ in history by
following him to the cross and receiving his life as he gives it to us under
the forms of the Eucharist.

Sacrifice

The Eucharist is a meal, the extension and completion of the Exodus Passover meal. As such it is a sacrificial meal. Sacrifice is at the center of the
work of salvation. Sacrifice is God's way of dealing with what is wrong in
history, which is to say, what is wrong with us, individually and collec-
tively. It is God's way of dealing with sin.

Sacrifice. All the ways we have of dealing with what is wrong with the world, whether that wrong is named "sin" or not, are in stark contrast to this. Our typical ways are through force (getting rid of what is wrong by destroying it or containing it or policing it), by education (teaching people right from wrong, and hoping that when they know the difference they will do what is right), by entertainment (distracting people from what is wrong with the world by giving them excitement and diversion, temporary vacations from the wrong), by economic improvement (providing incentives and opportunities to improve people's lives so that they will not out of despair and desperation, anger and retaliation, make a further mess out of things). None of these approaches is without merit. All of them in ways small and large make the world better. But none of them are God's way of accomplishing salvation. God's choice is sacrifice.

Sacrifice always involves material: flour, grain, lambs, goats, pigeons, bulls, incense. Biblical people built altars and offered sacrifices. Stuff. Leviticus is our most comprehensive source for how they did it. Leviticus is an extended schooling for training our imaginations to grasp that virtually everything that we do has to do with God but requires God's action to make it (us) fit for God. So we bring ourselves, our "bodies as a living sacrifice" (Rom. 12:1) represented by our offerings. These offerings are to be the best that we have, the best that we can do. But this "best" is not given to God to show him how good we are; it is not an attempt to gain his approval. These offerings are our best but they are also an acknowledgment that our best is not good enough. So we place our best on the altar to see what God can do with it, to see if he can do any better with it than we have been able to do. We let go of our best, give it up. So what happens next?

A priest builds a fire under the offering and burns it up. The fire transforms our gift (our lives) into smoke and fragrance that ascend to God. Our lives, whether well-intentioned or rebellious, our inadequate and sin-flawed lives, are changed before our eyes into what we cannot see but now hear as the priest declares us whole, forgiven, healed, restored. God has used the stuff of our sins to save us from our sins.

And Jesus became sin for us (2 Cor. 5:21). Offered up on the altar of the cross he became our salvation.

Typically, secularized salvation stories are rescue stories. A person from outside arrives and pulls us out of the trouble we are in. Jesus works from the inside, enters the troubled condition, receives it into himself, becomes the sacrifice that is transformed into the life of salvation. The cross of Christ is the sacrifice to sum up all sacrifices, the final sacrifice, the sacrifice that accomplished and accomplishes salvation.

Ritual

Jesus' most honored command produced a ritual — an ordered arrangement of actions and words that Christians reproduce wherever and whenever they want to "remember" and "proclaim" salvation. A ritual is a way of preserving continuity of action and integrity of language across time and among peoples of various habits and understandings, predispositions and inclinations. We commonly develop rituals to maintain fundamental human transactions. Rituals range from something as simple as shaking hands, to the solemnities of weddings for marriage and funerals at death, to the elaborate rites of royal coronations with their great processions and finery.

The usefulness of a ritual is that it takes a human action that is understood as essential to our ordinary lives and removes it from our immediate "say-so," protects it from our tinkering and revisions and editing, sets it apart from our moods and dispositions. There is more going on than I am aware of or can be responsible for. Reality is larger than me. A ritual puts me into the larger reality without requiring that I understand it or even "feel" it at the moment. The handshake and "hello," for instance, put me in a friendly place of encounter without requiring me to invent a greeting or comment each time appropriate to the circumstances. Or even think about it. It saves a lot of time, but it also maintains an appropriate connection to reality. "Rituals are a good signal to your unconscious that it is time to kick in," says Anne Lamott.[41] But there is another useful dimension to a ritual. It keeps us in touch with and preserves mystery. For reality is not only larger than me and my immediate circumstances, it is also beyond my understanding. Rituals preserve that mystery, protect certain essential aspects of reality from being reduced to the dimensions of my interest or intelligence or awareness. So the handshake keeps the mystery of a human man or woman represented in even the most casual human greeting from being reduced to my shifting emotions; marriage protects the mystery of sex and family from exploitation; funeral rites give the mystery of death dignity and witness to something far more than death; the royal coronation sets human rule under the transcendent sovereign mystery of God or gods.

A ritual protects common but essential elements of human life from reduction, degradation, exploitation. I cannot take charge of a ritual, I can only enter in — or not. Neither can I engage in a ritual by myself; others are involved. So a ritual, simply as ritual, prevents me from retaining any illusions that I am self-sufficient at the same time that it thrusts me into a life with others.

These reflections give texture to our understanding of the Eucharist as the focal practice for living out our salvation. When salvation is received eucharistically with the others who "do this" at the Lord's Table it cannot easily be pursued as a self-project; when salvation is received by eating the bread/flesh and drinking the wine/blood of Jesus, it cannot easily be reduced to a formula or abstraction. "Do this" (*poieite*, plural) is of necessity and by intention a corporate action.

Shape

Dom Gregory Dix, an Anglican monk in England, presented a paper in August 1941 that brought the phrase "The Shape of the Liturgy" into prominence among us. He did not exactly discover this "shape" — others before him had noted the elements — but he explored the implications and associations more extensively than anyone had done previously, creating a stunning piece of scholarly work. He observed that there is a fourfold shape to the eucharistic meal both as commanded in our Scriptures and as practiced ever since in the church. Four verbs — take, bless (or thank), break, give — shape the Supper.

This is St. Mark's record of the Supper: "And as they were eating, he took [*labōn*] bread, and blessed [*eulogēsas*], and broke [*eklasen*] it, and gave [*edōken*] it to them, and said, 'Take; this is my body.' And he took a cup, and when he had given thanks he gave it to them, and they all drank of it. And he said to them, 'This is my blood of the covenant, which is poured out for many'" (Mark 14:22-24 RSV; see also parallels).

Those four verbs — take, bless, break, give — occur in the same sequence in the stories of the feeding of the five thousand and four thousand.

Feeding the five thousand: "And taking [*labōn*] the five loaves and the two fish he looked up to heaven, and blessed [*eulogēsen*], and broke [*klasas*] the loaves, and gave [*edōken*] them to the disciples to set before the people . . ." (Mark 6:41 RSV and parallels).

Feeding the four thousand: "And he commanded the crowd to sit down on the ground; and he took [*elaben*] the seven loaves, and having given thanks [*eucharistēsas*] he broke [*eklasen*] them and gave [*edidou*] them to his disciples to set before the people . . ." (Mark 8:6 RSV and parallels).

St. John's narration of the feeding of the five thousand adds considerable more detail, including Jesus' "I am the bread of life" discourse. But the verbal pattern is the same, except for the omission of "broke": "Jesus then took [*the loaves*], and when he had given thanks [*eucharistēsas*], he distributed [*diedōken*] them . . ." (John 6:11 RSV).

St. Luke includes another meal in his Gospel, the supper at Emmaus, with the identical verbs in the same sequence: "When he was at table with them, he took [*labōn*] the bread and blessed [*eulogēsen*], and broke [*klasas*] it, and gave [*epedidou*] it to them. And their eyes were opened and they recognized him . . ." (Luke 24:30-31 RSV).

Years after Jesus had been host at these meals, St. Paul wrote to his troubled and fractious Corinthian congregation. One major area of trouble was the disorder around the eating of the Lord's Supper. In his rebuke and correction St. Paul uses the same verbs that the Gospel writers would place in their narratives: "For I received from the Lord what I also delivered to you, that the Lord Jesus on the night when he was betrayed took [*elaben*] bread, and when he had given thanks [*eucharistēsas*], he broke [*eklasen*] it, and said, 'This is my body which is for you. Do this in remembrance of me.' In the same way also the cup, after supper, saying, 'This cup is the new covenant in my blood. Do this, as often as you drink it, in remembrance of me.' For as often as you eat this bread and drink the cup, you proclaim the Lord's death until he comes" (1 Cor. 11:23-26). The final verb used by the Gospel writers, "give," does not occur here, but is clearly implied.

Matthew, Mark, Luke, John, and Paul give us accounts of Jesus' feeding the thousands, the twelve, and the two, using the verbs take, bless, break, and give to structure the Supper by which we remember and proclaim Christ and salvation. ("Give thanks" is twice used as a synonym for the second verb, "bless"). Early on in the Christian community, worship took on this eucharistic fourfold shape that has continued ever since.

*   *   *

Take Jesus takes what we bring him. Implicit in his taking is our offering. We offer what we have from the world of creation, from fields and rivers and seas: our onions and fish, our bread and wine, our goats and sheep;

the five barley loaves and two fish that an unnamed boy handed over to Jesus for the feeding of the five thousand (John 6:9); the simple meal Cleopas and friend set out for Jesus in the village of Emmaus; the fresh fish the seven disciples caught in the Sea of Galilee that Jesus included in his resurrection breakfast for them on the beach (John 21:10). There are always some among us who want to separate out, to distill the "spirituality" of life from the material, leaving an essence of pure soul. But these offerings that Jesus takes are emphatically material. The widow giving her mite (Luke 21:1-4), a nearly worthless piece of metal, was cited by Irenaeus as evidence of the sacred preciousness of the material in the economy of salvation.[42] But the offering is also emphatically personal; it is us, our sins and virtues, everything we are, even when it's not much. "There you are upon the table," said Augustine to his newly confirmed communicants, "there you are in the chalice."[43] We offer and he takes. He refuses nothing of who we are, what we have done.

This offering (the offertory) that Jesus takes from us, is the first movement of the Eucharist; it sets salvation in an ambience of sheer acceptance. God receives us and what we bring to him, just as we are. God does not extort; God does not exploit us; God does not force us. He takes only what we offer. "Coercion is no attribute of God."[44]

Those of us who are used to "making" our children (or students or employees) perform or behave or appear in certain prescribed ways "for their own good" have a particularly difficult time with this. But what is sometimes appropriate with our children and others until they have internalized moral habits and responsible behaviors is not a precedent for the way God treats us. He reveals himself as our Savior in Christ; he surrounds us with a bountiful creation; he brings us to his cross; he invites us to his Table. And he takes what we offer him and uses it as stuff for salvation. At every table we sit down to, we bring first of all and most of all ourselves. And Jesus takes it, takes us.

Bless What we offer to Jesus, Jesus offers to God with thanksgiving (*eucharist* means thanksgiving). He doesn't examine it for flaws, doesn't evaluate and appraise it, criticize or reject our offerings. "Two fish? Is that all you could come up with?" We can't imagine Jesus saying anything like that. He prays these offerings and the lives that back them up, offering what we offer to the Father.

The words that Jesus used in the blessing are not recorded for us. It is likely that it was a simple table blessing, thanks for the meal that had been set on the table, a prayer common at meals in the Judaism of his day and not unlike the prayers that we and our children offer at our breakfasts, lunches, and suppers.

But as Christians have continued to eat this Supper as a focused act of worship, the eucharistic prayer (the thanksgiving, the blessing) has been elaborated and expanded to include thanksgiving for creation, incarnation, and redemption, a rehearsal of Jesus' words instituting and commanding the keeping of the ritual, consecration of the bread and wine, prayer for the effects of Communion, and, at the conclusion, a doxology and the Lord's Prayer. The entire meaning of the Eucharist as it comprises Jesus' life and our lives is compressed into the prayer.

There is more. At the Supper with his disciples when Jesus prayed the blessing over the Meal, he told them plainly that this meal of bread and wine was at the same time, in some way or other (he didn't explain), his life, his flesh and blood, and that as they continued to eat and drink this Meal, they would be receiving him. The next day this flesh and blood was offered up on the cross as a sacrifice for our sins and became our salvation. The cross on Golgotha was the altar of salvation on which Jesus was sacrificed. Jesus is both the sacrifice and the priest who offers the sacrifice. That sacrifice accomplished our salvation. This is the act that centers and defines all of history.

And so when the Eucharist is enacted in our common worship, we understand that this same Jesus, the Jesus who is the Word of creation, incarnation, and redemption, who offered himself up, "a full, perfect, and sufficient sacrifice for the sins of the whole world," includes us in the offering, our bodies presented as a living sacrifice (Rom. 12:1), our flesh and blood saved by his flesh and blood, that "the bread which we break may be the communion of the body of Christ, and the cup of blessing which we bless, the communion of the blood of Christ."[45] It is not just the Last Supper that the Eucharist re-presents before God but, as Dix writes, "the sacrifice of Christ in His death and resurrection; and it makes this 'present' and operative by its effects in the communicants."[46]

This prayer of blessing gathers all of us and everything we are into everything that Christ is and does for us.

Break Our gifts don't remain what we bring. All too often we come to the Table with our best manners and a smug pose of impenetrable self-sufficiency. We are all surface, all role, polished and poised performers in the game of life. But the Jesus who saves us needs access to what is within us and so exposes our insides, our inadequacies, our "cover-ups." At the Table we are not permitted to be self-enclosed. We are not permitted to be self-sufficient. The breaking of our pride and self-approval is not a bad thing; it opens us to new life, to saving action. We come crusted over, hardened into ourselves. We soon discover that God is working deep within us, beneath our surface lies and poses, to bring new life. We cannot remain self-enclosed on this altar: "a broken and contrite heart, O God, you will not despise" (Ps. 51:17): the body broken, the blood poured out.

This third verb, break, to begin with was almost certainly simply the breaking and distribution of the loaf of bread. Paul, a page earlier in his Corinthian letter, used the symbolism of one loaf of bread which is "the body of Christ" as a metaphor for the basic unity of our common lives: "Because there is one bread, we who are many are one body, for we all partake of the one bread" (1 Cor. 10:17). But early on Christians saw in that broken bread from which we all eat at the Eucharist a pointer to Jesus on the cross, his body broken in sacrifice so that his life could become the salvation of the world. The best Greek manuscripts record Jesus' words at the Supper as "this is my body for you." But there are a number of other slightly later manuscripts in which the word "broken" *(klōmenon)* was inserted into the sentence, "this is my body *broken* for you" (see alternate reading of 1 Cor. 11:24), indicating that early worshipers connected the breaking of the bread and the "breaking" of Jesus on the cross.

Isaiah 53 supplied the imagery for this kind of developing reflection/meditation and provided a vocabulary that soon permeated the Christian understanding of Jesus' sufferings, his passion, as central to our salvation.

> But he was wounded for our transgressions,
>   Crushed for our iniquities;
> upon him was the punishment that made us whole,
>   and by his bruises we are healed.
>
> (v. 5)

> Yet it was the will of the LORD to crush him with pain.
> When you make his life an offering for sin. . . .
>
> (v. 10)

Because of this "broken" it is impossible to understand our participation in salvation as a life of untroubled serenity, a life apart from suffering, a life protected from disruption, a charmed life, a life exempt from pain and humiliation and rejection. This "broken" banishes even a hint that salvation might be a program of self-help. We discover this first in Jesus — the body broken, the blood poured out — and then we discover it in ourselves.

Give   The final verb: Jesus gives back what we bring him, who we are; and we receive what he gives. This is the Holy Communion. But it is no longer what we brought. It has been changed into what God gives, what we sing of as "amazing grace." Everything we bring to Jesus is given back, but lavishly — the twelve baskets witness the largesse (Mark 6:43); the seven baskets mark the generosity (Mark 8:8). Everything on the Table and everyone around the Table becomes gospel and is distributed to all who hunger and thirst after righteousness.

We eat the bread and drink the cup and know that Christ is in us, "the hope of glory" (Col. 1:27). We eat the bread and drink the cup and know that it is "Christ who lives in me" (Gal. 2:20). Paul uses the "in Christ" phrase over and over again — he is constantly elaborating the lived communion with Christ that is enacted in the Eucharist. Jesus could not have been more clear about it: this abundant life, this ransomed life, this salvation life is a life of communion, an intimate relationship of sacrificial love in and with Father, Son, and Holy Ghost.

The communion that we have in and with Christ reverberates in the communion we have with one another. A eucharistic life is a communal life through and through and from start to finish.

This means that there are no solitary Christians in the world of salvation. There are no do-it-yourself Christians. There are no self-help Christians. There are no Lone Ranger Christians. The moment the adjective intrudes it cancels the noun. Salvation is not a private deal with God. We are bound by the action of God in Christ to the entire creation that "waits with eager longing for the revealing of the children of God" (Rom. 8:19). Any understanding of salvation that separates us from others is false and sooner or later cripples our participation in what God in Christ is doing in history, saving the world.

*   *   *

"Do this" means the whole thing, the fourfold liturgical Eucharist that Christ commanded, the sacramental Meal. We cannot pick and choose between the verbs. It is an organic, rhythmic way of life that gets us in on everything that Christ is doing from the cross. This is the way we enter into, practice, and develop in the play of Christ in history. This is the shape of the Eucharist. This is the shape of the gospel. This is the shape of the Christian life. "Christianity came into being this way, the eucharistic meal. The Supper of the Lamb is its central event, established with the instruction that it be reenacted," writes Albert Borgmann.[47] For Christians, the Eucharist is the regular reenactment of the founding act.

Hospitality

> We cannot love God unless we love each other, and to love we must know each other. We know Him in the breaking of bread, and we know each other in the breaking of bread, and we are not alone any more. Heaven is a banquet and life is a banquet, too, even with a crust, where there is companionship.
>
> Dorothy Day[48]

The story of Abraham and Sarah at the oaks of Mamre preparing a meal for the three strangers (Gen. 18:1-15) has entered the Christian imagination as a defining moment for hospitality as Trinitarian presence. If we intend to live and give witness to Christ's work of salvation in the ordinary lives of our common days, we don't have to look far to find ways that are both in continuity with Christ's command, "Do this," and also immediately at hand. Salvation, eucharistically defined in our worship, continues to be expressed and lived out in daily acts of hospitality. The Eucharist in which we remember and proclaim salvation in Christ spills out of the chalice in the sanctuary and flows into the details of our common lives.

Meals

It is striking how much of Jesus' life is told in settings defined by meals.

Early on people noticed how frequently Jesus was seen at meals with people who were outsiders, men and women not considered acceptable in religious circles. Our term would probably be "the unsaved." He got a reputation for eating and drinking outside conventional settings and for not being very particular with whom he ate: "Look, a glutton and a drunkard, a friend of tax collectors and sinners!" (Luke 7:34).

One story in wide circulation in the early church was of a scandalous incident that took place when Jesus was having a meal at the home of a Pharisee named Simon. An uninvited woman slipped in and stood behind Jesus (he would have been reclining at the table). Weeping, she washed his feet with her tears. Then she dried his feet with her hair. And as if that were not enough, she ended up massaging his feet with an expensive perfume. And Jesus let her do it. Everyone, it seems, knew the woman was a local whore ("sinner" was the euphemism used by Simon). Under criticism by Simon, Jesus defended his acceptance of the woman at the meal on what we might term evangelistic grounds: "I tell you, her sins, which were many, have been forgiven." And then he dismissed the woman with a benediction: "Your faith has saved you; go in peace" (Luke 7:47 and 50).

At another meal with a Pharisee, a "leader of the Pharisees" this time, he challenged and rebuked the social snobbery that was a parody of hospitality and, in fact, destroyed hospitality (Luke 14:1-14).

Passing through Jericho one day, he invited himself to a meal with the disreputable Zacchaeus. And then he gave an evangelistic interpretation to what he was doing, eating with this man who was despised by all as a corrupt tax collector, by saying, "Today salvation has come to this house. . . . For the Son of Man came to seek out and to save the lost" (Luke 19:1-10).

Jesus frequently enjoyed the hospitality of his friends Mary, Martha, and Lazarus in Bethany. At one of these meals he made an unforgettable distinction between Martha's anxiety-ridden entertaining which was hardly hospitality and Mary's affectionate reception of their guest and leisurely entering into his conversation with them (Luke 10:39-42).

Two of Jesus' most powerful teachings on hospitality found their way into the common practice of the early church as visible witnesses to the reality of salvation being worked out in the world as we gather people into our homes and seat them at our tables for meals (Luke 14:12-14 and Matt. 25:31-46). Jesus frequently reinforced the centrality of hospitality by telling parables that featured food and drink, meals and banquets (Luke 14:15-24; 15:22-32; 16:19-21; 17:7-10). He was training the imaginations of his listeners (us!) to see salvation being worked out in a foreigner, a neighbor's midnight demand for bread, a beggar at a rich man's door. Both Luke and John give their final hospitality stories as unpretentious meals, the resurrection supper at Emmaus (Luke 24:13-35) and the resurrection breakfast on the Galilee beach (John 21:1-14).

Is it significant that Luke, who has more references in his Gospel to "save" and "salvation" (twenty-one as compared with fourteen each in Matthew and Mark and six in John) also has the most references to Jesus at meals or telling stories of meals? I think so. Luke's Gospel, in comparison to those of his Gospel-writing colleagues, is tilted in the direction of evangelism, making the connection between the message of salvation in history and the outsiders of history.

The frequency of hospitality references in the Epistles — Acts 4:32-35; Romans 16:23; Hebrews 13:1-3; 1 Peter 4:9; 1 John 3:16-18; 3 John 5-8 — shows how thoroughly the meal became a focal practice in the early church for participating in Jesus' work of salvation. The final citation, 3 John 5-8, is particularly instructive as it contrasts two church leaders, Gaius and Diotrephes, on the grounds of their practice of hospitality. Gaius was a hospitable man, sacrificial and generous in his hospitality to strangers, welcoming those who showed up as "fellow workers in the truth" (RSV). Diotrephes, by contrast, was full of himself, arrogantly refusing hospitality.

Joachim Jeremias, one of our finest scholars on matters eucharistic, observed the continuity of the final Meal with all these meals that Jesus had with all sorts and conditions of the people with whom he lived. His comment is trenchant: "In reality, the 'founding meal' is only one link in a long chain of meals which Jesus shared with his followers and which they continued after Easter . . . the last supper has its historical roots in this chain of gatherings."[49] Settings of hospitality, especially in connection with meals, are the most accessible and natural occasions for cultivating the focal practice of the Eucharist in our daily lives. Our continuing witness to and fear-of-the-Lord participation in the work of salvation is formed eucharistically around our kitchen tables. Daily meals with family, friends, and guests, acts of hospitality every one, are the most natural and frequent settings for working out the personal and social implications of salvation.

But there is a problem. The practice of hospitality has fallen on bad times. Fewer and fewer families sit down to a meal together. The meal, which used to be a gathering place for families, neighbors, and "the stranger at the gate," is on its way out. Given the prominence of the Supper in our worshiping lives, the prominence of meals in the Jesus work of salvation, it is surprising how little notice is given among us to the relationship between the Meal and our meals. Our surprise develops into a sense of urgency when we recognize that a primary, maybe *the* primary, venue for evangelism in Jesus' life was the meal. Is Jesus' preferred setting for playing out the work of salvation on this field of history only marginally available to us? By marginalizing meals of hospitality in our daily lives have we inadvertently diminished the work of evangelism? And is there anything to be done about it?

The Deconstruction of Hospitality

Of course there is something to be done about it. We haven't survived as a Christian community for two thousand years (four thousand if we count in our Hebrew predecessors) by being "conformed to this world" (Rom. 12:2), fitting into the sociological trends of the time, inattentively letting ourselves be assimilated to the practices of the world.

Perhaps the place to begin is with language. Hospitality and meals are complex acts that require attention to detail and involve persons who are for the most part named. Personal give-and-take is integral to whatever is going on. There are no abstractions in hospitality — particular persons are involved, beds have to be made, parsnips peeled, corn shucked, coffee brewed. And out of these irreducible particulars, organic and relational metaphors and similes flourish.

But for a long time now, the machine and its metaphors have dominated not only the way we live but the way we talk about the way we live. And the more machine the less person. The more machine the less relation. The more machine the less particularity. Machines can be mass produced and in return become machines of mass production, always doing the same thing in the same way. As the "myth of the machine"[50] achieves dominance in our thinking and speaking, our sense of the intricacies of soul and the particular workings of salvation atrophies markedly. The trouble and time involved in dealing with tardy or recalcitrant or inefficient persons are traded in for the convenience of getting things done quickly and predictably by technological devices.

As this exchange is made more and more often in more and more settings, the meal is the most conspicuous thing to go, and with the meal its metaphors. The "myth of the machine" dominates the imagination. Meals take time, meals are inefficient, meals are not "productive." And so meals are streamlined, made efficient, individualized — the personal and relational and communal are abbreviated as much as possible. The vast and encompassing "culture of the table" (Borgmann's phrase)[51] is pushed to the sidelines. The centrality of the meal in our lives is greatly diminished. We still eat, of course, but the intricate cultural world of the meal has disintegrated. The exponential rise of fast-food meals means that there is little leisure for conversation; the vast explosion of restaurants is evidence that far less food preparation and clean-up takes place in homes; in many homes the television set is the dominant presence at family meals, virtually eliminating personal relationships and conversations; the frequency with which pre-prepared and frozen meals are used erodes the culture of family recipes and common work. All this, and more, means that the meal is no longer easily accessible or natural as the setting in which to encounter the risen Christ in our ordinariness and dailiness.

But we still eat meals, all of us. And so the meal remains as a major condition in which we can, if we will, stay in close touch with history and participate in the eucharistic dynamics of salvation in history. But given the widespread and insidious deconstruction of hospitality, we need to be more deliberate and intentional about it. When we realize how integral acts of hospitality are in evangelism, maybe we will be more deliberate and intentional about it. A life of hospitality keeps us in intimate touch with our families and the traditions in which we are reared, personally available to friends and guests, morally related to the hungry and homeless, and, perhaps most important of all, participants in the context and conditions in which Jesus lived his life, using the language he used for the salvation of the world.

*   *   *

Another language move that contributes to the deconstruction of hospitality and the eucharistic life implicit in it is the disengagement of language from locale. The most frequent North American way of giving witness to the salvation that Christ accomplished on the cross (which is to say, evangelism) is verbal. The "going and making" kicked off by Jesus' command "Go therefore and make disciples of all nations . . ." (Matt. 28:19) is carried out among us primarily by saying something. Such witness and preaching is commonly detached from a local context that is textured with ongoing personal relationships of responsibility and work. The language is largely formulaic, dominated by the rhetoric of advertising and public relations. This is a language suitable for crowds and strangers but of dubious usefulness in conveying anything personal, and Jesus' work of salvation is nothing if not personal. These primarily verbal strategies of evangelism are characteristically directed to the people whom we do not know or don't know very well. This way of using words to give witness to salvation (the practice of evangelism) is decidedly marginal to what is biblically normative.

It is the devil's own work to detach the *language* of salvation from the *setting* of salvation, to separate words from personal relationships, to make salvation a "cause" or a "project" that can be conducted as efficiently and impersonally as possible. But the gospel will not permit it. In the story of our salvation, we find the Architect of our salvation going about his salvation work in the thick textures of place and person, and to a surprising extent, in the settings of a meal.

We must always keep in mind that the work of salvation is God's work in Jesus *in history*. And history is never a generality. History by its very nature is composed of specifics: locatable place, datable time, named people, identifiable events. The way we participate in salvation has to be in continuity with the way Jesus accomplished salvation, namely, in all the immediate details that make up history — not a generalized "world history" but a storied local and personal history. That is why the focal practice for participating in Jesus' work of salvation is not a detached verbal act but a meal, an event that employs all the senses and can occur only in specific places with named people, requiring a language that is personal and conversational. A meal engages personal participation at the most basic level of our lives. It is virtually impossible to be detached and uninvolved when we are sharing a meal with someone.

A Sacrificial Life

The word that pulses at the center of the holy Eucharist and the meals in our homes alike is "sacrifice." As we enter into this vast field of salvation and ask how we can be appropriately involved in Christ's work, the term "sacrifice" requires attention; for whatever we do in this business, we must do it after the manner of Jesus.

The focal event of Jesus' work of salvation is a sacrifice. There is no ambiguity here — he sacrificed his life on the cross of Calvary. Our Gospel witnesses make it clear that his death was no accidental miscarriage of Roman justice, no cruel Greek tragic fate that inexorably overtook him. Jesus *embraced* it as his vocation, telling his disciples well beforehand, "the Son of Man came not to be served but to serve, and to give his life a ransom for many" (Mark 10:45). He prepared them and us meticulously as he approached the high moment of sacrifice, three times telling them that he was going to suffer and be rejected and be killed (Mark 8:31; 9:31; 10:34). He also said he would rise again, but that would come later.

Three times Jesus plainly told them what he was doing. At the last minute he also prayed three times to the Father to provide another way of salvation for the world, a nonsacrificial way. But there was no other way. "*This* is the way; walk in it!" (Isa. 30:21, italics added). And when through that night of Gethsemane prayer it became as clear to him as he had already made it to his disciples that there were no alternatives, he agreed to give himself as the sacrifice for "us and for our salvation." He gave himself as the sacrifice that would set the world's wrongs right.

St. Paul, the definitive preacher and interpreter of Jesus, knew no other way. He took the cross of Christ as the text for his life and ministry. "I decided to know nothing among you except Jesus Christ, and him crucified" (1 Cor. 2:2). As he looked over his life retrospectively while writing to the Philippians, he was content to stay in the same track, "sharing [in Christ's] sufferings by becoming like him in his death" (Phil. 3:10). It was precisely *this* vocation that Jesus invited his disciples to take up: "If any want to become my followers, let them deny themselves and take up their cross and follow me" (Mark 8:34).

I don't know of any part of the Christian gospel that is more difficult to move from the pages of sacred Scripture and our honored volumes of theology into the assumptions and practices of our everyday Christian lives. Very few among us would dissent from what Jesus said, what Paul wrote, what Calvin preached, and yet — and yet when it comes down to actual assent, we more often than not find another way. We begin our morning prayers with Jesus, "Father, for you all things are possible; remove this cup from me; yet . . ." (Mark 14:36). And our "yet . . ." trails off; instead of completing Jesus' prayer ("not what I want but what you want") we begin entertaining other possibilities. If all things are possible for the Father, perhaps there is another way to do something about what is wrong with the world, a way by which I can help out and make things better other than through a sacrificial life. In the jargon of the day, we pray: "sacrifice is not one of my gifts — I want to serve God with my strength, with my giftedness." It's a strange thing, but sacrifice never seems to show up on anyone's Myers-Briggs profile.

For a people like us, trained in a culture of getting things done (pragmatism) and taking care of ourselves (individualism), sacrifice doesn't seem at all obvious; neither does it seem attractive. There is nothing about a life of sacrifice that appeals to our well-intentioned desire to make a difference in the wrongdoing in the world and to make things better for our neighbors and ourselves.

But the self-promotion and self-help ways of salvation, so popular among us, do nothing but spiral us further into the abyss. There is no other way but sacrifice. Annie Dillard, one of our unconventional but most passionate theologians, is blunt in her verdict: "a life without sacrifice is an abomination."[52]

Nonparticipation in Jesus' sacrifice as the means of salvation is damning. The failure of our substituted good intentions in the work of salvation could not be more conspicuous. There is only one Gospel way to participate in Jesus' work — live a sacrificial life in Jesus' name.

$$* \qquad * \qquad *$$

The trouble with a word like "sacrifice," though, is that it sounds grandiose and therefore easily blurs into generalities. The grand word is quickly smothered in a welter of telephone calls, committee meetings, job assignments, and political urgencies. But there *is* a way to keep it in focus without being grandiose, a humble and ordinary way — the way of eucharistic hospitality.

Hospitality is daily practice in keeping sacrifice local and immediate: a meal prepared and served to family and guests is a giving up of ourselves for another. All the food on the table is life given and offered so that others (we among them) can live. "Sacrifice and meal," Hans Urs von Balthasar observes, are "always interlinked."[53] Meals provide daily opportunities to be on both the giving and receiving ends of a sacrificial life, to see how it works in detail, to observe the emotions and effects, to discover the difficulties. When we are talking about the salvation of the world, a bowl of rice seems like an insignificant launching pad. But it wasn't too insignificant for Jesus. Will we replace Jesus' humility with our grandiosity? Preparing and cooking, serving and eating meals are Jesus-sanctioned activities that provide daily structure to our participation in the work of salvation.[54]

So what do we do? We take the meal with as much gospel seriousness as we take our Scriptures; we take the kitchen to be as essential in the work of salvation as is the sanctuary. Meals are front-line strategies countering the inexorable deconstruction of hospitality that is running amuck in the Western world today. The meal is a focal practice for reenacting in our dailiness all that is involved in the eucharistic meal in which we participate in the sacrifice of Christ for the salvation of the world.

The common meal is the primary way by which we take care of our physical need for food, our social need for conversation and intimacy, and our cultural need to carry on traditions and convey values. But, get this, it is also a primary way in which we cultivate a sacrificial life, congruent with Jesus' sacrificial, eucharistically defined life. The meal is an extraordinary coming together of life. All the food placed on the supper table was planted, tended, and harvested by men and women who brought skill and hard work to the planting and tending and harvesting. Unless we are farmers and gardeners, most if not all that is on our tables is the fruit of the work (and sometimes the affection) of others. The complex world of soil and weather is the huge hidden iceberg under the potatoes, celery, and lamb chops being served on the table. Everything served had to be harvested, hauled, and delivered. And then cut and chopped, ground and milled, roasted and boiled, seasoned and garnished. As the meal is served and eaten it develops into an act of communion: conversation, emotion, sensory delights, prayers, and recognitions work themselves into what materially is nothing but chemicals and calories. And then there is the cleaning and washing up, the storage of leftovers, preparation and anticipation already underway for the next meal. An enormously complex web of engagement is behind, underneath, and around even the simplest meal we serve or that is served to us. The preparation, serving, and eating of meals is perhaps the most complex cultural process that we human beings find ourselves in. It is a microcosm of the intricate realities that are combined to form the culture that gives meaning to the daily lives of us all: men, women, and children — and Jesus. But it is not culture in a museum sense; it is totally immediate, personal, and relational — relational with the materials of creation and the persons we live with. Because it is so inclusive (anyone and everyone can be included in the meal), so pervasive (we all have to eat), so comprehensive (taking in the entire range of our existence, physical and cultural), and unrelentingly social (we necessarily rely on uncounted named and unnamed others), the meal provides an endless supply of metaphors for virtually everything we do as human beings. These metaphors nearly always suggest something deeply personal and communal: giving and receiving ("blessed are those who hunger and thirst after righteousness for they shall be filled"), knowing and being known ("taste and see that the Lord is good"), accepting and being accepted, bounty and generosity ("land flowing with milk and honey"). The meal is capable of endless variations in necessity, pleasure, and communion.[55]

*   *   *

The four verbs that Jesus used at the Supper continue to put salvation into action every time we sit down to a meal. The first and last eucharistic verbs — "take" and "give" — are terms of generous exchange. Every table — kitchen table, picnic table, banquet table — is a place of giving and receiving. No one owns anything here. Everyone at the table shares a common need. All is grace. We recognize layer after layer of lavish generosity inherent in every meal. Our daily immersion in this generosity, the taking and giving at the heart of hospitality and at the heart of salvation, keeps us in daily touch with the world in which Christ works the salvation of the world.

The middle verbs of the Eucharist — "bless" and "break" — are terms of sacrifice. At the Lord's Table we are at the place of sacrifice, Jesus' sacrifice. We deliberately set ourselves obediently and expectantly in God's presence in order that our lives become formed sacrificially. Jesus' life, offered to the Father in blessing, was sacrificed to take away the sin of the world, and entered history as the salvation of the world. The life of sacrifice is deeply embedded in the common meal. The blessing and breaking reach into the commonplaces of our lives. In our meals, we participate in and practice the elements of a sacrificial life as one life is given so that another may live. It may be the life of a carrot or cucumber, it may be the life of a fish or duck, it may be the life of a lamb or heifer. But it is also our lives, given to the others in generosity and service. Eating a meal involves us in a complex, sacrificial world of blessing and breaking. Life feeds on life. We are not self-sufficient. We live by life and the lives given to and for us.

Everything in our lives that takes place at the Lord's Table can, if we will, inform and shape our lives as we return to our kitchen tables. What is before us supremely in Jesus on the cross and in the Eucharist gets worked into the way we live with and for others, expressed in language as everyday as "pass the cauliflower," or, as Jesus said in one of his most memorable salvation conversations, "Give me a drink" (John 4:7).

*   *   *

At the Holy Supper we take our places in the wildly generous world of salvation, lavish in grace. We participate in that salvation by receiving the sacrificed life of Jesus in the bread and wine, remembering and proclaiming "the Lord's death until he comes" (1 Cor. 11:26). We leave the Table. Where do we begin doing our daily part in the remembering and proclamation? We go home where our relationships are thickest and most textured, with the people with whom we have most access, and among the responsibilities that define our obedience. We join in the preparing, serving, and eating of meals with family and friends, neighbors and strangers, in breakfasts of cornflakes and toast, lunches of baloney sandwiches, and suppers of tuna casserole. Every meal — breakfast, lunch, and supper — whatever the menu, wherever and with whomever we eat it, puts us in the company of Jesus, who ate his meals with sinners and gave himself for us.

We initiate the remembrance and proclamation of salvation at the eucharistic table. We continue it at every meal to which we sit down. For the Christian, every meal derives from and extends the eucharistic meal into our daily eating and drinking, our tables at which the crucified and risen Christ is present as host.

All the elements of a eucharistically formed life are present every time we sit down to a meal and invoke Jesus as Host. It's a wonderful thing, really — that the most common action of our lives, eating meals, can reflect and continue the most profound of all transactions, salvation. The fusion of natural and supernatural that we witness and engage in the shape of the liturgy continues, or can continue, at our kitchen tables.

III

Christ Plays in Community

"Holy Father, protect them in your name that you have given me, so
that they may be one, as we are one. . . . I in them and you in me, that
they may become completely one, so that the world may know that
you have sent me and have loved them even as you have loved me."

JOHN 17:11, 23

We are all members of one another, and one of us is Jesus Christ. . . .

AUSTIN FARRER[1]

When we take time to look around and see where we are, we find ourselves in an incredibly beautiful country, various and exquisite. Breathtaking beauty. Heart-stopping wonders. We lift our eyes to the hills and see God: praise and gratitude spring spontaneously from our lips — thanks! We exult in creation.

But this beautiful country is also a dangerous country. There are crazy people out there with guns; there are typhoons and drunken drivers; lightning strikes at random; mosquitoes crash our picnics. We fasten our seatbelts, train our children not to speak to strangers, and apply insect repellent. Not infrequently we cry out — help! We are mired in history.

This beautiful and dangerous country is also, in some mysterious yet inescapable way, *my* country, *our* country. We are not tourists here; we are not spectators taking photographs of the cliffs and meadows, the quaint cottages and the odd people. We don't have the leisure to write excited letters to our friends about the beauties we admire and the dangers we fear. We are part of it: we don't just look and admire, or look and fear — we *respond*. And we *want* to respond, *want* to get in on it. Like a young child. We are content for a few years to let our parents cook meals and feed us, but at about three or four years we say, "Let me do it," or, "What can I do?" We say it long before we are able to do anything without making a mess of things, but that's not the point — we want to be part of what is going on. It's hardly a decision; we can't help it: everything out there touches something in here, in me, in you, in us: *Respondeo etsi mutabor* — "I respond although I will be changed."[2] Participation is in our genes. We insist on getting in on what is going on. It is one of the irrepressible features of this life of ours. We are not content to be spectators. We want to help, to participate in this creation, in this history. We know that, in some way or other, we are part of all this, and we want to get in on it. There is, of course, also abundant evidence of passivity and indolence in and around us. But it is never assumed to be a good thing, never admired. We have an intuitive sense that passivity is a symptom of loss, a deficiency, an anemia of spirit, something subhuman. And if we can't arouse ourselves, we find artificial stimulants to inject responsiveness into our lives even if it is nothing more than responding as a spectator to others who are playing the game.

*   *   *

Christ plays in the community of people with whom we live, and we want to get in on the play. We see what Christ does in creation and history and we want in on it, firsthand with our families and friends and neighbors. But difficulties arise. Soon or late those of us who follow Jesus find ourselves in the company of men and women who also want to get in on it. It doesn't take us long to realize that many of these fellow volunteers and workers aren't much to our liking, and some of them we actively dislike — a mixed bag of saints and sinners, the saints sometimes harder to put up with than the sinners. Jesus doesn't seem to be very discriminating in the children he lets into his kitchen to help with the cooking.

*   *   *

I was responsible for the spiritual care of such a community for most of my adult vocational life and have had considerable opportunity to reflect on what is involved.

When I became a pastor I didn't think much about the complexities of community in general and of a holy community in particular; I was absorbed in the theatrical glories of creation and the dramatic workings of salvation in history. I was moving from city to city, going from school to school. I was given gatherings of people to study with, work with, play with — but it was all fairly transient. And then it no longer was transient — this was it. A congregation, improbably named the people of God. These people for good or ill, but *these* people. I often found myself preferring the company of people outside my congregation, men and women who did not follow Jesus. Or worse, preferring the company of my sovereign self. But I soon found that my preferences were honored by neither Scripture nor Jesus.

I didn't come to the conviction easily, but finally there was no getting around it: there can be no maturity in the spiritual life, no obedience in following Jesus, no wholeness in the Christian life apart from an immersion and embrace of community. I am not myself by myself. Community,[3] not the highly vaunted individualism of our culture, is the setting in which Christ is at play.

Exploring the Neighborhood of the Community

When I was an adolescent, one of the visions that filled my head with flash and color and glory was the French Revolution. I actually knew very little about it. Some vague impressions, incidents, and names were mixed haphazardly in my mind to produce a drama of pure romance, excitement, and the triumph of righteousness. If I had had access then to my present vocabulary I would probably have used the word "holy" to sum it up: something spiritually blazing and extravagant and glorious.

I had this picture of idealistic, devoted men and women with the ringing affirmations of liberty, equality, fraternity on their lips, marching through a corrupt, sinful world and purging it with their righteous ideas and action. Names like Marat, Robespierre, and Danton had a ringing and righteous sound in my ears. Evil dungeons in the Bastille were deep shadows against which the fires of liberation burned purely. Heroism and villainy were in apocalyptic conflict. The guillotine was an instrument of the Last Judgment separating the sheep from the goats.

Thus my imagination, untroubled by facts, spun a wonderful fantasy of the glorious French Revolution.

When I arrived at college and looked through a catalogue of courses, I was delighted to find a course listed for the French Revolution. I had to wait a year to take it since first-year students were not admitted, but that only served to whet my appetite. Returning for my second year, my first move was to enroll in the course.

The class was one of the significant disappointments of my college years. I brought the kind of great expectations to it that adolescents often do to adult enterprises, but nothing of what I expected took place.

The professor was a slight, elderly woman with thin, wispy gray hair. She dressed in dark, shapeless silks, and spoke in a soft, timorous monotone. She was a wonderfully nice person and was academically well-qualified in her field of European history. But as a teacher of the French Revolution she was a disaster. She knew everything about the French but nothing about revolution.

I, meanwhile, knew practically nothing about the subject, and the few facts I had in my possession were nearly all of them wrong. What I possessed, in fact, was a vast ignorance about the whole business. But I was right about one thing: it was a revolution. Revolutions turn things inside out and upside down. Revolutions are titanic struggles between antagonistic wills. Revolutions excite the desire for a better life of freedom, *promise* a better life of freedom. Sometimes they make good on their promises and set people free. More often they don't. But after a revolution nothing is quite the same again.

Sitting in her classroom, though, day after day, no one would ever know that. Ill-fated Marat, murderous Charlotte Corday, the black Bastille, the bloody guillotine, venal and opportunistic Danton, giddy Marie-Antoinette, ox-like Louis XIV — all the players and props in that colorful and violent age were presented in the same platitudinous, tired, and pious voice. Everybody sounded the same in her lectures, all presented as neatly labeled specimens, butterflies on a mounting board on which a decade or so of dust had settled.

For a long time after that the French Revolution seemed to me a very great bore. Say the words "French Revolution" and I yawned.

*   *   *

A few years later I had become a pastor and was astonished to find men and women in my congregation yawning. Matt Ericson went to sleep every Sunday; he always made it through the first hymn but ten minutes later was sound asleep. Red Belton, an angry teenager, sat on the back pew out of sight of his parents and read comic books. Karl Strothheim, a bass in the choir, passed notes supplemented by whispers to Luther Olsen on stock market tips. One woman gave me hope — she brought a stenographic notebook with her every Sunday and wrote down in shorthand everything I said. At least one person was paying attention. Then I learned that she was getting ready to leave her husband and was using the hour of worship to practice her shorthand so that she could get a self-supporting job.

These were, most of them, good people, nice people. They were familiar with the Christian faith, knew the Christian stories, showed up on time for worship each Sunday. But they yawned. How could they do that? How could anyone go to sleep ten minutes after singing "Blessing and Honor and Glory and Power . . ."? How could anyone sustain interest in Batman when St. Paul's Romans was being read? How could anyone be content to practice shorthand when the resurrected Christ was present in word and sacrament? I had, it seemed, a whole congregation of saints and sinners who knew everything about the Christian life except that the gospel had redefined everything and everyone, set everything and everyone in a participating relation to a holy God. It came to me that holy was to Christian what revolution was to the French in the eighteenth century, the *energy* that created a community of free men and women plunged into a new life. The community that I was working with knew the word "Christian" pretty well, and identified themselves as Christians. But *holy?* Holy Spirit? Something blazing? A community bonfire?

I knew I had my work cut out for me. When I was ordained and then called to be pastor of a congregation, I had supposed that my task was to teach and preach the truth of the Scriptures so that these people would know God and how he works their salvation; I had supposed that my task was to help them make moral decisions so that they could live happily ever after with a clear conscience. I had supposed that my task was to pray with and for them, gathering them in the presence of a holy God who made heaven and earth and sent Jesus to die for their sins. Now I realized that more than accurate learning was at stake, more than moral behavior was at stake, more than getting them on their knees on a Sunday morning was at stake. *Life* was at stake — *their* lives, their *souls,* their *souls-in-community.* People can think correctly and behave rightly and worship politely and still live badly — live anemically, live individualistically self-enclosed lives, live bored and insipid and trivial lives.

That's when I got seriously interested in the word "holy" as an attribute of community, what Gerard Manley Hopkins described as "the dearest freshness deep down things."[4] I became interested in what "holy" meant in my workplace, my congregation, the people of God community to which I was assigned as a pastor. When I sensed that "holy" to congregation was what "revolution" was to French politics in the eighteenth century, it didn't take me long to realize that I was as ignorant of this world of church in the twentieth century as I had been earlier of the world of France in the eighteenth, an ignorance perpetuated by romanticizing fantasies. Just as I had little idea of what was involved in actual revolution, I was similarly unschooled in the holy. I started looking for signs of the holy, evidence of the holy — holy lives, holy community, Holy Spirit. And I started paying attention to what Scripture and theology told me about what was involved in being a part of this Holy Spirit–formed community. After a good bit of casting around, I found the place to begin was the resurrection of Jesus.

Kerygma: Jesus' Resurrection

The gospel, while honoring our experience, doesn't begin with our experience. We don't begin a holy life by wanting a holy life, desiring to be good, fulfilled, complete, or wanting to be included in the grand scheme of things. We have been anticipated, and the way we have been anticipated is by resurrection, Jesus' resurrection. Living a holy life, the Christian equivalent of revolution, begins with Jesus' resurrection.

The resurrection of Jesus establishes the entire Christian life in the action of God by the Holy Spirit. The Christian life begins as a community that is gathered at the place of impossibility, the tomb.

Just as Jesus' birth launches us into the creation and Jesus' death launches us into history, Jesus' resurrection launches us into living in community, the holy community — the community of the resurrection. Jesus' resurrection is the kerygmatic lift-off for living in the community of the Holy Spirit.

Jesus' resurrection is the final kerygmatic "piece" that, together with his birth and death, sets the good news, the gospel, in motion and creates the Christian life. Everything necessary for the Christian life is now laid out before us and put into action *in us*. The way we live our lives, the impulses and desires we have to get in on what God is doing in the wonders of creation and the mess of history, is activated now by Jesus' resurrection. There is no living worth its salt that is not the consequence of the action of God in Jesus through the Holy Spirit: "If the Spirit of him who raised Jesus from the dead dwells in you, he who raised Christ from the dead will give life to your mortal bodies also through his Spirit that dwells in you" (Rom. 8:11). Paul is tireless in the variations he plays on this theme. George Steiner speaks of the "rich nuances of the resurrection."[5] This is the kind of living that we designate *holy* living in the holy community. A resurrection life.

I am using the word "kerygmatic" to identify those pivotal moments in the life of Jesus — birth, death, resurrection — that so clearly reveal God to us, for us, and now in us. They are kerygmatic because they are an announcement, a proclamation of something that has happened quite apart from us but that makes present the reality in which we live. And makes it present in such a way that we realize that it is wonderfully good and that it is at hand for participation — ourselves no longer reduced to ourselves, having to take charge of ourselves and everyone around us, "to make something of ourselves" as we are so often told. Nor do we any longer understand ourselves as having to put up with everything that comes to us and make the best of it, because the resurrected Christ, raised by the Holy Spirit, is doing something about all of it.

Each of these moments is a proclamation: *this* — this birth of Jesus, this death of Jesus, this resurrection of Jesus — is something we cannot do for ourselves, cannot take credit for, cannot take over and run with, cannot reproduce in any way. It is done for us. We can only hear and believe and enter this God-for-us reality that is so generously given as both the context and the content of our lives.

There are symmetries in the birth/death/resurrection stories but there is also this difference: we experience birth and death, at least biologically, in what appear to us as natural conditions; but the resurrection is wholly supernatural. Jesus did not raise himself; he was raised. And we do not raise ourselves; we are raised.

$$* \qquad * \qquad *$$

It is critical that we get inside this and make it our own, critical that we realize not just that the resurrection happened but that it happens. Too often we make the resurrection only a matter of apologetics and melt the resurrection accounts down into an ingot of doctrine; for Jesus (and Paul interpreting Jesus) resurrection is primarily a matter of living in a wondrous creation, embracing a salvation history, and then taking our place in a holy community: *receive the Holy Spirit* (John 20:22). Receive this Holy Spirit by whom Jesus has just been raised from the dead so that you can continue to participate in Jesus' resurrection life in your prayers and obedience.

It happens, we do not make it happen. The more we get involved in what God is doing, the less we find ourselves running things; the more we participate in God's work as revealed in Jesus, the more is done to us and the more is done through us. The more we practice resurrection the less we are on our own or by ourselves, for we find that this resurrection that is so intensely and relationally personal in Father, Son, and Spirit at the same time plunges us into relationships with brothers and sisters we never knew we had: we are in community whether we like it or not. We do not choose to be in this community; by virtue of the resurrection of Jesus, this is the company we keep.

We live the Christian life out of a rich tradition of formation-by-resurrection. Jesus' resurrection provides the energy and conditions by which we "walk before the LORD in the land of the living" (Ps. 116:9). The resurrection of Jesus creates and makes available the reality in which we are formed as new creatures in Christ by the Holy Spirit. The do-it-yourself, self-help culture of North America has so thoroughly permeated our imaginations that we don't give much sustained attention to the biggest thing of all, resurrection. And the reason we don't give much attention to it is because the resurrection is not something we can use or manipulate or control or improve on. It is interesting that the world has had very little success in commercializing Easter, turning it into a commodity, the way it has Christmas. If we can't, as we say, "get a handle on it" and use it, we soon lose interest. But resurrection is not available for our use; it is exclusively God's operation.

*   *   *

All four Gospel writers conclude their Jesus story with his resurrection. But John does something additional which calls for special attention as we attend to the significance of the *community* of the resurrection.

The text that holds this in focus is this: "[Jesus] breathed on them [his assembled disciples] and said to them, 'Receive the Holy Spirit'" (John 20:22). A few days before the resurrection, on the evening before his crucifixion, Jesus had an extended conversation with his disciples that prepared them for his death and resurrection. Throughout that conversation he promised them over and over again, with variations, that when he was gone physically he would be present with them in the Spirit (John 14:15-17, 25-26; 15:26; 16:7-11, 13-14).

On the Day of Resurrection he made good on that promise: "Receive the Holy Spirit." He replaced himself with himself.

Resurrection is the work of the Holy Spirit in Jesus, raising him from the dead and presenting him before the disciples; resurrection is also the work of the Holy Spirit in those of us who believe in and follow Jesus.

The Day of Pentecost story, the story of the formation of the resurrection community, is told in Acts 1–2. It is the story of the descent of the Holy Spirit on Jesus' followers with the result that the life of Jesus was now lived in them. But there is also a pre-Pentecost story that took place fifty days before the actual event. It is the story behind the Pentecost story and

is, as many background stories turn out to be, essential for first understanding and then participating in the story that makes the headlines.

John is the only evangelist to tell the story (John 13–17). It is the story
of how Jesus spent his last night with his disciples. The disciples didn't
know that Jesus would be arrested later that night and killed before their
terrified eyes the next day. They didn't know that these marvelous years
with Jesus would terminate at noon the next day in a bloody, mocking, humiliating crucifixion. They didn't know that it was their last night with Jesus. And, of course, they had no idea that in three days there would be a
resurrection.

But Jesus knew. And so he set about preparing them to continue
what he had begun. They had no idea what was coming next. These unsus-
pecting, unaware disciples in coming months and years would speak and
do what Jesus had been doing, "in fact, will do greater works" (John 14:12).
But how?

How they did it is how we do it, how we will continue to follow Jesus
when we cannot see him. But be prepared for a surprise — or maybe I
should say, a disappointment; for Jesus doesn't do anything attention-
getting. He performs no dazzling miracle to remember him by, provides
no riveting metaphor to keep his message in focus. But if he does not use
miracle or metaphor — two things that he is very good at — what's left?
Yes, they are to continue Jesus' life when he is not physically there. But
how?

They've been eating supper together. Jesus gets up from the table,
takes a basin of water and a towel, and proceeds to wash the feet of his disciples. Peter objects, but Jesus overrides him and continues the washing
(John 13:1-11). And then Jesus begins to talk; he talks a long time — this is
the longest conversation or discourse of Jesus that we have reported to us.
The disciples listen. Eight times the disciples (five are named) make comments or ask questions, one-liners that Jesus weaves into the conversation
(John 13:12–16:33). Finally, Jesus prays. As he prays he gathers up the life
that they have lived together and fuses it into the life that the disciples will
continue to live, praying his life and work and their life and work into an
identity: it is going to be the same life whether people saw and heard Jesus
living it or will see and hear Peter and Thomas and Philip living it (John 17).

And that's it. This is how Jesus chooses to spend that evening with
his disciples preparing for the transition from Jesus present to Jesus absent. He begins by washing the feet of his disciples, down on his knees be-

fore each of them, getting his hands dirty with the dirt of their feet. He ends by praying to his Father and their Father that what they continue to do will be congruent with what he has been doing.

The pattern holds: whatever we do in Jesus' name, we begin on our knees before our friends and neighbors and conclude looking "up to heaven" praying to the Father. Washing dirty feet and praying to the Holy Father bookend our lives. We can't live Jesus' life, we can't do Jesus' work, without doing it within the boundaries that Jesus set.

But there is more here, much more. Between the washing and the prayer there is the conversation. Condensed into a single Jesus sentence the conversation is, "I tell you the truth: it is to your advantage that I go away, for if I do not go away, the Advocate will not come to you; but if I go, I will send him to you" (John 16:7).

*   *   *

The style of the conversation that prepares us for the pentecostal continuation of living the Jesus life in the Jesus way is as important as the words themselves. It is a style that cultivates relational participation. Compare John's story style with the three writers who preceded him in writing a Gospel.

Matthew, Mark, and Luke all write the Gospel story on the same pattern. The storyline follows Jesus for three or so years of public life, most of it in Galilee, and ends up in a final, climactic week in Jerusalem. Most of the action takes place during the three years in Galilee as our writers introduce us to what Jesus does and says and acquaint us with the various ways men and women respond to him: following, questioning, misunderstanding, some recognizing God revealed in him and believing, and some hating and finally killing him. They are all skilled writers and take us through Jesus' days with gathering momentum to that week of celebration, betrayal, mockery, rejection — and glory. In retrospect we can see that the main concern of all three writers is to get Jesus (and us) to Jerusalem and that final Passover week where the real action — suffering, crucifixion, resurrection — takes place. They provide just enough narrative material to make sure we understand that it is us and the world's salvation that is being brought to completion.

And then we pick up St. John's Gospel. From the first line we know that we are in a very different literary world. We find ourselves involved in a world of leisurely and extended conversation, discourses that expand and ruminate on something that has just happened (usually something Jesus has done). Unlike the pithy, aphoristic language from Jesus that we are used to, we are now in the company of Jesus as he takes his time, repeats himself, picks up a phrase and then drops it, circles around and picks it up again, like someone holding a gemstone up to the light and slowly turning it so that we notice the various refracted colors.

Matthew, Mark, and Luke write like kayakers on a fairly swift flowing river with occasional patches of whitewater; there is never any doubt but that they are going where the course of the river takes them. But John is more like a canoe on a quiet lake, drifting unhurried, paddling leisurely to take in aspects of the shoreline, noticing rock formations, observing a blue heron fishing in the rushes, pausing and drifting to sketch cloud patterns reflected in the glassy water.

Halfway through John's Gospel (chapter 12), it appears that the action might be picking up: Judas cynically criticizes Mary as she anoints Jesus; Palm Sunday euphoria trumps the plot to murder Lazarus; the crowd is aroused, responding to thunder from heaven and Jesus' prayer; Jesus quietly disappears into hiding and then suddenly emerges, crying out in fragments of urgent apocalyptic. The adrenalin is beginning to flow. Well-schooled by John's canonical brothers we, of course, know what's coming next. The real action — arrest, trial, crucifixion — will appear on the next page.

We turn the page. What is this? John abruptly interrupts the action and invites us into Jesus' longest conversation/discourse yet (John 13–17). In my Greek Bible (with notes) it is seventeen pages. The two longest discourses up until now have been the Bread of Life discourse (ch. 6) with six pages and the Light of the World discourse (ch. 8) with five pages.

What is John doing?

John is slowing us down. John is quieting us down. John is asking us to shut up and listen. John is telling us to turn off our cell phones, stow our palm pilots, and pay attention to this story that we think we know so well. John is inviting us into the company of Jesus for a time of spiritual formation. John is getting us ready for resurrection — and Pentecost.

* * *

We easily pick up the drift of the conversation. Jesus says two things over and over and over again. He tells his friends that he is leaving: "I am leaving the world and am going to the Father" (John 16:28). I count fifteen times in the conversation in which, one way or another, Jesus tells his disciples that he is leaving them. The second thing he says, and this also over and over and over, is that he is sending them the Holy Spirit: "whom I will send to you from the Father" (15:26). The Holy Spirit, also named the Advocate and the Spirit of Truth, is designated by name and pronouns twenty-six times. Fifteen times he tells them he is leaving; twenty-six times he refers to the Spirit that he and the Father are sending.

"I am leaving. . . . I am sending. . . ."

Jesus is leaving, the Holy Spirit is coming.

Jesus is leaving. They are not going to see him again. But the leaving is not abandonment (John 14:18). He will not be incommunicado (14:13). He is not walking off, forgetful, distracted.

The Holy Spirit is coming. This Holy Spirit will be in them, doing in them what Jesus did among them. The Holy Spirit, God's way of being present with us, will make their life and work continuous with Jesus' life and work. The way God was present to them in Jesus, God will be present to others in them.

The leaving and the sending work together, back and forth, back and forth. Jesus' absence from them becomes the Spirit's presence in them. Everything Jesus said and did among them is to be continued in what they (we!) say and do.

> I washed your feet; you wash one another's feet. (13:14)
> I have loved you; you love one another. (13:34; 15:12)
> You've seen me; you'll see the Father. (14:9)
> You've seen me work; you'll do my work. (14:12)
> I've been with you; the Spirit will be with you. (14:16-17)
> I live; you also will live. (14:19)
> You are in me; I am in you. (14:20)
> I am teaching you; the Spirit will teach/remind you. (14:25-26)
> Abide in me; I abide in you. (15:4)
> I was hated; you will be hated. (15:18-25)
> The Spirit will testify; you will testify. (15:26-27)
> I go away; the Spirit will come. (16:7)
> I haven't finished what I have to say; the Spirit will tell you. (16:12-15)

In the prayer (ch. 17), this congruence between what they have experienced in Jesus' presence and what they will experience in the Spirit's coming becomes even more explicit:

I am no longer in the world; they are in the world. (17:11)
Father, we are one; may they be one. (17:11, 22, 23)
I don't belong to the world; they don't belong to the world. (17:16)
You sent me into the world; I send them into the world. (17:18)
I sanctify myself; they are sanctified in truth. (17:19)
You are in me and I in you; may they also be in us. (17:21)
You love me; you love them. (17:23, 26)

*   *   *

The conversation is rambling and unsystematic. This is not what we ordinarily think of as good teaching. But Jesus is not making things clear, smoothing out ambiguities; he is making them vivid, pulsing. There is no outline and there are no transitions. Definitions are lacking. What the conversation does is immerse us in the presence of another, the presence of Jesus readying us for Spirit. We are soon listening more to who he is than what he says; we are drawn into this seamless web of relational attentiveness, leaving and sending, sensing within ourselves the pervasive, soul-permeating continuity between the absent Jesus and the present Spirit.

And there is also this about the conversation. It is exceedingly spare in the use of imperatives. Jesus is not telling us how to practice spiritual formation, "how to do it" — he is telling how it is done. Spiritual formation is primarily what the Spirit does, forming the resurrection life of Christ in us. There is not a whole lot we can do here any more than we can create the cosmos (that was the work of the Spirit in creation), any more than we can outfit Jesus for salvation (that was the work of the Spirit at Jesus' baptism). But there is a great deal that the Spirit can do — the resurrection community is the Spirit's work. What we can do, need to do, is be there — accept the leaving and the loss of the physically reassuring touch and companionship. Be there to accept what is sent by the Father in Jesus' name. Be there, receptive and obedient. Be there praying, "Here am I, the servant of the Lord; let it be with me according to your word" (Luke 1:38).

*   *   *

A number of years ago we got a call from our son: "Mom, Dad, Lynn's pregnant. We're going to have a baby." Their first child. But even more important, our first grandchild. Within days we were driving the two hours to Princeton Seminary where they were students. Jan was excited, brimming with anticipation. But I wasn't feeling much of anything. We had had three children of our own, I didn't see why this was so special — and there were still six months before we would see the baby. As we got closer to greeting them Jan's anticipation heightened, but somehow this pregnancy hadn't penetrated my emotions. I felt dull, flat, routine.

Driving back home the next day, I complained of my lack of ebullience, an emotion Jan had in excess. "What's wrong with me? Why don't I feel anything?" Jan said, "It's because you've never been pregnant."

"Well that's just great; so what am I going to do about that?"

She told me to build a cradle.

When we got home I went to the public library and found pictures of cradles. I decided on an early American hooded cradle, sketched out plans, went to a specialty woods shop, examined the stock, and chose some Honduras mahogany. Most afternoons I came home an hour or so early from my parish duties to my shop and worked on that cradle. I decided to finish it with applications of tung oil. I worked on each piece of the cradle with the finest grade of sandpaper, over and over. I then went to fine steel wool, over and over. Each application of tung oil deepened the color; after several applications it seemed like the wood glowed from within. I worked with each piece of the cradle, shaping it, holding it, rubbing it, over and over and over — and all the time anticipating the baby that would be in that cradle, over and over and over. Jan's prescription worked: I got pregnant. Week after week shaping that cradle, my hands and fingers working the wood, over and over anointing the oil that set the mahogany on fire from within, imagining the developing baby that would soon be swaddled in that cradle, praying in gratitude and anticipation for the life in Lynn's swelling womb. By the time the cradle was ready, I was ready, prepared to receive the gift of new life.

Think of the conversation as cradle building, the images and repetitions. The images: the continued life of Christ in us grounded in the physical act of kneeling and the material stuff of dirty feet, a basin of water and a towel (John 13); the life of Jesus continued in us offered in prayer to the Holy Father who, we can be very sure, is faithfully even now answering in us Jesus' prayer for us (John 17). And the repetitions: Jesus' words working deep into our praying imaginations, over and over and over — "I'm leaving. . . . I'm sending" — the emptiness, the fullness. Jesus visibly leaving, Spirit invisibly arriving. Resurrection.

As North Americans we are typically impatient with this kind of thing. When there is something important before us, especially something dramatic like Pentecost, we like to set goals and develop strategies. But that is not John's way. He tells us a Jesus story. He takes us into the company of Jesus in such a way that we are formed in the way of Jesus, takes us into the room where Jesus is praying to the Father for us, "that they may be one, as we are one, I in them and you in me" (John 17:22-23), a community of the resurrection. For resurrection takes place in a company of friends. It is not a private experience. It does not make us self-sufficient or autonomous.

Threat: Sectarianism

When Jesus said "Receive the Holy Spirit" (John 20:22), he said it to the assembled community. When St. Luke described the descent of the Holy Spirit it was upon the community, one hundred and twenty (at least) praying and waiting followers of Jesus "together in one place" (Acts 2:1).

We are a community. We are not ourselves by ourselves. We are born into communities, we live in communities, we die in communities. Human beings are not solitary, self-sufficient creatures. As we realize both the necessity and the nature of our lives in community, we also become aware of the difficulty, the complexity, and, as Christians who are following Jesus, the seductions all around us to find an easier way, a modified community, a reduced community customized to my preferences, a "gated community."

Just as gnosticism is the standard threat to living receptively and adorationally in the creation, and moralism is the ever-present threat to living sacrificially and hospitably in history, so sectarianism is the sin that "coucheth at the door" (Gen. 4:7 ASV), ready to pounce, endangering our life together lived generously and lovingly in the community.

Sectarianism is as common in the community in which Christ plays as gnosticism is in creation and moralism is in history. As in the first two threats, the boundaries and definitions are not fixed — it is more like a tendency, an ever-present pull to something smaller, a reduction that enables us to exercise control. Sectarianism involves deliberately and willfully leaving the large community, the "great congregation" that is featured so often in the Psalms, the whole company of heaven and earth, and embarking on a path of special interests with some others, whether few or many, who share similar tastes and concerns. But God's clear intent from the outset is to bless "all the families of the earth" (Gen. 12:3), and the anticipated hope is that "at the name of Jesus every knee should bend, in heaven and on earth and under the earth, and every tongue should confess that Jesus Christ is Lord, to the glory of God the Father" (Phil. 2:10-11).

Sectarianism is to the community what heresy is to theology, a willful removal of a part from the whole. The part is, of course, good — a work of God. But apart from the whole it is out of context and therefore diminished, disengaged from what it needs from the whole and from what what's left of the whole needs from it. We wouldn't tolerate someone marketing a Bible with some famous preacher's five favorite books selected from the complete sixty-six and bound in fine leather. We wouldn't put up with an art dealer cutting up a large Rembrandt canvas into two-inch squares and selling them off nicely framed. So why do we so often positively delight and celebrate the dividing up of the Jesus community into contentious and competitive groups? And why does Paul's rhetorical question, "Has Christ been divided?" (1 Cor. 1:13), continue to be ignored century after century after century?

*   *   *

We encounter ascending levels of complexity as we proceed from creation to history and now to community. A consideration of these complexities can clarify the nature of the sectarian threat. Creation itself is the study of a lifetime. Poets and scientists keep calling our attention to details that we are always overlooking. We have noted how the relative stability and "there-ness" of creation opens up into the "here-ness" of history marked by huge interpenetrating movements and events that develop exponentially as men and women act and speak, make love and war, explore and invent, buy and sell, have families and form governments. Journalists try to keep up with all that is happening hour by hour, day by day. Scholars try to understand and discern the meaning of what has happened. But this quite staggering complexity takes yet another quantum leap in complexity when we deal with souls-in-community, the "us-ness" of our common life. The world within and among us, our bodies and souls in community, is more complex than the worlds without us, these already formidable worlds of creation and history. It is demanding to analyze and comprehend the rain forests. It takes a keen and wide-ranging intelligence to piece together the history of the Aztec civilization. But the human soul-in-community? Where do we even start? There are mysteries here that do not yield to work in the laboratory or field studies. We human beings, most of us anyway, won't stand still long enough to be studied impersonally and objectively by some so-called expert. We won't be reduced. We refuse to be explained lest we be explained away.

It is understandable that we are overwhelmed and retreat from the complexities. Our primary sense of ourselves is, of course, me — "me, myself, and I," as we are wont to say. But after awhile we realize that there is more to existence than my needs, my wants, my impulses. Without our consent, birth lands us kicking and screaming on the playing field of creation and history. We are given a few weeks, maybe even months, of indulgence in me-ness, as if we were the sole occupants of the field, but then the long, slow, arduous process of socialization is launched, the development from me-ness to us-ness: there are others in this family, we live in a neighborhood, the glories of creation open up before us, the adventures and dangers, the surprises and catastrophes of history begin to penetrate our cocooned world, and then — lo and behold! — we find that we are inescapably *involved* in what is going on and there is no getting out of it. We are participants in the three-ring circus of creation, history, and community, whether we like it or not.

We can attempt to withdraw, and many of us try — pick up our marbles, as our children say, and go home. It is fairly common as a stock response. It seems like an easy option but it turns out not to be effective in the long run. It looks like we are stuck with one another ("all the families of the earth!") in the grand arena of creation and as the huge drama of history plays to a full house. But that doesn't mean we have to like it. And it doesn't mean that we can't try to arrange something less demanding, more manageable. How about a sect? Not exactly a denial of community but excluding as much of it as we are able and then redefining it to accommodate me.

*   *   *

The impulse to sectarianism has its roots in "selfism," the conceit that I don't need others as they are but only for what they can do for me. Selfism reduces life to my appetites and needs and preferences. Selfism results in expulsion from the Garden. But once out there "on our own," east of Eden, we find that we can't quite make it without a little help, so we join forces with a few others out of necessity, meanwhile fiercely insisting on our independence and excluding all who don't suit our preferences. We become a sect. Sects are composed of men and women who reinforce their basic selfism by banding together with others who are pursuing similar brands of selfism, liking the same foods, believing in the same idols, playing the same games, despising the same outsiders. Early on selfism developed into sectarianism in order to build a tower to heaven without having to bother with the God of heaven. The attempt disintegrated into a snake pit of sects, each incomprehensible to the other. Babel is the mother city of sectarianism. With the call of Abraham, the long, slow, complex, and still continuing movement to pull all these selves into a people of God community began. The birthing of the Jesus' community on the Day of Pentecost was an implicit but emphatic repudiation and then reversal of Babel sectarianism.

*　　*　　*

The Greeks, as so often in matters of human experience, provide us with just the right story, the seed story of selfism, that provides the root for sectarianism. It is the story of Narcissus.

Narcissus was a gloriously handsome young man. All the girls fell in love with him. They adored him, threw themselves at him, treated him like a glamorous celebrity with all the attributes of a god. But Narcissus paid the girls little mind. He rebuffed, ignored, and dismissed them. He scorned their adulation. Narcissus had no time for them; he was all the company he needed. He could not waste time on anyone; he required his full attention. One of the girls that Narcissus slighted prayed to the gods for redress, a prayer that was immediately answered. (Greek deities love answering these kinds of prayers.) The great goddess Nemesis was right there to answer the prayer of the girl with the broken heart, and she heard and stepped in to take care of Narcissus. In the Greek world, gods and goddesses don't let us get by with this kind of dehumanizing behavior. She decreed, "May he who loves not others love himself only." One day as Narcissus bent over a pool to get a drink of water he saw there his own reflection. Wow! He already knew he was important; he knew all the girls were falling all over themselves to get his attention. But he had no idea that he was *this* good-looking. He fell in love with his reflection immediately. He exclaimed, "Now I know what all those girls see in me, no wonder they are in love with me — *I'm* in love with me! How can I ever bear to quit looking at such loveliness that is me, mirrored in that water." Narcissus couldn't tear himself away from his image. Kneeling at the pool he pined away, fixed in one long, adoring gaze. The whole world was reduced to that image, the Narcissus-adoring self. Narcissus got smaller and smaller and smaller, until there was no Narcissus left; he had starved to death on a diet of self. Selfism is suicide. All that is left of Narcissus to this day is a white flower, a frail memorial in the cemetery of selfism.

*   *   *

Narcissus would seem to be an unlikely character to show up in companies of Christians. Men and women who are so radically reoriented in this grand creation overflowing with wonders, a people who have been so graciously invited into a place in history at the eucharistic table where there is so much to receive and share, would seem to be immune to at least the more gratuitous forms of self-absorption.

And yet the progeny of Narcissus keep showing up in our communities of created and saved souls. They are so glaringly out-of-place in the context of the biblical revelation that one would think that they would be noticed immediately and banned absolutely. More often they are welcomed and embellished, given roles of leadership and turned into celebrities. These are men and women whose lives have just been re-centered from self to Savior by worshiping a sovereign God, people who have been redefined from impersonal roles or functions to sons and daughters of God and brothers and sisters with one another. It is an odd phenomenon to observe followers of Jesus, suddenly obsessed with their wonderfully saved souls, setting about busily cultivating their own spiritualities. Self-spirituality has become the hallmark of our age. The spirituality of Me. A spirituality of self-centering, self-sufficiency, and self-development. All over the world at the present time we have people who have found themselves redefined by the revelation of God in Jesus' birth, death, and resurrection, going off and cultivating the divine within and abandoning spouses, children, friends, and congregations.

This is not only odd; it is outrageous. For one thing, it makes hash of our inclusion in Jesus' prayer for his about-to-be-scattered friends that "they may all be one. As you, Father, are in me and I am in you, may they

243

also be in us . . . that they may become completely one . . ." (John 17:21, 23). For another, it removes Jesus' primary and insistently repeated love command from its controlling and dominating place in our lives. None of us, of course, would think of eliminating the love command, but we routinely place it on the margins and so relativize it. We pick the people and places and occasions in which we will practice it. In other words, we confine it within the walls of a sect.

But holy living, resurrection living, is not a self-project. We are a *people* of God and cannot live holy lives, resurrection lives, as individuals. We are not a self-defined community; we are a God-defined community. The love that God pours out for and in us creates a community in which that love is reproduced in our love for one another.

*   *   *

Narcissism is seldom encountered in its pure Greek form. We develop ways to maintain our narcissistic predispositions without attracting (we hope) the notice of Nemesis. The usual way in which we avoid the appearance of crass individualism is through sectarianism. A sect is a front for narcissism. We gather with other people in the name of Jesus, but we pre-define them according to our own tastes and predispositions. This is just a cover for our individualism: we reduce the community to conditions congenial to the imperial self. The sectarian impulse is strong in all branches of the church because it provides such a convenient appearance of community without the difficulties of loving people we don't approve of, or letting Jesus pray us into relationship with the very men and women we've invested a good bit of time avoiding. A sect is accomplished by community reduction, getting rid of what does not please us, getting rid of what offends us, whether of ideas or people. We construct religious clubs instead of entering resurrection communities. Sects are termites in the Father's house.

The attempt to reduce the community of the resurrection to a sect is a perpetual threat. This is not what God had in mind when he poured out his Spirit on the praying followers of Jesus that memorable day in Jerusalem.[6]

Grounding Text (1): Deuteronomy

The Christian life is not a self-project. We are a *people* of God and cannot live the Christian life by ourselves. We live in community whether we want to or not, whether we admit to it or not. The Bible knows nothing of the solitary Christian. Having been created and saved we are now commanded to live out our creation and salvation in the community that Christ gathers by his Holy Spirit. Deuteronomy and Luke/Acts are major texts that ground us in this world, this community, in which Christ plays.

*　　*　　*

Deuteronomy occupies a strategic place in our understanding of what goes into being formed as a people of God. More than anything else it is about the formation of the community of God's people. It would be hard to over-estimate the power of this final book of the Pentateuch for shaping our participation in the community. Deuteronomy, presented in the voice of Moses, preaches the meaning and formation of holy community. Working off of the foundational material of creation and salvation narrated in the first four books of the Pentateuch, the language turns sermonic. After a long training (forty years!) the people are addressed as if they are capable of doing what they have been created and saved to do: live as the people of God in the promised land of God. Live holy lives. Live the creation/salvation revolution. It has taken them a long time to grow up; they are now poised at the threshold of maturity and called to love. Love is our most mature act as human beings. Both statistically and sermonically, the word "love" holds a prominent place in the book.

The Story

Deuteronomy is embedded in a story that gives contemporary poignancy to what it means for us to be gathered and formed into the resurrection community of the Holy Spirit. King Josiah and Prophet Jeremiah play principal roles in the story. The story takes place in and around the year 622 BC in Jerusalem and is recorded in 2 Kings 22–23 and 2 Chronicles 34–35.

Here's the story. Josiah became king when he was eight years old —

far too young, it would seem, to be a king. He became king at such a young age through an act of violence: His father, Amon, was murdered by a cabal of conspirators in a bloody palace coup. The assassins were immediately apprehended and killed by others who then rescued Josiah and promptly crowned him king. He was the youngest king ever to sit on Judah's throne. The year was about 640 BC. Josiah's reign would end thirty-one years later when the Egyptian pharaoh killed him in a battle at Megiddo (609 BC). Violence launched his kingship and violence ended it. But the thirty-one years of his reign were simply stunning, and in no small part because of Deuteronomy.

Josiah inherited a huge moral and political mess. His grandfather, King Manasseh, may have been the absolutely worst king Judah had ever experienced, ruling for a fifty-five-year reign that filled the country with every imaginable evil and even some unimaginable. Assyria was the dominant world power at the time. It had bullied the world for three hundred years and had acquired the distinction of making high art out of evil — cruelty, torture, lasciviousness, black magic, spirit-mediums, witches, sorcerers, child sacrifice. You name it. Manasseh, improbable as it seems considering his lineage as a leader of the people of God, was a great admirer of all things Assyrian and imported its evil by the truckload into Judah and Jerusalem. He constructed Assyria-inspired sex-and-religion shrines all over the country, erected obscene phallic pillars to the goddess Asherah, filled Solomon's temple with foul images and relics, and even built rooms in the temple for the use of male prostitutes. It's hard to imagine anything worse: a moral cesspool, a spiritual nightmare, creation polluted, salvation repudiated, the holy community in ruins. Amon, Josiah's father, continued Manasseh's course, but the assassination cut that short at two years. Such were the conditions faced by the eight-year-old Josiah when he was put on Judah's throne.

Presumably the same people who rescued Josiah from assassination by the assassins of his father surrounded, guided, and advised him through his childhood until he was mature enough to govern in his own right. We are not told that story. Did his mother Jedidah play a role? All we know is the results: at age sixteen he was seeking "the God of his ancestor David" (2 Chron. 34:3). By the time he was twenty he was acting as king on his own and began cleaning up the Manasseh mess, scrubbing the country clean of the sex-and-religion idolatries (34:3). He had embraced David as his mentor in all matters royal: he "walked in the ways of his ancestor David; he did not turn aside to the right or to the left" (34:2).

When Josiah was twenty-six years old, Hilkiah, the high priest, in the course of extensive repairs being carried out in the place of worship, found a scroll, the "book of the law of the LORD given through Moses" (2 Chron. 34:14). The book was Deuteronomy.[7] When it was read to Josiah, he immediately embraced it as his text for completing the reform that he had launched six years earlier. It was the defining moment of his kingship: he had his text. Without a moment's hesitation he set about the extensive rebuilding of his country as a community of the people of God.

*   *   *

Four years after Josiah launched his reform movement, Jeremiah received his call to be a prophet and began preaching repentance, using language that we can see has many affinities with words and phrases in the Deuteronomy scroll. The king and the prophet, it seems, were of one mind. In retrospect it seems clear enough that Deuteronomy provided the text that God used in the lives of Josiah and Jeremiah to pull the people of God back from the brink of extinction. One of our best Deuteronomy scholars is extravagant in his assessment: the reform "revolutionized all aspects of Israelite religion."[8]

Jeremiah and Josiah were roughly the same age. (An educated guess is that Jeremiah was two years older than Josiah.) Jeremiah grew up in a priest's home in the village of Anathoth only two miles and less than an hour's walk from the Jerusalem royal palace where Josiah lived. Were they boyhood friends? The scroll was discovered in the temple by the high priest Hilkiah. Jeremiah's father was a priest named Hilkiah. Was the priest who was Jeremiah's father the same man as the priest who discovered the Deuteronomy scroll? Maybe.

At any rate, at the discovery of the scroll, Josiah launched a vigorous reform movement throughout the country, using Deuteronomy as his text for reform. Within four years of the discovery of the scroll, Jeremiah received his call to be a prophet. There is no hard evidence that Josiah and Jeremiah were partners in the reform movement, but it sure looks like it. Jeremiah mentions Josiah's name four times (Jer. 3:6; 25:3; 36:1, 2) and alludes to him another time (Jer. 22:15-16). From the records we have of his preaching (the book of Jeremiah), we can see that much of his language reflects the language of Deuteronomy. After Josiah was killed in the battle at Megiddo in 609 BC, Jeremiah preached Josiah's funeral sermon (2 Chron. 35:25).

For thirteen years, Josiah and Jeremiah, the young king and the youthful prophet, were allies in leading a major reformation in Judah, restoring the ravished, decimated, corrupted people of God as a true worshiping community. Josiah tore down the sex-and-religion shrines and vile phallic pillars and smashed the furnaces used for child sacrifice — a top to bottom housecleaning. And Jeremiah preached his sermons of repentance and forgiveness, wept rivers of tears lamenting the depths of degradation to which the people had descended, exposed the venality and lies that passed for religion in the popular preaching of the day, challenged the superficial trivializing messages from the priests that assured the people that everything was just fine, that "healed the wound of my people lightly" (Jer. 6:14 RSV).

*   *   *

In one sense the reform didn't last long. Thirteen years to be exact. Then Egypt and Babylon got rid of Assyria (a good thing) but also conquered Judah (not a good thing), and Babylon soon hauled Judah off into exile. But in another sense the reform that Josiah led and Jeremiah preached formed a people of God that not only survived a massive political defeat, enslavement, and exile, but actually flourished. The Josianic reform, using Deuteronomy as its text, formed (re-formed) God's people into a community of worship and love that endured for another five hundred years, making its way through much suffering and withstanding many assaults until it would again be re-formed by the Holy Spirit as the resurrection community of Jesus Christ.

The Plains of Moab

Deuteronomy is a sermon — actually a series of sermons. It is the longest sermon in the Bible and maybe the longest sermon ever. Deuteronomy presents Moses, standing on the Plains of Moab with Israel assembled before him, preaching. It is his last sermon. When he completes it, he will leave his pulpit on the plains, climb a mountain, and die.

The setting is stirring and emotion-packed. Moses had entered the biblical story of salvation as a baby born under a death threat in Egypt. Now, 120 years later, eyesight sharp as ever and walking with a spring in his step, he preaches this immense sermon and dies, still brimming with words and life.

This sermon does what all sermons are intended to do: takes God's words, written and spoken in the past, takes the human experience, ancestral and personal, of the listening congregation, then reproduces the words and experience as a single event right now, in this present moment. A sermon changes words *about* God into words *from* God. It takes what we have heard or read of God and God's ways and turns them into a personal proclamation of God's good news. A sermon changes water into wine. A sermon changes bread nouns and wine verbs into the body and blood of Christ. A sermon makes personal again what was once present and personal to Isaac and Rebekah, to Ruth and Boaz, to David and Abigail, to Mary and Elizabeth, to Peter and Paul, to Priscilla and Aquila. To you. To me. No word that God has spoken is a mere literary artifact to be studied; no human experience is dead history merely to be regretted or admired. The continuous and insistent Mosaic repetitions of "today" and "this day" throughout these sermons keep attentions taut and responsive. The complete range of human experience is brought to life and salvation by the full revelation of God. That is what Moses is doing from his great pulpit on the Plains of Moab: Live this! Now!

Not only is the sermon the way this is done, but it has functioned continuously and powerfully in the community of God's people as a primary means for the grammatical conversion of language from them to us, from was to is, from then to now. Even when a sermon is clumsy or inept, when it keeps the language of the community local and personal it has its use.

The Plains of Moab are the last stop on the forty-year journey from Egyptian slavery to Promised Land freedom. The people of Israel have experienced a lot as a community: deliverance, wanderings, rebellions, wars, providence, worship, guidance. The people of Israel have heard a lot from God: commandments, covenant conditions, sacrificial procedures. And now, poised at the River Jordan, ready to cross over and possess the new land, Moses, preaching his great Plains of Moab sermon, makes sure that they don't leave any of it behind, not so much as one detail of their experience of God's revelation: he puts their entire experience of salvation and providence into the present tense (chapters 1–11); he puts the entire revelation of commandment and covenant into the present tense (chapters

12–28); and then he wraps it all up in a charge and a blessing to launch them into *today's* obedience and believing (chapters 29–34).

"Let's go."

*   *   *

Getting saved is easy; becoming a community is difficult — damnably difficult.

Nothing could have been easier from a human point of view in the story that we have before us than getting saved. These people, our ancestors in salvation, prepared a meal of lamb and vegetables and bread, ate it, and simply walked out of Egypt, walked away from four hundred years of slavery, following Moses east until they arrived at an impassible sea. There they watched as Moses stretched his staff over the waters. In astonishment they saw the waters divide all the way to the far side, exposing a dry roadway, probably paved with Sodom and Gomorrah asphalt. They crossed. On the far shore they looked back and saw the Egyptian horses and chariots in full pursuit. Terror-stricken, they huddled together as their doom hurtled toward them across the highway through the sea. And then, just as the Egyptian forces were all stretched out along the miraculous road, horses pounding, chariots rumbling, men shouting, the sea walls collapsed on the Egyptians. The people were saved. Stuttery Moses slipped into the unlikely role of cantor as if he had done it all his life and led them in singing the great anthem of salvation:

> "I will sing to the LORD, for he has triumphed gloriously;
>   horse and rider he has thrown into the sea.
> The LORD is my strength and my might,
>   and he has become my salvation;
> this is my God, and I will praise him,
>   my father's God, and I will exalt him.
> The LORD is a warrior;
>   the LORD is his name."

(Exod. 15:1-3)

The hills rang with the salvation hymn; over time it became the Israelites' national anthem. Miriam and the women got out their tambourines and began dancing. Salvation singing, salvation dancing.

And the people who had done nothing but walk and watch now began to sing and dance. What could be easier?

Three days later the people were complaining because the water tasted bad. God gave them fresh water (Exod. 15:23-25). A month and a half later they were complaining again because they didn't like the food. God gave them "bread from heaven," the marvelous manna, with instructions on how to receive it. But the people flouted the instructions and did it their own way, disobedient and willful (Exod. 16). Again there was a problem with the water and the disgruntled people took it out on Moses, so angry this time that they were ready to kill him (Exod. 17:1-7). In the first three months of their salvation, there are fourteen references to the people's incapacity for community.[9] When Moses' father-in-law Jethro met him in the wilderness, bringing Moses' wife and children to join him, Jethro was alarmed at what he saw: Moses was spending all his time from morning to evening settling the arguments and fights of his quarrelsome congregation. Jethro helped him to organize a judicial system so that he wouldn't have to do it all himself, but the fact that such a comprehensive system was needed at all testifies to the contentiousness of the people (Exod. 18:13-27). These saved people don't know the first thing about getting along with each other.

*   *   *

Moses begins his Plains of Moab sermon by rehearsing the events that preceded their arrival at this place. When they left Mount Sinai for Canaan they arrived in a mere eleven days at Kadesh Barnea at the threshold of the Promised Land (Deut. 1:2). But then their complaining, foot-dragging, disobedient spirit got to be too much — they weren't yet capable of living as a community in the new land — and God sent them back to Sinai to start over. It took thirty-eight more years to get back, prepared to enter the land, thirty-eight years of hard schooling in becoming a community capable of living freely obedient and loyal in love (2:14). Now on the Plains of Moab, Moses goes over what they have been through for the forty years, reminding them that it was their recalcitrance, their unresponsiveness, their reluctance to receive God's commands and promises that accounted for that forty years. It wasn't their enemies and it wasn't the forbidding terrain that stretched eleven days into forty years; it was because "you grumbled in your tents" (1:27).

Even after forty years of intense wilderness training, though, they are far from an ideal community. And, as we will soon find out, they never will be, any more than we will be. Utopian communities are not featured in the biblical story. But the people of Israel have made a start. Before he sends them off to inherit the land, Moses goes over the basics with them. He begins with what he started them off with at Sinai forty years earlier, Ten Words that set down the conditions for living in community; he adds to that a simple creed that provides a common focus; and then he goes over the instructions for living, selecting and revising the Sinai instructions that will guide them in the everyday affairs that lie just ahead of them.

"Ten Words": The Conditions

Conventionally we call them the Ten Commandments, but the Hebrew text speaks of the Ten Words (Deut. 4:13; 10:4; Exod. 34:28). The Ten Words establish the conditions necessary for a free, loving, and just community of God's people to develop and flourish. The three adjectives — free, loving, just — are basic to community.

Community is intricate and complex. It consists of many people of various moods, ideas, needs, experiences, gifts and injuries, desires and disappointments, blessings and losses, intelligence and stupidity, living in proximity and in respect for one another, and believingly in worship of God. It is not easy and it is not simple. The conditions, established by the Ten Words, at least make it possible. None of the conditions is onerous. All are both necessary and non-negotiable.

No community worth its salt has ever existed very long in ignorance or defiance of the conditions.

*　　*　　*

The Ten Words are arranged in pentads, two sets of five.[10] The first pentad sets down the God-conditions; the second pentad sets down the human-conditions. When the two pentads, one to five and six to ten, are set down in parallel columns, the first thing that strikes us is how differently they are formulated. Each word in the first pentad of God-conditions is formulated by including the phrase "the LORD your God" and is elaborated either by providing a context or motive or expansion or reason for the command. In the second pentad setting down the human-conditions each word is a bare, unadorned command: "Don't. . . ." And don't ask me why.

If we are going to live in community, dealing with the God whom we cannot see takes priority over dealing with the men and women we can see. And so that we don't, in our hurry to get on with the really practical things that are on our minds, brush past the invisible, fail to attend to the immense gravity of what is involved, reduce God to mere background, we are slowed down by strategies of expansion on each word: there are reasons here that you may not have thought of, there are consequences here that you might not be aware of, there is a context involved that sets this command in a world far larger than what you see around you right now. Here are five God-conditions apart from which you can never have community. Ponder. Realize. Imagine. Embrace. Worship.

And if we are going to live in community, dealing with the men and women whom we look at and see every live-long day has to be faced head on. This may not be as obvious as it appears, for there is nothing more common among us than turning the people among whom we live into abstractions, lumping them into categories, idealizing or demonizing them, dealing with them impersonally as principles or projects. The staccato, unqualified imperatives of the second pentad prevent us from projecting our likes and dislikes on others, depersonalizing them and then dealing with them however we decide is appropriate. Here are five human-conditions that cannot be violated if you are going to live in community, no matter what you feel or think. Name. Respect. Listen. Honor. Accept. Serve.

* * *

First Word: "I am the LORD your God, who brought you out of the land of Egypt, out of the house of slavery; you shall have no other gods before me." (Deut. 5:6-7)

First, God. God's presence in the present, the now, is where we also are present, the condition in which we live, we and our family and friends, our neighbors and the strangers who are among us, and, yes, our enemies. This is the neighborhood. And this God who lives here is about to tell us what to do. But his command does not come out of a vacuum; it comes from a rich, storied context of salvation from slavery. Before he tells us what to do, he tells us what he has done: he has saved us from a life of slavery. We are no longer slaves who have no choice in what we do or do not do. We are free to say yes or no. Our freedom is a gift of God's salvation. Do we understand this? Then we are ready to hear his first word: you shall have no other gods before me. Our choice.

Our choice, because God, having set us free, is not going to violate our freedom now by imposing himself upon us. The community in which we live is not formed by coercion. Nobody *has* to live here with these others whom God has saved. On the other hand, if we want to live in community, this is the first condition: God without rivals, God without secretly holding on to other options.

Second Word: "You shall not make for yourself an idol, whether in the form of anything that is in heaven above, or that is on the earth beneath, or that is in the water under the earth. You shall not bow down to them or worship them; for I the LORD your God am a jealous God, punishing children for the iniquity of parents, to the third and fourth generation of those who reject me, but showing steadfast love to the thousandth generation of those who love me and keep my commandments." (Deut. 5:8-10)

Idols are non-gods and as such are much more congenial to us than God, for we not only have the pleasure of making them, using our wonderful imaginations and skills in creative ways, but also of controlling them. They are gods with all the God taken out so that we can continue to be our own gods. There are innumerable ways in which we can make idols for ourselves. The possibilities are endless, ranging from the skies above to the earth around us to the sea beneath us. It is no wonder that idol-making and idol-worshiping have always been the most popular religious game in town.

And because it is so satisfying to us, it is difficult to see why there is anything so very wrong with it. It *is* a spiritual act, after all. We are dealing with what has transcendent meaning. We are worshiping, which is the religious act par excellence and therefore always a good thing. Except that at rock bottom there is nothing to it, or at least nothing of God to it.

Third Word: "You shall not take the name of the LORD your God in vain: for the LORD will not hold him guiltless who takes his name in vain." (Deut. 5:11 RSV)

God is not a name or concept to be bandied about frivolously. God is not verbal decoration to give color or enhancement to our speech. God is holy and sovereign. God is the one who gives meaning to our words, who determines life and everything in it. We do not give meaning to God; we cannot give emphasis or authority to who we are or what we are doing or saying by throwing in the name "God," no matter how impressive it sounds. When we reduce God to a name among other names, all names eventually become depersonalized, mere ciphers to identify others by function or role, without regard for the dignity and reverence inherent in every person and every thing. Eventually language itself loses its capacity for expressing wonder and adoration and intimacy, and, most of all, belief and love. A word — any word, but beginning with the name "God" — used "in vain" soon becomes flattened into words that are only useful in "getting and spending."

Blasphemy, using the name of God to curse or reject or dismiss, is only a more conspicuous use of God's name "in vain." All casual, thoughtless, clichéd uses of the name, and perhaps especially among those who consider themselves devout believers in God, fall under the warning. Language in itself, beginning with the name "God," is holy, a precious gift that makes it possible to live in community. A primary necessity for living in community is to tend reverently to the way we use language, beginning with the way we say "God," but then extending into the way we use language around the supper table, when buying groceries or a pair of shoes, and when answering the telephone.

Fourth Word: "Observe the sabbath day and keep it holy, as the LORD your God commanded you. Six days you shall labor and do all your work. But the seventh day is a sabbath to the LORD your God; you shall not do any work, you, or your son or your daughter, or your male or female slave, or your ox or your donkey, or any of your livestock, or the resident alien in your towns, so that your male and female slave may rest as well as you. Remember that you were a slave in the land of Egypt, and the LORD your God brought you out from there with a mighty hand and an outstretched arm; therefore the LORD your God commanded you to keep the sabbath day." (Deut. 5:12-15)

The sabbath command is one of the most frequently articulated commands in the Hebrew community, probably (if contemporary experience can be introduced as evidence) because it was so frequently violated. Why is it so difficult to "keep sabbath"? Why is the holiness of time so easily and thoughtlessly dismissed? Why does this solemn command, issued in the context of such august authority and undergirded with more supporting words than any of the other nine (idol-making comes in a close second), get treated with such short shrift? And why does this command, even when it is kept, so often in its very keeping get kept in a way that violates its basic meaning? Jesus, as he went about fulfilling the law, was frequently at odds with those who were keeping the sabbath but keeping it in such a way that nullified what was commanded.

Is it because we don't like letting go of the controls? Is it because we want to be important and if we aren't observed doing something in the community we won't be noticed? Is it because if we let down our guard someone will take advantage of us or take over our position? Maybe. Even probably.

But community cannot flourish without a sabbath. A kept sabbath keeps us out of one another's hair for at least one day a week. Sabbath breaks the stranglehold, emotional or physical, that some of us have on another, a stranglehold that prevents the spontaneities of love and sacrifice.

We notice that the reason given for sabbath-keeping here differs from that given in Exodus. In Exodus we are told to keep sabbath because God kept sabbath. Since he rested on the seventh day, we also rest on the seventh day, get back in step with the creation rhythms of work and rest. In Deuteronomy we are told that keeping sabbath is a matter of simple justice; it prevents the stronger from exploiting the weaker, whether parents over children, employers over workers, even masters over horses and mules. Everyone is given a day to recover the simple dignity of being himself, herself, in the community without regard to use or function or status. Even the dogs and cats are included.

Fifth Word: "Honor your father and your mother, as the LORD your God commanded you, so that your days may be long and that it may go well with you in the land that the LORD your God is giving you." (Deut. 5:16)

Why do mothers and fathers get included in this first pentad of the Ten Words, the pentad that sets down the God-conditions for living in community? Maybe to make it difficult to keep God shut off in a sacred compartment separate from everyday life? Maybe to insist that the way we deal with God always has its analogue in what we face in daily experience? And what human experience is more analogous to being children of God than having parents?

We are introduced into giving reverence and honor to God whom we cannot see by honoring parents whom we can see. The command to honor parents anchors the commands to honor God in the specificities of everyday life. Life with others takes place in the conditions (primarily persons) that are given to us, not conditions that we choose. And nothing is more unconditionally *given* than parents. None of us chooses our own parents. And we do not have an easy time growing up with our parents. After those first months and years of helplessness in which we are dependent on the care and love of father and mother, we gradually come to experience them as getting in the way of getting our own way. Nor do we for a long time, if ever, understand them; they precede us and much about them is beyond us, a mystery — we come to honor and respect what we do not yet know. Not all the time, of course, but often enough for even the most obtuse among us to realize that growing up does not mean simply becoming *my*-self. I am who I am only in a relation of honor and reverence to others — and the first and most enduring relation to others that we are aware of is to mother and father.

The appropriate disciplines that train us from disobedience to or incomprehension of parents into a way of life that honors father and mother also develop a way of life that honors God along the lines commanded by the first four words, this God who is beyond our understanding and who is also well known for getting in the way of getting our own way. That is why the dishonoring of parents is taken so seriously in the Hebrew community (Exod. 21:15, 17; Lev. 20:9; Deut. 27:16; Prov. 20:20; 30:11; Ezek. 22:7). Cursing God and cursing parents fall under the same sentence (cf. Lev. 24:15-16 with Exod. 21:17; Lev. 20:9; and Deut. 21:18-21). Philo in his commentary on the Decalogue drew the parallel between the honor due to God and the honor due to parents: "For parents are midway between the natures of God and man and partake of both. . . . Parents, in my opinion, are to their children what God is to the world . . . the difference being that God created the world, while parents created individual beings only."[11]

These are considerations that lead us to place the fifth word as the concluding command to the first pentad where "the LORD your God" appears in each commandment, rather than, as some do, placing it as the initial command in the second table that is concerned with human relations.

*　　*　　*

If the first pentad is understood as a detailed elaboration of what is involved in the command to love God (Deut. 6:5-6), the second pentad is understood as an exposition of the command to love one's neighbor (Lev. 19:18). The abrupt change of style gives this tablet a staccato austerity — no reasons given, no motivation suggested: five unqualified imperatives.

Sixth Word: "You shall not murder." (Deut. 5:17)

Life is sacred and inviolable. Not just my life but your life. We do not simplify our lives by getting rid of other lives no matter how inconvenient or disgusting or impossible they seem to us. No person can be excised from the membership by a vote of the membership, and certainly not by a veto.

Seventh Word: "Neither shall you commit adultery." (Deut. 5:18)

Marriage is sacred and inviolable. The intimacies of a vowed life together are protected against sexual predation. Sexual desire is not allowed a life of its own. Sexuality is a community, not a private affair.

Eighth Word: "Neither shall you steal." (Deut. 5:19)

Things are sacred and inviolable. The things of this world — trees and rivers, garden and wilderness, money and tools, chariots and chihuahuas — are gifts to the community that each of us is responsible for keeping and tending (Gen. 2:15). They are not loot for plunder. The things of this world are not up for grabs to the strongest and canniest.

Ninth Word: "Neither shall you bear false witness against your neighbor." (Deut. 5:20)

Words are sacred and inviolable. The Hebrew word translated here as "false" is the same word translated as "in vain" in the third word. Words used about or to neighbors are as sacred as those used about or to God. Frivolous and empty talk that demeans or trivializes persons is as sacrilegious as outright lies. Language is the community's lifeblood; if the circulatory system is diseased the community gets sick, sick from lies and gossip alike.

Tenth Word: "Neither shall you covet your neighbor's wife. Neither shall you desire your neighbor's house, or field, or male or female slave, or ox, or donkey, or anything that belongs to your neighbor."

The final word in the love-your-neighbor pentad penetrates to the heart. Up until now the commands have targeted overt actions. This one is an inner disposition — wanting what is another's, desiring what I don't have rather than appreciating what I do have. To covet is to fantasize a life other than what is given to me. When we habitually covet either people or things (usually both), it isn't long before we are plotting and scheming to impose our own will on them to get them by hook or crook. Nothing is sacred. Covetousness is a silent infestation of termites in the community; if it remains undetected, the joists eventually give way and the floor falls in. None of the preceding nine words is safe from the hidden and elusive workings of covetousness. Community vigilance is required.

Grammatically, the second pentad could be a single sentence, each word linked to the next by "and." "You shall not kill *and* you shall not commit adultery *and* you shall not . . ." and so on. The pentad is an unbroken chain of linked commands. None can function by itself. It's all or nothing.

*   *   *

Such are the conditions required for living in community. The Ten Words are often individualized as a code for personal morality. That is a weak way to view them; these are conditions for *community* living, living as God's people entire. In life as created by the word of God and life as experienced in history there are simply no private actions — everything is personal but nothing is private. Everything we do is connected with everything else. When any one of us violates even one of the condition-defining words, ramifications are immediate and sometimes immense in the community (although not always apparent).

"Hear, O Israel:" The Creed

"Hear, O Israel: The LORD is our God, the LORD alone." (Deut. 6:4)

Israel's creed. In Hebrew it is a mere six words: *Shema˓ Yisrael, YHWH elohēnu, YHWH ˒ehad.* But those six words were enough to keep Israel focused on and loyal to God alone. Israel was immersed in a culture of many gods. They rubbed shoulders with highly religious people who dispersed and expressed their religious affections and expectations in multiple ways. These cultures — Canaanite, Philistine, Moabite, Egyptian, Assyrian, Babylonian, and others — were colorful and exciting, a three-ring circus of gods and goddesses accompanied by sideshows promising the latest in underworld wonders and heavenly mysteries. Something for everybody. Israel's belief and worship was dull compared to the technicolor extravaganzas put on by their neighbors. But not their lives; lives in Israel were not dull. Their creed kept them lashed to reality, God-reality and God-truth. Their creed kept them from imagining that our lives are improved by collecting gods and goddesses — or anything else, for that matter; there was no need for accumulating things, or for searching out every nook and cranny of the world for new insights, novel experiences, exotic tales. Their creed gave their community a center and a centering: one LORD, the LORD alone.

But along with the fierce single-mindedness, the simple austerity, the undistracted seriousness of this creed, there is also evidence of a kind of playfulness that found its way into the reflections and prayers of our ancestors who read and prayed and copied these words into the Scripture scrolls of the worshiping community. The playfulness surfaced in a company of Hebrew scholars who lived in the eighth and ninth centuries of the Christian era in the Galilean seaside city of Tiberius, where they acquired the name "Masoretes."

The evidence of this playfulness shows up in the way they copied out the creed. Here's what they did: they copied the last letter of the first word, "hear" (shema'), larger than the other letters. And then they copied the last letter of the final word, "one" ('ehad), to match it. The last letter of the first word (ayin, or a) and the last letter of the last word (dalet or d) in the creed, copied in larger and bolder script, now stand out and spell the Hebrew word 'ad, meaning "witness." The creed is a witness to what orders and centers the community's life; and the community who recites the creed is likewise a witness. I find this winsome. This, it seems to me, is not frivolity but the playful seriousness of scholars who are imagining their way into the text, living their way into it, savoring its possibilities. They are not doggedly plunking down one letter after another, but see the letters alive, see the possibilities of participating in the life of the letter and inviting others to participate also. Israel's creed is not bare dogma regarding God; it is witness. And as we recite it we also become witnesses.

* * *

There is more. What is believed/witnessed is immediately put into action: "You shall love the LORD your God with all your heart, and with all your soul, and with all your might. Keep these words that I am commanding you today in your heart" (Deut. 6:5). Love is the only appropriate action for living out the creed. There are, of course, other actions that follow, but this is where it all starts, all the living that proceeds from the presence and nature and commands of God: "*love* the LORD your God."

No matter how right we are in what we believe about God, no matter how accurately we phrase our belief or how magnificently and persuasively we preach or write or declare it, if love does not shape the way we speak and act, we falsify the creed, we confess a lie. Believing without loving is what gives religion a bad name. Believing without loving destroys lives. Believing without loving turns the best of creeds into a weapon of oppression. A community that believes but does not love or marginalizes love, regardless of its belief system or doctrinal orthodoxy or "vision statement," soon, very soon, becomes a "synagogue of Satan" (Rev. 2:9).

The insistence that this creedal love must be with "all your heart, and with all your soul, and with all your might" leaves no room for interpreting this love as anything less than a way of life that undergirds and permeates everything that we do. This is not an option for those who are so inclined. This is not what we do after we have first mastered something else we sometimes call "the basics."

"Love" is the big word in Deuteronomy, the most characteristic word. But it is not a valentine word, not a sentimentalized word. It gathers all our feelings of affection and emotion and intimacy into something more foundational and enduring, a structure of fierce and exclusive allegiance to God. Without such a creedal structure, this structure provided in God's covenant with us, human love erodes or atrophies to whim and fancy.

Most significantly, this is the command that Jesus selects as the first and unrivaled command, the command on which all other commands hang when he answers the scribe's question, "Which commandment is the first of all?" (Mark 12:28-30).

"These are the Statutes and Ordinances": The Instructions for Living

After the Ten Words that set down the conditions for community and the Creed that centers the community in God alone and a life of love, we have several pages designed to facilitate the everyday gritty details of living together in community (Deut. 12–28). The Exodus/Leviticus instructions, given at Sinai forty years before, are pretty much behind the Israelites by now; they have served their purpose. They are not ignored, but most of them are not in need of repeating: those many pages of instructions for building the structure for worship, the furniture and artifacts for worship, altars and tables and candlesticks; descriptions of how the priests should dress; procedures for making sacrifices so that all of life could be reimagined and practiced in relation to God's generous mercy and forgiving grace. Moses leaves all that out of his Plains of Moab sermon.

Other parts he doesn't leave out, but revises in light of their imminent life together in the new land. There are a hundred details involved in daily living that can't be left up to the individual to decide on the spot: "what if" details. What if you unintentionally kill someone . . . ? What if a virgin is raped . . . ? What if . . . ?

If we are going to live in community we can't brush things like this aside, trusting them to be worked out between men and women of goodwill who are, after all, "saved." We have to deal with these housekeeping details of getting along with each other.

*　　　*　　　*

Moshe Weinfeld speaks of the "unique humanitarian approach" that distinguishes the "statutes and ordinances" of Deuteronomy.[12] The parade example of this is in the Ten Words. These are copied almost word for word from Exodus, except for word three regarding sabbath-keeping, where the reason that supports the command shifts from the theological (we keep sabbath because God rested on the seventh day) to a matter of social justice (our families and servants and animals need respite from unrelieved labor); and except for word ten, in which the first object of forbidden covetousness is "your neighbor's wife," giving a wife first consideration instead of "your neighbor's house," as the Exodus formulation has it (Exod. 20:17). That verse is the first of a number of instances in the statutes and ordinances of Deuteronomy in which consideration is given to the dignity of women.

*　　　*　　　*

In Exodus there are five pages of instructions ("ordinances") that provide guidance through the day-by-day exigencies of life in the wilderness (Exod. 21–23), and there are another nine pages in Leviticus (Lev. 17–26), all of which provide a starting point for Deuteronomy. These combined fourteen pages expand to twenty-six pages in Deuteronomy (Deut. 12–28) — daily life in the settled conditions of the new land is about to become much more complex. Many, perhaps most, of these instructions, are directed, detail by detail, to culturally determined local conditions that don't have much if anything to do with those of us living three thousand years later in a highly technologized democracy. But still, it is highly impressive that so much care is given to the details of living as the people of God in community. The Ten Words set down the conditions for living in community. The creed provides the unifying focus (God only) and integrating motive (love). But that said, there are still a multitude of "what if . . . ?" details that must be dealt with if community life is not going to be endlessly snarled in minutiae.

But in contrast to the earlier instructions, as set down in Exodus and Leviticus, Deuteronomy does not read like a civil-law book, dealing with matters of money in compensation for infractions. The overall tone here is "securing the protection of the individual and particularly of those persons in need of protection."[13] Matters of human rights are included, with special concern for women and the family, treatment of slaves and care for the poor, property rights, and even environmental rights — matters that must be considered, detail by detail, in our communities still. Overreaching and authoritative generalizations (The Ten Words! The creed!), necessary as they are, fundamental as they are, are no defense against the so-called "minor" sins ("the little foxes that ruin the vineyards," Song 2:15) that men and women of goodwill inadvertently, ignorantly (and sometimes, it must be admitted, with pious malice) inflict on the community. G. E. Wright, percipient in his study of this text, selected these "statutes and instructions" — so easily passed over and dismissed as arcane — as "the glory of the Deuteronomic code."[14]

Moses

Given the magnificence of Deuteronomy as the community is reimagined sermonically, the account of Moses at the conclusion is sobering. "Magnificent" is exactly the right word for Deuteronomy and for Moses in his leadership. We have been provided with a detailed grounding of the community in the actual conditions in which the people of Israel (and we, their ancestors) live out daily life. "Deuteronomy . . . attains a sober, earnest, and moving eloquence which sets the book apart from all other literature in the Bible."[15] But despite this sober and earnest eloquence, most of us are incorrigible romanticizers of matters "spiritual." We are prone to go off on tangents of utopian fantasy, following the line that if God is involved in all of this, and if we are involved rightly, the community that results will be quite idyllic. The Moses story that brings Deuteronomy to completion in Moses' two great poems, the song (ch. 32) and the blessing (ch. 33), prevents this great sermonic "making present" of our belief and obedience from vaporizing into an insubstantial romanticizing mist, prevents us from dissipating the lived-out actualities of salvation into sentimental songs or inspirational pep talks. The creation/salvation life isn't thinking about or talking about God, it is *living* God's gift of a free life of love in families and workplaces under conditions of difficulty, of failure, of disappointment, of heartbreak — conditions of sin and death. And Moses is one of the showcase instances in Scripture of failure and heartbreak, of the way in which conditions of sin and death are unavoidably inherent in community in general, but in the people of God community in particular.

We pray and ponder our way through this community-grounding text: realizing what it means to live together in obedience and love, to live imaginatively into that awful journey with its deaths and disobedience, we listen to the sermon that takes up everything at hand as stuff for hope and promise and then shapes it into responsibility, ability to respond; everyone becomes a participant in the words that made the world, made salvation, and now make community. This has to be the most unromantic rendition of community ever written: detailed, honest, particular, bracing, with no illusions.

*   *   *

After Moses had preached his sermon, he wrote it down, handed it over to the priests, and ordered them to read it every seventh year to the congregation — men, women, children, aliens — during the autumn Feast of Booths, the feast devoted to remembering God's providence through the forty wilderness years. Deuteronomy was to be their text for living; every seventh year they would get a refresher course (Deut. 31:9-13).

He then appointed Joshua to take over the leadership from him and take the people across the Jordan into the new land.

The scenario on display on the Plains of Moab that day is totally satisfying: a congregation of free people, thoroughly trained in worship and obedience, ready to enter a land of promise. Moses' sermon has just brought it all present and alive before them, those splendid sentences and stories reverberating in their ears. Joshua holds the reigns of leadership that Moses has just placed in his hands. Moses and Joshua stand before the Tent of Meeting; the pillar of cloud, God's presence among them, appears in confirmation and blessing. A dramatic, satisfying moment. A perfect ending.

Except. Except that there is one thing more. God has a private word with Moses. It couldn't have been pleasant for Moses to hear; and it certainly isn't pleasant for us to read. But if we are going to be prepared for the reality of living as a holy community, we must read it. Here it is:

"'Moses [I'm paraphrasing here], you are about to die and be buried with your ancestors. You'll no sooner be in your grave than this people will be up and whoring after the foreign gods of this country that they are entering. They will abandon me and violate the covenant that I've made with them (31:16). . . . So here's what I want you to do: Copy down this song and teach the people of Israel to sing it. They'll have it then as my witness against them (31:19) . . . when they begin fooling around with other gods and worshiping them (31:20). . . . When things start falling apart, with many terrible things happening, this song will be there with them as a witness to who they are and what went wrong. Their children won't forget this song; they'll be singing it.

"'Don't think I don't know what they are already scheming to do behind my back, behind your back. And they're not even in the land yet, this land I promised them' (31:21).

"So Moses wrote down this song that very day and taught it to the people of Israel" (31:22).

The song provides the rhythms and metaphors that will keep Israel's experience, both their sins and God's care for them, alive and present for understanding and sharpening the holy community's life of worship, love, and obedience in the generations that follow. But it can't have provided a very satisfying ending for Moses. He had done his best. He had preached his best and final sermon. He had written this stunning book of wisdom, love, and grace. He had transferred his authority into the competent hands of Joshua. The pillar of cloud had filled the air with the blazing light of God's presence. And then God whispers to Moses, "And one more thing, Moses — everything is about to fall to pieces; these people can't wait until you're out of here so they can dive into the orgiastic sex-and-fertility religion of the Canaanite culture. So write out one last message that can be read after you are dead — make it a song so the children can learn it and will be able to pick up the pieces and recover this holy community that you started and that you have served so faithfully and well these forty years."

*   *   *

Moses, at the end of his life, hands over leadership to Joshua, teaches the people his song, blesses the community tribe by tribe, and then trudges up Mount Nebo to Pisgah Peak with the entire Promised Land spread out before him in a wide-screen vista. There he dies. God buries him (ch. 34).

He dies, by all human accounting, a failure, and knowing that he is a failure, knowing that everything that he has worked for in leading, training, and praying for this community will unravel as soon as the people enter Canaan. It is a familiar story for readers of Scripture, even though frequently suppressed. What does this mean? It means that we have to revise our ideas of the holy community to conform to what is revealed in Scripture. It means that we cannot impose our paradisiacal visions of hanging out with lovely, upbeat, and beautiful people when we enter a Christian congregation. It means that God's way of working with us in community has virtually nothing to do with the world's idea of getting things done, of what "works" and what doesn't. It means that God hasn't changed his modus operandi of choosing the "low and despised in the world" (1 Cor. 1:28) to form his community. It means that we who want to get in on what God does in the way God does it in all matters of community, will have to give up pretensions of shaping an organization that the world will think is wonderful as we parade our accomplishments to the tune of "worship" or "evangelism."

Grounding Text (2): Luke/Acts

Of the original quartet of writers on Jesus, St. Luke alone continues the story as the apostles and disciples live it into the next generation. The remarkable thing, and Luke skillfully employs his literary art so that we don't miss it, is that it is essentially the same story, the Christ story recapitulated in the Christian story. Just as Moses gathers up the forty years of salvation history from the Red Sea to the Plains of Moab into his Deuteronomy sermon and converts them into the present, ready to be lived out in the Promised Land of Canaan, so Luke gathers up the thirty years of Jesus' life and puts them into his story of the first Christian community as it develops across the next thirty years or so of its existence, Christians living the Jesus life in the Roman empire.

*   *   *

The two-volume work of Luke/Acts places the life of Christ and the life of the Christian community each alongside the other. Jesus had told his disciples on that solemn night of leave-taking that his followers would continue the work that he had started: "Very truly, I tell you, the one who believes in me will also do the works that I do and, in fact, will do greater works than these, because I am going to the Father" (John 14:12). In his final prayer with and for them he places their lives and his in parallel: "As you have sent me into the world, so I have sent them into the world" (17:18).

It is St. Luke's task to make those two "sendings," the sending of Jesus into the world by the Father and the sending of us into the world by Jesus, explicit with plenty of detail.

*   *   *

The story of Jesus doesn't end with Jesus. It continues in the community of the men and women who repent, believe, and follow. The supernatural doesn't stop with Jesus. God's salvation, which became articulate, visible, and particular in Jesus, continues to be articulate, visible, and particular in the men and women who have been raised to new life in him, the community of the resurrection.

The Holy Spirit

St. Luke is, in all probability, the only Gentile writer in the New Testament. He is also the only Gospel writer who was not an eyewitness to Jesus. All that he knows of Jesus comes from others, especially the apostolic witnesses, but also anyone else he was able to get hold of. He says that he wrote only "after investigating everything carefully from the very first" (Luke 1:3). He has the unique experience among the Gospel writers of knowing Jesus exclusively through the work of the Holy Spirit in the community of Jesus' followers.

It is understandable, therefore, that the Holy Spirit should loom so large in Luke's thinking and dominate his vocabulary. The other Gospel writers saw and heard and touched Jesus, ate with him, walked the roads with him, prayed with him, listened to him teach and tell stories, watched while he was crucified, were witnesses to his resurrection, saw him ascend into heaven. All that came secondhand to Luke. Except that, as it turned out, it wasn't secondhand at all. The Holy Spirit, God's way of being present with us, made it all firsthand. So it is quite natural that Luke, whose experience of Jesus was exclusively by means of the Holy Spirit, should refer to the Holy Spirit more frequently than his Gospel-writing colleagues.[16]

His Gospel begins with a visitation of the Holy Spirit that results in conception; the book of Acts begins similarly, also with a visitation of the Holy Spirit that results in conception. In the Gospel it is Jesus, the Savior, who is conceived. In Acts it is the church, the company of the saved, that is conceived. The two Holy Spirit conceptions are meant to be understood as parallel beginnings in the parallel narratives: both Jesus Christ and the community of Jesus Christ similarly conceived by the Holy Spirit.

The Conception of Jesus

In Luke's Gospel, the conception of Jesus is paired with the prior conception of his cousin John. John is conceived by the Holy Spirit in the womb of Elizabeth, who is long past the years of childbearing. Six months later Jesus is conceived by the Holy Spirit in the womb of Mary, a virgin with no sexual experience. Elizabeth and Mary stand at the extremes of impossibility regarding conception, Elizabeth a barren post-menopausal old woman and Mary a young virgin.

The first reference to the Holy Spirit comes in the angel Gabriel's message to Zechariah announcing that he is going to become a father: "Your wife Elizabeth will bear you a son.... [E]ven before his birth he will be filled with the Holy Spirit" (Luke 1:13-15). Six months later, this same Gabriel shows up at Mary's home and announces to her that she is going to have a baby. When Mary challenges Gabriel's angelic naiveté in human reproductive matters — "That's impossible; I'm a virgin" — Gabriel tells her, "The Holy Spirit will come upon you, and the power of the Most High will overshadow you" (1:35).

There is more to come. When Mary visits Elizabeth, Elizabeth is "filled with the Holy Spirit" and blesses Mary (1:41). When Elizabeth gives birth to John, his father Zechariah is "filled with the Holy Spirit" and prophesies (1:67). Thirty-three days after Jesus' birth, his parents bring him to the temple for the Moses-prescribed "purification" ceremony; Simeon, introduced as a man on whom the "Holy Spirit rested" and one to whom the "Holy Spirit revealed . . ." (2:25-26), meets Mary and Joseph in the temple and, "guided by the Spirit" (2:27), takes the infant Jesus in his arms and blesses child and parents.

Is Luke making sure we understand that God is actively creating and confirming life in this setting of sheer impossibility? Seven times the Holy Spirit (or Spirit) is cited in these two opening chapters. Five times the action of the Holy Spirit is detailed in relation to five persons: the embryonic John, the virginal Mary, the great-with-child Elizabeth, the old priest Zechariah, and devout Simeon.

But the births themselves (and this is important to observe) are completely natural. A nine-month pregnancy preceded each birth. The babies born from these unlikely wombs (barren and virginal) had normal infancies, were weaned from the breast, gradually acquired the ability to eat solid food, one day rolled over and started to crawl, were soon walking, then running, made nonsense babbling sounds that overnight turned into words and then, quite astonishingly, into sentences.

The Holy Spirit, however miraculous in the conception of life itself, doesn't seem to shortcut or skip anything that is human. There is nothing in a Holy Spirit–conceived life that exempts that life from the common lot of humanity. It didn't skip anything in Jesus, "who in every respect has been tested as we are" (Heb. 4:15), and it doesn't skip anything in us. And that means, of course, that there is absolutely nothing in us that it is inaccessible to or incapable of holiness. Humanity itself is divinely precious. The long, complex, danger-filled, often painful process of growth from fetus to infancy to adulthood to parenthood and then on into old age is embraced and given meaning and dignity as God in Christ continues to be present in and for us by his Holy Spirit.

The Conception of the Community

Thirty-three or so years later, the last words of Jesus to his followers are, "you will receive power when the Holy Spirit has come upon you" (Acts 1:8). Jesus' friends are going to get their start the same way he got his, by the Holy Spirit. Jesus' followers are going to become a resurrection community in the world ("when the Holy Spirit has come upon you") in the same way that Jesus became the Savior of the world ("the Holy Spirit . . . upon you"). The operations of the Holy Spirit upon and in that septet of marginal Jews assembled in Luke 1–2 is about to be reproduced in Jesus' followers who are gathered in Jerusalem waiting for Jesus to send them "what my Father promised" (Luke 24:49; cf. Acts 1:4-5).

Fifty days after the fateful Passover in which Jesus was crucified, and ten days after his ascension into heaven, the Holy Spirit descended on the waiting believers in Jerusalem. On that day, the Day of Pentecost, the holy community of the church as we now know it was conceived. Mary the mother of Jesus is the only member of that core group of seven who was in on the conception and birth of Jesus who is also now present at this conception and birth of the community (Acts 1:14). The Holy Spirit that conceived Jesus in Mary's womb now conceives Jesus' community with a charter membership of 120 (at least) of Jesus' followers. And Mary is there to see and be part of it.

References to the Holy Spirit now quicken. The seventeen references to the Holy Spirit in Luke's Gospel increase to fifty-seven in Acts, a document about the same length as the Gospel. We are not to lose sight of the fundamental Jesus story line: what the community does and says and prays is continuous with what Jesus does and says and prays. This is the same Jesus story that we read in the Gospel but without Jesus being visibly and audibly present. The Holy Spirit is God's way of being present and active among us in the same way that he was in Jesus.

*   *   *

Twice, at the end of the Gospel and at the beginning of Acts, as Jesus tells his friends that he will send the Holy Spirit to them, he also says that this coming of the Spirit will be accompanied by *power*: "stay here in the city until you have been clothed with power from on high" (Luke 24:49); and "you will receive power when the Holy Spirit has come upon you" (Acts 1:8).

"Power" is a critical word for understanding what we can expect as the Holy Spirit "clothes us" and "comes upon us." But a dictionary is not a good place from which to determine its meaning. Dictionaries are wonderful tools and we would be the poorer without them, but in Gospel matters they are among the lesser helps. The reason is that everything in the Gospel is personal, relational, and embodied in particulars. There are no generalities. Every word is embedded in the Story and, in the most comprehensive sense, incarnate in Jesus, "the word made flesh." Isolated in a dictionary a word has no context and therefore no relationship, no "flesh." For those of us who are interested in living the truth and not just acquiring information, it is necessary to discover the meaning of a word by looking it up in the Story, not the dictionary.

The first two times that Luke employs the term "power" are instructive. The first is in Gabriel's annunciation to Mary: "The Holy Spirit will come upon you and the power of the Most High will overshadow you...." Here Holy Spirit power makes a woman pregnant. All five of the Holy Spirit references in Luke 1–2 are related to pregnancy and birth. This is a most interesting use of "power" and not at all the way it is conventionally used. Sexual impregnation is associated with intimacy and lovemaking, gentleness and mutuality. If the sexual act is impersonal or harsh or forced, it is understood as a violation. If we are careful to let the Story provide the meaning of "power," it is inconceivable (literally!) to understand power as anything impersonal or imposed by force. We can footnote Gabriel with a text from the prophet Zechariah: "Not by might, nor by power, but by my Spirit, says the LORD" (Zech. 4:6) — the kind of power that is synonymous with "might" is no part of the way the Spirit works.

The second occurrence of the term "power" by Luke is in the account of Jesus' temptation in the wilderness. Jesus is tempted by the devil to command stones to become bread, to become the ruler of all the kingdoms of the world, and to prove his divinity by performing a spectacular circus trick by diving off the pinnacle of the temple and having an angel save him at the last minute. Each is a temptation that has to do with the exercise of power: power to impose his will on the creation, power to impose his will on nations, and power to become a talk-of-the-town celebrity. Each of these exercises of power could be, and with Jesus most certainly would be, good: feeding a lot of people, ruling the whole world justly, demonstrating the miraculous, ever-present providence of God to the people on the street. Jesus said no to each one in turn. Why? Because in each case it would have been power used impersonally, power abstracted from relationships, power without any engagement in love, power imposed from the outside. Each instance — and Jesus' citations of sentences from the Story each time highlight this — would have been a use of power that was ripped out of the context of the Story and therefore ripped out of the participating context of people's lives. Whatever the power of the Spirit means, bullying force isn't part of it. It is certainly not what takes place when a fuse ignites a stick of dynamite (named after the Greek word for power, *dynamis*). The power of God is always exercised in personal ways, creating and saving and blessing. It is never an impersonal application of force from without.

After the three great refusals to use power to do good things in the wrong way, Luke tells us this: "Then Jesus, filled with the power of the Spirit, returned to Galilee. . . . He began to teach in their synagogues and was praised by everyone" (4:14-15). We observe in detail as the narrative continues that as Jesus teaches, whether in word or act, he is always personal and relational. Jesus, employing the "power of the Spirit," is set in explicit contrast to the three depersonalized, decontextualized uses of power in the wilderness: power to help the hungry, power to do justice, power to evangelize by miracle. The moment the community exercises power apart from the story of Jesus, tries to manipulate people or events in ways that short-circuit personal relationships and intimacies, we can be sure it is not the power of the Holy Spirit; it is the devil's work. The Holy Spirit, no matter how loudly or frequently or piously invoked in such settings, is a stranger to such religious blasphemies.[17]

The Prayers

If the Holy Spirit — God's way of being with us, working through us, and speaking to us — is the way in which continuity is maintained between the life of Jesus and the life of Jesus' community, prayer is the primary way in which the community actively receives and participates in that presence and working and speaking. Prayer is our way of being attentively present to God who is present to us in the Holy Spirit. So it is not surprising to find that St. Luke, whose task is to maintain and develop the organic continuities between Jesus and his company of followers, frequently brings us to prayer.

A Pentad of Prayers

Prayer is established as the common language of the community, the lingua franca if you will, as the conception, pregnancy, and birth stories of John and Jesus are set before us, these stories that form the necessary groundwork for the gospel story. Five prayers articulate a language of listening and believing, a language of receptive and responsive participation as God speaks the life of Jesus and the Jesus community into existence. The five prayers have been taken up by the community and used as a primer in forming the basic syntax of a people who owe their existence and identity to the presence and word of the Holy Spirit among them. They have been installed as basic elements in our life together, keeping us attentive and responsive to the Holy Spirit in and among us through the practice of prayer. They are commonly referred to in the church by the Latin word(s) that begin each prayer:

> The *Fiat mihi* (Luke 1:38)
> The *Magnificat* (1:46-55)
> The *Benedictus* (1:68-79)
> The *Gloria in excelsis* (2:14)
> The *Nunc dimittis* (2:29-32)

The *Fiat mihi*: ". . . let it be to me, according to your word," is Mary's response to the angel's announcement that she will conceive and bear a child, the "Son of God," by the Holy Spirit. Prayer begins when God addresses us. First God speaks; our response, our answer, is our prayer. This is basic to understanding the practice of prayer: we never initiate prayer, even though we think we do. Something has happened, *Someone* has spoken to us, before we open our mouths, whether we remember or are aware of it or not. Just as we learn to speak our mother tongue by first being immersed in the language of our mothers and fathers, siblings and others, so we learn prayer in response to what is being said to us, over and over, by the Holy Spirit in Scripture and song, in story and sermon, in heart-whispers and bold witness. On the basis of this prayer, the first prayer in the gospel story, many understand Mary as the archetypal Christian, the person who hears and receives, believes and submits to the word that conceives Christ in us.

The *Magnificat:* "My soul magnifies the Lord. . . ." The second in this pentad of prayers is, as is fitting, also by Mary. She now prays in response to the blessing of her aged relative Elizabeth, who is five months pregnant with John. Before she has prayed a half dozen words, we realize that this girl knows her family story, Holy Scripture, which tells the ways that God has been speaking and working among his people for two thousand years. We recognize that the words she uses in her prayer are taken and then recast from the prayer of Hannah, her ancestor from a thousand years earlier, the prayer Hannah prayed when she was miraculously pregnant with Samuel (1 Sam. 2:1-10). The heart of Mary's prayer, as it was for Hannah's, involves three great reversals in the way we experience the world when God conceives new life in us: God establishes his strength and disestablishes the proud (Luke 1:51); God puts down the people at the top and lifts up the people at the bottom (v. 52); God fills the hungry and sends the rich away empty (v. 53). The proud, the powerful, and the rich are reduced to size; God, the downtrodden, and the deprived are perceived truly, filled out in dimensions of majesty, wholeness, and dignity. Revolution (but in God's way, not ours) is on the horizon.

Mary's prayer takes us into a large, extensive world of God's promised word in the process of fulfillment. It is a world large with creation and wonder, history and salvation. Prayer enlarges our imagination and makes us grateful, joyful participants in what has been and is yet to come.

The *Benedictus:* "Blessed be the Lord God of Israel. . . ." Zechariah, speechless since the day that Gabriel announced to him the conception of John in Elizabeth's womb, gets his tongue back on the day his son is named and circumcised. The first thing he does is pray. His words, pent-up for nine months in his "womb," now burst into praise and prophecy. His earlier nonresponsive nonprayer to the word of God delivered by Gabriel is converted by the Holy Spirit into a blessing that gathers the revelation of God to Abraham, David, and all the holy prophets, and places this eight-day-old baby in their company, an eight-day-old prophet who will "go before the Lord to prepare his ways" (v. 76). The language is Isaianic. Salvation is on the way.

274

Zechariah's prayer takes us into the company of those whom God has used to work his will in this world and of those he will use. There is a great company of fathers and mothers, prophets and apostles, friends and neighbors who make up the community of the resurrection. Prayer brings us into the multigenerational conversations that gather around the throne.

The *Gloria:* "Glory to God in the highest heaven, and on earth peace. . . ." The setting is a field near Bethlehem. It is night. Shepherds are tending their sheep; this is their workplace. Jesus has just been born in a stable not far away. Suddenly the shepherds are flooded with light, an angel announces Jesus' birth, and then — then an incredible thing happens: a great choir of angels appears, singing praise to God in heaven and peace to us on earth. The prayer of the angels joins what originates in heaven with what takes place on earth, the first intimation we get of Jesus' instructive prayer, "on earth as it is in heaven."

The angels' prayer puts us in the company not only of the "communion of saints" as Zechariah's *Benedictus* does, but of the "whole company of heaven." However earthbound we feel, however humdrum and mundane our work is (shepherding in that society was equivalent to bagging groceries in ours), our prayers give us a place in a choir that expresses all the melodies and harmonies that heaven comprises.

The *Nunc dimittis:* ". . . now you are dismissing your servant in peace. . . ." This final prayer in the Lukan pentad is prayed in the temple, an institutional setting on a religious occasion. The occasion is that of "purification," prescribed by Moses for mothers forty days after giving birth (Lev. 12:2-8). When Joseph and Mary bring the infant Jesus to the temple for the ceremony ("what was customary under the law," v. 27), they are met by Simeon, who has been directed by the Holy Spirit to meet the parents and Jesus. This is the first of the five prayers to be offered in a public place.

Simeon's prayer is a prayer of completion. What he has been praying for all his life ("salvation . . . a light for revelation to the Gentiles . . . glory to . . . Israel . . .") is now present in this infant. Simeon takes the child in his arms and blesses him; he also blesses the parents. Simeon holds the purpose and meaning of his life in his arms. He is now ready to die. After a long life of hopeful prayer and faithful witness he steps aside and gives place to Jesus — a letting go, a relinquishment. His phrase "according to your word" is identical to what Mary prayed in the *fiat mihi.*

Mary and Simeon, the first and last pray-ers in this company, are a complementary pair: the young girl starting out in submission to God's word; the old man ending in submission to God's word. God's word not only initiates all prayer, it provides the grammar and vocabulary of prayer and brings all prayer to wholeness, to completion. God gets the first word in prayer; he also gets the last word. Mary and Simeon between them mark off the bounds and primary content for the language of the community, the language that we name "prayer," spoken submissively and believingly "according to your word."

These five prayers articulate the range of response to what the Holy Spirit does in creating and shaping community. These conception, pregnancy, and birth prayers provide a vocabulary and syntax for participation in the way the Spirit has been, is, and will be speaking and working in our lives.

Prayer Stories

St. Luke now tells us three stories, unmentioned by the other Gospel writers, that Jesus uses to teach his followers the basic nature and necessity of prayer, the prayers of the Neighbor, the Widow, and the Sinner.

The Neighbor at prayer (Luke 11:5-13) weaves prayer into the natural fabric of daily life. What is more natural than caring for a friend who arrives unexpectedly at midnight? What is more natural than to find oneself unprepared for such an unexpected demand on one's pantry? What is more natural than to not want to be disturbed, along with one's entire family, from deep sleep in the middle of the night? So Jesus places prayer (a conversation between a person and God) in a story between two neighbors, one unexpectedly needing something from the other, but at an inconvenient time and a time requiring disruption of normal routines.

Do we think that prayer is a formal ritual with protocols unique to it, with its own vocabulary and syntax, manners and gestures, assigned to designated times and places? Do we suppose that prayer is more or less an extra, a superfluity, what we do after human essentials are taken care of, what we engage in when and if we have time and inclination for it? If so, we think and suppose wrongly. Prayer is not ritualized language composed ceremonially for an audience with heavenly royalty. Our relation with God is as unpredictable, unplannable, and unrehearsed as life with our neighbors.

276

Jesus' commentary on the story extends our sense of prayer into the give and take of ordinary life, the life of asking and searching and knocking on doors. Jesus incorporates the asking and receiving relational language that is fundamental to the life of children and parents into our understanding of prayer.

The Widow at prayer (Luke 18:1-8) gives the weakest and least influential people in our society legitimacy and equal footing with the recognized power figures in society. Widows in the social structure in which Jesus lived were at the absolute bottom of authority and influence. They were not used to being listened to by anyone of rank; after a lifetime of being ignored it is hard to "pray always." But Blaise Pascal contended that God told us to pray in order to give us the "dignity of causality."[18] Prayer, conversation with God, is not conversation regulated by social or class distinctions, but conversation in which all men, women, and children, widows and judges, kings and beggars, the literate and the illiterate, poor and rich, the wise and fools, saints and sinners are equals, peers with identical access to the ear, the attention, the consideration of God.

We are not used to this, especially people at the low end of the "influence ladder." A lifetime of experience tells us that "if you know someone important" you are more likely to be listened to. Our lives are filled with letters of recommendation, letters of reference, endorsements, celebrity awards that give words credibility and ensure an audience. It is inevitable that these experiences seep into our practice of prayer. Especially if we are used to being ignored, put off or "put on hold," we will have internalized these diminishments for so long that we will hardly be bold in prayer like the Widow. Jesus says, in effect, "get used to it." Get used to being listened to by God.

Then Jesus steps out of the story and asks us, those of us who have been listening to the story, especially those of us who have gotten so used to not being listened to by anyone of importance and so have even quit asking God for what we need, "And yet, when the Son of Man comes, will he find faith on earth?" Will he find this sort of faithful, persistent refusal to abandon prayer among "his chosen ones who cry to him night and day"? Will we finally give up and quit praying because the deaf ear of the world has so flattened our expectations of being heard by God?

In the third story (Luke 18:9-14), the Sinner takes prayer to bedrock, digs down to hard granite, the rock-honest foundation from which an authentic life of prayer can develop. With feet on bedrock the Sinner is grounded in the conditions necessary for prayer: a desperate, gut sense of need and a heart sense that God is the only one who can do anything about it. Prayer is not casual. Prayer is not a whimsical nod upward. Prayer is urgent, nothing less than a life-and-death matter: "God, be merciful to me, a sinner!"

Pose, pretense, and posturing are primary dangers that threaten prayer. Ignorance is no impediment, and most emphatically not sin. The great temptation always crouching at the door of prayer is to use prayer as a way to avoid God: using God language to avoid God relationship; using the name of God as a screen behind which to hide from God. Clichés are the usual verbal giveaways of prayer that is, in fact, nonprayer.

The Pharisee is introduced as a foil to the Sinner. The Pharisee in the world around Jesus is the prototypical self-defined and self-conscious religious person, the person who has worked diligently to achieve righteous competence and pious expertise. In the course of acquiring the manners and morals of his chosen way of life (women were not admitted to the club), it was virtually impossible for the Pharisee not also to acquire a snob's sense of superiority over all the failed and messed-up wretches who filled the streets and alleys of the city. He uses the language of prayer to distance himself from these "others." And then he goes on to use the words of prayer to distance himself from God, turning God into a mirror before which he can preen in self-approval. The Pharisee's nonprayer is only conscious of me: I, I, I, I — four ego statements. Where is God in all this? An impersonal audience at best.

If the Neighbor at prayer introduces the holy language of prayer into the thrust and pull of ordinary life and if the Widow at prayer gives the underdogs from a discriminatory and unjust world a guaranteed hearing before the Judge of all the Earth, the Sinner at prayer unceremoniously gets rid of the gingerbread prayers that clutter so many lives and returns us to bedrock, to our need and God's mercy, so that we can get in on the life of Jesus firsthand. With the Neighbor, the Widow, and the Sinner working in our imaginations, there is not much that we are going to encounter in our lives of following Jesus that is not pray-able, which is to say that there is not much, if anything, ahead of us in which the Holy Spirit will not be doing in us what was done in Jesus.

The Praying Community

These five prayers that mark the beginning of the life of Jesus in Luke's Gospel and the three stories of prayer that urge our active participation in these prayers have narrative continuities in the book of Acts, where we read the story of the formation of the Jesus community. Here also, just as prayer is established as the basic language for those who participated in the Spirit's work in the conception, pregnancy, and birth of Jesus, prayer is similarly established as the basic language of the Jesus community as it is brought into being by the Spirit, and then continues to pray naturally, boldly, and honestly as it had learned to do through Jesus' stories.

*   *   *

Before Jesus left his followers by ascension into heaven, he "ordered them not to leave Jerusalem, but to wait there for the promise of the Father," what he then named as being "baptized with the Holy Spirit" (Acts 1:4-5). But they had other things on their minds; they wanted to know, "Lord, is this the time when you will restore the kingdom to Israel?" (1:6).

These followers still had a lot to learn. Jesus tells them to wait for the Holy Spirit. They are not listening; they interrupt by asking questions about timetables and agendas . . . "when?" But prayer is not the place where we get our curiosity satisfied, it is where we establish continuities with Jesus' life. It sounds very much as if their "kingdom" agenda had gotten in the way of hearing what Jesus had just told them. Jesus said, "wait"; they responded, "when?" And that "when" sounds suspiciously like "when will we get our kingdom assignments so we can start running things?" Jesus is talking about waiting until they are immersed in God's presence, which will be Jesus' presence in their lives, so that they will be able to continue what he had begun in them; they are asking when the real action is going to begin so they can take charge of kingdom-of-God leadership.

Jesus told them that the "when" was none of their business, that they were not competent for kingdom work as they were; receiving the Holy Spirit was their sole business at this time. The next thing was not a "next thing" — it would be the same thing, continuous (by means of the Holy Spirit) with what they had been living in his company all along. And then Jesus left.

This time they listened. They waited. And as they waited they prayed, "constantly devoting themselves to prayer" (1:14). One of their prayers while they waited was prayer for guidance in the replacement of Judas in the company of the Twelve. That prayer resulted in the choice of Matthias as an apostolic witness to the resurrection.

After ten days, these waiting and praying men and women received what Jesus and his Father had promised: the Holy Spirit, the active presence of Jesus and the Father in them. Their prayers were now more than *their* prayers — they prayed more than they were, more than they knew, "as the Spirit gave them ability" (2:4). Worshipers in Jerusalem, gathered from all over the Middle East for the Feast of Pentecost, hear them praying and are astonished to hear in "the native language of each" a witness to "God's deeds of power" in the prayers (2:6, 11).

People are puzzled; some jeer. Peter preaches a sermon that puts the whole thing in perspective: this is nothing new — this is in continuity with what God has been doing for a long time. For documentation he quotes a prophet whom they had been reading all their lives, Joel, and the prayers of David that they had been praying all their lives (Ps. 16, 132, 110), and then connects it all with Jesus. Many ("about three thousand") see the whole picture, are convinced, and are baptized. The Jesus community is up and running.

*   *   *

And praying. The community's common language is prayer (Acts 2:42). Prayer is both implicit and explicit in the story of the Jesus community that Luke continues to tell: when Peter and John are released from prison and return to the community to report, "they raised their voices together to God" and prayed (4:24-31); when the work of caring for the hospitality needs of the people gets to be too much, the Twelve call the community together and appoint deacons for that work so that they themselves can "devote themselves to prayer," nurturing and maintaining the primacy of their basic language of prayer, taking care that it not be diluted or dissipated (6:1-6); when Stephen is being killed by stoning, he prays — prayer is the language most natural to him, deepest within him (7:59); Saul in Damascus, blind and hungry for three days, prays for help, which then comes through Ananias and the Holy Spirit (9:10-19); in Joppa, Peter is taken to the home of Dorcas, who has just died, and "he knelt down and prayed" — his spontaneous response (9:36-43); all the action in the great, turning-point Cornelius story is fashioned in prayer (10:2, 9, 30-31); the community's first line of defense against the murderous machinations of King Herod Agrippa I is prayer (12:5, 12); when the community requires direction for expansion they pray (13:3); new churches are constituted and shaped by prayer (14:23); when the Council of Jerusalem decision is delivered, its prayer-filled composition is described in the wonderful phrase, "it has seemed good to the Holy Spirit and to us" (15:28); when Paul and Silas arrive in Philippi they seek out "a place of prayer" (16:13, 16); in the Philippian prison, Paul and Silas immediately make that also a chapel of prayer, "praying and singing" (16:25); Paul's tearful parting with the Ephesian elders concludes when "he knelt down with them all and prayed" (20:36); after a seven-day visit at Tyre, Luke, who is traveling with Paul at the time, reports that "we knelt down on the beach and prayed" (21:5); as Paul recounts his conversion story to a hostile crowd of Jews in Jerusalem he mentions that Jesus spoke to him "while I was praying in the temple" (22:17); on his last storm-tossed travel to Rome, just before the ship is wrecked, Paul addresses the crew, telling what happened while he was in prayer the night previous, a message of comfort and God-granted security (27:23-26); on the morning of the shipwreck, Paul addresses all the passengers and crew, 276 persons in all, and urges them to eat and give "thanks to God" (27:35-36); on Malta, the island of their shipwreck, when Paul learns that the father of a man who has befriended them is sick and near death, he "cured him by praying and putting his hands on him" (28:8).

The frequency and persistence of the language of prayer in the community of Jesus is evident throughout the narrative; it is also not obtrusive. We are not being urged to pray, or given examples of prayer. This is simply the way the community uses the language. Luke does not remark on it as anything unusual or contrived. Quite the opposite: prayer is the natural, unselfconscious language of the community.

The Unwanted

Another conspicuous feature of Luke's integrated narrative of Jesus and the Jesus community is the emphasis he places on the acceptance and inclusion of people who were used to being excluded: the outsiders, the unwanted, the uninvited. Luke is not unique in this, but he does go beyond his Gospel-writing colleagues. As a second-generation Christian is he observing an increase of concern for who is "in" and who is "out"? Are the old-timers trying to protect the "purity" of the community against dilution or contamination? It wouldn't be the first time.

By the time he sits down to write his Gospel and Acts, Luke, as a Gentile, most likely has had ample experience of being excluded from the community of Jesus by well-meaning guardians of God's integrity and holiness. He has observed how often and persistently the most hospitable place in the world, the community of the resurrection, can quickly become cruelly inhospitable.

*   *   *

In his Gospel, Luke tells three back-to-back stories of Jesus that throw the doors of the kingdom and its community open to those who in that culture were typically marked for exclusion, men and women Joel Green has described as "the least, the lost, and the left-out."[19]

The stories are told in the course of a conversation around a supper table. Jesus, Luke tells us in the passage leading up to this dinner, was walking along in the company of some religion scholars ("lawyers") and Pharisees. They were on their way to the house of a leader of the Pharisees for a Sabbath meal. But it wasn't, it seems, a relaxed stroll. His companions were "watching him closely" (Luke 14:1). "Watching him closely" (paratēroumenoi auton) connotes suspicion. This is the word Luke later uses in Acts to name the murderous watching of Paul by his enemies at the Jerusalem gates (Acts 9:23-24). Earlier in the Gospel he told us that the Pharisees were critically watching Jesus in order to "find an accusation against him" (Luke 6:7). And in the last week of Jesus' life, the chief priests "watched him and sent spies" in order to find grounds for executing him (Luke 20:20).

So on this Sabbath day, invited to a meal with this particular leader of the Pharisees, Jesus is being watched accusingly. They have seen what he has been doing, touching lepers, keeping company with women, telling flattering stories of Samaritans, including Gentiles as if they were equals, treating the hated tax-collectors and despised prostitutes with dignity. As they approach the house to which they have been invited, Jesus notices a man ill with dropsy and heals him, a provocative act bound to offend them — it's the Sabbath, remember. But then he turns the knife, infuriating his fellow guests with a question that put his action past criticism: "If one of you has a child or an ox that has fallen into a well, will you not immediately pull it out on a sabbath day?" (Luke 14:5). Jesus was providing plenty of fodder to feed their suspicions. Stories had been accumulating around Jesus; his enemies were busily collecting them as evidence. That's why they were *watching him closely*. Word was getting around that Jesus was inviting unwanted and unacceptable people into the kingdom, and they weren't about to let it happen if they could help it. Is this any way to form a community of the righteous?

By the time they enter the house and sit down to the Sabbath meal, the clean air of welcoming hospitality is thoroughly polluted by the grit and soot of accusatory suspicion, the sweet aroma of the meal ruined by the bad breath of these uptight community watchdogs. The meal, a setting that invites open and free conversation, is no longer that. The squint-eyed religious security police have set the tone.

*   *   *

The three stories that Jesus now tells feature the verb "call" *(kaleō)*; it is usually translated "invite." It is a hospitable word, inviting a person into a setting of relationship. But each of Jesus' stories discloses the inhospitality that can so easily hide behind hospitality.

The first story (14:7-11) skewers the pride of the brightest and best of the guests who are at the table. This is a table where guests are ranked by their proximity to the host. But Jesus notices that, instead of waiting to let the host place them, they have ranked themselves, each trying to snag the most honored place. Jesus asks them, "What if the host would have come in after all this elbowing and jostling and picked some poor wretch (a prostitute, say) that you just pushed into last place, and put her in the highest place that you had captured for yourself? What if he had demoted you to last place?" Humiliating.

The second story (14:12-14) is a bold sally at the host, calling into question his motives for inviting this particular company of guests to dinner. What on the surface looks like generous hospitality is, Jesus discerns, a self-serving strategy for securing dinner invitations from these guests — social insurance with an eye out for business contacts. "So, why didn't you invite that Samaritan who just moved in down the street and is a stranger in town?"

The third story (14:15-24) opens with a statement by an unnamed guest: "Blessed is anyone who will eat bread in the kingdom of God!" By this time the tension around the table would have been close to unbearable for both guests and host. Is this man hoping to clear the air, change the subject, shift the conversation to eating bread in the future kingdom of God in order to divert attention from Jesus' stories that were making everyone so uncomfortable and forcing them to face their present inhospitality? If he is it doesn't work.

The anonymous guest is referring to the great end-time banquet in heaven (mentioned earlier in 13:29) to which all the Pharisees around that table would assume that they, of course, have an invitation. But Jesus quickly picks up on the incompatibility between that assumption and their determined inhospitality toward all the socially disapproved outcasts that Jesus is insistent on inviting, "the poor, the crippled, the blind, and the lame" (14:21). Their suspicious and disapproving *watching* of him constitute, Jesus is saying, a rejection of God's invitation to the final banquet.

"Blessed is anyone who will eat bread in the kingdom of God" is, in the context, nothing but a diversionary pious, hot-air cliché. Jesus pounces and punctures it. "Oh, really. Do you have any idea how casually the people around this very table take God's invitation to come to dinner?"

He gives three examples: it is like someone who refuses to come to dinner because of the press of business ("I have bought a piece of land"); or refuses because a more attractive option has just come up ("I have bought five yoke of oxen and I am going to try them out"); or refuses because of an urgent demand ("I have just been married"). Lame excuses, every one. If there had been any intention to take the dinner invitation seriously, arrangements would have been made, even with regards to the marriage — especially with regards to the marriage.

The people around that table are eating a Sabbath meal, for them a weekly anticipation of the end-time kingdom banquet. The guests are all socially and theologically approved peers. It is common knowledge among them that there are clearly defined categories of people who would never be invited to such a meal. And these disapproved categories are the very people that Jesus is going out of his way to include in God's invitation. The refusal of his table companions to invite any of these, says Jesus, is a refusal to come to the dinner to which they themselves have been invited. Jesus' story exposes the outrageous sacrilege of refusing to invite people of whom we disapprove into the community while blandly assuming that our invitation to God's end-time banquet is a sure thing.

*   *   *

Jesus, working off of a text from Isaiah, from which he had earlier preached in the Nazareth synagogue, names the typical unwanted guests as the poor, the crippled, the lame, and the blind (Luke 14:13 and 14:21). Luke in his story-telling pulls in Samaritans, lepers (and others with ritually-defiling illnesses), the hated tax collectors, Gentiles, and women. He is demonstrating how Jesus and the Jesus community make it obvious that there are no unwanted guests in the company of those who follow Jesus.

Hostility to Samaritans by the disciples is confronted early on by Jesus and squashed (Luke 9:51-56). Later Jesus uses the despised Samaritan in one of his most well-known stories, forcing us in a most unforgettable way to quit trying to define a neighbor, ethically or socially, and to simply, without fanfare, become a neighbor to whomever we happen upon (Luke 10:29-37); the inclusion of Samaritans continues in the community in response to Philip's going among them (Acts 8:4-25). The status of Samaritan is combined with that of being a leper to bring a doubly unwanted person into the story of Jesus' healing and acceptance (Luke 17:11-19). The hated tax-collector Zacchaeus is given a prominent place of inclusion when Jesus singles him out and invites himself over for a meal (Luke 19:1-10). The major problem of what to do with Gentiles, introduced in the figure of the token Roman centurion stationed in Capernaum whose son Jesus healed (Luke 7:1-10), is picked up again with another centurion, Cornelius, in Caesarea (Acts 10) and then expanded exponentially (but not without considerable prayer and discussion!) at the specially called Council of Jerusalem (Acts 15). After that, with Paul taking the lead as the primary missionary, any and all Gentiles were included, no questions asked. Over half of the account of the formation of the community of Jesus is given over to the embrace and inclusion of Gentiles (Acts 13–28).

Among the "unwanted" who are invited and embraced in the community, women get equal billing with the Gentiles in Luke's time and attention. All the Gospel writers are inclusive of women, but Luke even more so than the others. We have already noticed the prominence of Elizabeth and Mary in the conception and birth stories of John and Jesus that open the Gospel. Luke includes several stories of women that don't appear in the other Gospels: the widow of Nain and the raising of her son (7:11-17); the prostitute who anointed Jesus' feet with perfume (7:36-50); the Mary and Martha story (10:38-42); the "bent over" woman who was healed on the Sabbath (13:10-21). Women's stories continue into the book of Acts: the unjust treatment of the gentile widows, dealt with by the appointment of deacons who will ensure equal treatment of all (6:1-6); the death of Dorcas in Joppa and Peter's prayer that brought her to life again (9:36-43); the amusing mini-drama in which Mary, John Mark's mother, and her excitable maid Rhoda leave the recently imprisoned Peter standing out in the street knocking at their door (12:12-17); the conversion of the businesswoman Lydia in Philippi (16:11-15); the rescue of the slave-girl from the men who are exploiting her (16:16-18); the naming of Damaris as a significant convert in Athens (17:34); the important role that Priscilla played, with her husband Aquila, in Paul's life in Corinth (18:1-4) and in Apollos's life in Ephesus (18:24-28).

Luke makes it clear that the presence of women in the Jesus story was normal: "The twelve . . . as well as some women" made up the troop of disciples (Luke 8:2); he inserts the poignant reference to the women, whom Jesus affectionately called "daughters of Jerusalem," weeping as they followed Jesus to his crucifixion (23:27-31); and we read that Jesus' "acquaintances, including the women who had followed him from Galilee," held vigil as he died on the cross (23:49).

This embracing inclusion continues, but quite naturally and without fanfare, into the subsequent community: as Jesus' followers wait obediently in prayer for the Holy Spirit the named Twelve are together "with certain women, including Mary" (Acts 1:14); Peter's sermon on the Day of Pentecost includes references from the prophet Joel to God's spirit being poured out upon "your daughters" and "even upon my slaves, both men and women" to document what had just happened (2:17-18); as the community expands into gentile Europe, "not a few Greek women" got in on it (17:12); when Paul has a stopover in Tyre while on his way to Jerusalem "wives and children" are among those who escort him to his ship (21:5); when Paul visits for a few days in Caesarea with the deacon Philip, we are told, almost as an aside, that Philip has four unmarried daughters who have "the gift of prophecy," apparently a natural and accepted part of the community's preaching life (21:8-9); even Paul's sister comes in for honorable mention as the mother of the young man who saves Paul's life from a murderous ambush (23:16).

Assessing the way that Luke includes and honors women, Joel Green concludes that "'the twelve' and 'the women' embody the meaning of discipleship for Luke."[20] And this in a world biased against the admissibility of women as witnesses. The puzzling thing, after two thousand years, is that though Gentiles have long since been accepted as full guests in the community, there are still many areas and situations in which women experience marginalization and sometimes outright exclusion from important aspects of the community's life.

The Trials

The Gospel of Luke and the Acts of the Apostles both conclude with trials, first before the religious and then before the political judicial systems of the day. The trials provide firsthand material for understanding what the community of Jesus can expect from the world and what that world can expect from us.

*   *   *

Jesus was first arraigned before the high priest Caiaphas and then handed over to the Roman governor Pilate and the Idumean King Herod Antipas (Luke 22:63–23:25). Thirty years or so later, Paul was arraigned first before the high priest Ananias and his religious council, the Sanhedrin (Acts 23:1-10), and then before the Roman governor Felix (Acts 24). Two years after that Felix was succeeded as governor by Festus, and Paul faced Festus and King Herod Agrippa II in the dock (Acts 24–26).

So first Jesus and then, thirty years later, Paul, found themselves on trial before both the religious and the political judicial systems of the day. Jesus and the community of Jesus, alike, are put on the defensive. Whatever it was that Jesus was proclaiming and the community was continuing to say and do found favor in neither the religious nor the political culture of the time. The leaders responsible for Jewish religion and Roman law, those who understood themselves to take orders respectively from God and Caesar, had a hard time dealing with Jesus and the community of Jesus. When all was said and done, the verdict from the "powers that be" decided against Jesus and the Jesus community.

Jesus on trial, Paul on trial: the two trials, separated by thirty years, give our only savior and our first pastor a pulpit before the leading rulers of the country, the ones who held all the power, the ones who shaped the culture. The striking thing about the two trials is that neither Jesus nor Paul makes much of an impression on the "powers." It is quite extraordinary, really. First Jesus and then Paul have the attention, even if briefly, of the most important leaders in that part of the world and fail to convert them, fail to bring them to their knees, fail even to get taken seriously by them. But it seems that the indifference was mutual; Jesus and Paul didn't take very seriously the courts in which they were being tried, either.

These trials force us, if we are to stay true to the story we are reading, to give up the notion that the Christian community, rightly and obediently lived, can somehow, if we just put our minds to it, be tarted up sufficiently to catch the admiring eye of the world. We have ample documentation by now to disabuse us of such stuff. Eighteen hundred years or so of Hebrew history capped by a full exposition in Jesus Christ tell us that God's revelation of himself is rejected far more often than it is accepted, is dismissed by far more people than embrace it, and has been either attacked or ignored by every major culture or civilization in which it has given its witness: magnificent Egypt, fierce Assyria, beautiful Babylon, artistic Greece, political Rome, Enlightenment France, Nazi Germany, Renaissance Italy, Marxist Russia, Maoist China, and pursuit-of-happiness America. The community of God's people has survived in all of these cultures and civilizations but always as a minority, always marginal to the mainstream, never statistically significant. Paul was acerbically brief: "not many were powerful, not many were of noble birth. . . . God chose what is low and despised in the world" (1 Cor. 1:26, 28).

It gives us pause. If we, as the continuing company of Jesus, seem to have achieved an easy accommodation with our society and culture, how did we pull off what Jesus and the community of Jesus failed to accomplish? How has it come to pass that after twenty centuries of rejection, North American Christians assume that acclaim by numbers is a certificate of divine approval?

The significance of the church has never been in King Number. Its message has seldom (hardly ever, in fact) been embraced by the mighty and powerful. Strategies are introduced from time to time to target "important" leaders, men and women in high places in government, business, or the media, for conversion. It is not a practice backed by biblical precedent. There are, of course, Christians in high places politically and prominent in the celebrity pantheon, but their position and standing doesn't seem to mean anything strategically significant in terms of God's kingdom.[21] To suppose that if we can just "place" Christian men and women in prominent positions of leadership, we are going to improve the efficacy of the community in its worship, missions, or evangelism, has no warrant in Scripture or history.

Jesus on Trial

Jesus was so indifferent to the courts in which he was on trial that he didn't even attempt to get a hearing for his mission and message.

The first court in which Jesus was tried was the Jewish religious council, the Sanhedrin, presided over by the high priest Caiaphas. Jesus was tried on charges of heresy, accused of claiming to be Messiah and so guilty of blasphemy.

Matthew and Mark report on the trial in similar ways to Luke. When he was given a chance to answer the blasphemy charges, "Jesus was silent" (Matt. 26:63). Pushed by Caiaphas to admit to his messianic identity, Jesus threw it back at him, "You have said so" (*su eipas*; in Mark it is "I am," *egō eimi*); he then briefly elaborated with allusions from Psalm 110 and Daniel 7: "From now on you will see the Son of Man seated at the right hand of Power and coming on the clouds of heaven" (Matt. 26:64, citing Ps. 110:1 and Dan. 7:13), he says, an outrageous claim in the ears of the high priest, which could only have added weight to the charge of blasphemy.

Jesus' answer to the question of whether he is Messiah or not is expanded in Luke's report in the form of an accusation: "If I tell you, you will not believe; and if I question you, you will not answer" and then adds the self-incriminating allusions from Psalm 110 and Daniel 7. To the direct question, "Are you, then, the Son of God?" Jesus responds with the indirect, "You say that I am" (Luke 22:67-70).

John's court reporting is the fullest of the four. Of Jesus' response to examination by the high priest Caiaphas and his father-in-law Annas only the Annas segment is reported. To Annas's questions, Jesus says this: "I have spoken openly to the world; I have always taught in synagogues and in the temple, where all the Jews come together. I have said nothing in secret. Why do you ask me? Ask those who heard what I said to them; they know what I said." At that, a soldier slaps Jesus in the face for his insolence. Jesus in return slaps (verbally) the soldier in the face: "If I have spoken wrongly, testify to the wrong. But if I have spoken rightly, why do you strike me?" (John 18:19-23).

None of the words of Jesus reported by the Gospel writers in the religious trial can really be called a defense. Jesus makes no attempt to clarify or refute the blasphemy charges being made against him. Ranging from laconically noncommittal to insolent, he neither affirms nor denies.

$$* \quad * \quad *$$

The political trial that immediately follows is for sedition. Jesus is accused of claiming to be king. The country was crawling at that time with revolutionary terrorist groups (zealots) who were determined to free themselves from Roman rule; Jesus is accused of being one of these terrorist leaders. The Roman governor, Pilate, presides over this trial.

Matthew, Mark, and Luke report that Jesus spoke only three words (two in Greek, *su legeis*), "You say so," in answer to Pilate's question, "Are you the King of the Jews?" (Matt. 27:11). When accused by the Jewish chief priests and elders who were there to give evidence against him, "he did not answer." When Pilate invited him to defend himself "he gave him no answer" (Matt. 27:12, 14).

Luke adds one detail of his own by reporting the appearance of Herod Antipas, the puppet king in Galilee and son of Herod the Great who thirty years or so earlier had ordered the massacre of babies in an unsuccessful attempt to kill Jesus. Pilate, having learned that Herod is in town, sends Jesus over to Herod to be questioned. Herod is delighted; he has been wanting to get a look at this man for a long time, this man who has been causing something of a stir in his jurisdiction of Galilee; he thinks he might even get to see a miracle. Does he have any idea that the man before him that day is none other than the man his father had tried to kill? But Herod fares no better than Pilate in getting anything out of Jesus: "Jesus gave him no answer" (Luke 23:9).

John, as he had done for the religious trial, provides a more extensive exchange. To the sedition question, "Are you the King of the Jews?" (John 18:33), Jesus answers, "Do you ask this on your own, or did others tell you about me?" Pilate replies, "I am not a Jew, am I? Your own nation and the chief priests have handed you over to me. What have you done?" Jesus answers, "My kingdom is not from this world. If my kingdom were from this world, my followers would be fighting to keep me from being handed over to the Jews. But as it is, my kingdom is not from here" (vv. 34-36).

Pilate's attention is aroused: "So you are a king?" Maybe sedition is afoot here after all. But Jesus answers, "You say that I am a king. For this I was born, and for this I came into the world, to testify to the truth. Everyone who belongs to the truth listens to my voice" (v. 37).

By now Pilate realizes that he is chasing rabbits and loses interest. Suddenly bored with the whole procedure, he terminates the examination with the cynical question, "What is truth?" (v. 38).

Pilate concludes that Jesus is innocent of the charge of sedition and proposes to set him free. But the angry objections of the Jewish priests and police intimidate him. Then complications set in. He gets word that Jesus claimed to be "the Son of God" (19:7). Suddenly Pilate gets cold feet. Superstitiously nervous, he realizes that he might not be dealing with a political matter here at all, namely, a threat to the government by a local zealot pretender to the throne. Is it possible that one of the old gods has made an appearance and Pilate might be in way over his head? What if he is dealing with a serious god instead of a man with delusions of being a king?

Pilate has one more go at Jesus. Returning to his courtroom, he says, "Where are you from?" Jesus doesn't answer. Infuriated at the insolence, Pilate says, "Do you refuse to speak to me? Do you not know that I have power to release you, and power to crucify you?" (19:9-10).

Jesus dismisses the threat: "You would have no power over me unless it had been given you from above; therefore the one who handed me over to you is guilty of a greater sin" (v. 11).

Does Pilate somehow now realize that he himself is the one on trial? It seems so, for now he tries his best to get himself off the hook and let Jesus go. He tries to get out of it, but he is not a man of strong character and caves in to the pressure from the crowd. He hands the "king" over for crucifixion (vv. 12-16).

Paul on Trial

Thirty years later when Paul gets his turn before the authorities, he at least gives his witness. In contrast to Jesus' taciturnity he is positively voluble. But he fares no better on the conversion front. He is listened to, but the listening seems pretty perfunctory.

Paul comes to trial in the Jewish religious court in Jerusalem in a roundabout way after being arrested on charges of disturbing the peace. Asian Jews accuse Paul of defiling the temple by bringing gentile Greeks into the holy place. There is a huge riot, and the angry mob drags Paul out of the temple, determined to kill him. The Roman tribune, responsible for policing the city, hears the uproar, comes running with his soldiers, and rescues Paul. Not knowing what is going on, the tribune first arrests Paul and then asks questions, trying to get to the bottom of the situation (Acts 21:27-36).

The tribune had assumed that Paul was a man he had been looking out for, an Egyptian revolutionary who had fomented a revolt and had set up a terrorist camp out in the wilderness with four thousand assassins. When he realizes his mistake, he lets Paul speak to the crowd. The crowd quiets down as Paul tells his story, tells them of his part in the killing of Stephen, gives witness to his Damascus Road conversion and God's commission to carry out a mission to the Gentiles. The mention of Gentiles sets the crowd off again and the tribune has to intervene once more to save Paul from being ripped apart. Determined to get to the root of the matter, he has Paul tied up and orders him whipped, expecting to torture the truth out of him. Paul pulls rank on the tribune by claiming his rights as a Roman citizen and the tribune calls off the whipping. Still curious, though, as to why the Jews are so murderously angry with Paul, he orders the Jewish religious court into session and brings Paul before it to have his case heard (Acts 21:37–22:30).

The high priest Ananias, a successor to Caiaphas, who had presided over Jesus' trial on the charge of blasphemy, is the presiding priest this time. The first words out of Paul's mouth turn the trial into a fight. Ananias, offended by Paul's opening remark, orders him slapped. Paul counters with verbal abuse, insulting the high priest. Paul follows this up by provoking a fierce argument among members of the court, an argument that turns violent. Fists must have been in use because the Roman tribune, fearing for Paul's life ("that they would tear Paul to pieces"), calls the whole thing off and hauls Paul off to the safety of the barracks (23:1-11).

By this time the Roman tribune knows that he is in over his head. The next day he sends Paul under guard the sixty or so miles down to Caesarea to the Roman governor Felix. Felix provided a safe place for him and made arrangements for a political trial.

This trial is in a Roman court. The high priest Ananias with his elders and lawyer from Jerusalem bring their case against Paul, charging him with instigating a riot in the temple and disturbing the peace.

Paul makes his defense before Governor Felix. He replies to the Jewish charges brought by their prosecuting lawyer, Tertullus. Governor Felix seems to listen with interest but procrastinates making a decision. So Paul is kept in custody indefinitely. But both Felix and his Jewish wife Drusilla find Paul interesting and frequently arrange for conversations with him in which they talk of "faith in Christ Jesus . . . justice, self-control, and the coming judgment" (Acts 24:24-25). Felix is clearly attracted by what Paul has to say but is also fearful of the implications. He is also clearly not interested in justice; he keeps Paul, unconvicted and unsentenced, in his prison, conveniently at hand for an amusing theological conversation when he is in the mood for it. The conversations go on for two years, but nothing seems to come of it. When Felix is succeeded as governor by Festus, he leaves Paul in prison "to grant the Jews a favor" (24:27). So much for the vaunted Roman justice system.

After two years in prison, Paul is brought to trial a second time in Caesarea, but this time before the newly appointed Governor Festus. The same old charges are brought by the Jews against Paul and Paul again denies them. Festus waffles; he wants to keep the Jews friendly. He probably suspects (from Felix?) that the charges are trumped up. Indecisively, he tries to buy time by suggesting that the trial be reconvened in Jerusalem. Paul, fed up with the indecisiveness, asserts his status as a Roman citizen and appeals to the emperor and the right to a trial in Rome. Festus, by this time glad to get rid of him, confers with his counselors and grants Paul's appeal: "to the emperor you will go" (Acts 25:12). So that is settled — finally!

Presumably, Paul is returned to prison to await deportation to Rome and a trial there. In a few days, King Herod Agrippa II and his sister Bernice arrive on a state visit to welcome the new governor. This is interesting — after all this time the "Herods" are still in the story. This Herod is the great-grandson of Herod the Great who tried to kill the infant Jesus. Like his great-uncle, Herod Antipas, who was curious to get a look at Jesus on trial in Jerusalem (Luke 23:8), Herod Agrippa II is curious about this Paul, this missionary of Jesus. His father, Herod Agrippa I, had killed James son of Zebedee and imprisoned Peter a number of years before (Acts 12:1-3). Herods keep showing up in this story.

Governor Festus indulges Herod Agrippa's curiosity and invites him to look Paul over and hear him speak. Festus makes something of a state occasion of the meeting, which is replete with military officers and prominent leaders of the city (25:23). And even though this is not a formal trial, more like a fact-finding hearing (Festus is trying to find a formal charge that would legitimate his appeal to the Roman court), Paul's speech before those assembled in the auditorium (26:2-29) is exceeded in length among the sermons and addresses in Acts only by Stephen's. It turns out to be not so much a defense as an impassioned sermon, complete with altar call: "King Agrippa, do you believe the prophets? I know that you believe. . . . I pray to God that not only you but also all who are listening to me today might become such as I am — except for these chains" (26:27-29).

What Paul says is very interesting, and King Agrippa and Bernice are certainly interested, but nobody in the courtroom seems to have been much affected by it. The primary motivation is curiosity regarding this jailbird preacher. Did they hope to see some supernatural fireworks to enliven their parasitical, bored, and indolent lives?

*   *   *

A member of the Herod family makes an appearance in each of the trials — Herod Antipas at Jesus' trial and Herod Agrippa II at Paul's trial. They play minor roles in the proceedings, mere walk-on parts, but their presence provokes this reflection: the Jesus community gave astonishingly little attention to the World.[22] If any name was synonymous with the World in that first Christian century it would have been Herod, any Herod. The Herods epitomized the vanities of the World, what we sometimes refer to as "worldliness," matters of influence and status, pomp and circumstance, self-indulgence, what still gets summarized in the phrase, "getting on in the world." It is more than curious that the Jesus community continues to court Herod-like people in hopes of gaining their approval, recruiting them as allies, and using their influence in the cause of the kingdom.

Herod Antipas and Herod Agrippa have long since receded into history as more or less stock figures for spiritual dilettantism and sham showmanship. But in their own time Antipas and Agrippa were impressive. All the same, the Jesus community was not impressed. The presence of Antipas and Agrippa at the trials gave the community access to men in positions of influence. The entire Herod family (five Herods are mentioned in the gospel story) permeated the cultural and social scene of the day. They were not necessarily liked, in fact they were often despised, but you had to admit that they knew how to "make it" in the world. Despite being members of a conquered people of Semitic stock in a world dominated by Roman politics and Greek culture, all the Herods managed to achieve celebrity status. If you wanted to "get ahead" in that kind of world, you couldn't do better than take a lesson or two from the Herods. They wrote the book on "leadership principles" for the world in which the Jesus community was being formed.

But the community showed no signs of being interested in their "book." Jesus and Paul on trial before the World could easily have interpreted the presence of a Herod at the trial as a link to influencing the Roman governors — the Herods, after all, were fellow countrymen with influential ties to Rome; the Herods could well serve as a bridge for getting the message of the gospel to the most powerful political and cultural leaders of the age.

The Herods more or less epitomize the kind of people that the Jesus community is so often drawn to in hopes of gaining their approval, recruiting them as allies, and using their influence in the cause of the kingdom.

But neither Jesus nor Paul did it. Basically their attitude is one of detached indifference. There is no fawning, no sign of what so often comes out among us in the presence of important people as, "Oh, what an opportunity! Let's make the most of this . . . these are influential leaders." Jesus virtually ignores them. Paul faithfully gives his witness but with no attempt to adapt or curry favor.

What is significant here for understanding the community vis à vis the World is this: the Herods offer the possibility of influence with Rome. These men are masters at "influence." Both Herods are curious about the men on trial: Antipas curious about Jesus, Agrippa curious about Paul. This curiosity is ripe for exploitation; it can be used for the kingdom. But neither Jesus nor Paul exploited it; they do not "use" it; they ignore it.

And why? Because Jesus and the Jesus community know that the conditions in which the gospel makes its way in the World have little to do with influence and wealth and power. The non-negotiable context from which they work is made up of Jesus, the cross, and the Trinity. Neither celebrity nor "opportunity" distracts either Jesus or the Jesus community.

The World is a seductive place. Once we begin to cater to its interests, appeal to its curiosities, shape our language to its idioms and syntax, embrace its criteria of relevance, we abandon our basic orientation.

Too often what took place at the trials of Jesus and Paul, trials that put Jesus and Paul in contrast to the way of the World, recedes from our awareness and is replaced by assumptions dominated by opportunity, technique, and accomplishment. Jesus and Paul were not seduced.

*   *   *

The Herodian dynasty stretched over sixty or so years, from the birth of Jesus and on through the formation and early development of the Christian community. The Herods were minor figures, almost insignificant in the story that Luke tells of Jesus and the Jesus community. But they and their ilk continue into our times to loom large in the imaginations of people, not excluding people in the Jesus community, people who want to make their mark in the world — "for Jesus." They represent a remarkable instance of a dynasty that was incredibly successful in achieving celebrity and influence and wealth in less than auspicious conditions. The Roman government was interested only in using them for its own purposes and the general Jewish population despised them. But they still managed to achieve prominence in the public eye, epitomizing what can be achieved in adverse circumstances. The Herodian world was a world of wealth and influence, a world of pomp and circumstance, a world of cruelty and self-promotion, a world of arrogance and self-indulgence. These were people who knew how to get things done. For those who want to do great things for God, the Herodians obviously offer great promise.

But nothing could be more obvious and clear than that Jesus and Paul took "the road less traveled," the way ending in death by crucifixion for Jesus and imprisonment and death for Paul.

Akōlutōs

Luke/Acts ends on a quiet note: Paul under house arrest in Rome, receiving visitors, having conversations; it concludes with the teasing final word *akōlutōs*, "unhindered" (28:31 RSV). *Akōlutōs* suggests a wide-open field for the holy community in an opened-wide world. Early in his Gospel Luke expands our imaginations to understand that nothing less than the entire world is the theater for telling the story of Jesus: "In those days a decree went out from Caesar Augustus that all the world should be enrolled" (2:1 RSV). And now, sixty-two or so years later, Paul is in Rome, the place where that decree was issued, but under house arrest, chained to a Roman soldier assigned to keep watch over him: Paul, forcibly confined to his lodgings and "preaching the kingdom of God and teaching about the Lord Jesus Christ quite openly and unhindered" (28:31 RSV). Unhindered? "All the emphasis," writes I. Howard Marshall, "lies on that last phrase."[23] Is this irony? Paul immobilized by Roman chains doesn't seem like a promising strategy for accomplishing the salvation of the world that was forecast when Jesus told the incipient community, "you shall receive power when the Holy Spirit has come upon you; and you shall be my witnesses ... to the end of the earth" (Acts 1:8 RSV). Or is "unhindered" Luke's carefully chosen final word for the *means* by which the Holy Spirit accomplishes the formation of the kingdom in this world?

In the geography of the first century, Rome is the whole world; the mythical "man on the street" couldn't think larger than Rome. Rome encompassed "the end of the earth," in the popular imagination. This is now where the Jesus community's leading preacher and teacher has been placed. The Jesus community, represented in the person of Paul under house arrest in Rome, is on its way to becoming a world community even though no one would be able to guess it at the time. This Jesus community is not parochial, not provincial, was never intended to be confined to a ghetto or an institution or bounded by matters of race or culture or politics. Already in Rome, unsupported by outward evidence, it is poised to receive all and sundry into its embrace.

Unhindered? Paul can't leave his house. He has just had a disappointing conversation with the leaders of the local Jewish community, who have never so much as heard of him and who, after they do hear him, walk away arguing over what he has said. As they go, Paul sends them off smarting under the lash of Isaiah's prophecy, "this people's heart has grown dull . . ." (Acts 28:20-27). He is no more successful with the Jewish leadership in Rome than he had been in Jerusalem. Meanwhile Christians, with Nero on the rampage, are being martyred wholesale in the city. Paul will soon be included in the killings. Unhindered?

There can be little question, given the care with which Luke uses words, that he means, quite literally, unhindered. But this is not the reductionist, literal usage of the pedantic, unstoried mind. Paul, and Luke who is writing the story of the Jesus community, are by now well-schooled in the *means* of grace, the *way* in which the Spirit works salvation and forms the community. Conversant with and well-practiced in this way, the way of Jesus, the way of the Spirit, the way of the cross, the way of resurrection, they know how these things are done. They have lived these narratives, these Gospel and Acts narratives, lived them from the inside, engaged them in prayer and obedience, and know that "unhindered" is exactly the right word to end on. The judicial foot-dragging that has Paul mired in prison, the religious obduracy that has isolated the Jewish leadership from the Jesus community, the massacres that are sickening the city with Christian corpses, do not qualify as hindrances. "Unhindered" stands as the last word.

Is it not obvious by now that all through this narrative of the formation of the Jesus community the means used are unconventional, countercultural, and alien to any person who knows nothing of resurrection? But once resurrection is introduced into the story, all the ways in which we work have to be rethought, re-imagined, and reworked. The world's means can no longer be employed for kingdom ends.

After assimilating just what it is that God has done and is doing in creation and salvation, this is the most difficult and at the same time the most important thing to embrace in the Christian life: that we become willing participants not only in *what* God does, but in the *way* he does it. We have all grown up and been immersed in a pre-resurrection world of means in which power and money, information and technology, lust and avarice, pride and anger are the usual and approved ways for accomplishing the work of the world. They work, as a matter of fact, very well. They work efficiently. A clever and determined person can get almost anything he or she wants by perfecting and practicing these ways. The Herods certainly did.

But if Luke's last word is right and accurately represents Paul and the Jesus community, these ancestors of ours are well on their way to a perceptive, discerning engagement in using the means, the only means, appropriate for doing gospel work.

"Unhindered" is just the right word. It tells us that all the difficulties or obstacles that loom large in an unbaptized imagination are simply of no account in the agenda of the kingdom, where the resurrection, the Spirit's action in bringing Jesus alive into this present, defines the means. "Unhindered" connotes a kind of effortlessness. Paul, representing the Jesus community in Rome and as such a witness to the resurrection, is no longer competing with the world's means. His *being there* is enough: available; accessible to others without raising his voice, without fighting his way free of the imprisoning chain, without being diminished by the unlistening, unseeing Jewish leadership; free to offer up in intercession the massacred bodies of the Christians on the altar of the cross of Jesus. It is not exactly doing nothing. Something like sacrifice is involved — in the words of one of our better spiritual theologians, "the suppression of self-consciousness, and a certain precise tilt of the will, so that the will becomes transparent and hollow, a channel for the work."[24]

This unforced presentness is not easily acquired, but it can be acquired — it must not be supposed to be a mere matter of temperament or circumstance. Both temperamentally and circumstantially Paul was the last person in the world to exemplify this resurrection equanimity. He first appears in these pages as a fire-eating persecutor of Christians, energetically engaged in locking them up and, in at least one instance, at the stoning of Stephen, an accomplice in killing them. He was by nature impetuous, emotional, and capable of bursts of anger, and in the course of his work and travels he got knocked around considerably. When Paul told the Philippians that he had "learned to be content" (Phil. 4:11) regardless of circumstances, it was in considerable measure because he had learned to live by the means of the Spirit in contrast to the means of the world.

Learning how to live as the community of Christ is largely a matter of becoming familiar with and disciplined to the means by which the Father, Son, and Holy Spirit work formationally among us: namely, by the Holy Spirit from God's side and prayerful obedience from ours, by hospitably including the unwanted outsiders of the world into the community, and by cultivating a detachment from the world's insiders and their ways, especially as these ways are exemplified in the leaders and celebrities.

The community of Jesus betrays its Master far more often and damagingly by the *way* it speaks and acts than by anything it ever says or does. Anger and arrogance, violence and manipulation rank far higher than theological error or moral lapses in desecrating the holy, resurrection community.

So — *unhindered*. This is a remarkable and memorable last word that Luke uses to characterize Paul and, by extension, the Jesus community. And it is timely today for the Jesus community, which is constantly tempted to use the world's means to do Jesus' work. *Unhindered:* content and relaxed, practiced and discerning in living the Jesus life in the Jesus way, living a congruence between the resurrection reality and the means by which we give witness and live obediently in it.

Cultivating Fear-of-the-Lord in Community: Baptism and Love

This is a most attractive life, this resurrection life. The birth and death of Jesus come together in an amazing and personal way in Jesus' resurrection. And now we find that *our* lives, *our* birth and death, come together in resurrection: Jesus' resurrection becomes our resurrection. We read Paul's words, "If you be raised with Christ . . ." (Col. 3:1), and we say, "If?" No, "Since. . . ." He has made us "alive together with Christ" (Eph. 2:5); "it is Christ who lives in me" (Gal. 2:20). The resurrection stories of our four evangelists are now fused by Paul into the language of personal and communal participation. The Christian life is a Jesus-resurrection life, a life that is accomplished by the Spirit.

But just as in the fields of creation and history we find that very often our spontaneous responses for "getting in on" what God has done and is doing are inappropriate, so also in community. Instead of participating in what God is already doing, we end up bypassing, avoiding, or interfering with it.

We bypass the community of Jesus when we cobble together a group of people whom we judge to have far more potential for carrying out Jesus' kingdom work than the merely baptized. We recruit motivated and talented leaders who can catch a vision and execute it with dispatch. We develop job descriptions for discipleship, uninformed by Scripture, and look for candidates.

We avoid the community of Jesus when we slip into a spectator role. We are not indifferent. We appreciate and praise. We admire and exclaim and are inspired. But we do it from the stands, paying for good box seats, supporting the community with our applause, and doing occasional volunteer tasks when we are so inclined.

We interfere with this Spirit-created community when we try to take over. We discover this wonderful gift of new life in Christ — purpose and meaning and gratitude are moving through our arteries; we can hardly help ourselves — and we move in and start giving orders to the Spirit on how we think the community should manage its affairs. We are, after all, reasonably accomplished in getting things done, doing good works, and motivating others. We know the truth and goals of the gospel. But we haven't taken the time to apprentice ourselves to the way of Jesus, the *way* he did it. And so we end up doing the right thing in the wrong way and gum up the works.

Bypass, avoidance, and interference present major and persistent difficulties in cultivating a life of Spirit-directed participation among those of us who in baptism are "raised with Christ," living together in the company of the resurrection. None of us is a stranger to the task of living and working with others. It is, after all, an ordinary part of growing up — we call it "socialization." We learn to do it in various settings, in the family, in school, at work, on athletic teams, playing in band and orchestra, belonging to Boy Scouts or Girl Scouts, Rotary or Lions. It is understandable that we will bring what we have learned in these various settings into the church. But more often than not what we have learned isn't appropriate in this community — worse than inappropriate, it is wrong. The community of the resurrection is unique. How do we participate appropriately in this holy community? Parallels and continuities with the other groupings of people with whom we associate in matters of means are minimal. We have to start over and ask, "What is the unique quality of this community to which I find myself invited, and how do I participate in it rightly?

The short answer to the "how" question, as in the parallel areas of creation and history, is to cultivate fear-of-the-Lord. As we cultivate fear-of the-Lord, we develop a reverent respect for what is going on, and then modestly but also in genuine delight begin doing what is there to be done. Practicing fear-of-the-Lord gradually but surely shifts our attention from a preoccupation with what we can or should do to an attentive absorption in what God has been doing and the way he continues doing it in Jesus by the Holy Spirit.

The focal practice for cultivating the fear-of-the-Lord in community is baptism that achieves mature formation in the practice of love.

Baptism

Christianity is *about* water: 'Everyone who thirsteth, come ye to the waters.' It's about baptism, for God's sake. It's about full immersion, about falling into something elemental and *wet*. Most of what we do in worldly life is geared toward our staying dry, looking good, not going under. But in baptism, in lakes and rain and tanks and fonts, you agree to do something that's a little sloppy because at the same time it's also holy, and absurd. It's about surrender, giving in to all those things we can't control; it's a willingness to let go of balance and decorum and get *drenched*.

Anne Lamott[25]

The Gospel accounts place baptism early and prominently in the story: first, John baptizing, preparing the way for Jesus and then baptizing Jesus: John baptizing, Jesus being baptized. Jesus' baptism at the Jordan was marked by the descent of the Spirit on and into him, accompanied by the voice from heaven, "this is my beloved son," confirming his identity, at which time he began his ministry of revealing the kingdom of God. Jesus at the Jordan was a replay of Genesis 1, as he stepped into the waters that "are without form and void" while the Spirit (the dove) hovered. Thirty years later the same Spirit descended on the charter community of Christians, at which time they began to speak the language and do the work of God's kingdom in the world. Their first act was to baptize three thousand converts on the Day of Pentecost. For virtually all our Christian traditions, with the Society of Friends (the Quakers) the one exception, the defining first act and word marking life in the community of the resurrection is holy baptism.

*   *   *

A pastor friend of mine was given the assignment of organizing a new congregation. A person in such a position needs all the help he or she can get. Virtually everything must begin from scratch. Early on a woman came to my friend and said, "Pastor, let me help you. I'm really good at organizing and motivating people. I've done a lot of community work and would love to use my experience and skills in getting this new church going." My friend said, "Oh, thank you. I'd love to have your help. How about if we begin with conversations, thinking and talking through what it is we will be doing together. Here is what I propose, that for the next six weeks or so we meet weekly for a couple of hours and read and discuss what John Calvin wrote on baptism. Baptism, either actually or in prospect, will define and account for what is distinctive in the people who will make up this congregation. A church community is not quite like anything else. We are dealing with souls here, entire lives with nothing remaindered, immersed in God." The woman lost interest after two weeks.

*   *   *

Baptism definitively places our unique and personal name in the company of the Trinity, Father, Son, and Holy Spirit. Because we do not baptize ourselves — it is always something done to us in the name of the three-personed God in the community — the resurrection life by which we become our true selves is accepted as previous to and outside of anything that we can do for ourselves. At that moment we are no longer merely ourselves by ourselves; from then on we are ourselves in the community of similarly baptized persons.

As we enter the community of the resurrection, holy baptism redefines our lives in Trinitarian terms. Baptism is at one and the same time death and resurrection, a renunciation and an embrace. In baptism we are named in the same breath as the Name — Father, Son, and Holy Spirit — and are on our way to understanding our lives comprehensively and in community as children of this three-personed God. We are turned around, no longer going our own way but living as members of the community that follows Jesus. We cannot be trusted to do anything on our own in this business. As Barth insisted so strenuously, we are always beginners with God.[26]

Trinity: The Name

The theological understanding of God as Trinity is the controlling center of what takes place in baptism. We are baptized in the name of the Trinity. Baptism is an immersion in the triune God, God the Father, God the Son, and God the Holy Spirit. The implications are enormous: we are now participants in the company of the God who creates heaven and earth, the God who enters history and establishes salvation as its definitive action, and the God who forms a community to worship and give witness to his words and work. God understood as Trinity, God in three persons, lays the essential conceptual groundwork for living in the community of the resurrection. Three features are immediately clear: baptism in the name of the three-personed God means that our core identity is, as is his, emphatically *personal*; baptism in the name of God the Father, God the Son, and God the Holy Spirit means we are now welcomed as full *participants* in everything of God; baptism in the name of the Trinity means there is more to God, far more, than we can ever comprehend; we are baptized into a *mystery*.

The personal By insisting that God is three-personed, Father, Son, and Holy Spirit — God inherently relational, God in community — we are given an understanding that God is emphatically personal. The only way that God reveals himself is personally. God is personal under the personal designations of Father, Son, and Holy Spirit and never in any other way: never impersonally as a force or an influence, never abstractly as an idea or truth or principle. And so, of course he can't be known impersonally or abstractly.

We are not used to this. We are schooled in institutions that train us in the acquisition of facts and data, of definitions and diagrams, of explanations and analysis. Our schools are very good at doing this. When we study persons, whether God or humans, we bring the same methods to the work: analyzing, defining, typing, charting, profiling. The uniquely personal and particular is expunged from the curriculum; and that means the removal of the most important things about us — love and hope and faith, sin and forgiveness and grace, obedience and loyalty and prayer — as significant for understanding and developing as persons. The fact is that when we are studied like specimens in a laboratory, what is learned is on the level of what is learned from an autopsy. The only way to know another is in a personal relationship, and that involves at least minimal levels of trust and risk.

Because of long training in our schools and an unbaptized imagination, we commonly bring these reductionist, depersonalized methods to our understanding of God. But when we do, we don't come up with much, for God is totally personal, *inter*personal, relational, giving and receiving, loving and directing. There is nothing in Father-Son-Spirit that is not communal. And so there is nothing to be learned of Father-Son-Spirit except by entering the communion, entering the company of the Trinity: praying and listening, being quiet and attentive, repenting and obeying, asking and waiting. Trained as we are in the schools, it is the easiest thing in the world to use words abstractly and to treat the gospel as information. But Trinity prevents us from doing that. Trinity warns us against supposing that we can lock ourselves in a room free of all people and distractions and just read, study, and meditate and then expect to know God. Trinity is our defense against every soul-destroying venture into the Christian life that depersonalizes the gospel or God or other people.

When we are baptized into the community in the name of the Trinity, our lives become relational in a more thoroughgoing and deeper way than ever, not only with God but with the membership of the baptized.

The participation By insisting that God is three-personed as Father, Son, and Holy Spirit we are given an understanding of God that welcomes participation. We are baptized *into* the communal life of the Trinity. The spiritual life is a participation in the being and work of God. God is never a nonparticipant in what he does. He does not delegate. He does not manage from an impersonal position. He does not separate himself from his community by ranks of angel-secretaries through whom we have to arrange an audience. Baptized, we begin to get a feel for what it means to participate in what we have assumed we were not adequate for or qualified to do.

We are not used to this. For most of us, as our responsibilities grow we acquire skills for doing our work efficiently, which usually means by not participating personally. We send memos, prepare work assignments, develop programs, set goals, organize committees. It is a lot easier to guide and motivate people from a distance than to "get involved" with them. It is a lot easier and faster to depend on technology for travel and communication, building and farming, entertainment and managing, than to plunge into whatever there is to be done. But every time we do, engagement with reality, whether the reality is persons or things, lessens, and there is consequently less of us, less life.

When we bring these managerial and technologized habits into our dealings with God, we soon end up dealing with an idol, a thing-god on which we can project our plans and projects, programs and piety. The world of religion is surfeited with this kind of thing. Some people make a lot of money helping people construct such thing-gods, or idea-gods. It seems to be very satisfying to a lot of people to listen to leaders tell them how to use God to their benefit — the leaders are so enthusiastic, so convincing!

But we can only participate in who God is, *as* he is. He is not for hire to implement our fantasies or demands. God is not an undefined sort of energy or function in place somewhere waiting for us to show up with the right technique or the correct password to swing him into action. He is already active, enormously and incessantly active, creating and saving, healing and blessing, forgiving and judging. He was active in this way as Father, Son, and Holy Spirit long before we showed up on the scene, and he has clearly made it known that he wants us in on what he is doing. He invites our participation. He welcomes us into the Trinitarian dance, what I earlier described as the *perichoresis*.

When we are baptized into the community in the name of the Trinity we are freshly defined as participants in the work and being of God. There are many ways of making our way in the world without getting overly involved with people and things. But not in the Christian life. The more we understand God as Trinity the more we realize that we are welcomed as participants in everything that God — Father, Son, and Holy Spirit — is up to. And what's more, every act of participation is unique — God has not enlisted us in a regimented army marching in lockstep. We are immersed in particulars, not absorbed into generalities.

The mystery It is commonly said that the Trinity is a mystery. And it certainly is. Large books are written by theologians probing the endless reaches of the mystery. But it is not a mystery veiled in darkness in which we can only grope and guess. It is a mystery in which we are given to understand that we will never know all there is of God. It is a mystery that prevents us from presuming to use what we know to control or manipulate God. It is a mystery in which we cultivate the posture of worship, adoring what we cannot wholly understand, receiving that for which we have yet no name. It is not a mystery that keeps us in the dark, but a mystery in which we are taken by the hand and gradually led into the light, a light to which our souls are not yet accustomed, but light nevertheless in which we recognize ourselves as persons in the company of a personal God, become participants in all the operations of God, and develop an identity of humility and receptivity, a not-knowing in the presence of the God who knows us.

With God and the Christian life there is always more, much more. So much more that if we keep that "more" in mind there will never be any chance of our reducing God to the dimensions of our needs or imaginations. The "more" is a mystery of light: the Trinity surpasses our understanding but not in an intimidating way; we are invited to be present and to worship.

God formulated as Trinity confronts us with a largeness, an immensity, a depth that we cannot manage or control or reduce to dealing with on our own terms. God is more than we can comprehend. "A God that can be understood is no God." We cannot "know" God in a way that explains everything about him. The only way that we can approach God is through worship: holy, holy, holy.

We aren't used to this. We want to be "in the know." Answers provide credentials for competence. Now that we are insiders in this community that early on in its existence acquired the reputation of "turning the world upside down" (Acts 17:6), we would like to make good on our reputation. Pressure develops, sometimes from within, sometimes from without, to be "relevant" to the society, to reduce God to fit people's needs, congregational expectations, or our own ambition. But God is never a commodity that we can use, never a truth that we can use to explain or prove what is by its nature beyond understanding. In a functionalized world, in which virtually everyone is trained to understand themselves in terms of what they can do, of their competence, of their expertise, we are confronted with the Trinity. In the Trinity we are faced with the reality that we are not in control, that we are not able to serve people on their terms but only on the terms of who God is in himself. We do not know enough — if we reduce God to what people want or what "works," we leave out too much; we leave out most, in fact, of God who dwells "in light inexpressible."

Trinity: The Naming

The focal practice of baptism is basic to our identity formation. In baptism we are named ". . . in the name. . . ." This is our identity; this is who we are. Me — Eugene, but not just Eugene — Eugene in the community of Father, Son, and Holy Spirit, but also the community that includes Dorcas and Richard, Fletcher and Charles, Mildred and Yvonne, George and Beulah. If you want to know who I am and what makes me tick, don't for heaven's sake look up my IQ or give me a Myers-Briggs profile or set me down before a Rorschach test. Study me in the company of Father, Son, and Holy Spirit.

*   *   *

The Trinity is of particular use to Christians in times of confusion. Our age certainly qualifies on that score. With the theological, religious, and cultural traditions in disarray, the options offered by opportunistic teachers and religion marketers for dealing with God and/or the soul are beyond calculation. In desperate times we are tempted to go for the quick answer and the efficient solution. But the quick answer is almost always the oversimplified answer, leaving out all the complexities of actual truth; the efficient solution is almost always the depersonalized solution, for persons take a lot of time and endless trouble. In such conditions the Trinity is our most practical theological formulation for staying in touch with Christian basics: it keeps us in touch with the immense largesse of God and at the same time the immediate personalness of God. Meditating and praying in the name of the Trinity is essential for keeping our lives both large and personal during these times when the devil is using every strategy he can come up with to make us small and mean.

From the moment we are newly named in the name of the Trinity we know ourselves in a new way, a unique way, a way counter to the naming directed to us by our parents and our teachers, our friends and our employers, our neighbors and our enemies. We suddenly acquire ears to hear Thoreau's different drummer. Our eyes are opened to see, with Moses, "him who is invisible" (Heb. 11:27). Our baptismal name summons us to a way of life that follows Jesus.

*   *   *

Two imperatives chart the way of the baptized Christian as we set out living together in the community of the resurrection. Neither is difficult to understand, but it takes a lifetime of attention and discipline to be shaped by them. The words are "Repent" and "Follow." A third imperative, "Pray," yokes and interiorizes them.

"Repent" is the no and "follow" the yes of the baptized life. The two words have to be worked out in changing conditions throughout the life of the community and in each of our lives. We never master either command to the extent that we graduate and go to higher things. These are basic and remain basic.

"Repent" is an action word: change direction. You are going the wrong way, thinking the wrong thoughts, imagining everything backward. The first thing we do as we begin our life in the community is to quit whatever we are doing. Regardless of what it is, it is almost sure to be wrong, no matter how hard we are trying, no matter how well intentioned. Virtually everything in the North American way of life has led us to think that we are in charge of our lives, that we are the measure of all things, that everything depends on us. We are traveling a broad road paved with good intentions, expertly engineered with the latest technologies to get us to where someone has told us we want to go, and we want to get there with the least inconvenience, efficiently and quickly. It is a heavily trafficked road, noisy and polluted, with many accidents and fatalities. But it does get us where we have been told that we want to go, so we put up with almost anything on the way.

And then the baptismal word comes: repent. Turn around. Change your way of thinking, your way of imagining. Leave the noise, the pollution, the clutter, the depersonalizing efficiency, the technology-enabled hurry. Just say a loud, authoritative, non-negotiable no. We are on holy ground and we need to protect it from profane stomping and trampling.

We begin the resurrection life not by adding something to our lives but by renouncing the frenetic ego life, clearing out the cultural and religious clutter, turning our backs on what we commonly summarize as "the world, the flesh, and the devil."

And then follow. Follow Jesus. Following Jesus is the baptismal yes that succeeds the no. We have renounced initiative and taken up obedience. We have renounced clamoring assertions in favor of quiet listening. We watch Jesus work, we listen to Jesus speak, we accompany Jesus into new relationships, to odd places and odd people. Keeping company with Jesus, observing what he does and listening to what he says, develops into a life of answering God, a life of responding to God, which is to say, a life of prayer.

Prayer is the baptismal language learned and spoken in the community of the baptized. For following Jesus is not a robotic, lockstep marching in a straight line after Jesus. The following gets inside us, becomes internalized, gets into our muscles and nerves; it becomes prayer. Prayer is what develops in us after we step out of the center and begin responding to the center, to Jesus. And that response is always physical — a following, for Jesus is going someplace: he is going to Jerusalem and he is going to the Father. We follow Jesus, joining the company of his followers, cultivating a life of prayer in Jesus' name, finding that the Spirit is praying in us and through us to the Father. We are in the world of the Trinity where all is attention and adoration, sacrifice and hospitality (communion), obedience and love.

Love

> Love is never abstract. It does not adhere to the universe or the planet
> or the nation or the institution or the profession, but to the singular
> sparrows of the street, the lilies of the field, "the least of these my
> brethren."
>
> Wendell Berry[27]

If baptism is the focal practice that provides us our resurrection identity in
the community in which Christ plays, love names the way of life congruent with that identity. Baptism forms us in the practice of love. We have
seen how Deuteronomy preaches love in profuse particularity as the
dominant characteristic of the community of God's people. We have observed that the early Christian community as presented in Luke/Acts
throws open its doors and generously invites in all the unwanted, "the
least, the lost, and the left-out." But this love is not an item in a catalogue
available on order to Christians; it is the way of life that permeates and
sums up the thinking and behavior of followers of Jesus in the company of
the Trinity. In parallel to Sabbath/wonder in creation and Eucharist/hospi-
tality in history, Baptism/love is the focal practice that cultivates the fear-
of-the-Lord in community.

But "love" is one of the slipperiest words in the language. There is no
other word in our society more messed up, misunderstood, perverted,
and misused as the word "love." Complicating things even further, it is a
word terribly vulnerable to cliché, more often than not flattened into
nonmeaning by chatter and gossip. It is all me-directed. It is all self. The
largeness of love is reduced to the mouse hole of the ego. It is often used by
the same person and in the same conversation in self-contradicting ways
— seriously and frivolously, soberly and sentimentally, thoughtfully and
teasingly. It is used in the worship of a holy God and as a euphemism for
loveless sex. It is used to reveal heart intimacies and commitments and as
a cover for telling every sort and variety of lie. An incalculable amount of
violence, both emotional and physical, occurs in relationships begun in
love. In no other human experience do we fail so frequently, get hurt so
badly, suffer so excruciatingly, and get deceived so cruelly as in love. Still,
we continue to long for love, dream of it, attempt it. Walker Percy titled
one of his novels *Love in the Ruins*, an epitaph far too many in our communities can claim for their own. So when the men and women of the Chris-

tian community are given the responsibility for telling one another that God loves them, that he commanded every one of us to love one another, and when we assume responsibility for giving guidance and instruction in the life of love, we know we have no easy task. In fact, it is difficult to imagine a more formidable, seemingly impossible, task. Because of the enormous importance this has for the way we live, it is important to get it right. We need to listen attentively to every conversation, read discerningly every book, if we hope ever to discern the truth and implications of the love word.

*   *   *

For understanding the difficult yet uncompromised necessity of love in Christian community, we can hardly do better than use the First Epistle of John for orientation. The letter (actually, it is more like a sermon) deals directly with an early, unidentified Christian community that is having a torturous and confused time with this foundational love component of Christian living. The writer (also unidentified but in the early traditions assumed to be John the Apostle) is a pastor. His task, which is also our task, is to insist first on the irreducible essentiality of love and then to clarify two of the more common ways in which love is deconstructed.

Establishing a Love Identity

The community that received this pastoral letter was pretty much a mess. In addressing their behavior, Pastor John uses the words and phrases "lie" or "liar" five times (1 John 1:6, 10; 2:4; 4:20; 5:10), "hate" four times (2:9, 11; 3:15; 4:20), "child of the devil" once (3:8), and "commits sin" once (3:4). He also makes references to failure or refusal to love (3:10, 14; 4:8), self-deceit (1:6), and refusal to help someone in need (3:17).

Not an ideal congregation by a long shot. And yet not unusual. This kind of thing is by no means rare in the people of God communities that are recounted in both Old and New Testaments. It is, in fact, the norm. And it continues to be the norm throughout our two thousand years of Christian history. These gatherings of saints and sinners in Jesus' name don't get along with one another very well. Anyone who joins a church expecting to be part of a happy and harmonious gathering of put-together people sooner or later is in for serious disappointment. We can also suspect that such a person hasn't read the Scriptures very carefully. There are exceptions, occasionally quite glorious exceptions, but Christian communities, all of them, are communities-in-progress, baptized sinners in various stages of development in the life of love.

Men and women are not admitted to the community by presenting credentials of love skills, nor do we maintain our place in the community by passing periodic peer reviews on love. We are here to be formed over our lifetimes into a community of the beloved, God's beloved who are being formed into a people who love God and one another in the way and on the terms in which God loves us. It's slow work. We are slow learners. And though God is unendingly patient with us, we are not very patient with one another. Outsiders, observing our embarrassingly slow and erratic progress in love, wonder why we bother. Well, we bother because God is love: he created us in love; he saved us in an act of love; he commanded us to love one another. Love is the ocean in which we swim. So what if many of us can only wade in the shallows, and others of us can barely dog paddle for short distances? We are learning and we see the possibility of one day taking long, relaxed, easy strokes into the deep.

And that is why this Johannine community in which lying and hating are so conspicuously in evidence is nevertheless consistently addressed in words that are affectionate and relational. These people are first identified as "little children" (teknia mou), an affectionate term that is used seven times (2:1, 12, 28; 3:7, 18; 4:4; 5:21). They carry the same identity in the eyes of God: "children of God" or, maybe better, "God's children" (tekna theou) is used four times (3:1, 2, 10; 5:2). "Beloved" (agapētoi), the same word used by the Father for Jesus at his baptism, is used of the community six times (2:7; 3:2, 21; 4:1, 7, 11). "Brothers" (adelphoi), here a gender-inclusive term used metaphorically (and sometimes translated as "brothers and sisters"), is used five times to identify members of the congregation within the intimacies of family life (3:10, 13, 15, 17; 5:16). "Fathers" (pateres) and "children" (paidia), again metaphors that define identity in terms of personal relationship, are each used twice (2:13, 14, 18).

These are all relational terms that occur in contexts of affection (but not of sentimentality). We can understand ourselves in community truly only when we understand ourselves in a love language, as beings created in the image of God who is love, as persons "born of God" (5:4, 18). Love, the relational term par excellence, is the foundational substratum that provides our fundamental identity in community.

Regardless of how well or badly we receive and give love, regardless of our performance or function or role, we are relational beings at the core and the community is in place to identify us as such, to name us "the beloved . . . little children . . . children of God . . ." against all the counter-identities served up by the world. We get labeled early and frequently in nonrelational terms: first-grader, smart, cute, average, short, second-string. As we enter adulthood nonrelational labels continue: married, widowed, divorced, lawyer, logger, butcher, teacher, leader, follower, wallflower.

These labels are inevitable and in many ways useful but the common element to them is that they are impersonal and partial; when they become all-encompassing, which they too frequently do, they distort our core identity. They say almost nothing, or what is even worse, the wrong thing, about who we actually are.

A primary task of the community of Jesus is to maintain this lifelong cultivation of love in all the messiness of its families, neighborhoods, congregations, and missions. Love is intricate, demanding, glorious, deeply human, and God-honoring, but — and here's the thing — never a finished product, never an accomplishment, always flawed in some degree or other. So why define our identity in terms that can never be satisfied? There are so many easier ways to give meaning and significance to our human condition: giving assent to a creed or keeping a prescribed moral code are the most common in congregations.

Belief and behavior are essential, but as the defining mark of the Christian they lack one thing — relationship. They are both prone to abstractions or programs. Abstractions (learning right belief) are good; programs (learning right behavior) are good; but it is also possible to master the abstractions and carry out the programs impersonally. In fact, it is far easier if it is done impersonally.

Teaching people to think rightly and accurately is largely a cognitive process. We learn the right words and acquire the appropriate images for thinking about, imagining, and responding to God in Christ. All this is important. Still, it is possible, and not only possible but common, to think rightly and live badly, live impersonally. Knowledge does not turn into acts of love automatically.

Training people to behave morally is largely a programmatic process. We are trained in right responses, in keeping assigned rules, in respecting boundaries, in avoiding danger and fulfilling goals. But again, it is possible, and not only possible but common, to behave impeccably but live badly, live selfishly.

We have an abundance of educational courses for teaching right thinking about God in the community — Bible studies, catechetical curricula, Sunday School classes. And we have many imaginative programs for training in behaviors that are obedient to the scriptural commands to help and heal, form missions, and evangelize the world. But whoever heard of a class on love? And whoever heard of a love program? And the reason is that love cannot be reduced to what can be taught in a classroom or what can be formulated in a program.

The attractiveness of a class is that it simplifies by excluding everything but the subject involved. There is nothing wrong with this, as such, and much that is good. We need to get our thinking straight, know who we are and what we are dealing with. The classroom deals primarily with concepts and understanding. But learning to love can't be reduced to ideas about love.

The attractiveness of a program is that it simplifies by depersonalizing: get everyone doing the same thing for the same goal. There is nothing wrong with this, as such, and much that is good. It can help us to accomplish agreed upon things in the community to the glory of God. But the practice of love is nothing if not personal. You can't simplify it into a function.

What is dangerous is not ideas but the academic mind that abstracts both things and people from particular relationships into concepts. And what is dangerous is not programs but the programmatic mind that routinely sets aside the personal in order to more efficiently achieve an impersonal cause. These are not only dangerous but sacrilegious, for it is precisely relational particularities and personal intimacies that are at the center of our God-given, Holy Spirit–formed identities as the beloved who are commanded to love.

What is required, if we are to take Pastor John's letter as guide to the cultivation of our identity as children of God, is to refuse ever to sacrifice our commitments as a community to Jesus' love command in favor of a simpler and more readily achieved identity based on a common creed or a common cause.

Baptism defines our identity by an immersion in the emphatically relational Trinity — Father, Son, and Holy Spirit. It is at the same time a redefinition of our lives in the love-defined community of the beloved —

God's loved children, love-created and love-commanded brothers and sisters.

The Deconstruction of Love

Love is the highest and most complete expression of God's revelation: "God is love" (1 John 4:16). And love is also the highest and most complete expression of the human person: "If we love one another . . . his love is perfected in us" (4:12).

In using 1 John as a text for the cultivation of love in the community of the beloved, it is apparent that in John's congregation the two primary "disturbers of the peace" in the practice of love are sin and antichrist, impediments to the practice of love that continue to plague our communities.

Sin The people with whom we live in community are all sinners, every last one of them. If we entertain illusions of building and developing communities that are sin-free, and then periodically cleaning house by making a clean sweep of anything that defiles or offends, we end up doing one of two things. We settle for appearances, slick and glossy, cozy and domestic, and end up with a community that is nothing but a moral club. Or we get angry and mean, railing against the assembled people, blaming them for being bad and incorrigible children, and take on the role of reformer with the task of making sure that everyone thinks and acts rightly.

There is much naiveté regarding sin in Christian communities. For a people whose text for living is the Bible, a book in which "all have sinned" (Rom. 3:23) is documented on virtually every page, this is an enormous irony. We settle for conventional appearances or reforming campaigns, neither of which is conspicuous for insight or discernment in the subtleties of sin as it works its way among us. We quit being diagnosticians of the soul and instead develop programs — educational, political, economic programs — all of which can be done (and often are done) without taking on the strenuous and personally involving relationships of love. In the process we marginalize practices that nurture love in the community: listening friendships, compassionate understanding, and, most of all, the forgiveness of sin. It is the forgiveness of sin that frees men and women to love, and in that freedom, commands them to love.

But to be forgiven for sin, first of all there must be the awareness that we sin and are sinners. And there must be a realization that sin is neither incidental nor "fixable."

It turns out that one of the major impediments to a life of love as it comes into our view in 1 John is that a good many people in the community were denying that they sinned. Pastor John is forthright: "If we say that we have no sin, we deceive ourselves . . ." (1:8); "If we say that we have not sinned, we make him a liar . . ." (1:10).

Why would people claim that they have no sin, that they do not sin? For a start, it makes life much simpler. It means that we don't have to bother with relationships; it means that we don't have to take men or women seriously; and it means that we don't have to deal with God in a personal way — for sin is basically a depersonalizing word or act. It is not, in essence, breaking a rule, but breaking a relationship.

John knows that we will never get love right if we don't get sin right, and the looming difficulty in getting sin right is our propensity to deny or minimize it. Euphemisms proliferate: mistake, bad call, poor judgment, error, wrong, negligent, slip, oversight, misstep, stupidity, screw-up, bungle, faux pas, and so on. But rarely, sin. We happen to live in a culture that has a low sense of sin. Here I distinguish sin from immorality or crime. Sin is a refused relationship with God that spills over into a wrong relationship with others — it is personal or it is nothing. Immorality and crime, on the other hand, are violations of rules or standards of the society, or violations of other people. Behavior is in question, not personal character. But sin is relational.

A refusal to deal with sin is a refusal to deal with relationships. And if we don't deal with relationships, we can't love. Love is the relational act par excellence just as sin is the de-relational act par excellence. If I say that I do not sin or that sin is a minor issue for me, in effect I am saying that love is not high on my agenda. George Herbert well knew that sin and love had to be treated in parallel if either is to be comprehended in depth: "there are two vast, spacious things. . . . Yet few there are, that sound them, Sin and Love."[28]

Well, John sounds them. He makes sin a big issue because he is making love a big issue. We cannot love impersonally; we cannot love by abstractions; we cannot love by acquiring information; we cannot love by completing a project. The *person* has to be involved in *these* persons: Father, Son, Holy Spirit; and in *these* persons: Herman, Abigail, Adolph, Jennifer.

When improvements need to be made in our communities, sin is not ordinarily targeted as the place to start. The usual launching pads for improving ourselves and the world around us are knowledge, power, and wealth. And the resources we assemble to deal with them are, in broad categories, schools, politics, business, medicine, and the judiciary.

We have schools to remedy ignorance. Ignorance incapacitates us from dealing rightly with the world and reality. We learn so that we can live better and more humanly. Knowledge is basic to living well. We use political processes to remedy weakness. Weakness leaves us helpless in the face of cruelty and injustice and oppression. Politics is a major way in which we exercise power in order to do good, to achieve justice, to alleviate suffering, to protect victims. Political structures (governments and organizations) are the primary locations of power to do good. We have businesses to make money that will free us from poverty. Poverty leaves us insecure and without resources to do anything beyond mere survival. Businesses provide the economic bases that give us an economy in which people can acquire enough money for a comfortable standard of living. And so on.

The interesting thing about these approaches to improving our communities is that we can spend our lives pursuing any or all of them and never bother our heads about sin. And neither do we need to bother our heads about love.

If what is wrong with the world is not sin but ignorance, what we need is to find the right formula, the right technique, the right thoughts to get back to our true origins, our real identity. We have all grown up in a culture in which there is a massive but mostly uncritical trust in education to solve our problems. We assume that if we can just improve our schools, our social and political and personal lives will improve. But after two hundred plus years of intense and sustained work on that foundation in America, there is little to support the hope. Our schools, with their symbolic stature as places for enlightenment, are seen by many now as dangerous to both body and mind. If what is wrong with the world is not sin but weakness, then we need to improve our political processes and get others to do the same. We need a president, senators, legislators, governors, judges, and mayors who will work for the weak, protect the vulnerable, control crime. We have, it turns out, one of the best working democracies in the world, but the social results are far from encouraging. Our citizens are given votes and influence and freedom. And they are conspicuous across the board for living badly, frivolously, addictively, and selfishly. If what is wrong with the world is not sin but lack of money, then we need to develop businesses, corporations, banks, and investment ventures all over the world to put people to work, extract crops and minerals and oil, make more money, and develop prosperity so that people will not have unmet needs and will be satisfied with their lives. We have been as successful as any nation in history in making money. But the fallout in greed, self-indulgence, exploitation, and dishonesty is appalling.

*   *   *

In 1910 G. K. Chesterton wrote a book with the title *What's Wrong with the World*. It was early in the century and the country was full of ideas and plans for making the world a better place to live. Socialists, anarchists, and utopians of various sorts were offering up proposals regarding poverty and economics, war and peace, ignorance and education, sickness and health, mediocrity and eugenics, proposals on how to set right what is wrong with the world. It was an optimistic age and the assumption in all the proposals was that all we had to do was find the right ideas and right technology and we could fix whatever was wrong. The daily newspapers were full of intelligent advice. But they were also impersonal, dealing with programs or plans that would redistribute income, enact legislation, develop mechanisms or tools, reform the educational system. None was without merit. But not one was personal. None identified the core "wrong," the refusal to deal relationally and responsibly with what is "right" with the world, namely, God. It is not surprising that neither the word "sin" nor the word "love" appeared in their proposals. Chesterton's book was a collection of his newspaper columns in which he called attention to the conspicuous omission of any sense of God or sin among his brilliant contemporaries. If I had to summarize Chesterton's weekly polemics directed to the pundits of the day who thought they could make the world better without bothering with God or sin, I would propose, simply, "me." What's wrong with the world? Me.

We are created to live in relationship and responsibility with one another and with our Creator and Savior. When we don't do it, it soon becomes apparent that there is something "wrong with the world" and that somewhere in that "wrong" there is a "me." That's the place, Pastor John tells us, to start doing something about it.

The only place, quite literally *the only place*, where sin is taken seri-

318

ously in community, is the Christian community, the congregation. But even here, strangely, not enough. Often enough the community of the resurrection takes its cues from the world around us and lets its identity be shaped by a pursuit of learning so that we can combat ignorance, a pursuit of power so that we can relieve weakness, a pursuit of money so that we can assist people to live a more fulfilling and satisfying life.

It is unlikely that the pastor who wrote 1 John would dispute that there is a great deal schools, governments, and businesses, along with the courts and hospitals, can and need to do as we live together on this planet earth. But first of all he insists that we cannot ignore or deny the huge fact of sin and that we are sinners. At the core of who we are, there is something wrong, something wrong relationally, wrong personally between us and our neighbors and God. The only way to deal with it is by forgiveness. If we deny that we are sinners, other than in generalities or through euphemisms, forgiveness has no meaning for us. And so we are incapacitated for what we are created and saved to do best, to love: to love God, to love Henry, to love Emily.

Sin, though, in 1 John, is not a condemning label; it is not an accusation. It is a diagnosis, a revelatory insight into our condition, so that we can know what do to and where to go to get in on a life of love, a *way of life* that is love, not love in teasing, illusive fragments. As a community we are oriented in a huge reality that frees us from sin as a cancer in the soul, frees us from sin as a silent wasting of love. The huge reality is forgiveness:

> [T]he blood of Jesus his Son cleanses us from all sin. (1:7)

> If we confess our sins, he who is faithful and just will forgive us our sins and cleanse us from all unrighteousness. (1:9)

> [I]f any one does sin, we have an advocate with the Father, Jesus Christ the righteous; and he is the expiation for our sins, and not for ours only but also for the sins of the whole world. (2:1-2 RSV)

> [He] sent his Son to be the expiation for our sins. (4:10)

Cleanse ... forgive ... expiation. ... A life of love in the community is secured by a life of forgiveness by God. That which we cannot do for ourselves through education or government or business is done for us by God in

Christ. This is the foundation, the only foundation, on which a community of love can be formed.

"Expiation" *(hilasmos)* is the Johannine word that gives the most resonance to this huge sin-absolving act, echoing centuries of Hebrew experience in having sins forgiven, the slate wiped clean. In it we see thousands and thousands and thousands of men and women for a thousand and more years walking away from the place of worship with hearts light, consciences cleansed; returning, with confidence that they were living in the presence of a gracious God who loved them, to their homes and workplaces freshly motivated and free to practice the love command in the community of the people of God. Sin, with all its accompanying disabilities, is taken out of the center and replaced by love — God's love accessible and active and energetic in the community of the beloved, and all of that now focused in the birth, life, death, and resurrection of Jesus Christ.

The denial of sin and the accompanying programs or strategies to develop a way of life that is indifferent to or marginalizes sin, is common enough to get a name: perfectionism. It is one of the deadliest sins in the book for resurrection communities. It is deadly because those who pursue this way are convinced that it is possible, if only they try hard enough and find the right principles or techniques, to live without sin. Since it is not possible (and Paul and John, at least, are adamant on this), they either deny that anything they are doing qualifies as sin, or else they acquire a veneer that gives a sinless appearance. It is deadly because it anaesthetizes any awareness of personal sin and therefore any awareness of Jesus in his primary and essential work of forgiveness on the cross, the unprecedented miracle of expiation *(hilasmos)*. This is why perfectionists so often become workaholics; by ignoring the ubiquity of sin they persist in the illusion that if they accomplish just one more mission, master just one more act of devotion, successfully avoid contamination with just one more sloppily living Christian, get one more program up and running, they will emerge head and shoulders above all others. Some of them accomplish impressive projects and manage stunning achievements, but they also end up without friends, often without family, without forgiveness because they never need it, and without love. Perfectionism assumes tragic proportions when an entire community is infected.

Perfectionism is essentially an adolescent sin. Adolescents, almost by definition, know nothing about sin. They know about "sins," the ten commandments kind of sins. But they assume that they will grow out of them in time, and are convinced that if everyone (their parents for a start) knew what they knew and shared their dreams, the world would soon be a better place.

But it won't. The Christian way does not eliminate sin in the community. Christians don't become sinless. The only sane (and biblical) approach to sin is through expiation/forgiveness, the sacrificial and operative center of which is Jesus Christ — forgiveness moved by love. Sin confessed and forgiven frees us to develop relationships of love with our Lord and with one another.

*   *   *

Having insisted that none of us is without sin, John goes on to insist that we must not practice sin, that is, not sin carelessly or deliberately or casually, as if it didn't make any difference. It does make a difference — it makes a difference in our ability to love and in others' ability to receive our love.

The first references to sin in John's letter tell us not to fool ourselves by denying that we sin (1:8, 10); later another pair of sentences occur that seem to cancel the first ones:

> Those . . . born of God do not sin . . . they cannot sin. (3:9; also 3:6)

> We know that those who are born of God do not sin. . . . (5:18)

What are we to make of this? First this: the sin that is at the forefront in the letter is the failure or refusal to love. The vast array of possible sins available to us is concentrated here in violations of love, in our relations with persons. Our identity as the beloved of God allows no other way of life than that of loving others. The blunt "cannot sin . . . does not sin" simply conveys this: no exceptions, no excuses.[29] And then this: what "cannot" be in persons who get their identity from being beloved children of God is a way of life, a lifestyle, that excludes love. Other translations make this clear with "keeps on sinning . . . continues to sin . . ." (NIV), which is to say, "makes a practice of sin." Christians are the community of the beloved. Being loved and loving make up our core identity. What we simply *cannot* do is take up a way of life that makes a practice, whether thoughtlessly or deliberately, of sinning, and in particular, of not loving, or even worse, of actually hating (2:9, 11; 3:13, 15; 4:20).[30]

Antichrist   The second element that "disturbs the peace" of the community of the beloved, contributing to the deconstruction of love as the defining and pervasive practice of their common life, is the presence of antichrists.

The Johannine letters are the only biblical documents in which the term "antichrist" appears (1 John 2:18, 22; 4:3; 2 John 7). In the context of the letters it is not difficult to get a sense of the word's meaning. Given the apocalyptic climate of our times, though, what needs to be noted is that it obviously is not referring to an evil counter-Christ who is out to take over the world — the blown-up, larger-than-life figure that fascinates so many in the doomsday crowd. For one thing, the term is plural, "many antichrists" (2:18).

But more significantly, Pastor John is referring to persons who remove humanity from Jesus, deny anything human in him at all, and represent him as a purely divine figure. We know that a lot of religious leaders were doing this at the time of the letter, and were acquiring quite a following. This sounds very "religious," very "spiritual," but in sober fact it is a flat denial of the incarnation. They deny that God has a body. They deny that in Jesus God became flesh and blood, the same flesh and blood as ours. They deny that "the Word became *flesh* and dwelt among us" (John 1:14 RSV, italics added). This incarnation, this becoming flesh, is the very genius and distinction of the Christian gospel.

This superspiritual Jesus sounds attractive when we first hear of it: supernatural, glorious, miraculous. In an age buzzing with "spiritualities" the way ours is, it is easy to consider this superspiritual Jesus as an improvement, a development into a higher form of spirituality.

But this dehumanized Jesus pulls the rug out from the community of the beloved. Love that is directed to a dehumanized Jesus dissolves into an aesthetics of the sublime. If Jesus is divested of all human features and characteristics, loving Jesus is stripped of all the details that have to do with the kind of life we are actually living with our family and neighbors. And here's the thing: a dehumanized Jesus is a lot easier and more pleasant to love than a difficult spouse, or an angry teenager, or a rude neighbor, or an insufferably boring brother-in-law — all of them so very, very human.

But this pastor knows nothing of a "spiritual" Jesus. The only Jesus John knows is a God-in-the-flesh Jesus that he has heard with his own ears, seen with his own eyes, touched with his own hands (1 John 1:1), had meals with, and walked with all over Galilee.

*   *   *

It's a curious thing, but Christian communities have always had a harder time dealing with, accepting, and following the Jesus who is flesh and blood like us than the Jesus who is "one with the Father." By far the most deadly and recurrent misconceptions of Jesus in our two thousand years of Christian living have had to do with those who would slight or ignore or deny his humanity. It seems to be much easier for many to believe in a Jesus who is all divinity and doesn't soil his hands with humanity than to believe in a Jesus with dirt under his fingernails. Jesus is great as a savior of souls and revealer of secrets of the spiritual life, but when it comes down to matters of making a living in a dog-eat-dog world or living in a quarreling family, Jesus is not much use.

Pastor John has no patience with such. He provides the community with a simple rule of thumb to separate Jesus truth from Jesus lies: "every spirit that confesses that Jesus Christ has come *in the flesh* is from God, and every spirit that does not confess Jesus is not from God. And this is the spirit of the antichrist" (1 John 4:3, italics added). The spirit of antichrist denies that Jesus was truly human, human in the way that we are human.

A dehumanized Jesus allows us to develop a practice of love that has nothing to do with actual people. We are free to practice a love of God that consists of a mix of music, mountains, and stories that fills our hearts with inspiring thoughts and feelings without all the distraction and bother of people. A dehumanized Jesus is a dehumanized God-with-us that gives us license to customize a life of love entirely to our own convenience, without involving us in sacrifice or patience. Loving a dehumanized Jesus means loving in a way that has nothing to do with anything particular men and women are doing in our community. We become lovers of ideas and feelings, lovers of ecstasy and novelty. But certainly not lovers of the God who so emphatically revealed himself in human flesh and blood. And certainly not lovers of our brothers and sisters, at least the ones who don't provide us with intimations of sublimity or ecstasy.

It is difficult to go to all the effort of loving people you don't especially like when we have this antichrist option before us, a christ who is not a Christ, a christ whom we can worship and adore and believe without troubling ourselves in dealing with the humanity within and around us. The antichrist option has always been a convenient loophole for not loving actual, named people. A lot of the men and women in John's community were taking advantage of it.

*   *   *

Sin and antichrist are parallel in deconstructing love as the primary practice in the community of the beloved. Sin reduces the people around us to roles or objects so that we can use them or manipulate them or condescendingly help them. They are depersonalized so that we don't have to be relational with them. And, of course, the moment that happens, there is no love — there cannot be any love, for love is a relationship or it is nothing. In a parallel way antichrist exalts the God who is among us to an idea or feeling, eliminating the humanity so that we can indulge in moods spiritual. Christ is dehumanized so that we don't have to be relational with God. And, of course, the moment that happens there is no love, for love is a relationship or it is nothing.

The life of community, at the core of which is love of God and love for neighbor, is lived out in the midst of sin and antichrists. The conditions are always there, there is no getting away from or around them. But we can be trained in an alert awareness of them.

We can be trained to recognize sin as an unwillingness to live in relationship and therefore in love. We can be trained to recognize the unrelational ways set before us in the community — principles and abstractions, causes and programs — and see them for what they are, substitutes for love. And instead of denying or ignoring them, we can confess our sin and receive absolution — return to our knees over and over and over again and receive Jesus' forgiveness and cleansing and get up off of our knees and love one another.

And we can be trained to recognize the antichrists as the men and women who tell us that Jesus wasn't human the way we are — "how could he be? He is God!" — and to recognize that for all their fancy talk about Christ, for all their superspiritualities, such people are just that, antichrists. When they tell us that mere people, ordinary people, aren't all that important — it's big ideas and urgent causes and stirring visions that real Christians are concerned with, not these dull and obnoxious people who pull us down — we can re-immerse ourselves in the story of Jesus. We can return to our knees and worship this Jesus in all the ordinariness of his humanity and then get up off our knees and go back to our families and friends afresh to love them.

*   *   *

The last line of 1 John is abrupt: "Little children, keep yourselves from idols." A non sequitur? He hasn't said a word about idols until now. But a second look reveals its appropriateness, maybe even its genius.

Pastor John has been teaching and training us in our identity as beloved children of God who love one another. He does it by centering on Jesus and insisting on his full humanity, which is to say his personal, relational life of love for us. He integrates this into an insistence on *our* full humanity, which is to say, our personal, relational life of love for one another.

He has warned us against the depersonalizing, the dehumanizing of Jesus — getting rid of his humanity so that we don't have to deal with our humanity. He has warned us against the depersonalizing, the dehumanizing of ourselves that occurs when we deny the most conspicuous evidence of our humanity, our sin, so we don't have to bother with the humanity of others. The two dehumanizing acts combined virtually eliminate the most human act of which we are capable, love.

He then steps back and gives us this memorable charge: "Little children, keep yourselves from idols."

Idols? Why does he introduce idols in his very last line? Why does he leave us with this as his last word? Just this: an idol is god with all the God taken out. God depersonalized, God derelationalized, a god that we can use and enlist and fantasize without ever once having to (maybe "getting to" is the better phrase) receive or give love, and then go on to live, however falteringly, at our most human. The essence of idolatry is depersonalization. The idol is a form of divinity that requires no personal relationship. The idol is a form of divinity that I can manipulate and control. The idol reverses the God/creature relationship: now I am the god and the idol is the creature.

The Community of Love

Overall, the most distinctive thing about Christian love is that it is commanded. Not urged, not encouraged, not striven for as a goal, but commanded: "The *commandment* we have from him is this: those who love God must love their brothers and sisters also" (1 John 4:21, italics added). And commanded not as one item among others but as the non-negotiable centerpiece of the community's life.

The task is daunting, but also unavoidable: nothing less than *community* (nobody goes it alone in this business); nothing other than *love* (God will settle for nothing less than the mature us, our essential humanity).

If community could be imposed it would at least be manageable. Coercion can provide uniformity and perfect order, but the result is not community; it is an ugly parody of community; it is Naziism. Community can flourish only in freedom. So the love that defines our common lives, even though commanded, has to be unforced, personal, freely given by the members of the community: ours must be lifetimes of accumulated acts of love — likely flawed, imperfect, juvenile, sputtery, but still love. Despite ourselves, loyal love.

We are immersed in great and marvelous realities — Creation! Salvation! Resurrection! — but when we come up dripping out of the waters of baptism and look around we observe to our surprise that the community of the baptized is made up of people just like us — unfinished, immature, neurotic, stumbling, singing out of tune much of the time, forgetful, and boorish. Is it credible that God would put all these matters of eternal significance into the hands of such as us? Many, having taken a good look at what they see, shake their heads and think not. But this is the perpetual difficulty of living a life of love in the community of the beloved. We had better get used to it.

The thing that I find so impressive here is how unrelenting John is in his insistence on love even though he knows how often we will fail at it. He knows as well as any of us that it is impossible to bring it off satisfactorily. But he still insists. He will not water it down. He will not qualify it in any way: "The commandment we have from him is *this*: those who love God must love their brothers and sisters also" (1 John 4:21, italics added). If we claim allegiance to Jesus but disobey the love command, John calls us liars (2:4). Blunt language. Not exactly what we think of as pastoral. But this pastor says it. No matter how good a line we talk or how well we gush inspirational language, if we hate brother or sister we're "in the darkness" (2:9, 11), which is to say, full of hot air and talking gibberish. If we refuse to love another, regardless of who the other is, we are Cain the murderer. Refusal to love is an act of murder! (3:15). *That* gets our attention. John leaves no loopholes. He even includes as a refusal to love something as seemingly minor and devoid of emotion, maybe even intention, as the failure to help someone in need (3:17).

An all too common response to this relentless, unqualified insistence on love is to scramble for definitions. What exactly does he mean by love? Define your terms, please. But we will find no relief in hair-splitting definitions.

Love is the most context-specific act in the entire spectrum of human behavior. There is no other single human act more dependent on and immersed in immediate context. A dictionary is nearly worthless in understanding and practicing love. Acts of love cannot be canned and then used off the shelf. Every act of love requires creative and personal giving, responding, and serving appropriate to — context specific to — both the person doing the loving and the person being loved. Because of the totally personal, particular, and uniquely contextual community dimensions involved in even the simplest act of love — the circumstantial complexity and inescapably local conditions — there is a sense in which we cannot tell a person how to love and so our Scriptures for the most part don't even try.

Instead of explanations or definitions or generalizations John settles for a name and the story that goes with it: Jesus. "We know love by this, that he [Jesus] laid down his life for us — and we ought to lay down our lives for one another" (3:16). Then he lets each of us find the particular but always personal and relational way to do it in the Jesus way: "We love because he first loved us" (4:19).

We learn how to love by being loved. Love is not built into our genes. A lot of very essential things in human life take place without learning or practice: we breathe, our hearts pump and circulate our blood, our sucking reflexes are fully developed when we come out of the womb, we kick and wave and scream, we cuddle and sleep and coo, all without schooling or training.

As we develop genetically, things come into play that do require teaching and training: reading and writing, social skills, artistic and athletic competence, emotional and relational understandings, how to repair a transmission, how to program a computer, how to get to the moon. At the top of these learned behaviors, these achieved identities, is love.

Everyone more or less knows this, but after we've reached the age of thirty or so, having failed at it so many times, it seems so out of reach that many of us settle for a human identity that is more accessible — like one associated with playing the violin, or playing a ten-handicap golf game, or repairing a transmission, or getting to the moon. When we run into John's barrage of sentences on love, it just doesn't seem very practical. We shrug our shoulders and say, "Well, I've tried it, tried it a lot. I don't seem to be very good at it, and the friends I've tried it on don't seem to be very good at it either. How about something a little more down-to-earth."

But John won't be deterred. He says, in effect, "This is about as down-to-earth as you can get. Don't you remember hearing *the Word became flesh and dwelt among us? . . .* Isn't *dwelt among us* down-to-earth? And *God so loved the world that he gave? . . .* Isn't *world* down-to-earth? You are the one he loves, and this world is the ground on which he loves you. I'm not putting anything alien or ill-fitting on you. This is who you are, your identity, *loved by God.* But being loved is not all there is to it. Being loved creates a person who can love, who *must* love. Getting love is a launch into giving love.

"This involves, of course, a radical purging of your imaginations of the barnacles, parasites, and grime that have accumulated around the word 'love' so that Jesus and the Jesus story become clear. It doesn't mean that everything that you have experienced or imagined or even fantasized of love is dead wrong. But most of it, if not all, has been a fragment of something larger, a single puzzle piece from a thousand-piece jigsaw puzzle. The whole story, the big picture on the box of jigsaw puzzle pieces, is the picture of how God loves, laid out plain enough in Jesus, who right now is living and alive in your community (Matt. 18:20). The story of Jesus is the story of a beloved who became a lover. Now you do it: love your brother, love your sister, love your neighbor."

And then John tells us this over and over and over again, relentlessly. Some comment that this is boring. Really? Maybe what the repetitions convey is patience. Maybe what John conveys by his repetitions is that this is going to take a long time. But that's okay; he isn't going to quit on us and God isn't going to quit on us. Nobody can rush or hurry these things. And no one can measure or evaluate anything so intricately complex and multifaceted. There are depths and mysteries here and a sacredness that must not be violated by meddling or interfering or engineering. Maybe all this love language is boring the way Ravel's *Bolero* is boring, the repetition of a simple theme over and over and over in different voices and decibels. But musicians don't find *Bolero* boring. And Christians who find themselves in the community of love don't find the love commands boring. John says "love" first one way, turns it around and says it again, shifts the tenses and gives that a try, puts it negatively and then positively and then negatively again. He appeals to our experience, he refreshes our memories with allusions from the Gospels, he insists on Jesus' present authority in all this, he raises his voice from time to time, throwing in salt and pepper words like "liar" and "murderer," "hate" and "antichrist." But every sentence comes out more or less the same: God loves you; Christ shows you how love works; now you love. Love, love, love, love. Just do it.

*   *   *

Love bade me welcome: yet my soul drew back,
    Guilty of dust and sin.
But quick-ey'd Love, observing me grow slack
    From my first entrance in,
Drew nearer to me, sweetly questioning,
    If I lack'd anything.

A guest, I answer'd, worthy to be here:
    Love said, You shall be he.
I the unkind, ungrateful? Ah my dear,
    I cannot look on thee.
Love took my hand, and smiling did reply,
    Who made the eyes but I?

Truth Lord, but I have marr'd them: let my shame
    Go where it doth deserve.
And know you not, says Love, who bore the blame?
    My dear, then I will serve.
You must sit down, says Love, and taste my meat:
    So I did sit and eat.[31]

As Kingfishers Catch Fire . . .

Forty years ago I found myself distracted. I was being tossed about by "every wind of doctrine" — except it was not winds of doctrines that were distracting me, but the winds of the times. It was the sixties and there was a lot going on: charismatic personalities like Kennedy and King, revolutionary goings on in the south, Timothy Leary and the drug culture, Earth Day and the flower children, Vietnam. . . . There was so much going on in the world, in the culture — so many important things to do, urgent voices telling me what had to be done. There was no "one thing needful" — there were many things needful, all clamoring for my attention.

I was living in a small town twenty miles from Baltimore, a town that was fast becoming a suburb. I had been assigned there by my denomination to gather a congregation and organize a church. I started out with a fair amount of confidence and with much energy. I was well supported organizationally and financially; the personal encouragement was strong. The mission that I had been called to lead was clearly articulated.

But as time went on I found myself increasingly at odds with my advisors on matters of means, the methods proposed for ensuring the numerical and financial viability of the congregation. I was given books to read on demographics and sociology. I was sent to seminars programming strategies for appealing to the suburban mindset.

It wasn't long before I was in crisis: a chasm had developed between the way I was preaching from the pulpit and the way I conducted our planning committee. I sensed that my attitude toward the men and women I was gathering into the congregation was silently shaped by how I was planning to use them to succeed as a new church pastor with little thought to serving their souls with the bread of life. I found myself thinking competitively regarding other churches in town, calculating ways in which I could beat them in the numbers game.

I had become very American in all matters of ways and means. I never wavered in my theological convictions, but I had a job to do — get a church up and running — and I was ready to use any means at hand to do it: appeal to the consumer instincts of people, use abstract principles to unify enthusiasm, shape goals using catchy slogans, create publicity images that provided ego-enhancement.

And then one day my wife and I attended a lecture in Baltimore at Johns Hopkins Hospital that showed me another way of being. Given my distracted condition, the timing was just right. The lecturer provided a defining image that has given shape to my life, both personally as a follower of Jesus and vocationally as I have been a companion to other followers of Jesus as a pastor and writer.

The lecturer was Paul Tournier, the Swiss physician who in midlife shifted the location of his medical practice from a consulting room with its examining table and supporting laboratories and surgeries, to his living room before a fireplace. For the rest of his life he used words, listened to and spoken in a setting of personal relationship, as the primary means for carrying out his healing vocation. He left a way of medical practice that was primarily focused on the body and embraced a medical practice that dealt primarily with the whole person, an integrated being of body, soul, and spirit. He wrote many books and I read them all. I don't think any of the books are still in print, and in retrospect I don't judge that they were great books. They were anecdotal in style, personal and storied, but there was a spirit of discerning grace that permeated the books that I found very attractive.

Driving the twenty miles home from Johns Hopkins, my wife and I commented appreciatively on the lecture, in the course of which she said, "Wasn't that translator great?" And I said, "What translator — there wasn't any translator." At which she said, "Eugene, he was lecturing in French. You don't know twenty words of French; of course there was a translator." And then I remembered her — a woman about his age, standing to the side and a little behind him, translating his French into English. She was so unobtrusive, so self-effacing, so modest in what she was doing that I forgot that she was there, and ten minutes after the lecture didn't even remember that she had been there.

But there was something else, Paul Tournier himself. During the lecture I had the growing feeling that who he was and what he was saying were completely congruent. He had been living for a long time in Switzerland; what he was now saying in Baltimore came across as an accurate and mature expression of all he had been living. Just as the translator was assimilated to the lecturer, her English words carrying not just the meaning but the spirit of his French words, so his words were one with his life — not just what he knew and what he had done, but who he was.

It was a memorable experience, the transparency of that man. No dissonance between word and spirit, no pretence. And the corresponding transparency of the woman. No ego, no self-consciousness. Later I remembered T. S. Eliot's comments on Charles Williams: "Some men are less than their works, some are more. Chas. Williams cannot be placed in either class. To have known the man would have been enough; to know his books is enough. . . . [He was] the same man in his life and in his writings."[1]

That's the sense I had that day about Tournier: he wrote what he lived, he lived what he wrote; in the lecture that day, in person in Baltimore, he was the same man as in his books written in Switzerland. A life of congruence. It is the best word I can come up with to designate what I am after in this conversation in spiritual theology.

* * *

The Christian life is the lifelong practice of attending to the details of congruence — congruence between ends and means, congruence between what we do and the way we do it. It is what we admire in an athlete whose body is accurately and gracefully responsive and totally submissive to the conditions of the event: Michael Jordan, for instance, at one with the court, the game, the basketball, and his fellow players. Or a musical performance in which Mozart, a Stradivarius, and Yitzak Perlman fuse and are inextinguishable from one another in the music. But it also occurs often enough in more modest venues: a child unselfconsciously at play, a conversation in which words become movements in a ballet revealing all manner of beauty and truth and goodness, a meal bringing friends into a quiet awareness of affection and celebration in a mingling of senses and spirits that brings something like a eucharistic dimension to the evening.

Congruence is what Gerard Manley Hopkins demonstrates in "As

Kingfishers Catch Fire," the sonnet that has provided the primary metaphor for this conversation in spiritual theology. We began with this sonnet, hoping that it would set the tone as Hopkins piles up a dazzling assemblage of images to fix our attention on this sense of rightness, of wholeness, that comes together when we realize the utter congruence between what a thing is and what it does: kingfisher, dragonfly, a stone tumbling into a well, a plucked violin string, the clapper of a bell sounding — what happens and the way it happens are seamless. He then proceeds to us men and women — "each mortal thing" — bodying forth who and what we are. But what kingfishers and falling stones and chiming bells do without effort requires development on our part, a formation into who we truly are, a becoming in which the means by which we live are congruent with the ends for which we live. But Hopkins's final image is not of us finally achieving what the dragonfly and plucked string do simply because it is determined by biology and physics; his final image is of how Christ lives and acts in us in such ways that our lives express this congruence of the inside and outside, this congruence of ends and means, Christ both the means and the end playing through our limbs and eyes to the Father through the features of our faces so that we find ourselves living the Christ life in the Christ way.

*　　*　　*

The words of Jesus that keep this in focus are, "I am the way, and the truth, and the life" (John 14:6).

For much of my life I have been trying to find ways to talk and write about the Christian life that will give witness to what is involved as God's Holy Spirit dwells formationally in us — which is to say, the Jesus *way*. Only when we do the Jesus truth in the Jesus way do we get the Jesus life.

I haven't found it to be easy.

It is easier to talk about what Christians believe, the truth of the gospel formulated in doctrines and creeds. We have accumulated a magnificent roster of eloquent and learned theologians and scholars who have taught us to think carefully and well about the revelation of God in Christ through the Holy Spirit. Many of us have studied them with appreciation and profit.

And it is easier to talk about what Christians do — the behavior that is appropriate to followers of Jesus, listed in commandments and moral codes, formulated in vision statements and mission strategies; life as performance. We've never lacked for teachers and parents and pastors to instruct us in the morals and manners of the kingdom of God.

But what tops the agenda for me is the Christian life as *lived,* lived with this sense of congruence between who Christ is and who I am; lived at this busy, heavily trafficked North American intersection with the kingdom of God; Christ playing in my limbs and eyes.

*   *   *

Two things absolutely basic to the Christian life are, unfortunately, counter to most things North American, which makes this intersection a confused place, clogged with accidents, snarled traffic, and short tempers. To begin with, the Christian life is not about us; it is about God. Christian spirituality is not a life-project for becoming a better person, it is not about developing a so-called "deeper life." We are in on it, to be sure. But we are not the subject. Nor are we the action. We get included by means of a few prepositions: God with us (Matt. 1:23), Christ in me (Gal. 2:20), God for us (Rom. 8:31). *With* . . *in* . . . *for* . . . : powerful, connecting, relation-forming words, but none of them making us either subject or predicate. We are the tag-end of a prepositional phrase.

The great weakness of North American spirituality is that it is all about *us:* fulfilling our potential, getting in on the blessings of God, expanding our influence, finding our gifts, getting a handle on principles by which we can get an edge over the competition. And the more there is of us, the less there is of God.

It is true that sooner or later in this life we are invited or commanded to do something. But in that doing we never become the subject of the Christian life, nor do we perform the action of the Christian life. What we are invited or commanded into is what I want to call prepositional-participation. The prepositions that join us to God and his action in us and in the world — the *with,* the *in,* the *for* — are very important, but they are essentially a matter of the ways and means of being in on, of participating in, what God is doing.

These ways and means are the second thing basic to the Christian life and also counter to most things North American. Ways and means must be appropriate to the ends they serve. We cannot participate in God's work but then insist on doing it in our own way. We cannot participate in building God's kingdom but then use the devil's methods and tools. Christ is the *way* as well as the truth and the life. When we don't do it his way, we mess up the truth and we miss out on the life.

My Montana neighbor, philosopher Albert Borgmann, is our most eloquent and also most important spokesman in these matters, exposing the dangers of letting technology determine the way we live our lives, dictate the means by which we, in his phrase, "take up with the world." It doesn't take a long while in his company, whether personally or through his books, to realize that the methods that we use today have plunged us into a major crisis, a crisis in the *way* we live. We have permitted a technology-saturated way of life to disengage us from what is essential to our humanity, whether in relation to things or people. As a result we live at secondhand: relationships atrophy, enjoyment diminishes, life thins out. Borgmann places the "culture of the table" — the preparing and serving and cleaning up after meals — at the center of the well-lived life. At the table everything involved in the preparation, serving, and eating of a meal requires *engagement* (an important word for Borgmann) — unless, of course, we use the available technology and buy TV meals and disengage from dealing firsthand with food and turn on the TV set as a substitute for human conversation, a corollary disengagement. Used without discrimination, technology discarnates our lives, the polar opposite of what takes place in Jesus in his incarnation, the *em-body-ment* of God among us. We can't live a life more like Jesus by embracing a way of life less like Jesus'.[2] Dr. Borgmann is head of the philosophy department at the University of Montana and has given a lifetime of sustained attention to understanding and discerning the ways technology affects the way we live, how the ways and means by which we do things (technology), if used unthinkingly or inappropriately, corrupt or destroy the very thing we set out to do. Borgmann is not anti-technology; in fact, he is very respectful of it. He just doesn't want it to ruin us — and it is ruining us. In great and thoughtful detail he is answering the question posed so brilliantly and insistently by Walker Percy in his several novels: "How does it happen that we know so much and can do so much and live so badly?"

This is the concern motivating a "kingfisher" life, the concern of spiritual theology: a focused attention on the *way* we live the Christian life, the *means* that we employ to embody the reality and carry out the commands of Jesus, who became flesh among us.

*   *   *

I want to say one more thing. This is slow work and cannot be hurried. It is also urgent work and can't be procrastinated. Life is deteriorating around us at a rapid pace. Life at the center — gospel life, kingdom life — is being compromised, distorted, and degraded at an alarming rate. At the North American intersection, slow and urgent are not compatible, they cancel one another out. But in the Christian way, patience and urgency are yoked. Urgent as this is, there is no hurry. There cannot be any hurry. Impatience is antithetical to a congruent life.

So what I want to say is, patience is prerequisite. Formation of spirit, cultivation of soul, realizing a lived congruence between the way and the truth — all this is slow work requiring endless patience. Unfortunately, patience is not held in high regard in our American society. We are in a hurry; we are addicted to shortcuts; we love fast cars and fast food. One of the most appreciated features of our vaunted technology is how fast we can get things and get things done.

But human life is endlessly complex, intricate, mysterious. There are no shortcuts to becoming the persons we are created to be. We can't pump up congruence by taking steroids. Patience is a difficult condition to come to terms with in a technology-saturated culture that is impatient — worse, contemptuous — of slowness. As a consequence, patience is jettisoned. And what happens is that the faster we move the less we become; our very speed diminishes us.

To talk about the spiritual theology under American conditions sometimes seems just absurd. It is such a seemingly fragile way of life in this culture of massive technology, arrogant leadership, pushing and shoving, insatiable consumerism. A Jesus way? Kingfishers and dragonflies? Stones tumbled over rim of roundy wells? So inefficient, so ineffective. And yet. And yet Jesus tells us to do it this way.

*   *   *

Rick Bass, a very good writer, is another Montana neighbor of mine. He lives in the Yaak, a wilderness area seventy miles north of my home. Besides being an excellent writer, he is a fervent environmentalist. I don't know him personally but have seen him in action, and like very much what I see. Environmentalists care deeply about this creation; but a lot of them are also pretty mean — angry, sometimes violent. Rick Bass is small of stature, elf-like, energetic and laughing, it seems, most of the time. He holds parties for the loggers and miners, working for common ground, developing a language of courtesy and understanding. He wrote an essay recently that I count as required reading for anyone who cares about living well, especially living well as North American followers of Jesus who are immersed in this impatient, shortcut-addicted culture.

He writes that it used to be that whenever he was confronted with a complex and difficult task he imagined himself patiently laying down one brick after another until eventually he got the job done. Slow, steady, careful work, brick by brick by brick. But he has recently changed his metaphor. He had been reading about glaciers. A glacier is the most powerful force the world has ever seen. Nothing, literally nothing, can stop a glacier. A glacier is formed by the falling of snow that accumulates over a period of time — an inch today, a quarter of an inch yesterday, a mere skiff of powder last week. As the snow deepens, the weight compresses. Ice is formed, and then more snow, which becomes more ice, year after year after year. Nothing happens for a long time, but when the glacier is sixty-four feet thick it starts to move, and once it starts nothing can stop it.

This is the metaphor that Rick Bass has embraced as he continues to do the writing and witness that is his vocation. He notes that one theory regarding the origin of glaciers is that they are "the result of a wobble, a hitch, in the earth's rotation. . . . glaciers get built or not built, simply, miraculously, because the earth is canting a single one-trillionth of a degree in *this* direction for a long period of time, rather than in *that* direction." And then this comment: "When I am alone in the woods, and the struggle seems insignificant or futile, or when I am in a public meeting and am being kicked all over the place, I tell myself that little things matter — and I believe that they do. I believe that even if your heart leans just a few degrees to the left or the right of center, that with enough resolve, which can substitute for mass, and enough time, a wobble will one day begin, and the ice will begin to form, where for a long time previous there might have been none.

"Keep it up for a lifetime or two or three, and then one day — it *must* — the ice will begin to slide."[3]

Or, to replace the metaphor with ours, we'll see . . . Christ playing in ten thousand places, lovely in limbs, lovely in eyes not his, to the Father through the features of men's and women's faces.

APPENDIX

Some Writers on Spiritual Theology

The single most important thing to understand in spiritual theology is that it is not *about* theology, not a body of information gathered in the classroom and from books; rather, it is a cultivated disposition to *live* theology, to live everything that God reveals to us in Scripture and Jesus and then live it in the neighborhood, in *our* neighborhood. Most of us know far more *about* God than we actually live in obedient faith *in* God.

Throughout this conversation my intent has been to invite my readers into participation in the Christian life, not just provide information about it. And so to conclude the conversation with a list of books to read could easily give the wrong signal. I don't want to overwhelm readers with more books and divert you from the real business of *living* the life of Christ.

And yet. And yet I do want to name a few writers who have been valued companions, warning me away from seductive options and fortifying my determination to live what God has revealed to me in Jesus Christ and not just give sermons or lectures or — God forbid! — write another book about it. Given the climate of this age in which there is so much sham and silliness regarding spirituality, I need perceptive and devout allies to keep me focused. But companions of this sort are not easy to either recognize or come by; it seems only courteous to introduce a few who have served me well. I'll keep my list short — seven of them, with annotations. None of them are "easy" reading — how could they be? Spiritual theology demands the most that we can bring to it. Making it easy inevitably falsifies it. Here are my seven:

Martin Buber, *I and Thou.*

More than any other writer, Buber has trained me to use language personally, relationally, intimately. He insists convincingly and relentlessly that
life is always interpersonal and requires a language that is personal and relational. The moment we turn either God or neighbor or thing into an It —
an Idea or a Cause or an Object, we distort or diminish the very thing we
thought we were pursuing. Spiritual theology is personal or it is nothing. (I
prefer the translation of Walter Kaufmann [New York: Scribner, 1970].)

Hans Urs von Balthasar, *Prayer.*

Prayer is language used in relation to God. If we do not pray what we understand and practice, we leave out the biggest part. Prayer is the most involving use of language available to us, but it also is at perpetual risk as we
become more and more preoccupied in using language when dealing with
things and people and events. Balthasar sets prayer in its largest possible
context, theologically and personally, and prevents us from trivializing it
or marginalizing it. Prayer is spiritual theology's first language. (Translated by A. V. Littledale [London: Geoffrey Chapman, 1963]; also available
in paperback from Ignatius Press in San Francisco.)

Fyodor Dostoevsky, *The Brothers Karamazov.*

Novelists are our masters in developing a narrative sense in us, a sense that
even the seemingly least significant details in our lives are eternally significant, that our stories are the form in which we live God's revelation. There
are many novelists who qualify as masters in this; Dostoevsky has been central for me. Without a strong sense of narrative, spiritual theology is in danger of atrophy by abstraction. (I recommend the translation by Richard
Pevear and Larissa Volokhonsky [San Francisco: North Point Press, 1990].)

Gerard Manley Hopkins, *The Poems of Gerard Manley Hopkins.*

Poets keep us attentive to the lived detail of life and keep our words accurate and honest. Again, as with novelists, there are many who qualify as
masters. Hopkins, priest and poet, ranks high on my list. The language of
spiritual theology is subject to constant assault by cliché and religious
cant. Without vigilance we end up mouthing pious platitudes. Poets are
essential allies in purifying the language. (The fourth edition, edited by
W. H. Gardner and N. H. MacKenzie [Oxford: Oxford University Press,
1967], is available in paperback.)

Wendell Berry, *What Are People For?*
Spiritual theology is under constant threat of assimilation by or reduction to the prevailing culture. We need discerning critics to keep us alert to the lies and illusions and betrayals to which spirituality is especially vulnerable. The prophetic bite and Christian winsomeness (a rare combination) of these and other essays keeps our identity as followers of Jesus in sharp focus. Berry's numerous novels and poems round out his witness. (San Francisco: North Point Press, 1990.)

Karl Barth, *The Christian Life.*
In this final but unfinished volume of the immense *Church Dogmatics,* a lifetime of prayed theology is harnessed to the Lord's Prayer. Barth made it only through the second petition before he died, but even as a fragment it stands as a powerful witness to spiritual theology as life that is prayed and prayer that is lived as Jesus taught us to pray. (Translated by Geoffrey W. Bromiley, subtitled *Church Dogmatics* IV/4: *Lecture Fragments* [Grand Rapids: Wm. B. Eerdmans Publishing Company, 1981.)

Rowan Williams, *Christian Spirituality.*
The prevailing distortion of spirituality in our day is that it is all about what we can do to live well before God, and then "happily ever after." Williams assembles a learned phalanx of protest against every so-called spirituality that sentimentalizes or commodifies the Christian life. The vigorous witness of these authoritative and formative figures from the first century to the sixteenth insists that the cross of Jesus (*not* our pursuit of happiness) is the essence and core of spiritual theology: suffering is involved, sacrifice is required. There is no other way. There is only the way of Jesus, the way of the cross, the way in which our "experience" is baptized in the death and resurrection of Jesus. We need to be conversant and at home with these witnesses so that we will not be seduced into thinking that spirituality can be customized to our comfort and convenience. (Atlanta: John Knox Press, 1979; published in England as *The Wound of Knowledge.*)

Notes

Notes to the Introduction

1. T. S. Eliot, "East Coker," in *The Complete Poems and Plays, 1909-1950* (New York: Harcourt, Brace and Co., 1952), p. 129.

2. In *The Poems of Gerard Manley Hopkins*, ed. W. H. Gardner and N. H. Mackenzie (London: Oxford University Press, 1967), p. 90.

3. A phrase from Reinhold Niebuhr in *The Nature and Destiny of Man*, vol. 2 (New York: Charles Scribner's Sons, 1941), p. 294.

4. Robert Browning, "A Grammarian's Funeral," in *The Poems and Plays of Robert Browning* (New York: Modern Library, 1934), p. 169.

5. William Barrett, "The Faith to Will," *The American Scholar* (Autumn 1978): 526.

6. See George Steiner, *Grammars of Creation* (New Haven: Yale University Press, 2001), p. 323.

Notes to the Prologue

1. Unless otherwise noted, all biblical citations are taken from the New Revised Standard Version of the Bible.

2. Eugen Rosenstock-Huessy, *The Fruit of Lips: Or Why Four Gospels*, ed. Marion Davis Battles (Pittsburgh: Pickwick Press, 1978), p. 85.

3. "The great human dogma is that the wind moves the trees. The great human heresy is that the trees move the wind." G. K. Chesterton, *Tremendous Trifles* (Beaconsfield, England: Darwen Finlayson, 1968 [first published, 1909]), p. 92.

4. Not all agree that there is a suggestion of bird-like hovering here. Some schol-

ars prefer to translate the phrase "a terrible storm" or "God's storm." Gerhard von Rad, *Genesis*, trans. John Marks (London: SCM Press, 1961), p. 47.

5. Gordon Fee has provided the definitive exegesis for the term. See *God's Empowering Presence* (Peabody, Mass.: Hendrickson, 1994), pp. 28ff.

6. "God's Grandeur," in *The Poems of Gerard Manley Hopkins*, ed. W. H. Gardner and N. H. Mackenzie (London: Oxford University Press, 1967), p. 66.

7. Lesslie Newbigin's reflection on the passage is pointed: "unbelief springs from the desire for a more 'spiritual' religion. The 'flesh' of Jesus — the concrete humanity of the Son of man — is the stumbling block because it forbids the kind of 'spirituality' which leaves each man free in the privacy of his own thoughts to give his allegiance to the 'truth' as he has himself discovered it. That kind of 'spiritual religion' is exactly 'the flesh' in biblical language. It is unbelief, and it is present in the midst of the disciples." *The Light Has Come* (Grand Rapids: Eerdmans, 1982), p. 89.

8. It is unfortunate that the word "soul" has deteriorated in popular speech to convey a kind of "spiritual" abstraction from real life, an ethereal otherworldly something-or-other that is remote from everyday stuff. But it is too good a word to abandon to the barbarians. The rich associations that have accumulated among us from centuries of Scripture reading and Christian conversation need to be preserved.

9. Johannes Pedersen provides us with an extensive study of the Hebrew understanding that "man, in his total essence, is a soul." See *Israel: Its Life and Culture* (London: Oxford University Press, 1926), vol. 1, pp. 99-181.

10. "Quietism" is the name associated with this approach. It was a popular form of spirituality in seventeenth-century France and was condemned as a heresy.

11. Rudolf Otto, *The Idea of the Holy* (London: Oxford University Press, 1923).

12. Bruce Waltke, "The Fear of the Lord: The Foundation for a Relationship with God," in *Alive to God: Studies in Spirituality Presented to James Houston*, ed. J. I. Packer and Loren Wilkinson (Downers Grove, Ill.: InterVarsity, 1996), pp. 17-33.

13. See Waltke, *Alive to God*, pp. 17-33.

14. Karl Barth, *Church Dogmatics* I/1 (Edinburgh: T&T Clark, 1936), p. 425.

15. *Perichoresis* is not a New Testament word and not all theologians today accept its appropriateness as an image for Trinity. It is a word from classical Greek and did not enter the Christian community's vocabulary until the eighth century when the Greek theologian John Damascene used the term to highlight the dynamic and interpersonal character of the Trinity in contrast to impersonal images and abstractions. Catherine LaCugna writes of "why the image of 'divine dance' has been used to translate *perichoresis*. Even if the philological warrant for this is scant, the metaphor of dance is effective. Choreography suggests the partnership of movement, symmetrical but not redundant, as each dancer expresses and at the same time fulfills him/herself towards the other. In inter-action and inter-course, the dancers (and the observers) experience one fluid motion of encompassing, permeating, enveloping, outstretching. There are neither leaders nor followers in the divine dance, only an eternal movement of recipro-

cal giving and receiving, giving again and receiving again. . . . The image of the dance forbids us to think of God as solitary. The idea of trinitarian *perichoresis* provides a marvelous point of entry into contemplating what it means to say that God is alive from all eternity in love." *God for Us: The Trinity and Christian Life* (San Francisco: HarperSanFrancisco, 1973), p. 272.

16. A most excellent discussion of the Trinity in the postmodern context is provided by Colin Gunton, *The One, the Three, and the Many: God, Creation, and the Culture of Modernity* (Cambridge: Cambridge University Press, 1993).

Notes to Chapter 1

1. Wendell Berry, *The Gift of Good Land* (San Francisco: North Point Press, 1981), p. 273.

2. There is a sequel. Johnny's Sunday absences continued for five years. And then he was back but now in a very different frame of mind. This time he was in pain. His wife had left him, his emotions were in chaos, his children a mess. Pain brought him back the second time and this time he stayed. But that is the subject of the next section, "Christ Plays in History."

3. Quoted by George Steiner, *Grammars of Creation* (New Haven: Yale University Press, 2001), p. 16.

4. Jesus is also designated "firstborn" in other contexts: "firstborn within a large family," Rom. 8:29; "firstborn from the dead," Col. 1:18 and Rev. 1:5; and "firstborn into the world," Heb. 1:6.

5. Karl Barth, *Church Dogmatics* III/1 (Edinburgh: T&T Clark, 1958), p. 28.

6. Raymond Brown, *The Birth of the Messiah* (Garden City, N.Y.: Doubleday, 1977), p. 314.

7. Brown, *Birth of the Messiah*, p. 314.

8. Karl Barth, *Credo* (New York: Charles Scribner's Sons, 1962), p. 68.

9. In Madeleine L'Engle, *The Weather of the Heart* (Wheaton, Ill.: Harold Shaw, 1978), p. 45.

10. See Philip Lee, *Against the Protestant Gnostics* (New York: Oxford University Press, 1987), especially pp. 13-44.

11. Eugen Rosenstock-Huessy, *The Fruit of Lips: Or Why Four Gospels*, ed. Marion Davis Battles (Pittsburgh: Pickwick Press, 1978), p. 86.

12. Isaiah 40:26, 28; 41:20; 42:5; 43:1, 7, 15; 45:7, 8, 12, 18; 54:16; 57:18; 65:17, 18 (2x).

13. Bruce Waltke, "The Creation Account in Genesis 1:1-3, Part IV: The Theology of Genesis 1," *Bibliotheca Sacra* (October 1975): 339.

14. Other rhythm-reinforcing repetitions: and it was so, 6x; and God saw that it was good, 7x; according to its kind, 10x; separated, 5x; made, 5x; called, 4x; created, 5x; gave, 2x; blessed, 2x; be fruitful and multiply, 2x; the heavens and the earth, 2x; firma-

ment, 9x; plants yielding seed and fruit trees bearing fruit in which is their seed, 3x; swarms of living creatures, 2x; birds, 5x; living creatures, 2x; cattle, 3x; creeping things, 4x; beasts of the earth, 4x; fish of the sea, 3x; lights, 6x.

15. Jon Levenson, *Creation and the Persistence of Evil* (Princeton, N.J.: Princeton University Press, 1988), p. 58.

16. Gregory of Nyssa, *The Life of Moses,* trans. Abraham J. Malherbe and Everett Ferguson (New York: Paulist, 1978), p. xv.

17. Wendell Berry, *Life Is a Miracle: An Essay against Modern Superstition* (Washington, D.C.: Counterpoint, 2000), p. 25.

18. Annie Dillard, *Teaching a Stone to Talk* (New York: Harper and Row, 1982), p. 40.

19. Lewis Mumford, *The Story of Utopias* (New York: Viking, [1922] 1962), pp. 2-3.

20. John Stott has assembled a lifetime of observations in his photographs and prose that catch the underlying created unity between what we see and what we believe as we become familiar with our place on earth. *The Birds Our Teachers* (Wheaton, Ill.: Harold Shaw, 1999).

21. Abraham Heschel called Sabbaths "cathedrals in time." *The Sabbath* (New York: Farrar, Straus, and Giroux, 1951), p. 8.

22. Hans Urs von Balthasar, *The Glory of the Lord* (San Francisco: Ignatius, 1982), vol. 1, p. 24.

23. "[T]he term 'Son of Man' throughout this gospel retains the sense of one who incorporates in Himself the people of God, or humanity in its ideal aspect . . . there is never any doubt that the evangelist is speaking of a real person, that is, of a concrete, historical individual of the human race, 'Jesus of Nazareth, the Son of Joseph' (1:45). He labours, grows weary, thirsts, feels joy and sorrow, weeps, suffers, and dies." C. H. Dodd, *The Interpretation of the Fourth Gospel* (Cambridge: Cambridge University Press, 1953), pp. 248-49.

24. In Alfred Corn, ed., *Incarnation: Contemporary Writers on the New Testament* (New York: Viking, 1990), p. 2.

25. The so-called authoritative *egō* occurs in Matthew 29 times, in Mark 17 times, in Luke 23 times, and in John 132 times. The full formula *egō eimi* is used by Matthew 5 times, Mark 3 times, Luke 4 times, and John 30 times. See G. M. Burge, in *Dictionary of Jesus and the Gospels,* ed. Joel B. Green and Scot McKnight (Downers Grove, Ill.: InterVarsity, 1992), pp. 354 and 356.

26. Reynolds Price, *Three Gospels* (New York: Scribner, 1996), pp. 158 and 148.

27. "He takes up a phrase or a word, plays with it, repeats it, turns it inside out, then drops it and revolves in a similar way round another, very often one that has been thrown up in the process of handling the first. We have to come to terms with this and accept it, otherwise we are simply baffled and irritated by his refusal to make his points and advance in an orderly manner." Austin Farrer, *A Rebirth of Images* (Westminster: Dacre, 1949), p. 26.

28. Edward Dahlberg, *Can These Bones Live?* (Ann Arbor: University of Michigan Press, 1967), p. 25.

29. William Temple, *Readings in St. John's Gospel* (London: Macmillan, 1959), p. xvii.

30. In *The Poems and Plays of Robert Browning* (New York: Modern Library, 1934), p. 301.

31. C. H. Dodd observes that "in the frequent Hebrew expression *othoth vumoftim, mofet* (Greek *teras*) means something wonderful or marvelous, a 'miracle' in the proper sense. But *oth* (Greek, *sēmeion*) does not necessarily connote the miraculous. It is used by itself for a pledge or token between man and man or between God and man...." *The Interpretation of the Fourth Gospel*, p. 141.

32. When Moses was being prepared to confront Pharaoh, God provided him with validating "signs," the same word *(sēmeion)* in the Greek translation of Exodus (Exod. 4:8-9) as John uses in his Gospel. Is there an echo of that in the confrontation here? Maybe.

33. This is the only time the phrase "signs and wonders" occurs in John, an echo, perhaps, of God's words to Moses, "though I multiply my signs and wonders in the land of Egypt, Pharaoh will not listen to you" (Exod. 7:3-4).

34. St. Teresa of Avila, "Meditations on the Song of Songs," in *The Collected Works of Teresa of Avila*, trans. Otilio Rodriguez and Kieran Kavanaugh (Washington, D.C.: Institute of Carmelite Studies, 1980), vol. 2, p. 246.

35. John uses "believe" only in its verbal form *(pisteuō)*, except for once as an adjective. He uses it ninety times in comparison to the thirty-four times of his three Gospel-writing colleagues combined. He uses "love" as a verb *(agapaō)* thirty-eight times compared to twenty-six times in the other three Gospels. The other verb for "love" in common use at the time *(phileō)*, he uses thirteen times compared to the eight instances in the other three Gospels.

36. I once heard this phrase in a sermon but no longer recall the preacher.

37. Karl Barth, *The Epistle to the Romans*, trans. Edwyn C. Hoskyns (London: Oxford University Press, 1933), p. 279.

38. Albert Borgmann is a professor of philosophy at the University of Montana. See his work, *Technology and the Character of Contemporary Life: A Philosophical Inquiry* (Chicago: University of Chicago Press, 1984).

39. In Wendell Berry, *A Timbered Choir* (Washington, D.C.: Counterpoint, 1998), p. 7.

40. The verb "rest" is used here. The noun, *shabbat*, as the name for the seventh day does not occur until Exodus 16:22-30.

41. Levenson, *Creation and the Persistence of Evil*, p. 100.

42. Peter T. Forsyth, *This Life and the Next*. Quoted by A. M. Ramsey, *P. T. Forsyth: Per Crucem ad Lucem* (London: SCM, 1974), p. 116.

43. Levenson, *Creation and the Persistence of Evil*, p. 111.

44. Levenson, *Creation and the Persistence of Evil*, p. xxi.

45. Quoted in Todd Eshtman, "Visiting Lake Wobegon," *The Lutheran* (February 2002).

46. Temple-building as participation in God's world-building is also evident in Solomon's temple, the other great building operation on display in our Scriptures. Extensive scholarly attention has been given to the detailed ways in which the Solomonic temple reflects and mirrors the world of creation and then receives its final Genesis stamp in Solomon's dedicatory prayer that is delivered in seven petitions (1 Kings 8:31-32, 33-34, 35-36, 37-40, 41-43, 44-45, 46-51). For a summary see Levenson, *Creation and the Persistence of Evil*, pp. 90-99.

47. "Philo's exegesis remains one of the most impressive attempts at a consistent symbolic interpretation, the influence of which for the later history can hardly be overestimated. For Philo the tabernacle was a representation of the universe, the tent signifying the spiritual world, the court the material. Moreover the four colors signified the four world elements, the lamp with its seven lights the seven planets and the twelve loaves of bread the twelve signs of the Zodiac and the twelve months of the year." Brevard Childs, *The Book of Exodus* (Philadelphia: Westminster, 1974), pp. 547-48.

48. Berry, *A Timbered Choir*, p. 14.

49. Quoted in Maise Ward, *Gilbert Keith Chesterton* (Baltimore: Penguin, [1944] 1958), p. 397.

50. T. S. Eliot's exquisite phrase for the ever-present but imprecisely noticed evidence of God at work among us in "The Four Quartets," *The Complete Poems and Plays, 1909-1950* (New York: Harcourt, Brace and Co., 1952), p. 136.

51. William Willimon, *The Pastor: The Theology and Practice of Ordained Ministry* (Nashville: Abingdon, 2000), p. 329.

Notes to Chapter 2

1. *Milosz's ABC'S* (New York: Farrar, Straus, and Giroux, 2001), p. 83.

2. Whether we think of God as a moralist or become moralists ourselves, the consequences are deadly. The song "Perfect" by Alanis Morisette, pointed out to me by a student, captures this well in lines like "If you're flawless, then you'll win my love" or "We'll love you just the way you are/If you're perfect" (from the album *Jagged Little Pill*, Maverick Records, 1995).

3. George A. F. Knight, *Theology As Narration* (Grand Rapids: Eerdmans, 1976), p. 20.

4. Donald E. Gowan, *Theology in Exodus* (Louisville: Westminster/John Knox, 1994), p. 6.

5. "Chinese Banyan" from William Meredith, *The Open Sea* (New York: Alfred Knopf, 1958).

6. "Pharaoh" literally means "Great House" and was used frequently to refer to the king of Egypt, perhaps much as we use the term "White House" to refer to the president, or maybe even as we say "Government" when we want to introduce a hint of distancing disapproval or contempt, as in "That's Government for you" or "You can't trust Government. . . ." See *Anchor Bible Dictionary*, vol. 5 (New York: Doubleday, 1992), pp. 288-89.

7. Gowan, *Theology in Exodus*, p. 2.

8. Peggy Rosenthal, "Poet of the Hidden God," *The Christian Century* (January 2001): 4-5.

9. R. S. Thomas, *Later Poems* (London: Papermac, 1984), p. 23.

10. The phrase is from St. John of the Cross, who lived and wrote in relentless opposition to self-indulgent spiritualities of all stripes. *The Collected Works of St. John of the Cross*, trans. Kieran Kavanaugh and Otilio Rodriguez (Washington, D.C.: Institute of Carmelite Studies, 1979), p. 122.

11. Gowan, *Theology in Exodus*: "God will do as Moses asks. He intends to reveal his name, but first he reserves his freedom not in any sense to be defined by a name. Israel will be able to address him, but not possess him" (p. 84).

12. Quoted in Brevard S. Childs, *The Book of Exodus* (Philadelphia: Westminster, 1974), p. 69.

13. Gerhard von Rad, *Old Testament Theology* (New York: Harper and Brothers, 1962), vol. 1, p. 185.

14. *Selected Poetry and Prose of William Blake*, ed. Northrop Frye (New York: Modern Library, 1953), p. 129.

15. Gowan, *Theology in Exodus*, p. 134.

16. See Peter Toon in *The New International Dictionary of the Christian Church*, ed. J. D. Douglas (Grand Rapids: Zondervan, 1974), p. 199; and Gregory Dix, *The Shape of the Liturgy* (London: Dacre, 1945), p. 436.

17. Knight, *Theology As Narration*, p. 106.

18. Donald Gowan's phrase for the Red Sea event. *Theology in Exodus*, p. 131.

19. Childs, *The Book of Exodus*, p. 238.

20. See J. F. Sawyer and H-J Fabry in *Theological Dictionary of the Old Testament*, vol. 4, ed. Johannes Botterweck and Helmer Ringgren (Grand Rapids: Eerdmans, 1990), pp. 441-63.

21. Latin for "god from a machine," referring to a device in Greek drama that used the machinery of ropes and pulleys to drop a god down to the stage to rescue someone by supernatural intervention from the entanglements of the plot.

22. Von Rad, *Old Testament Theology*, vol 1, p. 138.

23. Brevard Childs: "The poem praises God as the sole agent of salvation. Israel did not cooperate or even play a minor role. The figure of Moses is completely omitted. Yahweh alone effected the miracle at the sea." *The Book of Exodus*, p. 249.

24. George Steiner, *Real Presences* (Chicago: University of Chicago Press, 1989), p. 218.

25. Mary Doria Russell, *The Sparrow* (New York: Ballantine, 1996), p. 100.

26. From the hymn "Immortal, Invisible, God only Wise" by Walter Chalmers Smith, *The Hymbook* (Philadelphia: Presbyterian Church [USA], 1955).

27. Von Rad, *Old Testament Theology*, vol. 1, p. 13. See also Deut. 26:5-26; Josh. 24:2-13; Ps. 78:13, 53; 106:9.

28. Wallace Stegner, *When the Bluebird Sings to the Lemonade Springs* (New York: Random House, 1992), p. 181.

29. Reynolds Price, *Three Gospels* (New York: Scribner, 1996), p. 37.

30. See Austin Farrer, *St. Matthew and St. Mark* (Westminster: Dacre, 1954).

31. Sir Edwyn Hoskyns and Noel Davey, *The Riddle of the New Testament* (London: Faber and Faber, 1931), pp. 137ff.

32. H. C. G. Moule, *Veni Creator* (London: Hodder and Stoughton, 1890), p. 104.

33. Hans Urs von Balthasar, *The Glory of the Lord* (San Francisco: Ignatius, 1982), vol. 1, p. 151.

34. Jean Sulivan, *Morning Light* (New York: Paulist, 1988), p. 18.

35. Quoted by Belden Lane, *Landscapes of the Sacred* (New York: Paulist, 1998), p. 81.

36. I use, as the church has commonly done, the terms Eucharist, Meal, Supper, Table, and Communion as synonyms.

37. It is not clear from the text whether Jesus' Last Supper was, in fact, the Jewish Passover; the opinion of scholars is divided. But it is clear that it was prepared and eaten in the ambience of Passover and was understood to be in continuity with it, a salvation meal.

38. *The Presbyterian Hymnal* (Louisville: Westminster/John Knox, 1990).

39. A superb exposition of the meaning of the Eucharist exegetically, historically, and presently, for both Protestants and Catholics, is available in F. Dale Bruner, *Matthew, a Commentary*, vol. 2 (Dallas: Word, 1990), pp. 956-70.

40. Gregory Dix: "in the scriptures both of the Old and New Testament, *anamnēsis* and the cognate verb have the sense of 're-calling' or 're-presenting' before God an event in the past, so that it becomes *here and now operative by its effects*." *The Shape of the Liturgy*, p. 161.

41. Anne Lamott, *Bird by Bird* (New York: Pantheon, 1994), p. 117.

42. Dix, *The Shape of the Liturgy*, p. 117.

43. Quoted in Dix, *The Shape of the Liturgy*, p. 118.

44. *Epistle to Diognetus*, quoted by Douglas Steere in *Dimensions of Prayer* (New York: Harper and Row, 1962), p. 19.

45. The quoted portions are from the *Book of Common Worship* of the Presbyterian Church (USA), the service book that I have used most of my life.

46. Dix, *The Shape of the Liturgy*, p. 162.

47. Albert Borgmann, *Technology and the Character of Contemporary Life: A Philosophical Inquiry* (Chicago: University of Chicago Press, 1984), p. 207.

48. Dorothy Day, *The Long Loneliness* (San Francisco: Harper and Row, 1952), p. 285.

49. Joachim Jeremias, *New Testament Theology*, trans. John Bowden (London: SCM, 1971), part 1, pp. 289-90.

50. The phrase is from Lewis Mumford, *The Myth of the Machine*, vol. 1: *Technics and Human Development* (New York: Harcourt Brace Jovanovich, 1967).

51. Borgmann, *Technology and the Character of Contemporary Life*, pp. 201-6.

52. Annie Dillard, *Holy the Firm* (New York: Harper and Row, 1977), p. 15.

53. Hans Urs von Balthasar, *Mysterium Paschale: The Mystery of Easter*, trans. Aidan Nichols, O.P. (Grand Rapids: Eerdmans, 1993), p. 97.

54. Julian Green's comment is apropos in this context: "The devil is a great moralist and a great puritan. He suggests great austerities which he very well knows will bring about spiritual disasters. He never suggests small sacrifices, he aims at what is grand, sensational, at everything striking, at everything that stirs the imagination." *Julian Green Diary 1928-1957*, trans. Anne Green (New York: Carroll and Graf, 1985 [first published 1961]), p. 294.

55. Margaret Visser explores in immense and fascinating detail the extraordinary ramifications of the ordinary meal: *Much Depends Upon Dinner* (New York: Grove, 1986).

Notes to Chapter 3

1. Austin Farrer, *Lord, I Believe: Suggestions for Turning the Creed into Prayer* (Cambridge, Mass.: Cowley, 1989), p. 39.

2. Eugen Rosenstock-Huessy, *I Am an Impure Thinker* (Norwich, Vt.: Argo, 1970), p. 2.

3. The Bible furnishes us with a rich vocabulary that gives texture to the bare term "community": people, people of God, congregation, great congregation, church, chosen people, royal priesthood, holy nation, saints (always in the plural), chosen, Israel of God, household, temple, family, body, commonwealth. I will use them all. But note: *all* the terms are corporate.

4. Hopkins, "God's Grandeur," *The Poems of Gerard Manley Hopkins*, ed. W. H. Gardner and N. H. Mackensie (London: Oxford University Press, 1967), p. 66.p. 27.

5. George Steiner, *Errata* (New Haven: Yale University Press, 1997), p. 77.

6. There doesn't seem to be very much that we can do to eliminate the institutional sectarianism that we are all heir to. But any spirituality worthy of its salt can and must resist the attitudes and spirit of sectarianism and refuse to craft a spirituality formed on sectarian reductions or exclusions. Diversity in the body of Christ isn't nec-

essarily the same thing as sectarianism. Diversity in the community may, in fact, be a sign of health just as it is in the forest or on a farm. Denominations, as such, are not destructive, but when they function as sects, excluding and competing and prideful, they destroy that which they proclaim.

7. It is not named as such in Kings and Chronicles but was early recognized as Deuteronomy by Athanasius, Chrysostom, and Jerome, an identification confirmed by all scholars today.

8. Moshe Weinfeld, *Deuteronomy 1–11*, The Anchor Bible, vol. 5 (New York: Doubleday, 1991), p. 37.

9. The vocabulary is revealing: "complain" nine times (15:24; 16:2; 16:7 twice; 16:8 twice; 16:9; 16:12; 17:3); "quarrel" three times (17:2 twice; 17:7); and two instances of disobedience (16:20; 16:28).

10. Not everyone has arranged the Ten Words in the same way nor numbered them the same. For a discussion of the variations see Weinfeld, *Deuteronomy 1–11*, pp. 242-50.

11. See Weinfeld, *Deuteronomy 1–11*, p. 311.

12. Weinfeld, *Deuteronomy 1–11*, p. 20.

13. Weinfeld, *Deuteronomy 1–11*, p. 20. Also pp. 20-35 for details.

14. George Arthur Buttrick et al., eds., *Interpreter's Bible* (New York: Abingdon-Cokesbury, 1953), vol. 2, p. 474.

15. Buttrick et al., eds., *Interpreter's Bible*, vol. 2, p. 311.

16. Mark has only six places in which the Spirit is mentioned; Matthew twelve; John fifteen; and Luke seventeen (possibly eighteen); in Acts the Spirit appears fifty-seven times. See Joseph Fitzmyer, S.J., *The Gospel According to Luke (I–IX)*, The Anchor Bible (Garden City, N.Y.: Doubleday, 1981), p. 227.

17. In our Scriptures and in Jesus, power is consistently associated with weakness, humiliation, love, courage, hope, defeat: see Isaiah 53 and 1 Corinthians 11; Psalm 69 and 1 Corinthians 1; Mark 15 and 1 Peter 2.

18. Blaise Pascal, *Pensées and Provincial Letters* (New York: Modern Library, 1941), no. 513, p. 166.

19. Joel B. Green, *The Gospel of Luke* (Grand Rapids: Eerdmans, 1997), p. 24.

20. Green, *The Gospel of Luke*, p. 317.

21. Joseph, Daniel, and Esther are frequently mentioned biblical instances of persons living out their faith in the precincts of political power, but it must be noted that none of them was instrumental in converting the kingdoms in which they served. They were humbly giving faithful witness and providentially serving the people of God.

22. I am capitalizing "World" here to mark it off as the deliberately god-rejecting "world" as expressed in John's phrase, "Love not the world . . ." (1 John 2:15 KJV).

23. I. Howard Marshall, *The Acts of the Apostles* (Grand Rapids: Eerdmans, 1980), p. 427.

24. Annie Dillard, *Teaching a Stone to Talk* (New York: Harper and Row, 1982), p. 68.

25. Anne Lamott, *Traveling Mercies* (New York: Pantheon, 1999), p. 231.

26. Karl Barth, *The Christian Life* (Grand Rapids: Eerdmans, 1981), p. 80.

27. Wendell Berry, *What Are People For?* (San Francisco: North Point, 1990), p. 200.

28. George Herbert, "The Agony," in *Major Poets of the Earlier Seventeenth Century*, ed. Barbara K. Lewalski and Andrew J. Sabol (New York: Odyssey, 1973), p. 217.

29. J. L. Houldon compares this phrase to expressions common in ordinary speech, such as a parent saying, "little boys do not do so-and-so," knowing perfectly well that they do. See *A Commentary on the Johannine Epistles* (London: Adam and Charles Black, 1973), p. 94.

30. See B. F. Westcott, *The Epistles of John* (1883; repr. Grand Rapids: Eerdmans, 1979), p. 104.

31. George Herbert, "Love (3)," from *The Country Parson; The Temple*, ed. John N. Wall Jr. (New York: Paulist, 1981), p. 316.

Notes to the Epilogue

1. Quoted by W. H. Auden in the introduction to Charles Williams, *The Descent of the Dove* (New York: Meridian, 1956), p. v.

2. For a detailed analysis of the many ways this thinning out of life takes place within a culture in which technology is employed undiscriminatingly and unreflectively, see Albert Borgmann, *Technology and the Character of Contemporary Life*. Richard R. Gaillardetz has written a most useful interpretation of Borgmann's work in the explicit setting of our common Christian everydayness in *Transforming Our Days* (New York: Crossroad Publishing, 2000).

3. Rick Bass, *The Roadless Yaak* (Guilford, Conn.: Lyons, 2002), p. 114.

Index of Subjects and Names

Index of Scripture References